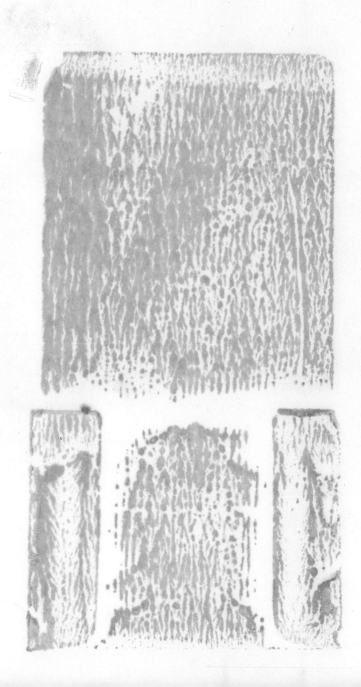

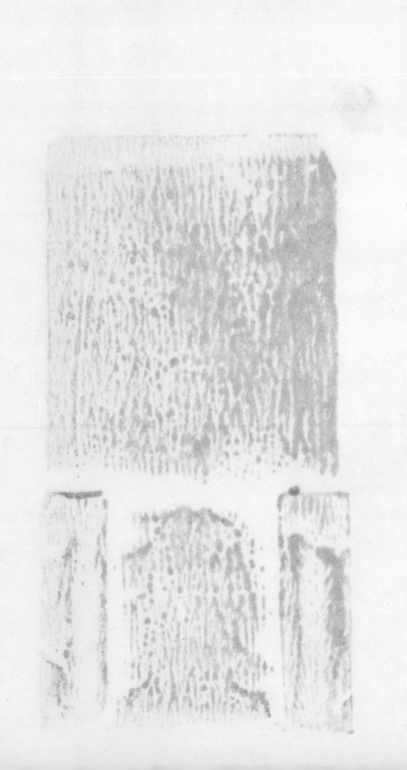

SCOTS BREED

PRESBYTERIAN HISTORICAL SOCIETY PUBLICATIONS

I *The Presbyterian Enterprise,* edited by Maurice W. Armstrong, Lefferts A. Loetscher and Charles A. Anderson (Westminster Press, 1956; reprint, 1963)

II *The Presbyterian Ministry in American Culture,* by Elwyn A. Smith (Westminster Press, 1962)

III *Journals of Charles Beatty, 1762-1769,* edited by Guy S. Klett (Pennsylvania State University Press, 1963)

IV *Hoosier Zion: The Presbyterians in Early Indiana,* by L. C. Rudolph (Yale University Press, 1963)

V *Presbyterianism in New York State: A History of the Synod and Its Predecessors,* by Robert Hastings Nichols, edited and completed by James Hastings Nichols (Westminster Press, 1963)

VI *Scots Breed and Susquehanna,* by Hubertis M. Cummings (University of Pittsburgh Press, 1964)

SCOTS BREED

AND SUSQUEHANNA

Hubertis M. Cummings

University of Pittsburgh Press

In loving memory of

SARAH

Wife of Thomas Simpson of Paxton

her granddaughter

SARAH ELDER

Wife of General James Wallace of Hanover

her granddaughter

SARAH ELDER COURDEN

her niece

SARAH COURDEN

Wife of Homer Hamilton Cummings

her daughter

SARAH ELLEN CUMMINGS

all of whom lived valiantly in the spirit

of their Scotch-Irish traditions.

Now a wild chorus swells the song:
Oft have I listen'd, and stood still,
As it came soften'd up the hill,
And deem'd it the lament of men
Who languish'd for their native glen;
And thought how sad would be such sound.
On Susquehanna's swampy ground,
Kentucky's wood-encumber'd brake,
Or wild Ontario's boundless lake,
Where heart-sick exiles, in the strain,
Recall'd fair Scotland's hills again!

Marmion, Canto III, IX.
Sir Walter Scott

PREFACE

THE PRESBYTERIAN HISTORICAL SOCIETY, Philadelphia, Pennsylvania is pleased to publish this work as the sixth in its series of monographs. It was the wish of Dr. Cummings, long a friend of the Society, that his history of the frontier Scots-Irish should appear under these auspices, and he so provided in his will when he died in 1963. The manuscript was completed in 1951 and is presented essentially as Dr. Cummings wrote it at that time.

The Society is indebted to Dr. Paul A. W. Wallace for his interest in the project and his assistance in the reading of proofs.

J. H. NICHOLS, *Secretary*
The Presbyterian Historical Society

CONTENTS

[ix

SCOTS BREED

SUSQUEHANNA AND HERITAGE

THE COMPLETE STORY of the Susquehanna River has never been told. Its beginning is in the mists of long gone aeons; its ending perhaps too far in the future.

White men first saw it only about three-and-a-half centuries ago. The commonwealth of Pennsylvania, in whose history it has played a very important role, is still seventeen years short of three hundred years in age. In one sense primordial and ageless, the Susquehanna in terms of human knowledge is the child of yesterday. It is an important river, for many reasons. It drains half the area of Pennsylvania, fills many lakes, is fed by many streams, and in turn feeds many others. A live past clings to the river as it clings to all that is best in the annals of Penn's Woods. The living present and the living future move in its course and along its banks with constant renewal of admonition and promise.

Often it has been called "Long Crooked River." As authentic a soubriquet would be "Long-Memoried River." For thousands of years it has attended and been changed by the pageant of Nature, and for hundreds of years it has attended and been changed by the pageant of Man. And it has played no mean role in either, whether at any given moment the action was catastrophic and tragic or serene and idyllic. In the three-and-a-half centuries of man's knowledge of the river, it has been like Shelly's *West Wind*, "destroyer and preserver."

Whether or not, like a river in classical Greece or Italy, the Susquehanna has a Genius, as a haunt of man it has a power. Men have been great and little before it, have sought to master it and failed—have sought to master with it and both succeeded and failed. Indian paths and roads of white men through its valleys or over its bordering hills have vanished. Bridges, canals, railroads, creations intended to use the river have disappeared. Canoe, battoe, raft, Durham boat, ark, steam tug, and coal dredge have challenged the Susquehanna through long decades and eventually vanished from its channel. Dams built in its

[1

course to feed the Commonwealth's great system of canals have crumbled like frost crystals in sunlight when spring or autumn freshets struck them at Athens and Towanda, at Muncy, Nanticoke, Shamokin, Frankstown, Huntingdon, Clark's Ferry, Columbia, and a score of other sites. Man's work in the river's current or at its side has been as the grass over which the Psalmist pictures the wind passing.

Yet in the Susquehanna today the mammoth dams at Safe Harbor, Holtwood, and Conewingo are evidence of man's perseverance and of the Susquehanna's power as ally and friend. The destroyer now preserves, gives man light for a thousand factories and for a million homes, and runs his railway trains as once it made possible the way of his canal boats. Were it not that, objectively considered, the Susquehanna is only a material and physical force, it might seem—like the ancient streams—a God.

Moreover, besides the wonders of history which attend the memories of the great inland stream, the wonders of nature have flourished beside it—mutable, elusive, constant, indestructible, their phenomena myriad. Cascades of mountain laurel in June fill woodland banks where the Susquehanna flows into Maryland. Broad expanses of blue water are dotted with grass-green or soft-willow-clad islands in summer from Columbia to Northumberland. The blunt ends of Accomac, Chickies, Blue Mountain, Peters', Berry's, Mahantango turn into velvet-black the peaks beyond silvery white surfaces against late twilight skies in October. Precipitous slopes bend to the water's edge gray-black in the early spring, emerald in July and August, brown, violet, and purple on clear November days, golden in the lowering western sun on January afternoons. Foliage ever changes in forms, hues, lights, and shadows as locusts and water-birches are replaced by maples, oaks, elms, hemlocks, pines, aspens, birches, or red-berried ash trees. Bottom lands are ribboned with roads to the west of the Wyalusing Hills; bluffs overlook a fair, untroubled champaign from Rummerfield to Tunkhannock. Masses of rhododendron crowd the woodland shores of the North Branch with a glorious density of green fronds and white and pink blossoms. Vistas open into a thousand valleys, with cloud and skies haloing each. Rocks on the shore lines; white-caps on the current on wild days of rain; filigree lights of pearl, or silver, or gold, in a million shimmering facets as sun or breeze touches a quiet surface during the ever lapsing hours of day or of moonlight; whirlpool, passionate swirl, and fury in a slate-colored storm. A poet might well devote all his art and affection to phrasing the river's visible majesty or the subtleties of its most delicate and evanescent charm.

THE PEOPLE

But the Susquehanna is not to be measured only in terms of power and beauty. For man it has been and will be long beyond our day background for human drama. From Captain John Smith's first glimpse of it in 1608 to the image of some tree-lined, half-sandy, half-rocky-bottomed reach of it which a youngster carried with him to bed after a happy day of swimming in 1951, the river has been close to human endeavor. First after the Indians to come to its shores were the English Quakers, then the trading and farming Scotch-Irish, then the Germans; and presently, in their turn, Czech, Slovene, Hungarian, Austrian, Serb, Italian, and Greek—each sharing in his generation the river's bounty and its discipline, its industry and its benefits.

In the pages which follow it is intended only to set down chapters from the story of one people, the Scots who once predominated on the river's banks and along its tributaries. Many of them lived there long and did important things, but in the mid-twentieth century they cannot be looked on except in retrospect. Their numbers and ratio have decreased; and alas, too often their virtues have been lost or diminished. It is well, indeed, that many of their best descendants have mingled with other stocks. But whatever their status now, they were to be reckoned with in the days of their initiative and eminence as Scotch-Irish, a name which has meant much to our country.

The Scotch-Irish were folk who wore their hearts upon their sleeves. To themselves they were always as important as the river which they labored to conquer. Paradoxically, throughout their lives they were certain they held something of royal blood in common with the great figures from Scottish history who in our time have grown all but legendary. And to understand the Scots bred along the Susquehanna one must know something of the personalities of those whose legends and memories came with their descendants.

Lights from olden days shine upon the Scotch-Irish from the Lady Devorgulla (Devorguilla) of Galloway, in 1275 A.D., the "Good" James Douglas in 1330, and Lady Napier, sister of the Marquess of Montrose in 1650.

Mid-twentieth-century Scotland offers little respect to the families to which Devorgulla was allied in marriage and lineage. But as daughter of Alan, Lord of Galloway, she inherited overlordship of tracts of country in southwestern Scotland broad enough to include three shires, enjoyed prerogatives greater than a princess, and through her mother had in her veins the blood of ancient Scottish royalty. Both Celtic and Norman in pedigree, she married John de Baliol, a nobleman who held fiefs in both England and France, and by her husband became mother to one Scottish king and grandmother to another. After her husband's death in 1269 she founded in his name and by his will the college which is one of the oldest at Oxford and, as Baliol, still registers heirs to the most venerable peerages of Scotland. But her Scottish womanliness was as great as either her wealth or power.

When John de Baliol died, Devorgulla had surgeons remove his heart from his body and enshrine it in a casket of silver which for long years she cherished as her most precious possession. When, for her friends among an order of Cistercian Monks, she founded the benefice of *Dulce Cor* on the banks of the River Nith south of Dumfries near Solway Firth, she requested that her own body be buried there in a tomb with the casket containing John de Baliol's heart lying on her breast. Today, still mindful of her wish and bounty, in a fair country-side the stately ruined arches of Sweetheart Abbey sustain the wistfulness of her quaint, enduring affection.

King Robert the Bruce of Scotland, a figure great in Scottish lore, did not lead in the years of his prime a notably pious and religious life. Hero of his country though he was, six weeks before he was crowned in Scotland at the end of March, 1306, he had slain his cousin, also the Lady Devorgulla's grandson John the Red Comyn, before the high altar of the Gray Friars Minorite Church in Dumfries. For that act of violence and impiety he bore papal excommunication through the twenty-three years of his subsequent monarchy. With contrition he vowed he would some day visit the Holy Sepulchre as a crusader. Failing that fond purpose in his lifetime, he requested his retainer Sir James de Douglas to carry his encasketed heart to the Holy Land. In obedience to his king's wish, the faithful liegeman set out on a solemn journey to Jerusalem, but died in Spain fighting the Moors. The royal heart of Bruce, recovered by Sir William Keith, was brought back to Scotland and buried at Melrose Abbey on Tweedside. And for six centuries since the death of Sir James "the Good," his Douglas descendants have borne on their family arms, amidst other devices, a shining bright heart, witness of their progenitor's bizarre and ancient fidelity.

Equally strange is the tale of James Graham, Marquess of Montrose, (1612-1650) and of his sister, the Lady Napier. That valiant nobleman and good soldier, faithful Presbyterian ruling elder though he was in the Church of Scotland, rose for his king, Charles II, after the dethronement and beheading of King Charles I in England. Battle after battle he fought to restore the younger Stewart (Stuart) to the Scottish throne; in the end he lost, was tried for treason by his Scottish and Presbyterian peers, and was condemned and sentenced to execution. At the Tolbooth in Edinburgh he was hanged like a felon in 1650, and drawn and quartered to boot. And when his mangled trunk was buried in the Boroughmuir, his sister Lady Napier sent servants secretly at night to remove the heart of her brother. This she had embalmed and enclosed in a casket and presently gave it to her youthful nephew, who was later the second Marquess of Montrose, and bade him cherish it in pledge of love and faith to his father.

When in 1660 Charles II was restored as monarch of his two kingdoms, one of his first acts was to honor Cavalier James Graham. The scattered remains of that loyal gentleman were gathered together and reburied with high ceremonial, this time in St. Giles. There, reinterred with his broken body, the heart of Montrose rests below a great window of stained glass, set to commemorate the virtues of the hero-martyr and to admit light to bay and arch of that great Edinburgh sanctuary for Presbyterian worship, the noblest of Scottish cathedrals.

Readers who understand these fantasies, and the emblems of devotion and dedication of these three great heroes out of the kingdom between Tweed and Solway on the south and Orkneys and Hebrides on the north will better understand the Scotch-Irish who came to make the Susquehanna their stamping ground for a century.

Those who came were Presbyterians assured of their inheritance through John Knox, the Protestant Reformation in Scotland, the Covenant of 1638, the Solemn League and Covenant of 1643, and latter-day civil and political disabilities in that northern Ireland where their sires had been "planted" by the Stewart kings of England and Scotland a century earlier. Many of them were more familiar with memories and tales of the Siege of Londonderry by the creatures of Catholic King James II of England and of the deliverance of that Irish city by the Protestant forces of King William III in 1689 than they were with the thirteenth-century exploits of Sir William Wallace or with the immemorial wanderings of the Stone of Scone. And they were more proud of having had kinsmen with the Prince of Orange in his victory on the banks of the Irish River Boyne in 1690 than they were of bearing the names of ancestors who had won with the Bruce on the wooded slopes and in the marshy waters of Bannockburn in 1314 or lost with the luckless Scottish King James IV at Flodden in 1513.

If most of them had forgotten the murder of James Sharp, Anglican Archbishop of St. Andrews, by Presbyterian hands on Magus Muir in 1679, at least one set of descendants had heard tales of the dishonor offered to the Reverend George Gillespie of Kirkaldy, when in 1661, thirteen years after his death, his tombstone was ripped out of the parish church and broken at the town cross by the common hangman in contempt for a co-author of the *Westminster Confession of Faith.* Another family remembered well their own tale of the shooting of John Brown of Priesthill by the dragoons of John Graham of Claverhouse in 1685 because that sainted "Christian Carrier" would not recant his Covenanting faith even on orders of the King's agent. And most of the Scotch-Irish who came had listened to parents' accounts of Presbyterian martyrdoms in the Grassmarket of Edinburgh or in the dungeons of the Bass Rock on the Firth of Forth.

If they came weary after two month's voyage in the dark and crowded hold of a narrow sailing ship out of Belfast or grieving at the death of friends and kinsmen on a pestilence-ridden vessel, they came hoping to have in Pennsylvania no more of any Test Act passed by a parliament of Queen Anne which debarred them as Presbyterians from holding political office in Ireland of even the most minor capacity. They had no illusions about all hardships left behind, and they came expecting to be free to live by the Westminster Confession and the Shorter Catechism rather than by the parliament-prescribed Anglican Prayer Book.

And, if few of them came with an attachment to the Stewart kings by whom and for whom their forebears in Scotland and Ireland had died, at least most of them came possessed of a multiple heritage which had been weaving for long hundreds of years. Indeed, like the poet George Noel Gordon Lord Byron, gifted, adventurous, mercurial, persevering, impatient, audacious, the Scotch-Irishman represented a crossing of races, ancient and manifold in origin.

The eighteenth-century emigrant from northern Ireland—from Londonderry, Belfast, Lisburn, and Donaghadee, from Counties Donegal, Londonderry, Antrim, and Down, from the shores of Lough Foyle and the banks of Lough Neagh—sprang from a very old mingling of races; and, when he had set to clearing the forests along the Susquehanna for farmsteads and trading posts, he had begun another chapter of a pilgrimage older than that designated by the hyphenated race name which men of a later day have given him.

Scot and Irishman in one by virtue of his father's and grandfather's migration from Scotland and his own recent residence in Ireland, he was in breed of an origin far more varied than any two names of peoples could suggest. The mores and passions, the joys and the adversities of epochs had become his inherited portion. He had grown out of various physical environments and contacts with many cultures, battle and industry, attitudes of religious faith and ideals of personal conduct. To know him fully one must know the inhabitants of early Britain and of old Caledonia, most northern and remote part of the isle: the Brython, the Roman, the Pict, the Scot, the Celt, the Saxon, the Norman, the Briton of King Arthur, the Irishman of Brian Boru, the Scot of William Wallace, the Englishman of Queen Elizabeth I, the lowlander of Andrew Melville, the highlander of Bonnie Prince Charles; and one must know the crevices in history which lurked within and between all that medley of races and national heroes and leaders. Completely to measure the stature of the Scotch-Irish who came to provincial Pennsylvania demands long historical retrospect.

For, when the compound proper name "Scotch-Irish" is employed in contemporary America, it is to designate a stock of folk whose progenitors two hundred years before had come into the colonies from Ireland, in whose veins was blood which had been nurtured in Scotland, and whose family names had been associated for a millennium and more with the annals of both Ireland and Scotland. They came not as O'Tooles, O'Haras, or O'Briens, not as Desmonds, Fitzgeralds, McCarthys, or Burkes. Rather they came as McQueens, McFarlands, McDonalds, McPhersons, McMillans. They came as Morrisons and Davisons, as Wallaces and Grahams, Gilchrists and Cummings, Pedans and Mitchells, Dixons, Gibsons, Murrays, and Simpsons. Some of them had parents and grandparents who had lived on Irish baronies and townlands, in Irish towns and counties. Donegal, Burt, Letterkenny, Down, Raphoe, Fermanagh, Londonderry, Drumore, Strabane, Monaghan, Tyrone, Lurgan, and Antrim—these, and a thousand more had been beloved place-names with tender memories of kinsmen and home.

But still quick in their spirits were older influences born of the associations of more remote sires in highland and lowland Scotland. They had inheritance from Inverness, Dumbartonshire, Argyle, Badenoch, and Galloway, from Ayrshire, Berwick, Kelso, the Lammermuirs, the Pentlands, the Grampian Mountains, Aberdeen, Perth, Edinburgh, Glasgow, and Stirling. In their veins were the excitement, energy, adventure, violence, challenge, courage, and endurance which once had dominated the Covenanter burghers of the Scottish cities, the Gaelic clansmen of the highlands, the borderers of race chiefly Saxon, who stirred continuously in Berwickshire and Roxburgh, counties of peel towers, reivers, and raids.

For, whatever they were in customs, dress, and beliefs, the Scotch-Irish who came in the eighteenth century into Pennsylvania to share the life of a continent had been for a thousand years Scots. Their breed was of Scotland. The history of Scottish culture was the dominant ethnic key to their stuff and quality. And theirs, in fact, continued to be Scottish hearts as they ranged the forests along the Susquehanna or broke its lower-lying valleys into farmlands. Fit to describe their mettle was the stanza with which the Borderer poet Walter Scott honored the circle of warriors who had fought to the last defending their defeated king at Flodden:

> The stubborn spearmen still made good
> Their dark impenetrable mood,
> Each stepping where his comrade stood,
>   The instant that he fell.
>
> No thought was there of dastard flight,
> Link't in the serried phalanx tight;
> Groom fought like noble, squire like knight,
>   And fearlessly and well.

And all that was dark and unfathomable in their temperament shone bright and transparent in the history of Pennsylvania and of the River Susquehanna.

CHAPTER I

PROVINCE LAW, 1728

"A PLAIN BLUNT SOLDIER"[1] Patrick Gordon called himself when he came to the Province in 1726. Nor does his portrait[2] which hangs in the gallery of the Historical Society of Pennsylvania belie his own estimate. Florid, gray-blue-eyed, long-and-even-nosed, firm-mouthed with just a suggestion of pucker between the short bow of his lower lip and the narrow rondure of his upper chin, he looks to have been soldierly enough when native emotions were not making him sensitive or shy. If his wig of long flaxen curls and the broad soft cushion of his throat or secondary lower chin oppose such an estimate, the tight unfrilled collar below and the steel cuirass binding his chest beneath the open braided velvet coat seem to corroborate the opinion which that deputy governor for the sons of William Penn had already formed of himself when he arrived in Philadelphia to take office. Clearly he was a person of resolution, whatever his breed as a Gordon or his Christian name of Patrick might imply as to birth and rearing.

Indeed, it is pleasant to accept the accounting for his personality which he offered in his inaugural address to the Assembly of Pennsylvania on August 2:

For knowing that I had been bred to the Camp, remote from the refined Politicks which often serve to perplex mankind, and that an honest Plainness, free from Art or Disguise, made up the main of my Character, amongst my Friends and Acquaintances, the Honble the Proprietors rightly Judged, that such a Person could form no views, but what would be openly avowed, and therefore be understood by every Man they could affect."[3]

But the proof of the pudding should be in the eating; and that Lieutenant Governor Patrick Gordon's bluntness was greater than his skill in matters of diplomacy need not at once be assumed. Certainly in the decade of his executive management of the Penn Proprietors' Colony of Pennsylvania a great many things took place which were not always to be explained by simplicity and candor.

[9

Moreover, it is not likely that John and Walter Winter would have concurred in the Governor's characterization of himself. Those two culprits would have said they had told their own story as they lay in irons in Chester Jail awaiting trial, in June 1728, and not too sure that they would escape hanging. But, unfortunately, the preliminaries to their narratives of themselves had occurred at a moment not quite opportune to authorities at work upon a problem of state.

Threats of war among the Indians settled in divers towns up and down the Susequehanna River were troubling Governor Gordon and Mr. James Logan of Philadelphia, the tried and trusted friend of William Penn the Founder and for a generation the best intermediary for the Indians' cause to the Assembly and Council of the Colony. On May 2, 1728, John Wright wrote from Hempfield of bitter resentment then being entertained in the neighboring Conestoga town.[4] Two prowling Shawnees had murdered a man and a woman of the Conestogoes. The Conestogoes had been cheated of the right to punish the murderers; for a party of Shawnees who purportedly were bringing those culprits to deliver them to the Conestogoes for justice had let the two escape.

Reaction had been swift. Seventeen young Conestogoes, armed and painted for war under command of Tilehausey, suddenly appeared at Mr. Wright's house in Hempfield. They would not tell that friend of James Logan where they were going. But some Conoys were going with them, and they had let it be rumored that they hoped "to cut off the whole nation of the Shawnees."[5] So in the writer's modestly ventured opinion it would have been well for Governor Gordon to come on Conestoga-wards before summer hunting.

Conestoga Town and events there had indeed become of prime importance. Its position near the east shore of the river in what was then upper Chester County was athwart the trail of Southern Indians scouting northwards and of Five Nations Indians scouting southwards. Moreover, it lay in 1728 at the western tip of the contemporary Pennsylvania frontier. Peace there, in no small sense, meant peace to the Province. If the traditional friendship of the Proprietary Government and of Philadelphia with the Indians, and the earnest purposes of William Penn and the Society of Friends toward the aborigines, were to be maintained, straws must not be left unturned among the Conestogoes. Already Patrick Gordon had been planning a visit to these.

Then handicaps began dogging his way. From up Susquehanna word came in late April of a bloody encounter between a band of white men and a sortie of Indians. The Governor and Mr. Logan had despatched messengers[6] to Olumapies, King of the Delawares at Shamokin; to Madame Montour in her village at the mouth of far distant Loyalsock Creek; and to Manawkyhickon, the Shawnee chieftain of even less determinate address. To each of these was sent as gift a matchcoat. Of each, faith and fidelity was desired, to their great friend and father, and to their league of friendship with him. The messengers had been instructed to deplore to Manawkyhickon that "we at Philadelphia are so great strangers to a man of his worth."[7] It was incumbent on them to invite that dignitary to attend the treaty which the Governor was planning to hold with the Indians when they returned from hunting. Furthermore, they expressed the hope that the Shawnees would convey to them anything he knew of what was transpiring among the Miamis or the Twightwees who lived among the French.

No answer had been forthcoming from distant Madame Montour. Olumapies sent a cordial response.[8] He believed, he said, that his gift had been sent him from a free and open heart. But he was troubled about Manawkyhickon. That Indian in a recent interlude had remarked, "if he did want war he could make a handle to his hatchet seventy fathoms long," and the Delawares "should see what that would do."[9] Olumapies had replied that he took that very evil of a man in Manawkyhickon's place, and he intended "to take all the care that in him lay to put a stop to his proceeding."[10]

Also, nearer Philadelphia the situation grew complex for Patrick Gordon. A petition "of the frontier inhabitants of the County of Philadelphia,"[11] signed on April 29, 1728, reached the Governor. Alarm and noise of Indians had been so great that several families had left their plantations with what they could carry away. Several mothers in childbed had been enforced to expose them "to coldness of the air"[12] in their flight, and their lives were in danger. The petitioners hoped for measures of Government which would relieve them of their fears of the Indians. Some eleven days later came a lament signed by seventy inhabitants of Colebrookdale, with the name John Roberts at the head of the list. Folk of that community had suffered from Indians falling upon their neighbors about Falkner's Swamp and Coshahopin.[13] Their wives and children, "that were more to them than life,"[14] were endangered, George Boone wrote on May 12 to the Governor, of the flight of the inhabitants from his neighborhood. He had only twenty men left with him to guard his mill and the thousand bushels of wheat and flour there. Would not the Governor and the Council take their cause into consideration? send them arms and ammunition? send some messengers to the Indians?[15]

But on the day before Boone's letter was forwarded, a murder of Indians, it would seem, not a murder by Indians, had occurred in old upper Chester County; and the ironmaster Samuel Nutt of "Malanton," Coventry Township, owner of Warwick Furnace, was writing about it to the Lieutenant Governor of Pennsylvania. John and Walter Winter's conduct had, in fact, become "disagreeable news" to relay for "a hearty friend and servant to command." The two men not only had killed one Indian man and two women, "without any cause given by the said Indians;"[16] more than that, they had then gone to George Boone with two Indian girls, one of them crippled, expecting to receive a reward.

Despite this unpleasant intelligence, and more so by reason of it, Patrick Gordon had to go on with the diplomacy of a plain blunt soldier if he was to protect what he deemed the interest of the Province.

Hue and cry for Walter Winter, John Winter, and Morgan Herbert, father-in-law to Walter, was instituted. On May 12 the three were examined by Edward Farmer and A. Hamilton, and their examinations were set down in a good clerkly hand, with the names of Walter and John Winter so closely subjoined as to be in the position of signatures, although certainly, as the examinations survive in manuscript form[17] today in the Pennsylvania Division of Public Records at Harrisburg, each name is in the hand of the clerk. One shows the script of Edward Farmer, the other that of A. Hamilton.

Of Walter Winter the first of the three examinations testified to behavior as follows:

A Dutchman from Tulpehocken told him on May 10 of two Christians wounded by prowling Indians in that more westerly settlement. Walter thereupon coursed his own neighborhood, desired settlers to get together in his house to defend themselves, returned to that house and busied himself making its windows fast against attack. Employed so, he was not disinclined to belief in word suddenly coming by way of John Roberts' son who brought appeal from his father. Lurking about the elder Roberts' house were several Indians. One of them had a bow and a great number of arrows. His father, the younger Roberts declared, was in danger of being killed.

Walter Winter and Morgan Herbert seized their guns, Winter's "being loaded with one bullet and ten swan shot,"[18] and started off for John Roberts' house. On their way they met John Winter, armed with a short gun, which he promptly exchanged for Herbert's longer one. Soon the three men were filing along the log which stretched across the run on the far side of which stood the house of the imperiled neighbor. In the moment of crossing Walter saw John Roberts standing in his doorway, gun in hand; and a few feet away on a wood pile near that door he beheld "an Indian man, some women and some girls."[19] As he looked, the Indian rose, took his bow, stepped backward, slipped an arrow from his shoulder, and put it to the string of his weapon.

The gesture of the redskin and his poise seemed hostile signs. Before the Indian could speed the missile which Walter Winter thought was being aimed at him, that intending rescuer of the Roberts' household presented his own gun and fired. In the same minute John Winter sent a second bullet from Morgan Herbert's musket.

Walter's shot hit the Indian; John's hit one of the women; and the party of three moved forward with a rush. The wounded brave, blood running from his breast, staggered away toward a swamp; the Indian girls ran in another direction. John Winter sped forward and brought one of these down with a blow which knocked her brains out. Walter seized the bow which the brave had dropped and with it and an arrow in hand pursued a second of the women, stopped her, and brought her back.

Such, as the examinant testified, was the story of the first day in which the two Winters had offended the laws of Pennsylvania and of the King. To his examiners he added a few details of the next morning in the vicinity of John Roberts'. Mrs. Roberts told him "the Indian boy"[20] had been in the house, and made three arrows there. He and his brother and Morgan Herbert took the corpses of the two Indian women slain by the single shot and the blow of John Winter "out of the Road and covered them with some leaves."[21]

This simple testimony, rude and unimaginative in its phrasing, was corroborated by that of John Winter in his examination by the same two examiners, Farmer and Hamilton. John told of the rumor of the Indian slaying and wounding of white men at Tulpehocken, of the coming of John Roberts' son to his brother's house, of his own joining with his brother and Morgan Herbert and his exchange of guns with the latter. He saw the log bridge over the run; saw Roberts in his door with his gun on his shoulder; saw Indians, he thought, "by the wood pile."[22] He saw the "Indian man"[23] rise up bow in hand, step back, begin putting arrow to his bowstring. He heard his brother Walter shoot, heard Walter call to him to shoot, and immediately shot among the Indians. His bullet killed one woman. He ran forward, struck another woman over the head "with the cock of his gun, and killed her."[24]

But the testimony of John Winter did more than corroborate in its own dull hardness of tone. It told of John Roberts striking at an Indian woman with an axe as she lay down; told of this wounded girl being found next morning at Taka Colie's cabin; and recounted that the slayers and others had "hauled them some distance from the Road," put the two dead Indian women "into a hole and covered them with some leaves."[25]

All this was on the 10th and 11th of May. On the 12th of that month, Morgan Herbert was examined, as were his son-in-law and John Winter. He testified to the same examiners to the truth of Walter Winter's deposition, except in one detail: He had not himself seen "John Roberts having a gun"[26] as he stood before his door.

Then, three days after Edward Farmer and Andrew Hamilton, Justices of the Peace of Philadelphia County, had taken down their examinations of the three frontiersmen of Cucussea, Chester County, those same dignitaries issued a warrant to the Sheriff of Philadelphia. The offenders had "set upon, assaulted and killed one Indian man and two Indian women being of our friends the Indians belonging to the Province of Pennsylvania."[27] Their notice added in a footnote that "hue and cry" had been "issued for apprehending John Roberts."[28]

The stage, in brief, had been set for Patrick Gordon's diplomacy. That mode of action must now embrace a second issue. Before May 10, 1728, the problem had been one of propitiating Olumapies, Madame Montour, and Manawkyhickon, at distant Shamokin and even farther than that up the Susquehanna; after May 11 the Governor must exercise every care with the Indians at Conestoga on the western frontier of upper Chester County.

An exciting force to new action had occurred; and the episode of the Winters became *entre-acte* to a main theme in political drama. The protagonist's purpose had to point upon Conestoga.

It was carried into effect there admirably. Governor Gordon had several cards to play in mid-month. He could inform the Assembly on May 15 that within the immediate future he was to meet with the Indians at Conestoga Town and that some of the Chiefs of the Five Nations would come presently to Philadelphia on a friendly visit.[29] On May 15 he could not only issue a timely proclamation for securing the peace of the Province, with narration in the midst of it of "a most barbarous murder—committed by some furious men on the bodies of three harmless and quiet natives, our friends,"[30] but supplement his decree with a promise that the malefactors should be tried and suffer a condign punishment. He could add to his propitiatory words to Indian chieftains along the Susquehanna, as he forwarded them on May 15 through John Scull and Anthony Zadowsky,[31] data of "four wicked white men" who had "killed a peaceable good Indian man and two women, which has raised a horror in me and all the good people about me."[32]

Moreover he could assert whether or not it was by effectual *coup d'état:* "But three of these villians are now in Irons in Chester Prison, the fourth is also taken, and they will shortly all be tried and suffer in some manner as if they had killed so many white People, for that we make no difference. We are all Brethren, and as one People. Tis true there are some very wicked Men amongst us, as there are some amongst all Nations, but when these men are guilty of such wicked Actions, we can do no more than put them to death. We kill them by our Laws that they may do no more mischief, and whether they hurt an Indian or a Whiteman, tis all the same, they must die for the one as for the other. When I heard of this I was much grieved, and I sent about twenty Men to find the Corpse to cover them with Shirts & strowds, and to bury them, and they are buried in ye Earth, and Covered with Strowds. We can do no more now for the dead but mourn for them, and we deeply mourn for this Wicked fact, but those who did it shall suffer for it according to their Wickedness, and must be Swept from amongst good Men and from the face of the Earth on which they are not fit to live."[33]

Ten days later Governor Gordon met with the Conestogoes in an Indian Council at their town, with a scattering of Delawares, Conoys, and Shawnees also gathered there, but with no chiefs of eminence named. He addressed them on William Penn's ideals and their strong league and chain of friendship with Pennsylvania; on his visit with the purpose of renewing the ancient friendship; briefly, on his disappointment that Olumapies and Opekasset were not present.[34] He praised their fidelity. He recapitulated their old vows to one another: paths free alike to Indians and Christians, the openness of their doors to one another, their mutual will to do no harm one to the other, their sincere intent to collaborate with each other in punishment of crimes committed amongst both or between them. For confirmation of their vows he gave the Conestogoes and their friends assembled with them 20 strowds, 20 duffles, 20 blankets, 20 shirts, a hundredweight of gunpowder, two hundredweight of lead, 500 flints, and 50 knives.[35]

He deplored the grievous news of the white murderers. He told of his mourning at that affair. He told of the promptitude with which the "three or four furious men" had been put into "irons in a dungeon to be tried by the laws of the Great King of all the English."[36]

He assured the Conestogoes of his policy of one justice to all, white man or Indian. He reviewed the affront of John Burt[37] of Snake Town who had been very abusive to the Indians after the killing of a white man eight months before at his house. He had sent men to arrest Burt; but that culprit had fled, and could not be punished. But, since an Englishman had been slain, Governor Gordon expected the Indians to "do us justice by apprehending the murderers that they may be punished, for we must be true and faithful to each other, that this spot may be wiped away and the chain be kept bright and clean."[38] He had issued a proclamation requiring "all our people to use"[39] the Indians well; he expected fair treatment in response from the Conestogoes, when he was himself willing to punish white men who did injustice to Indians.

In a few days Patrick Gordon had an answer from Olumapies and Opekasset.[40]

Those two had liked the letter which was carried by Nicholas Scull and Anthony Zadowsky to them. It had eased their minds. They bore nothing but love and good will to the Governor and all his people. They could not meet with him at Conestoga; but, if he pleased they would come in another eight days to meet him "at Molaton and discourse together in love."[41] (The date of their communication, as interpreted from the Delaware tongue by James Letort, was recorded by the emissaries on May 22).

On June 4 the meeting took place.[42] Again there were vocal preliminaries of William Penn and the chain of friendship. There were more gifts of strowds, blankets, shirts, powder, lead, flints, knives. Now in addition there were tobacco boxes, tobacco tongs, looking glasses, and vermilion. Again there was deploration of the offence of the murderers. Again there was mention of the dungeon and iron chains, with promises of equal justice. Once more there was description of the decent reburial of the three slain Indians with proper covering of shirts and strowds. And this time six handkerchiefs were given through Olumapies to the relatives of the dead to help them wipe away their tears; and there was additional solace offered in three strowds, three blankets, three duffles, and three shirts to cover the bodies of the dead, for a second occasion of hypothetical reburial.[43]

On June 19, 1728, at a Court of Oyer & Terminer & Jail Delivery held at Chester before David Lloyd, Richard Hill, and Jeremiah Langhorne, Esquires, John Winter and Walter Winter, earlier arraigned "for murdering an Indian Woman,"[44] were formally indicted. They "pleaded *not guilty*," and "for their trial put themselves upon God and the country."[45] A petty jury was called and appeared, consisting of

Henry Hays, George Ashbridge, William Horne, Peter Worrall, George Wood, Richard Jones, Abraham Lewis, Benjamin Clift, John Davis, Thomas Vernon, John Tomkins, and Evan Howell.[46] These jurors, "upon their respective oath and affirmation" said that the two men were "guilty of the murder aforesaid and must be hanged by the necks until they and each of them be dead."[47] Their case was recorded in the docket of the Supreme Court of the Province as "Dom. Rex a Jno. Winter & Walter Winter."[48]

Two days later Morgan Herbert, convicted as an accessory to their crime and so in the court's view likewise guilty of murder, was reprieved and recommended to the Governor's compassion and mercy, and was pardoned for not having actually participated in the deed of violence. On June 26, Patrick Gordon issued warrant for execution; and on Wednesday, July 3, John Winter and Walter Winter were hanged for having murdered "an Indian women called Quilee, otherwise Hannah."[49]

Thus did a *cause celèbre* of the old Pennsylvania frontier, in a year when Chester County was still the most western part of the jurisdiction of the Crown and the territory of the Proprietors in the Province, come to its termination. Two men who had acted with a precipitate violence and in a bloody deed, perished under the exercise of the law. They pleaded not guilty; their testimony to their conduct, which certainly had no clear justification, was set down in hands not their own, and diction which they could not probably have claimed to be in their own words. But more than their rash and furious act—extenuated by themselves because of desperate rumors from Tulpehocken and by their fears for John Roberts and his household—was against them.

Their irruption had affronted a necessary policy of state. Unarmed Pennsylvania dared not risk the disaffection of the Conestogoes, the Delawares, or the Five Nations. White men dared not slay Indians, unless they had every immediate evidence of the Indians' violence upon themselves. It was not an era when pioneers dared go berserk, or when the prosecuted dared plead "brain storms" or "impulse" in apology for themselves. Second-degree sentences were not to be thought of when the security of a domain was to be imperiled by a leniency of judgment. Unpremeditated behavior was as due for condign punishment as was premeditated behavior when it resulted in homicide.

It remains true, however, that, while that plain blunt soldier Governor Gordon made much, in his proclamations and treaties, of three or four furious men and of three Indians slain, the law in its final discipline was exercised for the murder of one Indian woman. John

Roberts, whose name had once stood at the head of an appeal of frontiersmen for protection from Philadelphia against the Indians, and for
whom hue and cry was raised for having part in the violence perpetrated by the Winters, eluded capture and trial, and disappeared
from history. He was, if the testimony of the two Winters as recorded
by Justices Edward and Hamilton had validity, as guilty as those two
culprits. Other frontiersmen, whose inconvenient petitions went un-
noticed by Council and Assembly in Philadelphia, would have pronounced him innocent.

And, had they dared to be vocal in 1728, other white Scotch-Irish
folk who were then settling in upper Chester County near the Susquehanna, would have considered the six handkerchiefs given by the
diplomat Patrick Gordon to Olumapies on June 4 as perquisites somewhat superfluous for Indian mourning.

CHAPTER 2

IMMIGRANTS

WHEN, IN 1701, Governor William Penn returned to England from his second and last visit to the province which in 1682 he had founded on the west banks of the Delaware River, he left behind one particularly valuable friend and agent. James Logan was a man of spirit and insight. No man in Proprietary Pennsylvania was ever to outrank him in practical sense or political acumen. Born in Ireland, educated in England as a Quaker, he was of Scottish descent —and, despite an overlay of culture and forbearance drawn from a lifetime association with the Society of Friends, Scottish in temper. Benjamin Franklin liked to tell of the man a story which illustrated his quality.

The "Canterbury," on which Penn and his young secretary were voyaging to America in 1699, was chased by a pirate and had to make prompt show of resistance. The Proprietor and his other Quaker friends retired below decks at once. It was not in their creed to respond to violence with violence. James Logan remained above, quartered to a gun, ready to participate in any action which might ensue. The marauding vessel made off when she found the "Canterbury" prepared for battle; and Penn, reappearing from below hatches, rebuked his subordinates for resorting to arms. Logan replied bluntly: "I being thy servant, why did thee not order me to come down, but thee was willing enough that I should stay and help fight the ship when thee thought there was danger."[1]

Later years were not to testify that Logan had changed either fundamental breed or creed. He grew into a man of parts in Pennsylvania, availed eventually as secretary and president to the Provincial Council, scholar, scientist, writer, collector of books; and in his fine house "Stenton" he was recognized by both Indians and Philadelphians as the nonpareil of wisdom and gentlemanliness. Yet his shrewdness as a man of affairs and diplomat never left him. One eminent modern

[19

writer has written of him, "He was a born chess player," like Shakespeare's Polonius finding out directions "by indirections."[2] Moreover, he had ideas for frontiers.

On November 18, 1729, he wrote to another trusty servant of the Penns: "About this time (1720) a considerable Number of good Sober People came in from Ireland, who wanted to be Settled, at ye same time it happen'd that we were under some apprehensions from northern Indians of whose claims to the Lands on Sasquehannah I was not then sensible. . . . I therefore thought it might be prudent to plant a settlement of fresh men as those who formerly had so bravely defended Derry and Inniskillen as a frontier in case of any Disturbance. Accordingly the Township of Donegal was settled some few by Warr[ts] at the certain price of 10 pounds per hund but more so, without any."[3]

In brief, James Logan, their fellow countryman in origin, had scented in the Scots immigrants from Ulster both a record of valor and a practical use. In a *sub rosa* sort of way they were to be the advance guard of a Quaker civilization.

Scots had then been coming for twelve years, but neither quite unobserved nor ceremoniously heralded. Letters from 1717 to 1729, in the correspondence of gentlemen, made reference to the numbers of them arriving. Few comments on them were complimentary. No really cordial welcome greeted them. No poetry emanated to declare their initiative and fortitude as they steered for the "stern and rockbound coast."

It seemed enough, during that decade of 1717-1727, that earlier settlers in Pennsylvania should know they were coming, disembarking at Lewes, Newcastle, and Philadelphia from ships inward bound from Dublin, Belfast, and Londonderry, and after examinations of ship captains' papers spreading westward into Newcastle County, northernmost of the Penns's three Lower Counties on the Delaware and in Chester County. Only folk on whom their settlements there began to impinge were notably aware of their presence. Dully factual were the first annals of them in America.

Two letters of Jonathan Dickinson gave them scant notice in the year 1717. On October 17 he wrote, "This summer we had 12 or 13 sail of ships from the North of Ireland with a swarm of people;"[4] on October 23 he commented: "from the North of Ireland many hundreds" arrived "in about four months"[5] at Philadelphia. Again in November, 1719, Dickinson reported that twelve ships laden with passengers from Ireland had recently come to Philadelphia. Eight years later more began to be said of them. Writing on November 23, 1727, to John Penn, eldest son of the Proprietor William by his second marriage, the observant James Logan remarked: "We have from the North of Ireland great numbers yearly," folk who reported that twice as many would come in 1728 and who themselves, as he put it, settled "generally towards the Maryland line where no lands can honestly be sold till the dispute with Lord Baltimore is decided."[6] He did not expand upon the implications in his commentary, although they were present.

But by 1728 the Ulster Scots were certainly not leaving Ireland unheeded. Archbishop Boulter, Lord Primate of the Anglican Church there, knew what was going on, and in communications to Ministers of State in England deprecated events. In March, 1728, he deplored that the "humor of going to America continued," accounting for the exodus by the "scarcity of provisions"[7] at home, and estimating that seven ships about to embark from Belfast would be carrying a thousand passengers to the colonies. On November 23, addressing the Duke of Newcastle at length, he lamented many points in the current state of Irish affairs. Agents of the colonies and shipmasters, he said, were deluding the people with stories of great plenty and estates to be had by them in America, in that manner playing upon the necessities of the poor. The people were complaining (He seemed to think falsely!) of oppressions from their fellow subjects, finding in those an excuse for going. Many were making the mistake of hiring themselves to persons of substance for their passage or contracting with masters of ships for four years of servitude to them. The whole North was in a ferment, people every day engaging to go next year. The humor was spreading like a contagious distemper. No one could cure the general madness. Worst of all, it "affects only Protestants"—and in that part of the country "which is the seat of our linen manufacture."[8]

Interesting message from a high-placed ecclesiastic! But there was a counterpart. A Lord-Justice, eager to know the cause of the deplored exodus, turned to two Presbyterian ministers, Francis Iredel and Robert Craighead; and these presently brought answer from the Presbytery of Tyrone: "The bad seasons for three years past [Ireland had had a famine in 1727-1728.], together with the high price of lands and tithes, have all contributed to the general ruin."[9] Nor did that Presbytery, while it grieved at the ruins of families who were "daily leaving their houses and lands desolate," forget to enumerate another reason for the departure: "the disabilities arising from the Sacramental Test [of 1704], which excluded them from all places of public trust and honor under the government."[10]

So much for attitudes in Ireland toward emigrating Scotch-Irishmen. The Primate read into their going a material loss to the country more than any political or social wrong to them. The Presbytery of Tyrone insisted on mention of discrimination against Presbyterians in Ulster no less than on mention of material hardship.

But a mind which could be more impartial and objective had grown aware of Irishmen landing in Philadelphia. Benjamin Franklin had begun publishing *The Pennsylvania Gazette* as his own venture in October, 1729. Not yet twenty-four years old, but already a man of both experience and initiative, he busily garnered, rewrote, and supplemented foreign news and correspondence. All London news brought into Philadelphia by ship captains in letters and journals were his quarry, as were ideas from everywhere. He was a newsman *par excellence*. Believing in the freedom of the press, he wrote with candor. Tersely, then, in the November 20th issue of his *Gazette*, not quite two months old under its new simplified name, he summed up reports from the newspapers of England: "The English papers have of late been frequent in their accounts of the unhappy circumstances of the Common People of Ireland; That Poverty, Wretchedness, Misery and Want are become almost universal among them; That . . . there is not Corn enough rais'd for their Subsistence one year with another; and at the same Time the Trade and Manufactures of the Nation being cramp'd and discourag'd, the labouring People have little to do, and consequently are not able to purchase Bread at its present dear Rate: That the Taxes are nevertheless exceeding heavy, and Money very scarce; and add to all this, that their griping, avaricious Landlords exercise over them the most merciless Racking Tyranny and Oppression. Hence it is that such Swarms of them are driven over into America."[11]

The objectively minded Franklin, like neither a timorous Primate disturbed for Ireland's material sake nor an outspoken but politically disabled group of Presbyterians in Tyrone, read conditions with a commoner's eye. Moreover, he appended to his account a statement from Robert Gambie of Londonderry of July, 1729. This told that 25 ships, each carrying 120 to 140 passengers, were that summer leaving Londonderry for America, and that many more were "going from Belfast, and the Ports near Colrain, besides great numbers fom Dublin, Newry, and round the Coast."[12] Where and when the exodus "will end God only knows."[13] Well might landlords request—as at the time they requested—that the Presbyterian Synod meeting at Dublin "use their

Influence with the People, in persuading them not to desert the kingdom."[14]

Through Franklin's *Gazette*, then, Philadelphians had notice of what further they might be expecting out of Ireland. As the Palatine Germans were coming and would be coming, so also the swarms of Irish might continue to be expected. Moreover other burghers in the Province than James Logan and Benjamin Franklin were conscious of the multitudes of immigrants landing at all the ports up and down the Delaware. Certainly as early as March, 1727, both folk and officialdom had grown uneasy and suspicious with regard to them. Speaking to the Assembly at the end of that month, Lieutenant Governor Patrick Gordon deplored circumstances in Pennsylvania: "We have seen large quantities of the Counterfeit Bills of our neighboring Colony diffused in this Province, to the great loss of its Inhabitants, and I am credibly informed, the Design has been laid to pour in upon us a Flood of our own Bills counterfeited from Ireland, where they have artfully imitated most of those of Jersey, that it requires more skill to distinguish them than is to be expected amongst Country People."[15] It was wise, thought Philadelphians, to keep an eye on the Irish now obviously in their midst, threading their way westward through Chester County to the Susquehanna, filling up Newcastle townships on the lower Delaware, squatting on unwarranted lands in both districts. They might not be "foreigners" like the Palatines. But they were a suspect group of people. Church of England folk and members of the Society of Friends, Assembly and Provincial Council had better watch them. And watch and suspect they did.

The spring of 1728 brought its example of violence in the slaying of hapless Indians at Malanton in Chester County in May; and hanging of John and Walter Winter for the offence on July 3 at Chester Jail was hardly an event to quiet suspicion. Indeed, in December of that year, Governor Gordon was still playing cautious. On the 17th, he addressed the Assembly, offering to that body, then made up chiefly of Quakers, compliments to "the ancient Settlers, the most substantial and judicious of the Inhabitants . . . most deeply interested in the Peace and Prosperity of the Country . . . generally everywhere easie."[16] Contrasting with these, he cited the dissatisfied, who were now, unhappily, "joined by other turbulent spirits from abroad."[17] Those latter, he regretted, thought "fit to discharge themselves here, to the Disquiet of a good and peaceable People."[18] "Having been uneasy at home through the meanness of their condition or Want of Room to display their busy humors," they have brought with them little beyond a "Noise and Clamor to distinguish them"—although certainly, from the speaker's point of view, they "cannot point out one real grievance in the Administration."[19]

Yet Patrick Gordon was not without hope as he spoke. He intended to suffer no remissness in his government which it was in his power to prevent or remedy. He confidently believed that folk who had been misled and remonstrant would "on due reflection recover themselves, and see how much Union and Order are preferable to Division and Confusion."[20] In the not distant future he expected them to "study the Ways that lead to their own Peace, as well as that of the Public."[21] Reflection seemed to him "the only thing wanting to render the people of Pennsylvania as happy amongst themselves as any now in the Universe."[22]

Equanimity in Quaker Assembly and deputy-executive was not, however, to be free of English authority. Gordon admitted on that December day in 1728 that he had had positive orders from Britain to provide by a proper law against the crowds of foreigners pouring in upon Pennsylvania. He and his Assembly must be on guard to prevent an English Plantation from being turned into a Colony of Aliens. It would require their thoughts how to withstand "an importation of Irish Papists and Convicts, of whom some of the most notorious," he was again 'credibly informed,' "have of late been landed in this River."[23]

So Philadelphians, who cherished peace and the material good of the Province, kept on thinking through the winter of 1728-1729; and on March 31, both the Assembly (which indeed, two days earlier had appealed for exercise of it) and the citizens were ready for Patrick Gordon's Proclamation of the Riot Act. All wished that "Riots and Rioters shall be punished by the Laws of England."[24] They deplored that into a colony first settled "by a sober and religious People, whose religious Principle was, and still is well known to be, against the Use of Arms," had come great numbers "of dissolute and disorderly Persons."[25] These, knowing Philadelphians "have no military forces," had "of late taken the liberty to menace and threaten both private persons and 'Members of this House.' "[26] Accordingly Assemblymen appealed to the Governor for measures to bring to an end "Disturbance of the Peace" and restore the "Publick Service of the Country."[27]

But a more potent means of handling the problem of the Scotch-Irish in Pennsylvania was to be found during the course of the year 1729 than the reading of an Act against tumults and disturbances.

Since its founding in 1681 as a proprietary Colony under the Penns,

Pennsylvania had had but three counties: Philadelphia, Bucks, and Chester, all fronting on the Delaware but at first bounded to the west and the north very indefinitely. In intervening years, by agreements with Colonel Thomas Dongan of New York in 1696, a Susquehanna Indians' deed in 1700, and a release by the Delaware Indians in 1718 of the lands between the Delaware and Susquehanna Rivers from Duck Creek to the Lehigh Hills, the original territory of the Province had been much extended. In theory, at least, Chester County had by then moved its terrain westward beyond the Susquehanna and northwestward to creeks like the Chickies and the Conewago, emptying into the Susquehanna from its east banks. Settlement in that hinterland toward the Susquehanna and the Kittochtinny Mountains was very slow; and there was virtually none west of the river during the first quarter of the eighteenth century. But, once the Scotch-Irish had penetrated Newcastle County to the south with some thoroughness, set up homes and established Presbyterian meeting places along Christiana, Cedar, White Clay, and other creeks there, tributary to the Delaware, they began filling up the Chester frontier toward Susquehanna. By 1720 they had been building cabins for their families and log churches for their worship in Nottingham Township bordering on Maryland, and were confidently ensconced from Octorara Creek, emptying into the Susquehanna some ten miles above Chesapeake Bay, to as far upstream as Pequea Creek, Conestoga Creek, and Conestoga Manor, which had been ordered surveyed in 1718 and which still in 1728 afforded the protection of the Penns to their friends and allies, the Conestoga Indians of Conestoga Town. By 1721 Scotch-Irishmen, settled along Chickisalunga (modern Chickies) Creek, northwestern boundary of this old "Conestoga" region, were applying to Newcastle Presbytery for missionaries to be sent among them for the founding of Presbyterian congregations. And there, little recked of by Philadelphians, a community was in embryo which under its eventual township name, Donegal, would become famous in Presbyterian and American history.

In 1729, then, the thing to do was to create Pennsylvania's fourth county. "Barkus," to resort to the language of Charles Dickens, "was willin'." Two intermediaries to the purpose were found in John Wright and Thomas Edwards, leading spirits in Upper Chester County (that is, the part of Chester County most remote from the down-Province Delaware River). A petition[28] was drawn; and out of the names attached to it 120 were in origin definitely Scotch-Irish, another 20 either Scotch or Welsh, and the remainder German or English.

Andersons, Moores, Scotts, Galbraiths, Hayes, Mitchells, Alisons, Whites, Blacks, Campbells, Stuarts, Maybanes, Patersons, Robinsons, Clarks, McKuons, Musgroves, Burns, and Woodrows[29] from the North of Ireland, and numerous other families of patronymics as Scotch-Irish as their own, were very cordial to having a county and a county seat in their midst for the easier administration of law and the maintenance of order.

Wright and Edwards copied the wording of the petition, and recorded entry of the names of their Scotch-Irish neighbors. On February 6, 1729, Governor Gordon had the document in his hands to lay before Council; on February 7 the Council decided to apprise the Assembly of the project; on February 20 the Assembly concurred in the design, and a warrant for the necessary survey of boundaries was ordered. Before May 2 the commissioners for the purpose reported completion of the survey; and in that month Lancaster County was erected by action of the Assembly and consent of the Governor. In October, 1729, four representatives sat for Lancaster in the Pennsylvania Assembly, and settlers on the Susquehanna were for the first time participant in the government of the Province. Three of their Assemblymen were men already known to the authorities: John Wright, Thomas Edwards, and Thomas Read. The fourth, James Mitchell, bore a name brought from Northern Ireland.

The petition in itself was a charter of liberties and responsibilities, a better measure than the fulminations of state. Patrick Gordon sponsored it on the ground that law was needed in those parts "on Susquehannah" where "the worst seek a shelter in homes of Impunity"[30] by reason of their distance from the regular administration of justice. But in its own comprehensive test it described the need of frontiersmen for a county town where elections and courts could be held in their own midst. They wished to have public offices near to them; justices and constables to protect them from thieves, vagabonds, and evil people in their own environment. When they had to look to law for redress in their material business—which, as they were far from markets, and, as money was scarce, was transacted chiefly by barter—they felt that the courts of Chester were altogether too remote for their purses to meet the expenses of the journeys necessary to the bringing of a suit. Eighty or a hundred miles from a seat of law made the expense of recovering a just debt prohibitive. It was cheaper to let a debt of forty shillings lapse than to have a debtor jailed by resort to an execution that distance away. As for a runaway servant, better let him make off into Maryland than to be at suit to retrieve him from a neighbor who was helping him escape.

Moreover, in matters merely economic, a county and county seat were important to them. In a county town closer at hand tax funds could be more readily built up to meet the cost of highway and bridge repairs. It would be far better, too, for them to be able to elect more commissioners and assessors. One of each of those in a vast circle in which 500 families resided was entirely inadequate to convenience. In sum, the Scotch-Irish of Lancaster County, who had come from an Ireland in which by reasons of their Presbyterianism they had had no privilege of civil office, were ready, when they signed their petition, to collaborate with Governor Gordon and the Pennsylvania Assembly for the "Public Good." They had come into a land where, however shady their repute might be with the Friends in Philadelphia, their religion was no longer a political disability.

Division lines had been adopted for a new region of civil and political authority; a county town was in the offing; a race of immigrants from Ulster were free to name the townships forming among them. They might, if they chose, behave themselves and be proper wards of the Proprietary Government of John, Thomas, and Richard Penn and loyal subjects of King George II. Good James Logan of "Stenton" did not forget that through their position and by their spirit they might also contribute another value to the Province.

From their own point of view those thousands of Scotch-Irishmen who came into Pennsylvania between 1717 and 1729 came as strangers into a new country rather than as novices to civilization. Of earthly goods they brought little; yet they brought with them habits and aptitudes. Moreover, for their way of life preparation had been made by men of Ulster arriving in earlier decades in Maryland, Delaware, and Philadelphia. As early as 1683 the Reverend Mr. Francis Makemie, of Ramelton County, Donegal, Ireland, a licentiate of the Presbytery of the Laggan in the year 1681, came, and through his spiritual labors on the Eastern Shore organized the Scotch-Irish wing of American Presbyterianism. Within the next twenty-five years of his ministry he became founder and pastor of four churches at Manokin, Rehoboth, Snow Hill, and Wicomico. Inspired by his wisdom and valor, Presbyterianism had spread into numerous communities. Before 1698 there were congregations not only in Lewes and Newcastle, Delaware, but one also in Philadelphia. During the next decade churches sprang up along White Clay, Red Clay, and Brandywine Creeks, whose waters made their way to the Delaware River through Newcastle County;

and at the Head of Elk Creek on both sides of the Pennsylvania-Maryland boundary. In 1708 there were prospering congregations at the Head of Christiana Creek and the Rock. The year 1714 brought into existence three more churches, Norriton, Abington, and Great Valley, in what was then Chester County (and has since become Montgomery County and Chester). By 1717 three Presbyteries, Snow Hill, (Maryland), Newcastle (Delaware), and Philadelphia, were ready to meet with the Presbytery of Long Island and form the first Synod in the Colonies. Before the immigrants of the third decade of the eighteenth century reached the lands between the Delaware and the Susquehanna River, the mettle of the Scots was already displaying itself with honor and confidence. The arrivals in 1720-1730 found that honest evidences of their culture had preceded them. They were prompt to add to a good beginning.

Donegal Township, chiefly occupied by Scotch-Irish before 1729, when it was formally designated by that name in the erection of Lancaster County, had a congregation of Presbyterians as early as 1721, with missionary supplies being sent to it from Newcastle Presbytery. For several years this group was served by the Reverend Messrs. George Gillespie and Adam Boyd, who had churches of their own at Christiana Head and Octorara. In 1727 James Anderson was installed as the first pastor of Donegal Church under the authority of Newcastle. In 1729 Presbyterians in two other communities adjacent to Donegal on the north but both fronting the east bank of the Susquehanna, Derry and Paxton, were ready for organization, and Mr. Anderson, who three years later became senior clerical member of a new Presbytery, was diligently serving these as a supply by instruction of the same Newcastle body. In 1732, so numerous settlers became in the westernmost parts of Lancaster County that not only Derry and Paxton Churches (today both in Dauphin County) were founded and provided with a pastor from the University of Edinburgh, but Donegal Presbytery came into being. The frontier had churches from below the Pennsylvania-Maryland line (not yet exactly determined) to within a few miles of the mouth of Paxton Creek, emptying into the Susquehanna at the Indian village of Peixtan, just southward of what would soon become Harris' Ferry and later Harrisburg. John Harris already had a trading post there; and settled just above him on the river were the Scotch-Irish families of Thomas Simpson and Thomas Forster.

The hardihood of the Scots from Ulster was, in fact, again facing west. The men whom it dominated had brought out of Ireland two names which spelled honor and an earlier beloved home to them:

Donegal and Derry. In their memories were images of villages and baronies on the western and eastern slopes of the Foyle River; and in their hearts was pride in the old achievements of Londonderry. But not the voyage of either Maeldun or Saint Columba was now to be undertaken; another adventure had begun for scions of the Scots of the Plantation in Ireland, and of the Presbytery of the Laggan.

It was pursued ardently. Creek mouth by creek mouth, creek side by creek side in the next few decades, it moved northward and westward mastering the shores of Susquehanna and the inmost reaches of its tributaries. When the Scotch-Irish pilgrims of the adventure crossed the Susquehanna, they were pioneers prompt to carry the ideals of the Scot into the Cumberland Valley, the Valley of the Shenandoah in Virginia, and southwestwardly to the Carolinas. Presbyterian clerics moved on missions from Donegal Presbytery to preach the Word and comfort the saints in the wildernesses of a new country, as once the followers of Saint Columba had voyaged from Daire Calgaich to Iona and Scotland.

Yet for thousands of the immigrants the fifteen years after 1730 were a period of settlement rather than one of search on still farther horizons. Forests had to be leveled by the swing of axes; tree stumps pulled or burnt out; forests floors turned into arable fields; and first harvests gathered from fertile, but difficult, new, and untamed soil. Cabins had to be set, crude tools to be made, first mills to be built, first diminutive barns and sheds, first log churches. Highways and lanes had to be plotted, surveyed, cut through woods and rocks, directed through mountain gaps, paralleled with creeks, bent around hill bases, or sped along old Indian paths. Labor made its unremitting demands. On purses fell expenses for warrants and patents to land, for surveyors' bills and land office fees. There was for the majority of the settlers more toil than romance, more burden than pastime. Shelter was more necessary than entertainment, livelihood than festivity. Clothing had to be manufactured from the hides of cattle, the skins of wild beasts, wool from a scattering of sheep, linen from sparse new fields of flax. From religion as much as any source not immediately material and gain-producing had to come interest and pleasure, or relief for man, wife, and child from the rigors of industry.

But religion had its zest in what was to be the era of the two Wesleys in England, and of George Whitefield and William Tennent and his sons in America; and Presbyterianism had among the Scotch-Irish not only apostles and saints, but zealots and rebels. Between the two rivers Delaware and Susquehanna, in Pennsylvania's four counties raged considerable spiritual fever. First ministers among the Scotch-Irish in the early colonial presbyteries were graduates of Scottish or Irish colleges and universities. The lack of sufficient numbers of these inspired William Tennent—whose Presbyterianism, because he had once been a deacon and priest in the Established Church of Ireland, smacked too much of Anglicanism for a number of his fellow divines—to found an institution for the training of divinity students and ministers.

In the late 1720's this Edinburgh University scholar and cousin on his mother's side to the Friend, James Logan of "Stenton," began with a log school on Neshaminy Creek, some twenty miles from Philadelphia in Bucks County, at a point where he also enjoyed a pastorate. A man of marked gifts, and a teacher of unusually fine parts, Tennent attracted to his college and taught with the aid of his four sons—whom he had already himself taught—a cluster of brilliant young Presbyterians. His pupils, once they had been examined, licensed, and ordained by the Presbyteries of Lewes, Newcastle, and New Brunswick (New Jersey), rivaled clerical colleagues who had studied in Old World universities. Moreover, they put even more of fervor into their preaching, and looked askance at the manners and the morals of their fellow clerics. Indeed, in 1740, Gilbert Tennent, most eminent of William's sons, went so far as to preach at Nottingham (then thought of as in Pennsylvania) on the theme "The Danger of an Unconverted Ministry, Considered in a Sermon on Mark 6:34." His sermon, presently printed, touched off a schism which was to keep Presbyterians split into "Old Side" and "New Side" for twenty years.

So it was as well that the Synod by an adopting Act in 1729 required of all ministers, before they could be ordained, subscription to the Westminster Confession of Faith. Only that wise measure kept the Scotch-Irish together in one Calvinist fold. Their pastors contested with each other. Congregations vied with each other in piety or passion. Families quarreled, or—what was worse—left their labors to throng to preachings in the fields of the New Siders or of George Whitefield in his periodic visits to the Colonies. From Philadelphia westward to the Susquehanna at Pequea and Upper Octorara the eloquent Whitefield carried his message against sin or failure to respond to grace. Old Side clergymen objected to Whitefield, descanted on the disorderliness and divisiveness of their New Side brethren, and censured them in resolutions at meetings of Presbytery. Churches and Presbyteries split in their memberships.

Donegal Presbytery and Newcastle Presbytery parted company with respect to methods of grace, Donegal adhering to Old Side ways and Newcastle embracing New. Into the limits set by earlier perambulation for the Reverend William Bertram of Derry Church and for John Elder of Paxton, came in 1745 New Side John Roan, pupil of William Tennent. In the next few years that former Ulster Scot and disciple educated in the Log College at Neshaminy had far more followers in New Side churches in Derry, Paxton, and Donegal than subscribed themselves Presbyterians in the Old Side flocks of the Messrs. Bertram, Elder, and Richard Sankey. Old Side Derry Church was in Donegal Presbytery; New Side Derry belonged with Mr. Roan to Newcastle; Mr. Roan's third church, Donegal, in the geographical midst of Donegal Township, was, contradictorily enough, allied to the same Delaware River presbytery.

Gilbert Tennent's text in the famous sermon which touched off the lasting division was, "And Jesus, when he came out, saw much people, and was moved with compassion toward them because they were as sheep not having a shepherd: and he began to teach them many things."

But the choice of Mark 6:34 was prophetic of more than schism in connection with the Presbyterian Scotch-Irish. The Tennent Log College emerged no more from idiosyncrasy than from the wish to provide for a need. There was in the Scotch-Irish, inherited from their Scottish forebears, a hunger for education. Schooling was second nature to them. Tennent's devotion to teaching was matched at many other points within a few years at many Scotch-Irish communities between Delaware and Susquehanna. Learning and doctrine had equal opportunity and fervor.

It was almost conventional for the Scotch-Irish pastor, whether Old Side or New, to administer education as faithfully as he prepared his sermons or administered the sacraments. At Faggs Manor in Chester County the Reverend Samuel Blair presided over one classical academy. His brother, John Blair, served in the same capacity near at hand, and carried his gifts for teaching with him when in later years he had migrated to a charge west of the Susquehanna. Samuel Finley, destined to be an early President of the College of New Jersey, had a classical school at Nottingham nurturing boys there who like Benjamin Rush and Richard Stockton would be leaders in their country's life. Francis Alison in 1743 began a career of teaching at New London, Chester County, which would presently make him in other fields the admired master and friend of college presidents, teachers, historians, governors, assemblymen, and three signers of the Declaration of Independence.

All these initiated a trend which would move westward and northward with every effectual settlement of the Scotch-Irish. By Scotch-Irish pastors the humanist culture and classical learning which had prospered in European universities during the Renaissance was brought into Pennsylvania and perpetuated in support of the reformed religion of Calvin and Knox.

It would not, however, be fair to say that the Scotch-Irish of frontier Pennsylvania were as equable in all things as they were constant in their zeal. The minutes of Old Donegal Presbytery testify often enough to the opposite of moderation and equanimity.

Presbyterians quarreled not only about concepts of Christian behavior. Pastors quarreled with church members who did not pay their pledges of support. Church members quarreled with pastors for prohibiting them from the sealing ordinances of the Church, for refusing baptism to their children or communion to themselves because, as the pastors maintained, their subscriptions were unpaid. If there were rebukes to members for drunkenness, fornication, and flagrant misconduct, there were charges brought to Presbytery against such practices by clergy too—with painful investigation, proof of guilt or innocence established, and rebuke or vindication all diligently recorded. The *fama clamosa*, or outcry against individual sin, had many an entry. There was scarcely an aspect of human life on which elders or ministers might not turn their eyes. Husband or wife might resort to *fama clamosa* with equal privilege to obtain justification or redress.

Nor did her being a pastor's helpmate always restrain a woman from bringing to ecclesiastical adjudication her "clamorous protest." Donegal Presbytery was shaken in 1737 by the outcry of the wife of the Reverend Mr. Thomas Creaghead of Pequea. That spirited lady had been debarred from the communion table by her own husband in the presence of his flock and would not be content with her spouse's decision. She resorted to the authority of the Presbytery.

For a summer and autumn, before reconciliation was effected between the two contestants and the wife was re-admitted to the Sacraments, Presbytery's business became everybody's business. Members of distant Paxton Church made it clear to senior clerics of Donegal that they would not attend worship if Mr. Creaghead was sent to them as a supply when, on the prospective retirement of Mr. William Bertram, they were looking for a new shepherd. Strange spectacle for the dignified young licentiate, John Elder, to contemplate at Pequea in

October as he came before Presbytery to qualify by a sermon and receive instruction to supply for four sabbaths at Paxton Church in
further test of his merits! Sober warning to a man intending for the
ministry, and still unwed.

But neither then nor now was the Scot to be summed up in either
mutable fervor or litigiousness. Perseverance is a trait again and again
illustrated in him. A conviction once born in the Scot is never lightly
foregone. Among the Scotch-Irish settled between the two great rivers
of Pennsylvania were descendants of the Scottish Covenanters; and
persuasions as to what was right in their Christian faith for the immigrants still survived among loyal adherents to an old Presbyterian
ideal in Scotland. At Braehead in that country, in 1743, the Reverend
John McMillan and Mr. Thomas Mairn instituted themselves as the
Reformed Presbytery of Scotland, determined to reassemble in one
organization the scattered remnants of the Solemn League and Covenant and of those followers of Richard Cameron who would not accept
the Presbyterian State Church of Scotland established in William and
Mary's reign. Four years later they ordained into the ministry McMillan's pupil, John Cuthbertson, intending to have him minister to scattered Covenanters in Ireland.

They could not have chosen a better pillar for their dream of a re-
Covenanted Church. But it was in America rather than in Ireland that
John Cuthbertson of Ayrshire aspired to help. The children of an old
School of Presbyterianism were eager for a type of leadership which
antedated subscription to the *Westminster Confession of Faith*; and
into their Macedonia between Delaware and Susquehanna in 1751
came that indefatigable missionary. He was four months over thirty-
three years when he arrived, peerless in energy and devotion to his
errand.

Factually he set down as the first entry in his American diary: "After
being forty-six days, Twenty and six-tenth hours at sea from Londonderry Loch, landed safely at Newcastle August 5th, 1751, about eight
in the forenoon;"[31] and promptly he set off for his mission. On the
second day after his arrival he rode fifteen miles to John Ross's of
New London Manor, Chester County; on August 9 he fared on to
Joseph Walker's in Middle Octorara. After two days with that host he
rode three miles to preach two sermons, on Psalm 8 and Song of Solo-
mon 3, and lecture on Luke 12:22-31 in a tent set up for services on his
first Sabbath Day in the Colonies. Next morning he set off on his horse,
and after limiting his rides to nine and eight miles on the 12th and
13th, was ready to preach again in the Pequea Valley two more ser-

mons on new texts and to lecture on Matthew 11:25-30 at Wednesday midweek services. On the 15th he rode not less than forty miles into Lancaster, and then on to Swatara Creek. Five more days and he was preaching a sermon, reading a lecture on Hebrews 4:14, and baptising the daughters in three families—all early enough for him to ride 18 miles farther on that August 20, cross the Susquehanna, and arrive at Walter Buchanan's house on the Conodoguinet Creek. There, on the next day he preached two sermons again, baptised three more children; and rode on 20 more miles into the Cumberland Valley. In his journal he made entry, "Give all praise to God," but at the end of the day admitted that he was "weary" and had been "molested." On August 22 he was at Rocky Spring (within five miles of modern Chambersburg) ready as ever in the calling to which he had been ordained at Braehead.

For Irish Saint Columba, sixth century apostle of Christian doctrine to Scotland, himself could not have been more impassioned than John Cuthbertson. As that Covenanter missionary was in his first three weeks in America, so was he to be for the next forty years. Other Presbyterian pastors had their fixed places of abode; their one, two, or three churches, their numerous concentrated congregations. Cuthbertson had chiefly the cabins of his friends, tents set up nearby, or open fields where folk gathered about him more numerously, as often they did. But he made of every home which he visited a sanctuary; and he visited thousands, conducting baptism here, the ceremony of marriage there, endlessly preaching and lecturing, never twice on the same text, and on rarer occasions administering communion.

To find in Christian annals a more persevering and constant saint would be difficult. Itinerant man of God, he rendered his service here, there, in Maryland, Pennsylvania, Delaware, New York, and New England, but most of all in the frontier counties of Penn's Province. He traveled on horseback, walked or led his horse in shadows of night and density of forest. He sailed, rowed, or walked on the ice, over the Susquehanna and other rivers and streams. Compass and blazed trees were his guides, or the instinct of his beast. He met sun and blizzard, as his diary testified, burning sun or rain, copperheads, rattlesnakes, treacherous Indians. On his long rides he studied the Bible and its commentaries, preparing for ever new sermons.

Adventurer of a faith, pilgrim of an eternity in his own way, he was both an individualist and the symbol of a race which had come restless and untiring into a new land. No true mold of Christianity seemed unrecoverable to him; no purpose of Christian dedication unfulfillable.

CHAPTER 3

SUSQUEHANNA

REDUCED TO A MAP and looked on from above, the rivers of the northeastern and eastern seaboard of the United States suggest a forest which by some odd transmutation has been flattened into one severe geometric plane.

A myriad of trees, trunk, bough, and branch, lie in one level experience, intricate and unpatterned except that the bases of all the horizontal trunks rest upon the coastal waters of a sea which is pictured more open but otherwise as flat as themselves. So closely are they drawn by map makers, whether first seventeenth- and eighteenth-century discoverers for the white man or twentieth-century draftsmen preparing textbook geographies for school children, that branches and boughs seem to interlace. But no terminal cartographic twigs of any two trees ever actually cross, and no branches of any two ever actually enmesh. All have a separateness which would be nonexistent in a forest of vertical trees; and all, as they stretch fork and bough in their horizontal plane, frame but a paradox.

The map reader, as he regards them, knows that they are not trees. For him today they are only a part in a network of lanes, roads, pikes, by-passes, superhighways, railroad systems, canal systems, air ports and air routes, mountains, mountain ranges, valleys and plains, meadows and pastures, swamps, bottom lands and hillside fields plowed and harrowed or planted and ripe for harvest. Briefly their limned shapes hint a story of agriculture, industry, and transportation; and a bird's eye view of them seldom takes us far into thought. To us they are rivers and creeks which have names for themselves and their branches. They are keys to a business errand on a new marketing of wares; to a picnic; to an afternoon of swimming at some new romantic hole; to a motor tour with family and dog; to a weekend of fishing along a distant, perhaps happily little-known, and perfect trout-brook; to a hunting lodge in the very heart of deer country with the splendors

[35

of autumn all about, and the season open for both does and bucks in a year of plenty and indulgent commonwealth laws.

Yet there in the cartographic plane of the American eastern seaboard are the river-trees; from Penobscot and Kennebec, to Charles, to Connecticut and Hudson, to Delaware and Susquehanna, to Potomac and Rappahannock and James, to Roanoke and Savannah, to Altamaha and St. Johns. And there, at halfway point for the eye moving south, its course ending in the Atlantic Ocean at the foot of the Chesapeake Bay, flat in the vast intricacy of intertwisting but separate black lines, the Susquehanna—a river-tree yet more intricate in figure than any of its neighbors.

It has been called "the Long Crooked River;" and certainly its crooks and bends, as—apart from compulsions of map-making—it winds around Appalachian mountain bases and through the valleys of Pennsylvania, reveal a complexity no less challenging than its overall length.

In nature and in fact it is a vast flattened tree-form of water always in motion. It is forever being born from ten thousand springs at ten thousand points of birth in upland springs and initial mountain rills. As a tree takes energy into it from breathing leaves at the ends of twigs that it may reinforce the vigor being gathered into it below the soil by filament root-ends, so the river draws its strength from particles of moisture oozing through leaf-mould or pebbles at the miniature terminals of its tiniest branches. The Susquehanna River is always being reborn of the confluence of a thousand infinitesimal tributaries, children themselves of cloud and mountain and sun. Yet its life is coeval with the age of these parents, and its history, primordial, primitive, modern, and contemporary, is as ancient as the history of these prime powers in the physical world. Moreover, it is not less complicated.

Indeed, to put the story of the Susquehanna together would require more than the cartographer. All the king's horses and men, all of his geographers and geologists, his chemists and physicists, his farmers and astronomers, his traders and travelers, his historiographers, archaeologists, paleontologists, entomologists, antiquarians, his scientists, his artists and artisans, his poets, philosophers, historians, both laymen and professional—could well join their efforts in the task and leave it unaccomplished. The shape of things to come and the shape of things past are both in the story. Complete rendering of them is still faraway; and the whole tale of the river is by no means to be confined between the material shores of all its physiographic tributaries. It cannot be summed in an ascent from Chesapeake Bay to Octorara Creek, Pequea

Creek, Conestoga, Chickiesalunga, Conewago, Swatara, and ever northward until all its conjunctures have been passed beyond Juniata, West Branch, and North Branch, and one far upstream terminal has been reached in a meadow spring in Cambria County, Pennsylvania, and another, two hundred miles away, at Otsego Lake and Cooperstown in the State of New York. Nor can it be measured in either the annals of Pennsylvania or of the United States of America when those two political and social entities are conceived of in terms of a transplantation to the Western Hemisphere of the white man's culture in Europe. Neither voyage on its surface nor the official archives of a Province later to become a Commonwealth opened to British settlement suffice to set forth the full history of the Susquehanna River. Nor can we sufficiently trace it in the little we know today of the aboriginal Indian tribes and nations who long ruled its shores and mastered or followed its currents. We do best to remember that in its completeness it exceeds boundaries of both time and space.

Yet when we approach the River's mystery first by avenues of race culture, or ethnographically, we catch first sense of Susquehanna territory as a land occupied by human beings when we enumerate Algonquins and Iroquoians, as larger Indian races once occupying the northeastern part of the United States from Virginia and Ohio to upper New York State and Maine to Canada, and when we attempt subtler distinctions among Iroquois, Delawares, Shawnees, Conoys and Susquehannocks (Conestogas), or divide the Iroquois Six Nations into the Onondagas, the Cayugas, the Senecas, the Mohawks, the Oneidas, and the Tuscaroras.

Most closely identifiable with the River and its tributaries, in times since the first coming of white men to it in the seventeenth century, have been the Susquehannocks, the Iroquois, and the Delawares. The Iroquoians, whose generic name embraced considerably more tribes than the Six Nations, occupied intermittently country from the Great Lakes and the upper St. Lawrence River to northern Pennsylvania and Ohio. The Delawares, or Lenni Lenape, possessed the territory bounding the river, whose name the white man transferred to them, from the New Jersey Coast to the westernmost tips of its tributaries, the Schuylkill and the Lehigh; and, in the course of the eighteenth century, by arrangements with the Proprietaries of Pennsylvania and the Confederacy of the Six Nations tribes, the North Branch of the Susquehanna including the fair Wyoming Valley. We cannot hope to regard the whole history of the Susquehanna, and omit any one of these.

But, more limitedly, the history of the Ulster Scots who reached the banks of the River between 1718 and 1729 is bound in with the history of the vanishing race of the Susquehannocks and their scions the Conestogas; with the Delawares migrating westwardly and northwestwardly in those same decades when they too might have been spreading along the tributaries of Susquehanna; and with the Six Nations whose Council, far away at Onondaga in western New York Province, kept its eye on every stirring of folk, white man or Indians, along the River, by means of an all-seeing chieftain stationed at Shamokin, where North Branch and West Branch met. Between 1675 and 1779 as a matter of fact, the Susquehanna belonged successively to the Susquehannocks, the Delawares, the Six Nations, and the Scotch-Irish, whatever Land Office records in that century might say. Shawnees were there in that hundred years, and Conoys, and Nanticokes, but as scattered and nomadic rather than as constant and longseated owners. Only in an occasional place name were they to leave permanent monuments to themselves. No one of those three tribes has left a great tale of itself on the River.

It was different with the Susquehannocks. Nearer although these were to extinction than Shawnees and Mingoes, they have a story, one which is set down in the white man's colonial records and one which they carried in their hearts. Aspects of it in fragments of weapons, utensils, or ornaments remained in covered graves or covered pits of refuse where once their forts or villages flourished. Pictures of birds and animals or men cut into rocks downstream from the Conewago Falls reflect their life in forms romantic and mystifying to archaeologists who in the twentieth century study them.

First white man to write of their race was Captain John Smith;[1] and they entered into European history when first they were seen at the head of Chesapeake Bay in the summer of 1608 by him. His *General History of Virginia,* printed four years later, introduced them to English readers as an affable and handsome people. Sixty of them came to visit Smith, bringing "skins, bows, arrows, targets, beads, swords, and tobacco pipes for presents."[2] "Such great and well proportioned men are seldom seen, for they seemed like giants to the English."[3] Yet they were of "an honest and simple disposition"; indeed, Smith and his companions had much ado to keep the Susquehannocks from "adoring the discoverers as Gods."[4] They had a language whose resonance was in proportion to their size; it sounded "from them as if it were a great noise in a vault, or cave, as an Echo."[5]

Smith's description of their dress in words and his printer's portrayal of it in a drawing made it both deft and beautiful. Never could bearskin or wolfskin be adapted to better sartorial advantage for shoulders, throat, chest, and midriff; and the double-fringed loincloth devised by the printer added lithe grace to the figure. Long bow and staff contributed to an athletic carriage; and the middle forelock trained back like a crest over the head, with side locks streaming free over the two ears, increased the nobility and handsomeness of countenance.[6] At their entrance into the history of Europeans the lords of Susquehanna seemed cast for a great part on the opening up of a continent to the subjects of British sovereigns.

But that was not the view taken of them sixty-seven years later by Colonel John Washington, commander in 1675 of the army of Virginia.[7]

The interval had brought them many a defeat by Five Nations Indians. On them was blamed an act of atrocity in the forty-year-old Province of Maryland, which might have been charged as directly to their Iroquoian foes. The government of Maryland, meditating retaliation, called upon Virginia for aid in an expedition against the Susquehannock fort at Piscataway. Forces under the command of Colonel Washington, with Major Thomas Truman of Maryland his subordinate officer and aide, moved on that palisaded Indian redoubt in September.

It stood north not far from the junction of a tidewater river which emptied into the Potomac, upstream from that more famous river's entrance into Chesapeake Bay. Earthworks surrounded its main extent. A great circle of wigwams stood within its enclosure. Scattered trees or lines of trees rose here and there. From its main center the smoke of council fires often climbed lazily skyward. Outside were another wigwam or two, small fields of maize which the Susquehannocks cultivated, or clearings in which their few cattle grazed. It was chiefly a place of rendezvous against an invading enemy of their own race. In the past decade they had both experienced and administered horrible deeds of war in their struggle with their Iroquoian kinsmen up the Bay and along the Susquehanna. Of white men they expected warfare more honest and more merciful if they expected it at all. Moreover they did not confess to the white man's murder of which they were suspected.

When, then, the army of Marylanders and Virginians appeared on the march, they were surprised rather than startled into defense. Passively they received two messengers who came forward from Major Truman's staff to invite their chief Harignera to a conference, regretted they must announce that that leader had but recently died, and amiably responded to the request which followed that they send six other of their sachems to visit with the officers of Maryland and Virginia. Away from their people the six chiefs listened through his interpreter to Thomas Truman's inquiries; knew nothing of the atrocities perpetrated by Indians in the two provinces; were of opinion they must have been performed by Senecas. Advised that the horses of white men were fleet and Indian runners themselves swift, they even consented to act as guides for the Virginians and Marylanders in a pursuit of the Five Nations tribe who had, they believed, committed the barbarities mentioned.

In fact, they seemed so wholly amenable that the white officers ventured to make their inquiries over into accusations. Colonels Washington and Mason of Virginia bluntly charged that the murders had been done on the south side of the Potomac, quite out of Seneca territory: they asseverated that Susquehannocks had been the criminals.

Offended, the sachems presented Major Truman a paper and a silver medal with black and yellow ribbon attached, once given them as a pledge of protection and friendship by Cecil Calvert, Lord Baltimore and Governor of Maryland. As long as sun and moon should endure, it guaranteed them the faith of Maryland as their ally. The Marylander was a man of honor. The first conference broke up, and the chiefs returned at nightfall into Fort Piscataway, with promise to treat again with the white men on the next day.

True to their Susquehannock word, they emerged on the morrow, but now into the midst of an incensed army of Virginians. The feelings of men had been played upon during the night by Captain John Allen, a ranger, who brought into camp the mangled bodies of several white victims of an Indian raid. The bloody evidences of savage barbarity were for the common soldier complete enough *corpus delicti;* and Colonel John Washington could bank on the support of his troops. Again the sachems heard the charges against their people; again they denied guilt.

Then suddenly, although they came as the emissaries of a friendly people, they found themselves seized and bound. Major Truman objected to the procedure forthrightly. He counseled moderation, delay, a more proper inquiry. But his Virginian superior prevailed. John Washington reasoned that his army had come to destroy Fort Piscataway and any forces in it which resisted. He was confident that the sachems were already as good as dead men. His subalterns demanded importunately what should be done with the six Susquehannock chieftains. "We shall get the Fort today," responded Washington; "why keep them any longer, let us knock them on the head."

So to the disgrace of Virginia, to the soiling of the white man's honor in the oldest and proudest of King Charles II's colonies in America, seven years before William Penn founded his city of brotherly love and laid open a province into which men of Scots breed could one day freely come, five princes of the race which long had dominated the whole Susquehanna were knocked on the head. For Virginia prevailed over Maryland in the affair.

But neither Virginian nor Marylander took the Fort in a day. On short supplies the chiefless Susquehannocks maintained heroic defense of earthworks and palisades, while food and numbers of warriors both dwindled. Then, having destroyed all resources left in Piscataway, they outwitted their napping white man besiegers and made their escape on a November night. Around Maryland and Virginia they sped for a winter of horror, avenging themselves in many an act of blood. Later, remnants of their race settled in Susquehanna towns above the Chesapeake; and scions of them were still remembering their story when the deputy governors of the Penns had begun allying themselves with the Conestogas. When Donegal Township in Lancaster County was founded in Pennsylvania, the name of Conotocarius, "Destroyer of Villages," was still being applied among their children and their children's children to John Washington, son of an Anglican clergyman dispossessed in Cromwell's time and on his death in 1677 a wealthy landowner on the lower Potomac—a man whose great-grandson would be far more famous and, happily, far more honorable than himself. Fort Piscataway had become a blot on a great family's escutcheon; the tragedy of five trustful chiefs had become a prophetic note in the history of a river which flowed a hundred miles north of it.

Other memories, too, centered in the Susquehanna River in the years when Scotch-Irishmen in their new township of Donegal looked from lofty Chickies Rock down over that broad and swift running stream bending to the south and west around the rugged and precipitous slopes of Accomac Mountain and Round Top, or from their new Derry, farther northwest, beheld the rude, dashing splendors of its waters at the Falls below Conewago Creek. Its course, wide, clear, and smooth, or rock-broken and roaring, was a course of physical power and terror, defiant and challenging. The hills and uplands along it; its fields low-lying or high; its close wooded shores; its occasional shallows, with swamps paralleling its banks; its sandy alder-bearing or willow-bearing islands; its rocky islands covered with spruce or black locust or oak—all had been, and still were to be, background to the action and catastrophe of men.

Indians remembered that long ago the Susquehannock village of Meanock[8] above the mouth of Octorara Creek had been abandoned; and that later more powerful Susquehannock forts twenty-five miles farther upstream on the west shore of the River had been reduced and annihilated by Five Nations' attacks. Only Fort Conestoga remained of three forts on the headlands between the mouths of Conestoga and Chickiesalunga Creeks. Farther up the mighty current which had given their race its name the Susquehannocks had no villages or forts after 1729. To the northwest on the River the Conoy Indians had supplanted them and occupied a village on the east bank looking toward the Falls. Between Swatara and Paxton Creeks was one Shawnee town; and, across the stream from these, between the Yellow Breeches and Conodoguinet Creek, another. At the junction of the Juniata with the Susquehanna, on the Big Island (now Haldeman's) there and in the triangle of land bordered by the Rivers meeting other Shawnees lived.

For the next thirty miles northward to Shamokin there was no permanent Indian settlement. The mountainous river banks were inhospitable, offering only trails rather than secure places of shelter or sites encouraging for tillage; and, moreover, at Shamokin, where North Branch and West Branch met, was established the southernmost outpost of the Six Nations' power. There the famous Oneida chieftain Shickellamy, governor and watchdog for the powerful Iroquois, kept eye upon the Province of Pennsylvania and upon the Delaware Indians who were ever being pressed westward and southwestward into all the forks and tributaries of Susquehanna.

Nearest neighbor to Shickellamy and like him vested in Six Nations' authority was Madame Montour with a village some thirty miles to the northwest on the West Branch where Loyalsock Creek emptied.[9] That able and enigmatic woman, often vouched for by visitors as a French lady and French-speaking, ruled both as matriarch and counselor. Her word was law; and her half-blood, acquired out of wedlock by union of French and Indian, was no barrier to the acceptance of her wisdom amid the Iroquoian folk. They had adopted her in young maidenhood and one of their warriors, the Seneca Carondowanna, had married her. Canadian French and New York English alike sought her interest; but she had become "in mode of life," as Conrad Weiser once put it, "a complete Indian,"[10] and in all things she planned first for the security of the Five Nations. For her as for

Shickellamy the Susquehannocks were a defeated race belonging to a dim past; and for him, as for her, the children of Onas (as William Penn was thought of among Indians) in Philadelphia and outlying counties were of interest mainly as they kept Onondagas, Senecas, Oneidas, Cayugas, Mohawks, and Tuscaroras, when they had become Six Nations, a superior confederacy.

Helpful to that purpose had been two influences, although not influences undertaken in voluntary cooperation. Of these the first was an event in Pennsylvania history which brings no honor to the participants in it; and the second was an able peacemaker and honest diplomat.

In its physical and geographic aspects the "Walking Purchase"[11] of 1737 was more immediately connected with the Delaware River territory than with Susquehanna lands, though it had its effect there, too. That notorious transaction, effectuated by Mr. Thomas Penn, heir of William Penn and at the time serving for his father's family as the active Proprietor, and by Messrs. James Logan and James Steele as his advisers, took shape as the completion of an old bargain made between certain Delaware chiefs and the Founder of Pennsylvania in the early 1680's. Slowly it came into form. In 1734 Mr. Penn produced a copy of an old deed, the original having been purportedly lost, which had sold to his progenitor all the land from the westerly branch of Neshaminy Creek back to the Delaware "as far as a man can go in one day and a half." The Delawares for a long time demurred, neither liking the apparently candid terms of the document nor wishing to part with other lands without having a new share in the proceeds of sale of them to settlers. In fact, they had been making some private deals of their own with inhabitants lately arriving. Almost three years elapsed before the Indians consented to have the ancient contract carried into effect. Then at the end of August, 1737, three "walkers" for Mr. Penn who turned into runners made their way over hill and dale on a northeast, rather than an east, line to the Delaware; and the sons of William Penn gained for their Province a tract of land which would later make three counties, and the eastern boundary of which gave them new control of the river for another sixty miles.

In virtue of an ancient deed the Delawares had to vacate regions of their old domain far beyond the Lehigh, distribute themselves among their kinsmen in Wyoming Valley on the North Branch of the Susquehanna, or filter, wherever they might, along the watercourses which flowed out of the Kittochtinny Hills or the Blue Ridge and joined with the Susquehanna south of its great junction at Shamokin. Not many of them did so contentedly.

But the day of the Six Nations had come; and Conrad Weiser, interpreter for the Province of Pennsylvania and shrewd mainspring in the development of its Indian policy, was every day cementing the friendship between Onondaga, longhouse and capital of the Iroquois, and the children of Onas. He had had no hand in the perpetration of the fraudulent Walk. His wisdom in the averting of after effects from it by visiting among the Shawnees and adding their influence to that of the Six Nations to prevent a general desertion of the Indians to the French interest kept frontier and Philadelphian conditions in equilibrium. No ardent admirer of the Scotch-Irish (whom he always designated as the Irish) Weiser as much as any man kept the Susquehanna River open to their adventuring. There was scarce a point of it northward of Shamokin, on one Branch or the other, which he had not visited on his journeys of diplomacy; and he and Shickellamy had become the main effectual instruments of its laws and its justice in the last decade before 1744. Men of Scots breed might be its new adventurers between 1729 and that year; the Oneida chieftain and Weiser ruled the trails which they attempted northward or into the Juniata Valley.

Yet certainly by the early 1730's the Scotch-Irishmen were asserting themselves farther and farther upstream. John Harris, reputedly of Yorkshire birth, licensed as a trader by the Lancaster County Court in 1730 and apparently operating at his trading post near the mouth of Paxton Creek, acquired on December 17, 1733, by patent and deed, 600 acres fronting the River.[12] Northwards of his tract Thomas Simpson, Thomas Forster, and Thomas McKee had secured by warrant and survey, during that same year, some 300 acres each[13]—the land over which the stately tree-lined residential front of the City of Harrisburg would in the next two centuries rise. Three pioneers of Scots blood were, in fact, breaking their fields above Harris' for what, little as they expected it then, would grow into an activating culture in a commonwealth and be, at the least physically, the site of the great state's capital. Moreover, just a few years later, northwards of their tracts, Robert Chambers and James Armstrong of the same Scotch-Irish stock settled on patents.

Ready, indeed, to take upon them the mould of the frontier and fitted by the pilgrim tradition of their sires to determine that mould, were an advance guard of the heirs of Scottish clansmen and borderers.

They did not take position demurely. Thomas McKee was more

for trading than farming; and almost at once was buying and selling at remoter points on the River, rivaling John Harris in his journeying rather than competing with him in business, but in 1742 carrying on lively in his trade opposite the mouth of West Mahantango Creek. Of him has many an adventure been told. But it was the Armstrong family who quite unintentionally provided for Paxton Township its first *cause celèbre;* furnished the Presbyterian members of the Reverend Mr. John Elder's Paxton Church with a topic for awesome conversation; and made the government in Philadelphia uneasy on the eve of a new Indian treaty being prepared for at the fifteen-year-old borough of Lancaster.

James Armstrong was in 1744 a justice of the County, although not too handy at taking down the script of depositions. His kinsmen, Alexander and John Armstrong, were both traders. Already these two knew the trails to Shamokin, and across the River, beyond the Big Island, the paths along Juniata on towards Allegheny. There they had sleeping-places. They knew the best stops at which to unpack their horses and spread out their wares alluringly before Indian eyes: coarse duffels or matchcoats to be drawn around redmen's shoulders for warmth or for ornament, shirts, mirrors, knives, scissors, occasional axes or hoes, bracelets of glass, trinkets for adults of either sex, toys for children, other lightweighted but tempting geegaws or utensils. And John, whom all folk, Scotch-Irish or Indian, called Jack, knew how to set prices to his own advantage in skins, deer, beaver, wildcat, fox, or raccoon. Furthermore, when he bartered on promise, he bartered sternly. It is possible that he attended worship faithfully enough when on Sabbath Days he was in Paxton; but certainly on weekdays he drove bargains with the reputed hardness of his race.

So, at any rate, reasoned one Delaware Indian who, retaliating in his own fashion rather than in kind, was occasion to a unique narrative framed by nine frontier deponents and set down for them in his unmistakable handwriting by their pastor John Elder on April 19, 1744, in the presence of Justice James Armstrong.

The signatories were Alexander Armstrong, Thomas McKee, Francis Ellis, John Forster, William Baskins, James Berry, John Watt, James Armstrong, and David Denny—of whom three, Ellis, Baskins, and Berry employed only their marks in signing, the last named shaping his as a diminutive animal, perhaps intended appropriately for a packhorse.[14] Mr. Elder made faithful copy of their attestation, leaving it, despite his clerical training and his meticulous script, entirely their own prose.[15]

The subscribers deposed that they had suspected that Jack Armstrong and his two men, James Smith and Woodworth Arnold, otherwise unaccountably missing, were murdered by Indians. They had put their heads together at Joseph Chambers' house, and there resolved to go in a body up the River to Shamokin to talk with the Delaware King and Shickellamy of their suspicion.

King Olumapies and his Council ordered eight Delawares to go with the deponents to James Berry's house, and from there to join the Paxton men on their quest to find the missing trio of traders.

From Berry's house, north of Wiconisco Creek, three of the Indians ran away in the night. The other five Delawares set out next morning with the white searchers and remained with them on their journey to the Juniata and the last "supposed sleeping place" of Armstrong. Arrived there, the Scotch-Irishmen dispersed themselves "in order to find out the corpse of the deceased"; and James Berry, coming to a white oak with three notches in it, found close to it a shoulder bone which set all thinking, when he brought it to the others for inspection.

They supposed the bone—as John Elder wrote down for them—"to be John Armstrong's" and believed "that he himself was eaten by the Indians." Less factually, they recorded, one of them handed it then "to the said five Indians to know which bone it was."

Different "sentiments" were passed; but on being put into the hand of one Delaware, whom they suspected of the still unproved crime, that Indian's "nose gushed out with blood, and he directly handed it to another." There (lest their asseveration be taken for mere superstition) they prefaced with an additional "They Testify and Say."[16]

Finding no other clue at the sleeping-place, the party "steered along a path about three or four miles to the Narrows of Juniata, where the Allegheny Road Crosses" and where they surmised "the said murder" to have been committed. They sat down for a conference on how to renew their "discovery." They divided into two groups, one of white men only, the other of white men and Indians. Then, not dexterous scouting with eyes always watchful of their Indian companions, but a circling of "Bawled Eagles" (they would be known to later Pennsylvanians as turkey buzzards) served them best.

On an island down stream they found the body of James Smith. In that same moment of finding, their Indian attendants, then on the off shore, disappeared; and "three shots of guns" away in the distance hinted that the Delawares had fled. The discoverers responded with a fire of three guns; and knew, having no other answer in signal, that the redskins had deserted them. Troubled, but not daunted, they resumed their errand. Down stream on the "Creek" side there were other bald eagles in the air, and not far away was the mangled body of Woodworth Arnold.

Nightfall was approaching. They thought it best to camp at the familiar sleeping-place and turned thither again. There the dog which had accompanied one of the deponents on the long search barked for the first time during the whole expedition; and, warned by him, the searchers stood "upon their guard behind trees, with their guns cocked, that night." On the morning which followed they returned to the two dead servants of Armstrong, took blunt note of mutilation and barbarity, and buried the bodies "decently as circumstances would allow." In their deposition they testified to ghastly cuts with toma-hawk, and a hole in one skull "which these Deponents does believe to be a bullet hole." They testified that they saw no more of the Indians whom Olumapies had ordered to accompany them; and, indicating that they thought "it dangerous to return the same way they went out," they chose the Allegheny road back to John Harris' (avoiding it would seem, the lower Juniata, and striking southwest toward Augh-wick before they ventured to turn eastward again to Paxton.)

Their scouting and their melancholy errand had taught them no great love or trust of Indians. But the mood and purpose which had taken them on their difficult and perilous journey were not satisfied. Furthermore they were not wholly without friends; and partial jus-tice, at least, could be effected after a fashion.

Three days after the date of their deposition, Thomas Cookson, in Lancaster making preparations of provender for prospective Indian guests there, was acting with despatch and forethought. Word had come from Shamokin that the Delaware John Mushemeelin had con-fessed to the murder of Armstrong. It was believed there that one "John a son of Neshalleeny"[17] of the same tribe, had killed James Smith and Woodworth Arnold. Shickellamy's sons and other Six Na-tions Indians on the great chief's orders escorted the two culprits as far into the settlements as James Berry's for trial by the Provincial authorities. Then at that place, fearing the resentment of other Dela-wares, the emissaries let Neshalleeny's son escape. Mr. Cookson made it clear by letter to Governor Thomas in Philadelphia that he would have the one criminal securely held in the Lancaster jail. Mushe-meelin expected to be kept there "until the Indians come down to the Treaty"; he preferred to be executed the Indian way, and he thought "it very hard" that the other Indian should be released. He did not believe Shickellamy's sons' reason for letting that accomplice abscond was a true reason. The agent of the Proprietary Government in Lancaster only thought it prudent to have Philadelphia informed of conditions on the frontier. But certainly he set into motion an episode in diplomacy.[18]

Conrad Weiser's wisdom was brought into the business. From his home in Tulpehocken, on the instructions of George Thomas he sped to Shamokin and Shickellamy. Two weeks later he was writing from that point a long report,[19] marshaling and sifting the information which he gleaned from Olumapies and the overlord of that Delaware chieftain, Shickellamy.

From Olumapies' statement he advised Governor Thomas that John Armstrong had been buried by the murderer himself, and his fellows' bodies by "those that searched for them."[20] The aged chief deplored that his tribesmen had been instigated by the Evil Spirit to the crime. Efforts were being made to gather and restore the slain trader's goods. The Delawares would make up in skins for whatever parts were "wanting." Their hearts were in mourning. In their sorrow they could say nothing more.

Of Shickellamy's declarations Weiser wrote at full length.[21] Olumapies, it seemed, was at fault. Mushemeelin, admittedly, had killed Armstrong, who on an earlier occasion had exacted from the Indian both his horse and his rifle for a debt which he owed the trader in skins. There was no question of the young Delaware's resentment and motive for revenge on that score. But during the investigation for Mushemeelin's accomplices within his tribe King Olumapies was drunk and failed to examine things properly. So he picked out and held as guilty Neshalleeny's innocent son. That youthful brave had been accused of complicity in sheer spite by Mushemeelin, who had killed, Shickellamy said, all three of the traders.

In fact, the Six Nations' chieftain furnished the most concrete and prolific details of the slaying, of the stealing of the goods, of an informer on the murderer and the companion Delaware thieves who made off with the packs, of conjuring by which to detect beyond all doubt the criminals, of measures adopted to get these into right custody and so preserve the chain of friendship between Delawares and Philadelphia. But Shickellamy did not fail to exonerate his own sons of their subsequent responsibility in letting the son of Neshalleeny escape at James Berry's trading post. Rather he made them very emphatic in insisting that the prisoners be delivered to Alexander Armstrong; his son "Jak" instructed the Delaware escort, if they were afraid to deliver them, quite precisely as to an alternative behavior: "They might separate their heads from their bodies, and lay them in the canoe, and carry them to Alexander to roast and eat them; that would satisfy his revenge as he wants to eat Indians."

So much for Shickellamy's power of narration and Conrad Weiser's skill as a scribe to him. The Delawares were abashed enough not to make trouble at Lancaster later. At the end of June, 1744, another treaty had become Provincial history. One Indian victim of Pennsylvania law at Philadelphia on November 5 was not enough to launch a war of Delawares upon that city. Mushemeelin was spared dying in the way Indians might have executed him; and young Neshalleeny's escape, whatever the motive or connivings behind it, served in the more general purpose of peace.

Today the story of Jack Armstrong has little currency in Susquehanna country. Few motorists realize, as they speed along the Juniata on their way to Lewistown or the West and pass through Jacks Narrows, that they are traversing a precipitous valley which takes its name from a murdered trader's sleeping place and violent death. The unsolved tale of the man is but another dim part of history.

But it was not so to Alexander Armstrong in 1744. The Public Records of Pennsylvania still preserve, besides the deposition of the man and his Paxton neighbors, Thomas Cookson's letter and Conrad Weiser's report, two manuscript letters of that second member of a Scotch-Irish family. One was addressed to Olumapies;[22] the other to Shickellamy.[23] Both called for justice and delivery of "all the murders." Neither indicated belief that John Armstrong had not been eaten by his slayers or that Alexander (Shickellamy's Jak to the contrary) had any desire to roast and eat Indians.

There was, however, something strangely pathetic in the Scotch-Irishman's appeal to Shickellamy. He began his request "to the King's great Councellor" with the words "My Great Friend, I write to you as you are a man that I hope will do your friend good."[24] He stated his wish. He asserted his wish not "to fall out or quarrel with you without you make us do it."[25] Then, in the closing sentence of his brief text, he reminded his addressee, "I am your hurted friend and brother."[26]

We do not know how much or how little he may have repined at the escape of Neshalleeny's kinsman, or actually whether he ever learned of how sentence overtook the confessed murderer and how report of it was printed in Benjamin Franklin's *Gazette*. What, unfortunately, we do know was that few of his Scotch-Irish fellow-countrymen in the eighteenth century were to believe in Indians very long as their friends. The shores, the main currents, the side creeks of a great river were all too often to bear other stories of disaster and treachery, involving Scots breed and Indian. Newer traditions would supplant lore of the proud Susquehannocks. A vanishing aborigine culture would have no more beauty and significance for the average Scotch-Irishman than it had for the missionary David Brainerd.

In September, 1745, ten months after the execution of Mushemeelin, that impassioned mystic and Presbyterian saint witnessed in trembling dismay ceremonies on a Susquehanna River beach which men in the mid-twentieth century would travel a thousand miles to see at Taos or Santa Fe. In the spring which preceded, the Shawnees on the Big Island at the mouth of the Juniata had been friendly towards his Christianizing them. Now, as the autumn neared, their natively pagan hearts were set upon a great sacrifice and dance.

Through the day, indifferent to Brainerd's zealous efforts, they prepared for this.

"In the evening they met together, nearly a hundred of them, and danced around a large fire, having made ready ten fat deer for the sacrifice. The fat of the inwards they burnt in the fire while they were dancing, and sometimes raised the flame to a prodigious height; at the same time yelling and shouting in such a manner that they might easily have been heard two miles or more. They continued their sacred dance nearly all night, after which they ate the flesh of the sacrifice, and so retired each one to his own lodging."[27]

All that joyous ceremonial ecstasy he pictured in his journal as beautifully as Homer might have described a hecatomb to Phoebus Apollo. But the twenty-seven-year-old representative of the Society in Scotland for the Propagation of Christian Knowledge stood back in solitary grief at their idolatrous revel. When it was ended he crept, pained and oppressed in body and spirit, "into a little crib made for corn and slept there on the poles."[28]

Next day was the Lord's Day, and his attempts on the holy morning to instruct the Indians were unavailing. Again they were bent on other pursuit than hearing the Gospel. Rather than that, they "gathered together all their powwows, or conjurers, and set about half a dozen of them playing their juggling tricks."[29] He knew now that their celebration was designed that it might drive off an epidemic of fever and bloody flux which had been troubling them. Yet there was no sympathy in him for their distracted motions, their singing, their howling. They extended their hands to the utmost stretch, and spread all their fingers "to push something away, or at least keep it off at arm's end."[30] They stroked their faces with their hands. They spurted water from their lips "fine as mist." They sat flat on the earth, bowed their faces to the ground, wrung their sides, twisted their faces, turned up their eyes. They chanted, peeped, muttered with warmth and vigor, some of them more fervent and devout in the business than others.

All the while he stood, Bible in hand, not more than thirty feet from them, resolute "to spoil their sport and prevent their receiving any answers from the infernal world."[31] Through the three hours of their charms and incantations he kept himself undiscovered and un-interrupting. At the end of that time his Christian heart rejoiced that they had received no answer at all; and thereupon he attempted discourse with the Juniata Indians upon his own faith.

It was in vain, however, he "named the name of Christ."[32] All that he could do on that Sabbath Day was to enter in his journal descriptions of customs from which his soul recoiled in utter disillusionment. And on the next day he made another distressful entry, recording that his missionary labors had been to no purpose. Moreover, he added of that island—near which were the trading posts of English John Harris, Scotch-Irish Thomas McKee, James Berry, and the Armstrong brothers—that the Indians "live so near the white people they are always in the way of strong liquor, as well as of the examples of *nominal* Christians; which renders it unspeakably difficult to treat with them about Christianity."[33]

That ancient tribal customs of the Shawnees might have had even more weight in their religion, as they danced and chanted, than had whiskey seems not to have occurred to the pious young Calvinist. Lost wholly on him was the magical firelight, with red bodies moving rhythmic within it, on what has since been known as Haldeman's Island.

CHAPTER 4

TRADERS, RIVERMEN, SETTLERS

THE INFANT John Harris, Jr., had been christened at Christ Church in Philadelphia on September 22, 1728,[1] his parents adhering then to the Church of England. But it was now the year 1753; and Harris, trader and ferryman who had five years before inherited the elder son's portion of his father's plantation and trading post on the Susquehanna just upstream from the mouth of Paxton Creek, had become a Presbyterian member of the Rev. Mr. Elder's Paxton Church. To the same congregation belonged his neighbors on the same east bank of the river to the north: the Simpsons, the Forsters, the Chambers, and the Armstrongs, all Scotch-Irish folk. By the minister of this congregation Harris' sister Elizabeth had been married in 1744[2] to another Scotch-Irishman. Indeed, four years before the death of the elder John Harris, first English settler in the area which has become modern Harrisburg, the Harrises were in the way of becoming, whether they wished it or not, foster children of the Ulster Scots who for a decade and a half had been rivaling the authority of the Six Nations on the lower Susquehanna.

October of 1753 came, and Elizabeth Harris' husband required thirty-eight pounds. At his brother-in-law's request, twenty-six-year-old John Harris, Jr., drew his leather bound receipt book from his pocket on the eighteenth day of October, wrote into it a receipt for the amount, and added an acknowledgment of a note for the same sum, held by him against his kinsman by marriage. That far voyager took the little pocket volume from Harris' hand; entered, in two scrawls below the receipt, an *I* with three crude cross bars and an emphatic capital *F*, and returned the book. Harris took it back; and, completing the record of receipt, wrote *John* before the *I* and *Finley* after the *F*, *his* above and *mark* beneath the two blunt letters.[3]

John Finley did not need learning. He kept his accounts in his head. His hands served him well at the reins of a pack horse, the oar of a boat, the paddle of a canoe. They tied traders' knots well, they sorted goods with dexterity, they maneuvered a rifle expertly if occasion required. In other respects beyond writing they were valuable adjuncts to his supple knees and swift-moving legs. They were useful almost as a brain in numerous ways. John Harris' brother-in-law was a fleet, far-seeking traveler of woods and stream, a lover of quest and adventure like Maeldun and St. Columba. The lure was not for him Irish seas or the westward waves of the Atlantic, for him it was Allegheny and Ohio, regions of river and forest far to the west of Susquehanna, full of a strange and novel beauty, marked here or there at the mouth of a creek or a tributary river by a settlement of Shawnees or of Delawares or of Six Nations Indians. Already in the late autumn of 1752 John Finley of Paxton Township in Lancaster County had visited Kentucky,[4] and fallen in love with a land which he fifteen years later inspired one Daniel Boone, his friend, to explore. There had been adventure before he got back to Harris Ferry ten months later and in new need of funds on October 18, 1753. But neither of the two men who bent over Harris' receipt book on that day knew in what positions of honor their two names would be held in two future commonwealths.

What they then knew were trade on the frontier, traders, Indians, and settlers; the stirrings of history were to them both only wonderings as yet about their neighbors and fellow traders beyond a mountain or river horizon. And they did not know in that October, as they talked amid Harris' stores, what had become of John Trotter,[5] their fellow trader in the township and on the paths to Ohio. They could guess that he had died, perhaps like Jack Armstrong in 1744; or that Frenchmen had crossed his path at some distant point and, pretending he was trespassing on lands of the King of France, seized his goods and person. Finley had had his acquaintance with *messieurs* and Indians. He remembered one affray clearly enough in far Ohio. From it he and James Lowrey had got back to the settlements on Susquehanna;[6] other of his fellow-traders he had small doubt had been carried Canadawards—to be charged with trespass before French justices.

Yet, while he and Harris talked, the story of John Trotter of Paxton was still in the making. Chief Justice William Allen in Philadelphia would himself not hear it for another five months; and Thomas McKee might continue for a long time to come hoping for repayment for an assortment of Indian goods had of him on note by Trotter in the summer of 1752.[7]

That former apprentice in trade to good Robert Young of Lancaster County, John Trotter, had moved ambitiously, in fact. He allied himself with a partner, Timothy Reerdon; and off the two set with four hundred pounds worth of goods, current money of the Province. Beyond Donegal and Paxton, beyond Carlisle and Aughwick, the path to Allegheny beckoned. To the west and northwest they knew were regions which men called Ohio and Erie, mountainous, river-channeled, peopled by wild beasts, herds of buffalo, Indians of many a tribe.

And what for young men were better than adventure and gain? If the well-known Conrad Weiser, the affable George Croghan, and Andrew Montour, the French Indian, whom all Paxton men knew, found Logstown on the Ohio no impossible journey, their juniors were not to be stay-at-homes—not when their blood had been drawn from Scotland and Ireland.

So August of 1752 beheld John Trotter, the trader, with his hired servant James McLaughlen, bartering Thomas McKee's stock at "an Indian Delaware town called Attiga, an ancient Town—situate on the River Ohio, pretty near halfway between Logstown and Venango, according to the course of the River."[8] But the river there (it was really the Allegheny) had "a very large Bent;"[9] and Attiga, Trotter believed, was as near to Venango as to Logstown. It would be no further exploit to turn to that last place than to make for Logstown. At the least, the trader and his man, having had a sample of Indian hospitality in the Delaware Town, risked passing on from there with two horse loads of goods; and adventure fell to their lot.

Suddenly, opposite Venango, before they could trade a penny's worth, a hundred-and-ten Frenchmen surrounded them, seized their persons and their horses and took away their goods. The mid-August day became a day of beginning; and the destination of Trotter and McLaughlen was to be farther than John Finley's fair land of Kentucky. On the morrow, in fact, the two Lancaster County men, their hands tied behind them with "hoppicos,"[10] strands of wild hemp, their legs fettered by somewhat the same means, and their bodies tied one to the other, were driven for a time before their captors. Only thick woods and slow progress made the Frenchmen relent enough to loose their victims; and then on the third day of their being prisoners Trotter and McLaughlen came to a "New Fort built on the side of the Lake of Canada."[11] What was more they saw a new road cut by the French, and great guns "being hauled along it toward positions in another fort already building."

They were not permitted, however, to study all the works of war being prepared for the Canadian army of King Louis XV. Promptly, instead, they were put into irons, confined in an outhouse, and held under guard. Four days they remained so. Then they were transferred to a bateau carried along the Lake to a small wooden fort at its head. Another day they were put into a cart which set out about noon and were driven to a large stone fort by nightfall. There was respite of two or three hours. After that, still in irons, they were set upon a larger bateau, equipped with both oars and sails, and were off on a voyage on another of the Great Lakes (whose name, like that of the first lake, the prisoners were not given to know). The sailing vessel brought them to Fort Cateraqui. Thence they were borne to Montreal, where they were jailed for four days with their irons still upon them. In that same fettered condition they were carried by sloop to Quebec and held there for thirty days more in jail.[12]

Here, however, they had at least one novelty in experience. Jacob Evans, fellow-trader of the Province of Pennsylvania and friend of John Finley, and now prisoner to the French, was put with them. He had had a longer journey with his captors than they. They all compared notes on the Ohio country. Three men, as they were next carried overseas from Quebec to Rochelle in France on a Man-of-War of thirty-six guns, could exchange stories or gestures at cheer. Through the month which followed at Rochelle, on the bread and water to which their fare was limited, they could plan together if ever luck was again to be theirs.[13]

The day of release came. The extended but simple deposition to which John Trotter affixed his mark (for he was as innocent of writing as was John Finley of Paxton!) before Judge Allen on March 22, 1754[14] rounded out his tale with both a surprise and noteworthy action, proper contributions from a Scotch-Irishman. Monsieur Menarrou, Commanding Officer at the Rochelle Jail, set them at liberty and provided them with a pass. (The deponent neglected to say at what English minister's suggestion the reprieve had come; John Patten's had come on the instance of Lord Albemarle; nor did he in his testimony repine that like Patten he had no restitution for his confiscated goods!) Delivery from jail was its own opportunity and reward. Trotter, Evans, and McLaughlen begged their way from Rochelle to Bordeaux. From that latter port Trotter and Evans embarked on the "*Betty and Sally,* Captain Snead*"* for Philadelphia; McLaughlen remained behind for want of "convenience" on the vessel.[15] They came to port on Saturday, March 16, 1754. Six days later the trader John Trotter, who had set out for Attiga and Venango, who had gone farther from Paxton even than the brother-in-law of John Harris, attested his deposition with a modest cross $+$;[16] and forthwith dropped out of history.

Except in their adventures and discoveries, perhaps, Finley and Trotter were not unique as Scotch-Irish traders on the Pennsylvania frontier. Hardly had Lancaster County been erected when active figures in New Donegal took to enterprise of their sort. Before their coming, James LeTort, Antony Sadosky, Peter Bezaillon, Joseph Jessop, Nicole Godin,[17] and other men of French blood, some of them refugees from the persecution of Calvinists in the era of the Revocation of the Edict of Nantes, others of origin in France yet more indeterminate, had been licensed as traders. These pursued their calling diligently along Susquehanna; and two of them, LeTort and Peter Bezaillon, transmitted their names to springs and hamlets and roads.

But Donegal and Paxton men were early to outnumber their predecessors whatever their race; and to press their journeyings or trade farther afield. James Galbreath, Jr., was plying his bargains along Chickiesalunga not long after 1718.[18] John Burt traded with the Indians of Conestoga before 1723 and by 1727 was dealing with them beyond the Swatara at "Snaketown," where his careless dealings in rum and affronts to his purchasers led to attack on him by several of his drunken victims, as well as to the killing of Thomas Wright, a fellow at that post.[19] James Patterson of Donegal, first licensed in 1723, when the county was still Chester, was operating on both sides of the Susquehanna near Conestoga before 1725, and as early as 1734 had ventured as far west as Allegheny.[20]

Families like that of Lazarus Lowrey[21] of the same township, all whose five sons engaged in Indian trade, and whose son James married a daughter of Patterson, were not numerous. But whole family connections, including in-laws, often pursued the business; and the Lowreys certainly embraced it with zest.

In 1730 the father was granted a license to trade with the Indians and to sell them liquor "by the small."[22] Before his death in fair repute in Philadelphia in 1755, that trader and substantial landholder along Chickiesalunga had made frequent trips to barter his goods into the Ohio country.[23] His son John, who had journeyed with him to the west of Allegheny before 1740, managed to have himself blown to bits in 1749 by a gamesome Indian's casting a spark[24] into a keg of powder near which he was sitting in distant Ohio. But that ending did not deter his brother James, Susanna Patterson's husband, from being the companion often of George Croghan, "King of Traders" (although not of Scotch-Irish breed), on divers occasions.[25] Where the Irishman out of Dublin went, (alternately suspect and emissary of the Provincial Government in Philadelphia) the Lowreys were willing to follow. An offer for his scalp by the French Commandant at Detroit failed to keep James out of Ohio; but it may have been added reason for his making a successful escape from the bloody affray in Kentucky[26] which led to Jacob Evans and several other of his companions being carried as prisoners into Canada in 1753.

Daniel Lowrey and Lazarus, Jr., won lesser eminence as traders; but their brother Alexander, apart from his not having so violent a death as John's, matched their father and his son James in final repute. He was only eighteen in 1744 when he began trading with the Indians on his own responsibility,[27] but before that year he had been apprentice to his father in the Ohio Country. Like few other Scotch-Irishmen he acquired the language of several tribes of the aborigines; and his skill in maintaining partnerships with such shrewd merchants in Lancaster City as Edward Shippen and the Jewish Joseph Simon[28] testified to his powers as a maker of bargains. Eventually he had trading posts and assistants at Carlisle, Logstown, and the Forks of the Ohio. When Lewis Evans' map of Ohio was published in 1755 the cartographer owed much of his accurate information to Alexander Lowrey.[29]

That flower of his family had recorded of him only one inimical contact with the Indians; and on that occasion his undaunted nerve, supplemented by his tireless feints and ability as a runner,[30] saved life and further career for him. He was to survive the War for Independence by twenty-two years, and at the venerable age of seventy-nine to be buried as Esquire Lowrey beneath a proud marble tomb in Donegal Presbyterian Churchyard. There his ashes would moulder in a grave near the dust of many another high-spirited family of frontiersmen, pastors, and soldiers of the Revolution: Andersons, Pattersons, Galbraiths, Hayes, Tates, Pedans, Scotts, and McFarquhars.

If in one individual man of Scots blood more of the spirit of quest could be summed up than was in the entire family of the Lowreys, or in the sole person of John Finley, Hugh Crawford[31] deserved that recognition. His trading on the frontiers began in 1739.[31] After that he was seldom of one place. Everyone knew him: Conrad Weiser, George Croghan, Andrew Montour, Christopher Gist, Finley, the Lowreys, and, by report at least, officialdom in Philadelphia. He traded in partnership now with one, now with another; and most of the places which all the traders together knew in their experience, he learned on his own particular travels. Far to the west of Paxton he ranged on the Juniata, far to the west of Juniata into Allegheny, westward to Ohio and Kentucky.[32] He exchanged strowds and knives for the Indians' peltry, but he did not fail to marvel at two mastodon's teeth discovered along Big Bone Lick and turned over to Gist, surveyor for the Ohio Company of Virginia, when in 1751 Gist, another far adventurer, visited Kentucky. As if he had been the poet Chaucer's Knight, Crawford was in much the same years on the Miamis, the Scioto, and the Wabash. Indian town after Indian town he visited on his expeditions, and no man took canoes or pack-horses farther than he. He was at Pickawillany on the Big Miami in May, 1748; at the Lower Shawnee Town (today Chillicothe) in January, 1752.[33]

Remembered today as the first settler to have a warrant for a tract near the Standing Stone on the Juniata,[34] which he conveyed to Croghan in 1760, to make future opportunity, as it were, for that second trader to become the founder of Huntingdon at the junction of the Raystown and Frankstown Branches of that fair confluent to Susquehanna; chosen escort to Pontiac when that haughty, but fortunately frustrated chieftain had to be humbled before Sir William Johnson at Oswego in 1766;[35] and in the next year an invaluable aide to Mason and Dixon, as those surveyors established the historic line separating Maryland and Pennsylvania[36]—for three decades Crawford played the game of merchant, traveler, warrior in General Forbes's army, and when times required, counselor, prisoner, rescuer of himself from French and Indian hands. And, when death came in 1770, he bequeathed as chief item in his estate a tract of land called "Crawford's Sleeping Place, on Youghiogheny River, twenty miles above Fort Pitt."[37] Both his breed and his calling spoke for themselves to the end.

The endeavors of Thomas McKee were not quite so far flung, but no other name, except perhaps that of the ferryman Harris, was to be as celebrated for trading on the broad current of Susquehanna below the junction of the river's two main Branches. Tireless as John Finley, colorful as Croghan, he began his enterprise as early as 1742-1743[38] on or opposite the Big Island on the west side of the river just above the mouth of the Juniata. Only one other trader had a post then farther north, his rival and friend James Berry, at the mouth of Wiconisco; but Berry was never to rival McKee in success and eminence. Berry would gain other notoriety, be known to have accepted of Jack Armstrong the horse which Mushemeelin resented losing, be remembered among Paxton folk as the ranger who discovered the shoulder bone of that victim of Mushemeelin's murderous craft, and leave his name on Berry's Mountain. Thomas McKee had his own story to tell to Deputy Governor George Thomas in January, 1743,[39] a whole year and more before joining himself with the Paxton investigators of Armstrong's death.

McKee told his story well. Early one frosty morning men came from the Island to the deponent's house, saying they "had heard the Dead Halloa, and were much surprised at it";[40] and a few moments later he himself was hearing that uncanny cry shouted repeatedly from across the water. It was no time to be faint-hearted. He took a canoe at once and with his servant sped over to the Big Island and promptly asked the meaning of the calls.

To his courteous inquiry, "How do you do, my friends?" ten Five Nations Indians answered nothing at all, and withdrew into the circle of their Shawnee hosts.

The Council House was already in use for a conference of warriors. McKee made bold enough to be admitted to the circle and listened as the leader of the ten Iroquois told of a war expedition in which he and his followers had been against some Southern Indians. On the Shenandoah river a party of Virginians fell upon them and slew four of their companions.

Dissatisfaction with white men was obvious. But Thomas McKee interposed firmly that none of the disorders of which the Five Nations group complained had been committed in Pennsylvania. To which one Shawnee retorted that white people were all of a color. Another questioned audaciously whether the Iroquois had met any of McKee's men on the Juniata seeking to purchase skins. A third remarked bluntly that they had not. "If they had, they would have cut them off."[41]

The white trader realized that offices of friendship had grown important. Promptly he rose up, withdrew, called one old Shawnee to his side, and presented his Indian familiar with three twists of tobacco. To his friend he admitted his fear of rashness from the Iroquois, and he argued that the warriors of the Five Nations must be reminded by the Shawnees of their treaty of peace with Pennsylvania.

The Shawnee mediated with his fellow tribesmen and came back to McKee to report that the Council approved his advice. Only a few Shawnees had found his warning disagreeable.

The trader—who said nothing to Governor Thomas of his indiscretion in having passed over to the Big Island in the first place—became wary. While he studied the situation a white woman approached him who long before had been the victim of a raid in Carolina and now was a trusted captive.[42] She told him that the Iroquois had not really relented from their purpose. They had merely pretended that the decision about him was being left to the Shawnees. Another council was about to be held at some distance. Thomas McKee had better make his escape, else he would be cut off.

The admonition was enough. McKee told his servant what the woman had said in her Indian tongue. Then the two men slipped away—"privately,"[43] as he put it. Scotch-Irish pioneers were not given to narrating each perilous step in an escape.

But the trader experienced genuine enough internal qualms. It was no small grief to him to leave among the Shawnees and the Iroquois "his considerable quantity of goods,"[44] both on the Big Island and at his post opposite on the east side of the Susquehanna. No wonder he felt deeply in 1744 the wrong done to Alexander Armstrong's brother, or that he joined with the party of rangers who sought the evidences of crime at the Narrows of Juniata, or stood with his companions as the Rev. John Elder wrote down their deposition for them in April of that year.

Yet there was mettle in Thomas McKee. Zest for trade was in his blood; and within another year or so he had sagely chosen another post for his enterprise farther upstream than James Berry's, north of East Mahantango Creek.[45] Moreover, he had chosen a position just across from the mouth of the other Mahantango Creek in the west bank, on the very threshold of the Juniata Path to Allegheny. The advantages of chief arteries of traffic were as well known to him as gasoline stations and roadhouses are to twentieth-century traveling salesmen. And his hand would stay in the game.

In those two decades after the erection of Lancaster County in 1729, during which the traders were pushing their ventures farther and farther along the rivers of inland America, other active Scotch-Irish folk were busy occupying more and more tracts along the tributaries to Susquehanna. In the 1730's they pressed farther upstream than Chickiesalunga, Conoy, and Conewago Creeks. Busily the emigrants coming west over Chester and Lancaster Counties to Donegal ascended the Swatara. As Derry, along that Creek, filled up, newly arriving settlers found their way upstream along its course; and Hanover Township came into being with a goodly settlement of Youngs, Stewarts, Reeds, Dixons, and Murrays on its fertile banks. Along the Swatara's branch, the Manada, farmsteads were cleared and occupied by Wilsons and Wallaces, other Stewarts, Greens, Barnetts, Browns, and Robinsons;[46] and these pioneers knew of neighbors to the north and west of them along Paxton Creek south of Blue Mountain. Subsistence farming was for all the rule of the years from 1730 to 1750.

Each farm family had to have its cabin—or its loghouse of two-and-a-half stories, as more prosperity or more children came; its hogpen; its cow stalls; its sheds or its grain cribs; its half-acre of flax; its pasturage for a half-dozen sheep; or its two or three cows. A family must spin its own linen, produce its own wool. From new fields and from forest and stream on its own tract, too often neither a legally warranted nor a patented one, must come the family's food. The women must turn the yield of flax and the wool from the sheep into clothing. The hide of the deer shot in the woods or of the steer garnered out of the miniature herd of the family had to provide leggings and shoes. Little was to be bought by money, which seldom came to hand. In exchange for necessities like salt, iron, glass, and spices a family must supply itself with corn, wheat, butter, and other home-produced commodities for barter.

If the returns for labor were shelter, nourishment, and clothing, not a great deal else was expected. Good cheer, God-respecting gratitude, family affections and pastimes, loyalties in the neighborhood must suffice. The family circle must prove its own and its friends' and kinsmen's inspiration and reward. As much of creature comfort as possible, nothing of luxury, required planning and hard work.

But not even this little, when we judge the dimensions of prosperity by mid-twentieth century standards, was to be had legally by all. Numerous emigrant Scotch-Irish came into Pennsylvania without the means to purchase lands. Indeed, they often had little more than the pioneering spirit.

They looked over the unoccupied vastness of the lands in the Susquehanna country, and realized that for winning a heritage for themselves they had only the labor of their own hands. Squatter sovereignty became for them like that possession which commonly folk say today is "nine-tenths of the law." They settled on land which they found empty, or they moved on ambitiously to land which they had learned by hearsay to be fertile and untaken. When the Provincial authorities created new counties, York in the summer of 1749 and Cumberland in January, 1750, and the Land Office offered more great tracts for purchase, poorer or more adventurous Scotch-Irish preferred to settle beyond the new limits.

So an exercise of the authority of the Province became relevant in 1750. The Scotch-Irish had, as appearances at least went, disturbed both the Six Nations at Onondaga and the Council and Deputy Governor in Philadelphia. Along Tuscarora, or Path Valley, and above Sherman's Creek toward Juniata, whole families had established themselves on land still unpurchased by the Penns and still loved by the Indians as favorite hunting fields. Action, Governor James Hamilton and Secretary Richard Peters regarded as imperative; and those two officials were confirmed in their attitude by the two sons of the late Shickellamy (now agents in their father's stead for the Six Nations at Shamokin), and by Andrew Montour.[47] If the squatters were suffered to remain along the Tuscarora Path and on the plantations which they had set up to the northwest of Sherman's Creek, other unwarranted interlopers would press into other Indian lands; and violent retaliation might be anticipated from angered and imprudent Iroquois—for not all of the subjects to the Onondaga Council were strictly responsive to their chieftains. To be warned seemed the part of wisdom.

Secretary Peters had not forgotten the behavior of certain truculent "Irish" folk on the Manor of Mask,[48] in Marsh Creek in York County several years earlier. Provincial officers had found there the small respect of frontiersmen for law and order. Back inhabitants had defied the Surveyor-General of Pennsylvania, the Secretary of the Province, and a staff of surveyors and chain-carriers who were making survey of unpatented lands on which farmsteads had already been established. Instruments had been torn from their hands by excited Scotch-Irishmen, who kept muttering, "No Manor should be laid out there; they would pay for land on common, not on manorial terms."[49] Threats of invoking the Riot Act had availed nothing at Marsh Creek. The frontiersmen, not the law, had prevailed; the survey had been frustrated on land already purchased for the Proprietary Penns. Mr. Peters wished no comparable flouting of Philadelphia upon lands beyond Susquehanna which were still owned by the Indians, and which were claimed as domain by the Six Nations.

So he moved with caution in the spring of 1750. In mid-May he gathered around him the Sheriff of new Cumberland County and six Justices, the most substantial residents of that new seat of government: Matthew Dill, George Croghan, Thomas Wilson, John Finley, Benjamin Chambers, and James Galbraith,[50] before advancing onwards from Carlisle to accomplish the command of Governor James Hamilton. Their route took the *posse comitatus* through Croghan's (now Sterrett's) Gap to Sherman's Creek, which empties into the Susquehanna some two miles below the mouth of the Big Juniata, and over that Creek into the valley and woods lying between it and the next creek to the north and northeast, the Little Juniata. As the Secretary himself summarized afterwards, the party came to one of the best hunting grounds of the Indians "situate twenty-five miles from the mouth of the Big Juniata and about ten miles north of the Blue Hills";[51] and there there were five cabins or log houses.

Promptly Richard Peters and his aides set to questioning the occupants, four of whom were called before the magistrates. By what right or authority had William White, the brothers George and William Galloway, David Hiddleston, and George Cahoon possessed themselves of those lands and erected cabins on them?

Frankly the interrogated squatters replied that they had done so "by no right or authority"; they believed "that the land belonged to the Proprietors of Pennsylvania."[52]

"Did they not know they were acting against the law and in contempt of frequent notices given them by the Governor's Proclamation?"

The challenged Scotch-Irishmen admitted as frankly that they had no defense to offer for themselves; and three of them submitted themselves to the mercy of the law. But not so the two Galloways. While the six Justices took White, Hiddleston, and Cahoon into custody, those two brothers got clear of the Sheriff and shouted back from a distance: "You may take our land and houses. Do what you please with them. We deliver them to you with all our heart; but you'll not carry us to your jail."[53] And defiantly they made off (Whatever memories of chagrin might be recalled to Secretary Peters' mind from the Manor of Mask in 1745!).

That was the sum of action on Tuesday, May 22. Then, with three men in custody, official duties were resumed on the morning of the next day; and an inconvenience was discovered. Nobody was at home in the fifth loghouse but the children. Andrew Lycans and his wife were expected "soon." More could not be reported of them by their progeny. The course of law had then to determine itself. The fifth squatter was desired quite as much as the three already in charge of the Sheriff; and those three volunteered good-naturedly to assist their captors. William White, David Hiddleston, and George Cahoon offered to become security jointly and severally for Andrew's appearance in court. They entered, like generous neighbors, into a recognizance of one hundred pounds; and consented to execute bonds to the Proprietaries in the sum of five hundred pounds, reciting the fact that they had been trespassers, and had no right to settle on the lands, and gave it into the possession of Mr. Peters for the Proprietors.

Thereupon drama followed upon legal procedure. The magistrates emptied of their contents the cabins of the two absconded Galloways; remembered the defiant permission of the two brothers to do what they pleased with their lands and houses, and on Mr. Peters' order set the houses afire.[54]

The two fires were the beginning of a series. David Hiddleston, more amenable to discipline than the Galloways, had the privilege of removing his goods from his cabin, then saw that acknowledged possession of the Proprietors burned.[55] Other late occupants had experience like his. The return of Lycans suddenly introduced variety into the Sheriff's and the Secretary's progress of state.

On the twenty-fifth, before the posse were ready to move on to the mouth of Big Juniata, Andrew showed no appreciation of the recognizance which his neighbors had given for him. He did not choose to be removed with them to jail; truculently he presented a loaded gun and declared he would shoot the first magistrate who approached him.

There was a scuffle. Lycans was overpowered; suffered an indignity which the Galloways had escaped in helping to carry his goods out of his own cabin; saw the cabin burn; and, into the bargain, was borne off in custody, with Lancaster Jail his destination,[56] and his children left to fend for themselves or be cared for by the families of other unseated fathers.

The whole business reflected but little honor on the Provincial Government, Secretary Peters, or Governor Hamilton—even though the offending squatters, Andrew Lycans included, were released in a few weeks.[57] Six Nations' rights seemed protected on the frontiers; peace between Philadelphia and the Six Nations (already firmly cemented) continued fully assured, the authority of Taghneckdoarus, son of Shickellamy, was maintained as against Scotch-Irish contestants of it; and other factious Scotch-Irish folk besides those settled on Marsh Creek had grievances which they would hold in their Scotch-Irish way against their Provincial lawgivers. Ultimately it did the Penns no good that cabins were burned presently all the way down Path Valley toward Maryland,[58] even though in the summer of 1754 they bought from the Six Nations all the territory which the Iroquois were so assiduously salvaging from Scotch-Irish interlopers in 1750, and a great deal more of excellent hunting land. The majesty of Proprietary law asserted itself, aided paradoxically enough by a cluster of Scotch-Irish Justices; and the rights of Tuscaroras, Senecas, Onondagas, Cayugas, Mohawks, and Oneidas, for themselves and their nephews the Delawares were preserved. The cost was a dispossessing of some sixty-three emigrants from Ulster of their rude log homes, and the destruction of half of these at Little Juniata, Sherman's Creek, the Big Cove, Aughwick, and the length of Path Valley. Following the episode, one of the dispossessed, Simon Girty of Sherman's Creek, died the following year in a drunken brawl in Paxton, leaving a widow, several children, and one namesake son who later made his father's name as famous as that of any desperado and outlaw in Pennsylvania.

Yet, despite dispossession, the children of Ulster were entering securely into their destined heritage in 1750 along Susquehanna and its tributaries and on both sides of its main course. The Penns knew little of whom they really were buying for in 1754, and the next two years after that date suspended but did not forestall the future in Pennsylvania of the breed of Pict and Scot of Enniskillen and Londonderry.

CHAPTER 5

BACK INHABITANTS

In the general course of American history 1754 stands out as a year of transition, anticipatory rather than momentous. Colonials of the time realized little of currents joining on the eve of terror and violence.

The Pennsylvania Gazette, seldom seen on the frontier, offered its pages quietly enough to Philadelphians. Some readers perused curiously its advertisements of anything from pickled sturgeon to cinnamon and nutmegs, ladies' combs or gentlemen's snuff, the rigging of a dismantled brigantine or a grist mill, an English servant lad's time for three years or a few likely men servants bred to country uses.

Others noted its "freshest" foreign advices with concern, although few of them gave any particular attention to a notice from Paris, published in the issue of July 25, to the effect that Madame la Dauphine was "now actually in the fifth Month of her Pregnancy, and enjoys a perfect State of Health." (A prospective grandchild to King Louis XV, who already had a son to succeed him, meant little to a Pennsylvanian, although it was to mean much.)

Occasional readers went deeper than a husband's blunt notice of his wife's elopement and his intentions to pay no further bills for her, or scanned dubiously Christopher Marshall's boast that thousands had been cured of "most of the distempers incident to human nature" by taking the "Royal Patent Medicinal Powder,"[1] which his drug shop could supply.

Not too many persons read diligently a pair of "domestic" advices. Yet those two items were there just the same. One was a letter from Colonel James Innes,[2] an officer writing from Winchester, Virginia, of date July 12, telling of the descent of the French on Fort Necessity and Colonel George Washington. The second[3] was a detailed transcription of the seven articles by which capitulation of that fort was forced upon the young Virginia officer by Monsieur Coulon de Villiers, excellent strategist.

[67

And those items should have been news to more than Virginians. But Philadelphia, with its Assembly still by majority Quaker, was only slightly interested in military matters. Washington, on his disappointed mission to the Forks of the Ohio, seemed at most but to be serving the commercial and political purposes of the Ohio Company, a group of Virginians who were seeking trade and land there—miles and mountains beyond the tracts of territory which Thomas and Richard Penn had just been acquiring by a sort of side issue at the Albany Congress. Moreover, decisions at that great conference, going on then in the Province of New York, seemed far more important to Pennsylvania generally. Only officialdom, Governor Hamilton, Secretary Peters, the Indian Interpreter Conrad Weiser, Indian Agent George Croghan, were alert to eventualities—unless one should add Andrew Montour, friend of the Six Nations, who in 1754 was to become a key figure in the movements of diplomacy on the Susquehanna and along tangent parts of Allegheny.

French Andrew was a figure familiar to Pennsylvanians and not unknown to Virginians. Son to Madam Montour, female ruler of an Indian town at the mouth of Loyalsook Creek, a half-breed sprung from an uneven and mysterious parentage French and Indian, he had inherited his mother's kind of wisdom and power; and, as she—despite her mixed and alien origin—retained the confidence of Philadelphia authorities decade after decade, so he commanded a sometimes grudged but never wholly withheld deference from the Province.

Count Zinzendorf has left a bizarre verbal picture[4] of Montour. His cast of countenance was decidedly European. He could have passed as a continental, had not his face been encircled with a broad band of paint, applied with bear's fat. Besides, he wore his European garments in 1742 with a difference. His brown broadcloth coat with the scarlet lapel waistcoat beneath was smart enough, but his shirt hung loose over his breeches; a neckerchief of black cordovan decked with silver bangles took the place of a stock; stockings, shoes, and hat were not enough to present him as a gentleman of the *beau monde* when great earrings hung with pendants of brass and wires plaited like a basket handle completed the spectacle of him. Andrew was suited to the backwoods rather than to a portrait by Watteau, and apparently he disappointed Zinzendorf when, being addressed in French by that nobleman, he responded in English.

Yet, even drunk, Montour was to be reckoned with. Conrad Weiser, as interpreter, had served with him on various missions, and knew how mercurial the half-breed could be; but Weiser held on cautiously to

Montour's values. He wrote of Andrew's drunkenness to the Secretary of Pennsylvania in August, 1754, and of his abuse of himself, the Governor, and Mr. Peters while in his intoxication.[5] He wrote that he had left him drunk at Aughwick, with one leg in a stocking but no shoe, and the other in a shoe but no stocking, and swearing terribly. But before Conrad himself had got to Carlisle, Montour had arrived and was ready to greet him with a cordial handclasp and a fervent apology for his late offense. He was there a whole day before Weiser, and had not so much as looked into his own quarters on Sherman's Creek lest meeting with the honest German be delayed.

Child of an irregular blending of cultures and agent of competing masters on divers occasions, he was essentially a man of the boundaries rather than an inhabitant of bounds. Nothing could be more natural than that he should have been with Conrad Weiser at Logstown in 1748;[6] with George Croghan at Pickawillany on the Miami in November, 1748;[7] with the two sons of Shickellamy at the burning of the cabins along Sherman's Creek in the spring of 1750;[8] again in Ohio in the winter of 1751-1752;[9] in the command of eighteen white men, traders and woodsmen, fighting on the side of George Washington at Fort Necessity on July 3, 1754, and losing with Washington to Coulon de Villiers. He was always until that date unquestionably loyal to British colonials, whether in Virginia or Pennsylvania, never suspected of collusion with their French enemies in the west or the north, and interested in any enterprise designed for the security of the English in America.

There was much to interest him after the retreat of Washington from the Forks of the Ohio and the fall of Fort Necessity. The French, driving away the Virginians, had built Fort Duquesne where the Virginians had hoped to be firmly established. Back inhabitants in Pennsylvania were everywhere becoming apprehensive. The Quaker Assembly in Philadelphia was refusing to set up taxes for defense for two reasons: a native pacifism and the insistence that, if the people of Pennsylvania were to have levies made on their possessions, the Penns, Proprietors of the Province, must likewise submit to taxation on their estates—a taxation from which the Proprietors declared they were in principle exempt. Other provinces, Virginia and Maryland, were readying for some counterstroke against the French to offset the Virginian failures of the spring and summer. In England measures were being promoted at Whitehall for an army of British regulars to be sent into America. On Will's Creek, Maryland, in the autumn of 1754, new levies of Virginia militiamen were assembling. And Andrew Montour knew of these various movements through divers agents of the Governor and the Council in Philadelphia, always more alert to frontier action and necessities than reticent Assemblymen.

So during the winter, before the expedition commanded by General Edward Braddock matured by dint of the Crown's efforts in England and the active official collaboration of Virginia and Maryland, French Andrew became the captain of a company of Scotch-Irishmen of Harris' Ferry and Paxton.[10]

If a trifle novel, that fact was not altogether remarkable. For Indians had become common experience in Scotch-Irishmen's lives. Commonly, men in Paxton knew in October, 1754, of John Harris' Indian guests. The two Half-Kings, Monacatootha and Tanacharisson, appeared at the Ferry on the first day of the month;[11] and in the next night the eminent Tanacharisson, late intimate associate of George Washington and severe censor of that commander's choice of site for Fort Necessity, died in the house of his host.

Tanacharisson's death was an event of moment. Troubled by it, John Harris turned to the other Six Nations chiefs who had accompanied the two Half-Kings. "Where," he asked, "did they choose to bury him?"[12] Monacatootha and others answered that they all looked upon Tanacharisson as like one of the English.[13] He had died among the children of Onas; let him be buried among William Penn's people. Indeed, they were of opinion that if "he was buried well, it would be a very good thing."[14]

Monacatootha desired that the melancholy news of the death be forwarded with all despatch to the Governor of Virginia. Other Indians stood about blaming the French for their friend's death; a conjuror of theirs had inquired into the cause of his illness, and found it came "by bewitching."[15] Twenty remained to witness the interment, which was achieved with state and expense enough for Harris to be compensated two months later by the Government to the amount of ten pounds, fifteen shillings, and fourpence, with an additional five pounds "for his trouble."[16]

It was a time for appeasing the Six Nations; Pennsylvanians clung to the friendship of the Iroquois. Andrew Montour, earlier by Indian name Sattelihu, had been declared a counselor of the Six Nations by the Oneida chieftain Scarroyady in October, 1754, at a treaty in Carlisle, in the presence of Pennsylvania Commissioners Richard Peters, Isaac Norris, and Benjamin Franklin.[17] "A horn was then set upon his head"[18] by the spokesman for the great tribes, and Andrew became Eghuisera. He was a leader who counted in the esteem of legislator and frontiersman, however far short of exquisiteness his attire as a gentleman might be and whatever his addiction to drink.

French Andrew's appearance at Harris' Ferry in December, 1754, was signal for as great excitement there, in fact, as the Half-King's death amidst his entourage had been in October. Montour come on a recruiting errand.

Promptly he enlisted the interest of the ferryman's brother William Harris with promise of a lieutenancy when they got on to the forces now gathering at Will's Creek in Maryland.[19] That young man inclining to join up, other youths of Paxton gathered around with enthusiasm. A number of the Indians who had come with Monacatootha and Tanacharisson joined Captain Montour's company.[20] By the end of the month the half-breed had a full complement of Scotch-Irishmen and Six Nations braves. The elder Harris encouraged the whole process. Montour counseled the Indian families at the trading post above Paxton Creek to stay on with their friend there, and wrote to Secretary Richard Peters at Philadelphia promising him that they would be maintained with but small cost to the Province, and assuring him that John Harris' "kind usage to the Indians this fall has been of much service; it ought properly to be rewarded."[21] Harris himself was highly pleased with the whole business. He wrote to Edward Shippen in Lancaster of his satisfaction in it. He hoped Andrew's "company would act their part so well as to be a credit to our *River Men*, of which almost the whole consists."[22]

Then, by way of Aughwick, where they were to be joined by more Indians, a band of back inhabitants, sons of settlers along Susquehanna, were in early January, 1755, off to camp and a still undeclared war for which Virginia chiefly was laying preparation. Sons of traders and farmers, kinsmen and juniors of the men who in 1744 had scouted on Juniata looking for the body of Jack Armstrong were going by Indian paths and Pennsylvania creek routes to join Edward Braddock before that general of his Majesty George II had so much as arrived in America.

So far as trustworthy annals of history are concerned, they were bound more for mystery than for glory. No muster roll of them survives today. John Finley has been believed to have been of them and to have met Daniel Boone for the first time when the two men served in the campaign of disaster which ensued.[23] Any central Pennsylvanian of military note during the War of the Revolution is likely to be written of as having served in Braddock's army. The fact is that we do not know who of John Harris' young Scotch-Irish friends actually served with Montour. Yet the truth that some went with him, and that some of them died in the venture which culminated in the debacle of July 9, 1755, lent poignancy to the aftermath of Braddock's defeat. They, and the men of their race, had little to do with the shaping of the expedition. Designed in England, helped most by officialdom in Virginia and Maryland, encouraged by Secretary Peters and Governor Robert Hunter Morris of Pennsylvania without aid of Assembly, supplied with provisions and fodder by the merchant Edward Shippen to his own no small material profit, provided with horses and wagons by Benjamin Franklin—who did less well materially by that help than he had expected—dominated by a military martinet, the campaign, which closed in wholly unwarrantable tragedy at Turtle Creek, six miles short of Fort Duquesne, was felt more in result than it was in participation and purpose by the Scotch-Irish along the Susquehanna and its tributaries.

The outcome was to dog them with adversity and terror for many a year. Far more their portion to bear than the effect of their behavior were the eventualities which hurled themselves brutally upon them in the autumn of 1755. The pusillanimous Colonel Thomas Dunbar, aide to General Braddock and successor to his command after Braddock's defeat and death, dismissed what was left of his Maryland and Virginia militia to their homes, ordered an Independent Company to garrison the wounded who had been got back to Fort Cumberland on Will's Creek, and himself made for Philadelphia with an unengaged and undefeated twelve hundred men of the King's army and a hundred officers. Dunbar's mind was on comfortable winter quarters for the rearguard as soon as the catastrophe of the vanguard had been reported to him. He was not a man to enjoy terror. That was left for the frontiersman.

On these the Indians struck without need of abetting by the French, contempt motivating as much as hate. A band of Shawnees went on pillage there, a band of Delawares here. Scotch-Irish river men had much to anticipate, much to confront. Settlers fled from Tuscarora Valley and from Juniata; Shippensburg, Wright's, Carlisle, and Harris' Ferry were initial points of stop on their flight.

The Susquehanna seemed again the western boundary of civilization. Down that great river, by rumor and hearsay, ominous news came to Harris in mid-October.[24] Penn's Creek, West Mahantango Creek, and Mahanoy Creek were all confused in first accounts; what was imprinted most firm in the minds of listening folk was that there had been an atrocity, that many were killed. Once more men of Paxton—

Thomas Forster, John Harris, Thomas McKee, and Adam Terrance—
had to act for and with settlers all along the east bank.

Again they had on their hands an expedition of inquiry.[25] They
learned much. Fourteen persons, German and Scotch-Irish, had been
scalped and slain near their houses, and eleven others been carried
away; these were folk who had established themselves, not on the
Mahanoy or the Mahantango, but along Penn's Creek beyond George
Gabriel's trading post at the mouth of that tributary. They lay in
death before their own doors, or in the burned ruins of their homes.
Neighbors found them, buried their bodies, fled the valley, and from
Reading appealed to the Government in Philadelphia for succor and
restitution.

Only the forty Scotch-Irish scouts of Adam Terrance's party arrived
early enough to comprehend the meaning of the spectacle and of all
its implications; and they studied mutilations not so much as causes
but to identify the perpetrators of the manifold crimes. Their study
took them and their horses back to the east side of the river over the
great ford upstream from Penn's Creek and on to Shamokin. It was
second nature to the Susquehanna men to consult the Indians at that
former capital of Shickellamy.

Many were there: Andrew Montour and Monacatootha the Half-
King and others, and more were assembling.[26] By day they had one
thing to tell aloud to their white visitors; by night other things to
whisper. It was West Branch Indians, they said, who killed the Penn's
Creek folk;[27] those offenders had sent a hatchet and two English scalps
up to Indians on the North Branch urging them "to strike with them,
if they are men."[28] The friendly Six Nations Indians at Shamokin were
not enough to withstand a body of French with fifteen hundred other
Indians, "Picts, Ottaways, Onandox, Delawares, and Shawnees,"[29] who
were not many days' march away from Pennsylvania and Virginia and
headed toward those two provinces. Montour was full of warning for
John Harris; and also he was ready with particular advice to give to
the Paxton men. He suggested it would be safer for them to return
southwards along the east shore.[30]

But many of the Delawares at Shamokin were in war paint,[31] as
was French Andrew himself; and Thomas McKee observed carefully
while Adam Terrance, who understood the Delaware tongue, kept his
ears open in the one night the party stayed at Shamokin.

One Delaware said to another: "What are the English come here
for?"

The reply was "To kill us, I suppose."[32] Then there was the further inquiry: "Can we not then send off some of our nimble young men to give our friends notice and have them come help us?"[33]

A war song followed. Then Terrance saw two well armed braves speed off in one canoe across the river, and another pair in a second strike off down stream. Like Thomas McKee, he mistrusted signs and the war paint of Montour.

On the next morning (It was October 25) the Harris-Terrance company, forbearing to follow advice so notably insisted on, reforded the river and "marched"[34] off peaceably on the west side. They had maintained civility and a friendly manner at the famous Six Nations' outpost. Now they chose to follow their own counsel.

But the snare they feared had been laid on the west bank. John Harris, Adam Terrance, and Conrad Weiser all had something to say of it later in attestations and letters to Philadelphia officialdom. Ten miles down stream, opposite the mouth of Mahanoy Creek, where midcurrent were willow-covered islands and bushes to conceal them, Indians were lying in wait. As the Scotch-Irish turned east again at the ford above Mahanoy leading them back to their own east shore, a brisk fire suddenly greeted them accompanied by hideous "hallowing."[35]

The party broke. Half of them galloped back in retreat. John Harris and some fifteen other of the cavalcade took to trees along the bank and returned fire. They killed four of their assailants on the spot. But, as they made forward again on horseback, another man mounted behind Harris on the same animal was shot and fell into the water. Another missile wounded the horse, and the good trader and ferryman had to abandon his beast and swim. Four other Paxton men, not so expert as he, were drowned.[36] Adam Terrance had the view of one of the men whom he lost being tomahawked.[37]

But the majority of the Scotch-Irish scouts escaped the ambush. Some together and some straggling on alone on one shore or the other, they got down Susquehanna to their own houses and people, and told their several stories.

John Harris wrote the proper reminder to Governor Morris: "I hope our journey, though with fatigue, and loss of our substance, and some of our lives, will be of service to our country."[38] He thought his companions and himself wise in "discovering our enemy, who will be our ruin if not timely prevented."[39]

It must have been at about the same date that a letter from Colonel George Washington reached Andrew Montour. That Virginian gentleman, on the day after composing this message of October 10, admitted to Governor Dinwiddie in a copy forwarded to him, "it savors a little of flattery—but this I hope is justifiable on such occasions."[40] His greeting, in fact, was very cordial. Braddock had slighted Montour's advice; not so Washington. His letter to the half-breed was an invitation from his "real Friend and Assured Humble Servant" to come, family and all, "to reside among us."[41] The writer was "enraptured"[42] at having learned Montour had been in a march at the head of three hundred Indians toward Venango. He wished to be remembered, too, to his good friend Monacatootha. He hoped he might have "an opportunity of doing something equal to your wishes."[43]

What "Dear Montour" thought of his correspondent's courtesy, history has not told us. But it is true that whatever his intentions as he talked to the men of Paxton at Shamokin on October 24, he did not desert to the French. He was back at John Harris' on October 31, with a report of a whole body of Indians in the French interest encamped at George Gabriel's, with a rumor that a French fort was to be erected "in ten days hence"[44] at Shamokin. Eight days later he was in Philadelphia at the side of Scarroyady, reporting to Governor, Council, and Assembly what might be expected on the two branches of Susquehanna.[45] His feelings were probably at one with those of his companion, on the afternoon of November 8, when the Oneida threw his belts down on the table before the pacifist Quakers declaring that if the Province did not fight on the side of the Six Nations, they would go somewhere else for protection.

Montour, the bizarre, the drunken, the mysterious, the mercurial, the affable, may have helped. At any rate the winter of 1755-1756 beheld the first measures of defense beginning on the frontier and in Philadelphia.

At neither point did they spring from His Majesty's officer Colonel Dunbar. In Philadelphia the means for untying the Gordian knot of no defense was found during the last two months of 1755. Mr. Thomas Penn wrote from England in October to Secretary Peters and Deputy Governor Morris informing them of an offer: Out of arrears in their quitrents in the Province his Receiver-General, Richard Hockley, was to pay a free gift of £5,000[46] from the Proprietors as a contribution to the cost of protection. That meant that out of annual fees still unpaid by Pennsylvania settlers on their patents to tracts of land, a fund could be raised for aiding them. It was up to the Assembly in December to create further means.

The Assembly forewent its principle of making the Penns pay in taxes as it made all other property-holders pay; accepted the concession (although certainly it was not a surrender of the Proprietary position of being non-taxable!); and voted £50,000[47] by levying of taxes on the people. By hook or crook, pacifist Assemblymen who had read the handwriting on the wall, and the wealthy sons of William Penn who would not abandon their prerogatives of tax exemption at length supplied means toward salvaging Pennsylvania from the French and the Indians. A program of fort-building could begin at strategic points in the mountains, on the Delaware, the Susquehanna, and the Juniata. Companies of militia could be recruited and officered at the expense of the Province.

In 1756 an era of forts properly began for the mountain passes or valleys and the river junctions of Pennsylvania—along the Blue Ridge, here north there south of the gaps from Delaware to Susquehanna, a line of diminutive log fortresses came into being: Fort Dupui above Easton, Fort Allen northwards of Allentown, Fort Lebanon, Fort Swatara, Fort Manada, on southwestwardly to Fort Hunter six miles above Harris' Ferry. West of Susquehanna were Fort Granville on the Juniata and Allegheny Path beyond the Long Narrows, Fort Shirley on Aughwick Creek at Croghan's familiar post and Conrad Weiser's meeting place with Indians, Fort Littleton in the same valley twenty miles to the southwest, Fort Morris at Shippensburg, and Fort Lowther at Carlisle.[48] Before the end of the year Fort Augusta[49] was built upstream upon the Susquehanna at Shamokin, designed to protect from French or Indian invasion at the confluence of the West and North Branches, and destined to supplant in importance Shickellamy's old council post for the Six Nations.

But these small stockaded defenses could be nothing without men. Nor could the able and prudent Colonel Conrad Weiser of Heidelberg, for the first season commander of companies and forts between Easton and Hunter's Mills, cover the whole territory. Riflemen and scouts had to be found and leaders for them in every locality threatened by the general danger. John Armstrong, eminent citizen of Carlisle, became Lieutenant Colonel in command there. Squire Adam Read, farmer on Swatara and resident of Hanover Township, Lancaster County, was commissioned as captain. Trader Thomas McKee, veteran of the Paxton men, who had scoured Juniata eleven years earlier on the quest for the slayers of Jack Armstrong and had been lately a hero in the Penn's Creek expedition, was named to the same rank.[50]

Armstrong, Read, and McKee were, in fact, the first three Scotch-Irishmen named by the provincial authorities to military office to serve in the command of other Scotch-Irishmen for the defense of their Scotch-Irish neighbors and of Pennsylvania. The duties of Read and McKee, beyond recruitment and reception and maintenance of stores, were simple. One headed a company of Hanover rangers, who patrolled Blue Mountain from Swatara Gap to Hunter's Mill, possession of a son-in-law of the original settler there, Joseph Chambers; the other a company of Paxton rangers who patrolled the east bank of Susquehanna from Hunter's northwards. Their men were divided into groups of ten or twelve who deployed back and forth between fortified farmhouse stations. Once a day the six- to ten-mile interval of farmland and forest between every two loop-holed, unstockaded farm houses was covered, in the effort to detect or to drive off any Indians lurking or raiding. Nights were spent at the stations with the family of the farmer or trader living there. Through the first half of the year folk in the townships bordering on Susquehanna had no more effectual protection than that simple arrangement under Captains Read and McKee. In fact and in spirit—beyond sparse allowances of muskets, powder, blankets, and provender—they were their own defenders. More than in officials in Philadelphia the assurance of their safety lay in the leadership of men like James Galbreath, John Harris, Thomas Forster, Adam Read, Thomas McKee, and the Rev. Messrs John Roan of New Side Derry Presbyterian Church, and John Elder and Richard Sankey of Old Side Paxton and Hanover Churches.

But that assurance was not impregnable. Violence came despite the vigilance and the valor of Scotch-Irish rangers. Not even the gradual advance of Colonel William Clapham with four hundred Provincial militia and riflemen up Susquehanna in midsummer from McKee's headquarters at Fort Hunter toward Shamokin made all settlers secure. Slaying and rapine by the Indians came in August, in the very vicinity of Forts Robinson and Manada at Manada Gap, upon Hanover folk. Their neighborhood was already sheltering the wounded Andrew Lycans, once burned from his cabin in Sherman's Valley by the Provincial authorities, and in March, 1756, driven with the remnants of his household and family out of a new warranted tract and home along Wiconisco Creek. He had been carried with these over three mountains in flight from an Indian raid and a bloody encounter in which contestants on both sides had been killed.[51] In the Lancaster County frontier township, while men nursed him unavailingly toward strength, his presence and weakness were both symbol and warning. Then closer bolts from the storm which John Harris and the Rev. Mr. Elder had been predicting to the Secretary and the Governor came in August.

James Ellis, soldier of Captain Frederick Smith's Company detailed at James Brown's loghouse station toward Manada, had a crop of wheat more than ready for cutting in a field two miles beyond that gap. On August 6[52] he prevailed with his corporal and some nine other scouts to repair thither and reap. Presently, with guards set and watching, they were busy with scythes and tying up bottles of wheat. Three Indians crept to position at one panel of the snake fence, fired on them suddenly, with the first shot killed their officer and with another wounded a second reaper as he stood gun in one hand and sheaf of grain in the other. A sinister howling and mad running and dashing of red devils followed as the rest of the party leaped to their guns. One Indian darted forth to seize the gun of the wounded scout and was driven off by his comrades, but made a fleet escape through the actual midst of them. Then the savages cleared away in retreat.

The nine white men hid the body of their fallen corporal, and, carrying their wounded companion, made for their fort. There they found missing James Brown, soldier and landlord.[53] Next day that descendant of John Brown of Priesthill, Scottish martyr shot down by Claverhouse's dragoons in 1685, was discovered killed and scalped near Ellis' wheat field. His gun, his shoes, and his jacket had been wrested from him and borne off by the redskins.

All this was a story to be recounted by Captain Adam Reed to Philadelphia officialdom. That frontier officer wrote factually, but not extenuatingly so far as his men were concerned. Indeed, he appended to his narrative the crisp commentary: "The rising ground above the field was clear of standing timber and the grubs [tree stumps] were low; so that they kept a bad look out."[54]

But the fact that a corporal's squad had been caught napping and the corporal and Brown been slain did not hide the truth from Hanover Township that Indians were lurking around Manada. Within two more weeks other Indian bands struck.

Eluding the scouts of the community and spreading east and west to the south of the Gap, they fell on families in their homes or at work in their fields. Ten men and women were killed and one boy, all persons with Scotch-Irish names, Craig, Galloway, Gibson, Berryhill, Fleming, Beatty, McClelland, and the like.[55] Another twelve, children and adults, male and female, and of similar surnames, were carried away prisoners. Joseph Barnett, farmer and devout Presbyterian of Hanover, became the central figure of an episode and story.[56]

He was at work in his own mountainside fields three miles from Manada with his neighbor James Mackey helping when sudden word of the incursion reached them. The two men sprang for their rifles, sprang aback their horses, and started away to raise or to join a party of pursuit. As he adjusted his firing piece, Mackey observed to Barnett, "I've run my bullet down hard to kill dead."

But before they had found other neighbors, they ran upon a file of savages, and were luckless. As James Mackey lifted his gun, an Indian's bullet pierced his right arm. The weapon dropped from his hands, and a second bullet went through his heart.

More fortunate, Barnett himself received two shots, one in the shoulder and another in his arm, as the foe began retreat from his fire. When they had fled, he fell from his horse, which ran home to the family loghouse. Exhausted and limp, his next neighbor dead, the wounded man crept into a patch of buckwheat. There presently other Hanover men found him. But it was with uncheering news: many folk besides James Mackey were dead; twelve had been abducted; the raiders had escaped. By them had been taken not only Mackey's son James, but Joseph Barnett's boy William. The father had survived for both joy and suffering. His own wife and his two infant sons had been spared. But he was left with an arm in which a bone was shattered and which he would never use wholly again; and his first-born was a child prisoner of Indians. That fact meant most of all in pain and anxiety.

Yet it was beginning and not ending, and cause for a quest. Barnett himself became a pilgrim journeying on the paths to Allegheny year after year, looking for a son. Folk back in Hanover, Provincial officers at one post or another on toward Ohio, alike came to know him as the father who still sought his child, responsive now to this rumor of William's whereabouts, now to that. Seven years were to pass before reunion of parent and boy brought happiness into a full family circle and a neighborhood. Yet, before fruition this ordeal and battle came to many another Scotch-Irish group. For their race, indeed, the summer of 1756 continued bitterly real and unidyllic.

Until September 7, it was, in fact, the summer of Delawares and Shawnees. Especially horrible were circumstances connected with Fort Granville on the Juniata.

Twenty-four rangers and militiamen, under the command of Lieutenant Edward Armstrong, manned the redoubt[57] named for the English statesman John Carteret, Earl of Granville, as Forts Lowther, Halifax, and Pitt later were named for generals and counselors of George II. It was a small stockaded structure. On July 30 it had gathered into it for protection a few straggling families. Siege came suddenly.

The defenders resisted the assault successfully for an afternoon and a night. On the second day their assailants, managing by means of a ravine to hide themselves for a time, emerged within forty feet of the stockade. One sortie hurled burning brands against it and set it afire. Another band kept up a brisk shooting. In vain young Armstrong and his men fought the blaze and returned fire. An opening in the palisades exposed the gallant officer and a bullet killed him. Other men were wounded and a second one died. Overtures for surrender were made by the enemy to the trapped folk. The Indians promised quarter. John Turner, who had married Simon Girty's widow, made the mistake of trusting them and opened the gate to the red foe. The garrison and three women and several children were promptly taken prisoners, and Fort Granville was razed to the ground. Of the few pitiful places of defense west of Susquehanna for the anxious people of frontier Pennsylvania one more was gone; and Braddock's defeat was now a year old.

Turner himself was to rue the impulsive act which had been forced upon him. With other captives he was borne to that Delaware Indian town on the Allegheny River which the trader John Trotter four years earlier had known as Attiga and now called Kittanning, equally distant from Venango on the north and from Logstown to the west downstream from the Forks of Ohio.

Here he was to experience no comfort. Rather, his captors, who must have despised his surrender, proceeded forthwith to their own style of *auto da fé*.[58]

No Spanish Inquisition spectacle could have excelled in terror the man's fate. The red monsters tied him to a black post. Several made a great fire and in it heated their gun barrels. Others danced madly around his figure, as their ruthless fellows ran the heated weapons through his body. For three hours they tormented him so. Then one Indian scalped him; another held up an Indian boy before the tortured victim; and that infant scion of the braves struck with a hatchet the finishing stroke into John Turner's head. Bloody stroke of mercy from a blood-indifferent child!

Andrew Montour had not ultimately gone French. The Six Nations had not deserted their English allies in Virginia, Pennsylvania, and New York. Merchants and artisans, ministers and lawyers, teachers and clerks remained safe in the colonial seaboard cities of America. On the Susquehanna, miles away from Kittanning, at Forts Halifax and Augusta, Colonel Clapham was establishing defense. Other points in the Province continued pregnable.

It was as well, in September of 1756, that there was a valiant Scotch-Irishman in command at Carlisle—one who felt that he must act whether anybody else did. Colonel John Armstrong became the hope of the frontier, more even than he knew—although the death of his junior brother Edward Armstrong at Fort Granville might have added spur to his determination and courage.

CHAPTER 6

BY FAVOR OF PROVIDENCE

THE DEGREE OF Colonel Armstrong's relationship to Trader Jack Armstrong is today indeterminate. He was the son of James Armstrong and member of the second generation of a Scotch-Irish family in America. From a Presbyterian baptism he had drawn the same Christian name John; but that, of course, could be no infallible testimony to kinship. Nor is evidence highly dependable that his father, before settling beyond Susquehanna, had been Justice of the Peace James Armstrong of Paxton in 1744; that names persist is small proof. But the patronymics of the Armstrongs, like those of Benjamin Chambers and his brothers,[1] are inseparable from either the history of the Scotch-Irish in America or white-man myths of the Susquehanna. They belong there as authentically as Jack Armstrong's name belongs to Jack's Mountain and Jack's Narrows of Juniata River lore.

Two James Armstrongs' signatures appeared on the deposition which Parson John Elder wrote down on April 19, 1744, one as that of the Justice before whom it was made, the other as that of a deponent.[2] With them was also the signature of Alexander Armstrong, grieving brother of the murdered man; and, apart from the macabre attestation of all the signers of that document, the name of another member of their clan, Robert Armstrong, survived for many years on the Susquehanna at a trading post not far south of Shamokin.

James, Robert, Joseph, and Benjamin Chambers likewise carried weight on the Scotch-Irish frontier, and still carry it today. They were early among settlers on Susquehanna, at a more northern outpost, it might be said, than where their fellow countrymen, the Simpsons and the Forsters, were establishing themselves in the same third decade of the eighteenth century. The mouth of Fishing Creek above Blue Mountain was their first place of settlement. There Joseph flourished long enough to break the acres of his farm, set up a mill, and develop enough property to encourage Samuel Hunter to woo his

[81

daughter, win her father's consent, and on Joseph's death acquire both farm and mill.[3]

Indeed, by that very creditable act Hunter obtained an eminence, without intending any sly practice, which should have been his father-in-law's. There was to be no more famous frontier fort in colonial Pennsylvania than Hunter's; and Joseph Chambers' name grew shadowy on Susquehanna only because a son-in-law was in the 1750's duly and legally settled upon the land which Chambers had first broken. What would later become McAllister's and was for many years Fort Hunter, was earlier Chambers'. The name Chambers stood out first in an historic episode when in 1744 the champions of murdered Jack Armstrong met at Joseph's house; then the pioneer farmer's and miller's name lapsed as eventlessly away as the current of his mill race slipping into the broad course of the river.

Of Joseph Chambers' brothers the story was to be more detailed. Longer lived and more nomadic, they moved on in the 1730's into still unpurchased and still unconstituted Cumberland County. By the time the County was erected in 1750, each was established for himself at the head of a creek, Robert at Middle Spring outside Shippensburg, James at the Big Spring where Newville would eventually take shape, and Benjamin at the Falling Springs farther south and west.

In years to come Chambers would be better remembered in the famous golden-wide valley than Edward Shippen and there would be no lovelier city and college town in all the commonwealth than Chambersburg, which was honored in immortalizing his patronymic. Indeed, all four of the sons of Major James Chambers, who had served as an Orangeman in the army of King William III,[4] were the sturdy forerunners of a brave tomorrow in Pennsylvania.

But if Benjamin Chambers was celebrated later on as the founder of a fair burgh, and in 1757 was reputed as the most truculent guardian of a frontier fort, John Armstrong was the outstanding Scotch-Irish figure of the summer and autumn of 1756. Thirty-nine years old, he was a man ripe in wisdom and experience. For two years, moreover, he had had the confidence of the executive government in Philadelphia.

The year 1754 was not only the year in which George Washington lost Fort Necessity, in which an ill destined male son was born to the Dauphine of France, or in which there was first official talk at the Albany Congress of a union of American Colonies. It was the year when Pennsylvania first grew wary of Yankees. Indeed, that summer the Province began keeping its political eye upon Connecticut men.

It had long been the hope of the Proprietors that the Six Nations should give them full legal possession of the Wyoming Valley on the North Branch of the River. That beautiful region was a favorite hunting ground of the Indians. Delawares occupied it. The Six Nations played fair, and left them in undisturbed position. Further they would not go at any time than to promise that, if they should ever sell the great tract, it would be only to the Penns. So matters still stood in July, when they signed away a yet larger tract[5] west and north of Cumberland County—in fact, all those hills, mountains, watersheds, and valleys from which the two branches of the Juniata flowed separately and among which they presently united into one swift current that sped on to join Susquehanna. This Indian empire of thousands of square miles, with all "rights, privileges, hereditaments, and appurtenances whatsoever thereunto belonging"[6]—the phraseology was, of course, that of the purchasers—was conceded to the children of Brother Onas for a total of eight hundred pounds,[7] the second half of which sum would be paid when occupation by the white man should properly begin.[8] (In the next hundred years it would be divided into eight counties.) From the angle of commerce the bargain was a felicitous one.

Yet the comfort of it was galled by a counterbalancing spur to Proprietary and governmental anxiety. One John Henry Lydius, suspected by Conrad Weiser and Pennsylvania's commissioners at Albany to be a French agent, "known" by Governor Robert Hunter Morris to be a Roman Catholic,"[9] widely reputed for drunkenness and given to drinking with Indians, had suddenly played a brilliant rogue's part. While other folk at Albany were projecting a union of colonies, and legislators for Pennsylvania were effecting the great purchase for the Proprietors, he stole a march on both, and bought Wyoming in a manner independently but not quite uniquely his own.

His procedure was fraudulent. He secured signatures to his purchase from a number of Six Nations Indians who were either qualified by no sanction at all from their tribes or were too inebriated, when they signed, to know what they were doing. But Pennsylvania realized, when in July the interloper began his traffic with both Oneidas and Mohawks, that Lydius' machinations were not in the interest of France, but designed to abet buyers in Connecticut.

Governor James Hamilton had already been on the alert. In the autumn Governor Morris, then new to his office, acted. Aware that the notorious deed negotiated by the maneuver of Lydius was a deed purporting sale to hundreds of Connecticut men contemplating settlement on the Susquehanna, in October, he assumed caution, courtesy, and pertinent inquiry. To Governor Fitch of Connecticut he wrote frankly in November, recounting to that gentleman a great deal of earlier Pennsylvania history and still more of Lydius' behavior[10]—of which he did not say he had been fully informed through Daniel Claus, Indian interpreter and agent—and confidant of Colonel William Johnson of Johnson Hall, New York. But, before he addressed that chief executive, Morris had sent an investigation to study facts and purposes for him in the New England colony. When John Armstrong of Carlisle presented his official letter to Thomas Fitch in December, the emissary had already, through a month of residence there and association with leading figures in Stamford and New Haven, framed a full report[11] on the scheme of the Susquehanna Company of Connecticut, and of personal and governmental attitudes toward it.

Almost as in a charter, in fact, Armstrong drew up his details of information: a merchant in Stamford avouched that the deed had been secured from several Six Nations chiefs;[12] that the purchasers of it had the countenance of the Government of Connecticut;[13] that, expecting to settle four hundred persons on the tract early in the next spring, these would be glad "how soon the matter had a fair trial and was brought to issue"[14] if the Proprietaries of Pennsylvania had any objection. At New Haven two military officers, the Governor, the President of "New Haven" College, and sundry other gentlemen insisted that an insinuation that the purchasers had had the license of their Government to purchase was a mistaken one.[15] A convention,[16] however, had met in Hartford, chosen Committee, Treasurer, and Clerk to represent them, and through those officials, under the name of the Susquehanna Company, were claiming as theirs "the Forty-Second Degree of Northern Latitude,"[17] from ten miles eastward of the easternmost branch of the River Susquehanna to the end of two degree of Longitude to the westward.

Of this Committee John Armstrong indicated who were the members, and called attention to the fact that Mr. George Wyllys, Treasurer to the Company, was also the Secretary of the Colony of Connecticut.[18] Further he reported that the leaders in the project were "men of great natural understanding as well as considerable acquirements."[19] Since summer the number of subscribers had grown from five hundred to eight hundred. Moreover, although the generality of "more knowing people" regarded the scheme as wild and preposterous, there were others who "cried up"[20] the antiquity of Connecticut's early charter claims to the territory; and Governor Morris' agent summed up briefly arguments pro and con on the subject of these.

Yet Armstrong gave more weight to other points. He predicted the subscribers, anticipating trouble with the Indians whom French encroachments were forcing back into Wyoming, would not risk settlement. He was of opinion that the distance of the lands they were pretending to was too far from their own seat of government. He believed, when the Governor's letters were put before the two Houses of Assembly in Connecticut, a stop would be made there to any considerable number's immigration to the territory; but it was "highly probable that matters are carried to so great a length some number will come."[21] Two other probabilities, also, were rumored: the Susquehanna Company Committee, by appealing to the populace of the colony, would presently put at the head of their government authorities who would confirm their "Indian Title";[22] one or two of the Committee were going to England in the next spring to solicit His Majesty for a new charter of incorporation for Connecticut which should include the tract as part of its lands.[23]

In brief, the transmission of this manifold news was a better piece of work than the news itself. Robert Hunter Morris had chosen effectually in Armstrong, although neither he nor his investigator had prevision of the train of events which would in after years succeed upon their measures of inquiry and warning. What most Morris divined of the episode was that the frontier gentleman from Carlisle was an able one.

The year 1755 came with its equivocal expectations of good from the Braddock campaign. Morris wished—but wished it without the encouragement of Pennsylvania's Assembly—to offer every support to that proud enterprise. It was but logical, then, that the Deputy Governor should in March choose the versatile Armstrong to head the commission of Pennsylvanians who should select a route west for Braddock's army and superintend the building of road to speed the prospective expedition.[24]

Armstrong rose to his responsibilities as well as any man might. With George Croghan, James Burd, William Buchanan, and Adam Hoops, he visited Fort Cumberland; had the disagreeable experience there of seeing what His Majesty's Commissary General Sir John St. Clair was like;[25] studied streams, mountains, and valleys, and with his aides drew a draught for the road which Morris desired; described engineering tasks ahead; and named costs.[26] Eventually it was not to his discredit that the Assembly never properly provisioned the workers cutting and building the road chosen or appropriated adequate funds for the expense of it; or that the impetuous Braddock and the stormy St. Clair never used it when built. What mattered most was that in 1755 Armstrong learned considerably more of masters and men from the *débacle* into which a King's General led his troops. In 1756 he followed a method more normal to the procedure of frontiersmen who knew more intimately the quality of their foes than did that luckless martinet in military tactics.

Seven companies, one of them led by himself personally and containing in all about three hundred men, made up Lieutenant Colonel Armstrong's command. From both sides of Susquehanna, from Lancaster and Cumberland Counties, recruits and officers came. Among them were McCormicks, Carruthers, Forsters, Kellys, Scotts, Morrows, Andersons, Findleys, Robinsons, Chambers, and Swans.[27] Their captains, lieutenants, and ensigns bore names just as Scottish: Hamilton, Mercer, Hogg, Ward, Armstrong, Potter, and Steel. Among these latter, indeed, were Hance Hamilton, Dr. Hugh Mercer, James Potter, and the Rev. Captain John Steel.[28] Two of these would be generals like Armstrong himself in George Washington's army within another twenty years, by appointment of Continental Congress. For all there were distinctions and honors ahead.

Military stores were slower in coming—the Province was more interested at the time in planning for and provisioning Fort Augusta at Shamokin. But in August Armstrong and his men were ready to march.[29] Several companies proceeded from Carlisle. At Aughwick, now become Fort Shirley, these were met by others gathering there from scattered military stations in the mountain-rimmed valleys of the border; and on the 30th[30] the combined forces set forth, men and officers bearing with them as the usual thing their personally owned weapons.

Four days were required to get them to the Beaver Dams, a few miles from Frankstown on what John Armstrong called the North Branch of Juniata.[31] It was a long trek which took them down Aughwick Creek to the mainstream of the Juniata; then by Jack's Narrows along that River to a crossing of the Raystown Branch, keeping them far to west of fallen Fort Granville; then northerly up the Frankstown Branch, passing the Standing Stone to their right; then bending with that Branch and its valley to the south of Water Street, and following the old path to Allegheny by whatever trails advance scouts advised or safety permitted. Watchfulness and sense of peril attended every mile and hour of it.

Yet the skill of their pathfinders and of their commander could interpret a fair omen well. Just three miles short of Allegheny Mountain, lofty barrier to the west and the north of their Beaver Dams camp, a few of Armstrong's men discovered the tracks of two Indians. This pair had killed a cub bear, and left marks of their progress at fires made for cooking its meat. The freshness of the signs left by them revealed two points for a frontier army to regard cheerfully: the Indians had preceded by only twenty-four hours; they had moved on unaware that seven Scotch-Irish companies were almost within sight and scent.[32] It was a "particular Providence in our favor,"[33] thought Presbyterians.

So next morning, on their fifth day from Fort Shirley, Armstrong and his men decamped, and made forwards. Their scaling of Allegheny Mountain, arduous and exhausting feat, they left undescribed and unrecorded. Somewhere near where they crossed it, canal and railway engineers a hundred years later would conquer that barrier in the favor of east-west transportation and travel, and the achievement would be heralded in many a work on the Pennsylvania Canal and the Portage Railroad. The eighteenth-century kindred of St. Columba and Maeldun took the challenge of the great "Hill" in their stride. They anticipated neither heralding nor subsequent tribute; and on the evening of their sixth day, September 5, were out of the Susequehanna watershed in broad clear fields beyond a divide and moving along streams which flowed into another river whose own waters would in due time empty into the Mississippi and the Gulf of Mexico. Something had been learned by Colonel John Armstrong and his companies of Scotch-Irish traders who had preceded them into the West. They knew Indian ways. Now the army of them was fifty miles from Attiga, or Kittanning, where John Turner had so recently died under redskin atrocity.

Strategy, labor, ordeal were ahead. An officer, a pilot, and two soldiers were sent forward to reconnoitre the town and bring back information of its situation and of the position of the enemy there.[34] A third day, and this party was met returning. To Colonel Armstrong they reported roads to be entirely clear of the foe; his army, they declared, had not been detected.[35] So, confident of their scouts' testimony, the seven companies continued their march, planning to be within striking range of Attiga by nightfall and to attack the town on the next morning.

But disappointment came. As they were still making forward two hours after dark, a guide brought sudden news that two or three Indians were bivouacked but a few perches ahead; they had built a fire by the roadside. Colonel Armstrong[36] at once ordered the rear to retreat "with all possible silence" for a hundred perches to make momentary retirement possible for the front while he and his staff consulted on tactics. As these talked, the pilot again returned and assured them there were at most three or four Indians by the fire; he was certain of his observation.

At once an officer suggested they immediately surround the enemy group and cut them off. Others advised, however, that to risk that was too hazardous; they dared not let one Indian escape and warn the town. Further, the effort would delay their campaign critically in another respect. He reminded them that they had planned to post their several detachments by the light of the moon. It would be a mistake to lose one hour of advantage during the night, if they were to surprise and attack successfully at daybreak. Best, they all thought, to leave one party with a lieutenant to watch the trio of warriors so near at hand; the pilot could guide the twelve men chosen to the best point for watching them through the night, until they could cut all off by day. The main force should advance without these.

That was not easy, however. A circuit off the road was imperative; this meant both stealth and hardship. The Scotch-Irish army, deploying, was retarded by stones and fallen timber in the woods. Every clink of a stone or crack of a bough might be signal to the encamped foe by the roadside. Within six miles of Attiga their horses had to be left behind, with the army's stock of blankets and baggage.[37] Then, as Armstrong's men advanced, doubt of the competence of their chief guide smote them.

Did he really know the exact site of the town? The right number of the enemy? The best paths?[38] Over hills and valleys the troops of Hamilton, Steel, and Mercer struggled on dubiously. The moon declined lower and lower.

But presently they had a better guide than their pilot. The beating of a drum and whooping of warriors at a dance[39] gave them the direction of Attiga; and, just before the moon set, the front emerged on the River Ohio (the Allegheny) one hundred perches downstream from the town. It was up to them to make the best of the last rays, and station their posts. Then a new cause for fearing to be discovered came: an Indian was whistling "in a very singular manner"[40] but thirty perches away.

Instantly all the troops sat down; order for complete silence was passed to the rear; apprehensively Colonel Armstrong turned to John

Baker, their most helpful scout, "Wasn't that signal to Attiga of their approach?"[41]

"No," answered Baker stoically; "it's just a young brave calling his squaw after his dance. He will now kindle a fire, clean his gun, and shoot it once before he goes to sleep."[42]

The Scotch-Irish lay quiet and hushed. The young warrior's gun went off. His fire became perceptible in a corn field thirty perches away. Other fires began to dot the field. Baker whispered: "They're being lighted to drive off gnats, the night's warm, the Indians will be asleep by them soon, and they will go out."[43] With relief the men from Carlisle and Lancaster and Cumberland Counties in the front waited, and perceived the truth of the man's interpretation.

Daybreak came; the van of Armstrong's army, after their long thirty mile march since yesterday morning, were most of them sleeping; as they had been moving in a long defile, the three companies in the rear were not yet quite brought up over the last precipice. Immediate tactics were of critical importance.

To these their commander despatched messengers with directions, and then, with the aid of his officers, roused his weary soldiers. To some he gave orders to take the end of the hill at which the front lay, march along its crest one hundred perches and as much farther as was required to take them above the upper or main part of the settlement and the corn field in which he presumed the warrior Indians were gathered and sleeping. He reserved a more numerous force. The men in this major body he instructed to withhold action until the detachment moving along the hill should have gained its position.

But, unfortunately, to reach that objective took a greater time than had been anticipated; full daylight came; it was no longer safe not to attack. Sallies had to be made on the cornfield. Parties moved with expedition into the maneuver, some upon the rousing warriors, others on the houses which day had revealed. At once, wakened Indians leaped up; their Delaware chieftain, Captain Jacobs, destroyer of Fort Granville in July, was heard by English prisoners giving the first war-whoop; other Indians cried that the white men had come; still others called to their children and squaws to get into the woods.

Groups of the Scotch-Irish, "with great eagerness,"[44] said their Colonel later, passed on from fringes of the forest into the field. Fire greeted them from there, and from across the river. Other of Armstrong's men in the same moment began their fusillade on the huts. From Captain Jacobs' house the fire was returned with "a great deal of resolution,"[45] and the commander turned with promptness to that point of crisis. There he beheld "sundry of our people"[46] wounded and killed. Constant fire from the portholes of the chief's abode was taking severe toll. Before that stronghold could be reduced, he was aware that the other lesser houses must be fired. To that task, on instruction from him, his men and officers concentrated with spirit.

Boldly they exposed themselves as they proceeded with their work of destruction. Sternly they called to the Indians, bidding them surrender themselves as prisoners or be trapped and burned. The savage retort came from one enemy: he was accept burning rather than capture, and would kill four or five white men ere he died. Precipitate carnage continued. The smoke grew thicker; the fire approached the larger house more closely.

One Indian inside it began singing. A squaw was heard crying from within, and the harsh rebuke of her by the sachems. Two Indians and a squaw sprang out, none the less, made for the cornfield, and were shot down by Armstrong's men. Captain Jacob himself tumbled out of the cock loft, was felled, stripped of his powder horn and pouch, and—when there was leisure for it later—scalped.

Excitement and action were both now intense as the fires. Indeed, as they went on with their unrelenting labor, a grim sense of entertainment came into the Scotch-Irish assailants. Colonel Armstrong had been wounded in the shoulder by a musket ball from the fortified house; his subalterns and his riflemen were falling wounded or dead. Their comrades experienced "agreeably"[47] the reports of charged guns firing off as the conflagration reached each unraised weapon. Every house seemed to abound with bags of ammunition and large kegs of gun powder. Each vast explosion of these bore cheerful witness to the destruction of the huge French-supplied stores of the Indians. In the dreadful moments of their own losses, the attackers at Kittanning rejoiced in the stern carnage of their victory. Their long arduous march west had not been in vain. The zest of reward was in them.

Then, at last, Jacobs' house itself caught fire. Its magazine of powder blew up thunderously. The roof sprang in fragments toward the sky. White spectators saw the severed leg and thigh of an adult Indian and the body of a three- or four-year-old child hurtling upward from a fiery abyss, carried so high "they appeared as nothing,"[48] and then falling far off into the cornfield. Attiga itself had ended in ruin.

Comparative calm followed. Officers and men could take measure of their success, behold their own dead, succor their wounded. English prisoners found in the town could be gathered and interviewed. The tired fighting men could compare notes with one another and their leaders.

The man who had acquired Captain Jacobs' powder-horn and pouch learned that they were a gift from a French officer, who had accepted in exchange the boots of Lieutenant Edward Armstrong,[49] slain at Fort Granville six weeks earlier and despoiled there by the Delawares. A rescued prisoner testified to the authenticity of the proudly possessed scalp of that dead chief; no other Indian had ever worn his hair in the manner of it. Other prisoners identified the scalp of Jacobs' squaw, and the locks of a young Delaware called the King's Son.

There were more sobering discoveries also. Captain Mercer had been struck in the arm early in the action. He had been carried to the top of the hill. There, as his friends, officers and men, gathered around their wounded surgeon, several of them saw a considerable party of Indians[50] cross the Ohio and take to the hill on the far side. The spectacle of their escape was ominous. Were they of sufficient number to surround the Scotch-Irish, or to cut them off?

John Armstrong thought. Withdrawal seemed imperative. But he would not consent to any flight in fear of a hidden enemy; and he saw to it that every last hut was burned before he ordered his army to spread out on the hill. Then, if he repined because that command, looking as it did to retreat, prevented more thorough search of the cornfield and the riverside and obliged his men to leave sundry scalps behind—"and doubtless some squaws, children, and English prisoners"[51] —he had the satisfaction of knowing what a quantity of goods had been burnt. It was enough, some of the released captives assured him, to last the boastful Indians for a two-year war. At length, having given his initial instructions, Armstrong was himself ready to proceed to the hill, have his wounded shoulder tied up and the blood stopped.

As he was being dressed, still other information made him alert to perils environing his army. Transmitted also by prisoners, this was to to the effect that on that very day two batteaux of Frenchmen and a large party of other Delaware and French Indians had designed to join Captain Jacobs at Kittanning. These, it was said, had been intended to accompany the Delaware chief on a march, to be begun on the morrow, for George Croghan's Fort or Fort Shirley. Indeed, twenty-four warriors had been sent out the previous evening on an errand of evil intent: either to spy that fort, or to raid back inhabitants of the Province.

All was a challenge to the commander. He conferred with his staff.[52] With them he wondered whether there had not been more Indians near that roadside fire seen by their pilot the night before. Wonder became conviction: there must have been more warriors. The query came as to how Lieutenant Hogg might have fared in his watching of them, or attacking. Moreover Colonel Armstrong knew that the provisions for his seven companies were "scaffolded"[53] thirty miles to the rear. Their horses, their blankets, and even the men's haversacks and the food in them had been left behind in Hogg's charge.[54]

Apprehension crept into Armstrong. In the hour of triumph he was aware he must act prudently. The height of the Scotch-Irish exploit had been reached. It was wisest now to retreat warily. He gave orders not to wait for the cutting down of the cornfield. He instructed his subordinates to collect all the wounded, capture all the Indian horses available, prepare for the withdrawal. They must not now risk destruction of themselves.

Hunger, want of sleep, apparent reversal of campaign began to tell upon the spirit of the army. Exaltation waned. Fears of being waylaid and surrounded aggravated the sudden dismay of even experienced woodsmen. The march back became very slow, for sundry miles not exceeding two miles an hour. Occasional hidden Indians fired from the brush on one wing or another of the retiring column. One victim of their cross fire was wounded in both legs.

Groups of men became separated from the main line. Captain Mercer was induced by several of his men to let them take him "into the road a nigh way,"[55] and to leave Ensign John Scott in charge of the main body of his company; and both he and Scott were soon missing. A detachment despatched in search returned without finding either.

In due course Armstrong reached the point where the Indian fire had been discovered on the previous night. There he found a sergeant and several men of Mercer's company who had decamped after the engagement at Kittanning.

It was no tale of honor, but one rather of mixed truths which they had to relate.

On their flight they had found Lieutenant Hogg severely wounded in two parts of his body.[56] He had strength enough to tell that when he had attacked in the morning, the number of Indians who had made their fire proved considerably superior in number to his own dozen riflemen. The pilot had, in fact, quite underestimated their strength. Three of Hogg's best men were killed by the first retort; his others had been demoralized forthwith and run away. He himself fell into a thicket and kept hidden.

Now, they admitted, James Hogg was dead. They had put him

on horseback even as he narrated his story. Then other Indians fired on the rescuing party; and a new second wound in the belly had ended the young officer.

So much appeared truth to Armstrong. But the cowardly sergeant overtold his tale.[57] His commander could not believe that the man and his fellows had stood a large number of Indians for five rounds, nor that they had beheld without running the killing and scalping of Hogg and "sundry other"[58] Scotch-Irish. Yet what concerned him more now than either his young officer's death or the deserter's narrative was the effect of this last on his men. Only with difficulty could his captains keep their companies from scattering. They could not prevail on them to collect what horses and baggage the Indians had left after their conquest of Lieutenant Hogg and his party.[59]

John Armstrong, in fact, fighting pretty much in the Indian's own way, had won a battle. At the end of long hazardous ordeal and military pilgrimage he had "by Divine Assistance"[60] prevailed.

But the color of the frontier marked his achievement both in the enacting and his subsequent taking stock of it.

An estimated thirty or forty Indians killed or mortally wounded was a fine toll against the enemy. The method of estimate was crude enough. Once the houses at Attiga had been burnt and the main firing ceased, his men ranged the cornfield looking for scalps as well as prisoners. Then there was an experience of regret; withdrawal was ordered when they had gathered but a dozen scalps. Later four or five of these were to be found missing.

To the frontiersman's view that paucity and that loss were a misfortune. In April, 1756, Governor Robert Hunter Morris had proclaimed not only a bounty of one-hundred-and-fifty pieces of eight for each adult male Indian enemy captured, but also a bounty of one-hundred-and-thirty pieces for every male Indian's scalp taken.[61] Moreover those bounties had been offered in good hard money, Spanish dollars. Indian scalps, in brief, had a commodity value; cornfield and river banks not wholly combed for them helped to dispirit Scotch-Irish warriors who were, they knew, acting under authority of the Executive Council of Pennsylvania.

But the importance of Armstrong's victory at Kittanning, despite the enforced retirement from position and the confession in withdrawal which followed, was genuine. Neither the number of enemies destroyed nor the number of English prisoners recovered was very great. The victor himself found the gain over the common enemy, Indian and French, "far from being satisfactory."[62] Piously he acknowledged, in his report from Fort Littleton on September 14 to the Governor, now William Denny serving as the Penns' new deputy, that "we must not despise the smallest degree of success that God is pleased to give . . . at a time of such general calamity."[63] He was in nothing prone to boast. But, through his prisoners, he had learned the strength of the French at Fort Duquesne and the sources of their provisions there and at their other three forts on the Ohio; he had won the first victory in Pennsylvania after the rout of Braddock's army; he had paved the way for the subsequent exploits of Forbes in 1758 and Bouquet in 1763; he had demonstrated despite exceptions—there are always exceptions among Scots—the spirit of the back inhabitants of the Province in strategy, endurance, discipline, and attack. Through his guidance the Scotch-Irish shone with a new honor in American history; and he gave thanks to God.

The leopard, however, had not changed his spots. Harmony had not fully come into Scotch-Irish hearts, or unison of attitude reached consummation on the frontier. In their study of measures of protection for the settlers in Cumberland Valley the Armstrongs and the Chambers were not at one. John Armstrong acted with and for officialdom in the Province; Benjamin Chambers[64] acted for his own immediate cluster of Scotch-Irish neighbors in Conococheague.

Indeed, he maintained his own private fort at the Falling Spring, where it joined that larger creek. Government or no Government in Philadelphia, he stood for his individual defense and his individual rights. The Lieutenant Governor and members of Council protested that his precautions did not square with their system of defenses for Pennsylvania beyond Susquehanna. It was argued that his "two four-pound cannon mounted,"[65] with only a few country people to man them, were likely to be captured by the Indians. If Chambers' log-house and stockade were stormed, and these guns taken, they might be carried east and used in assault upon Fort Morris at Shippenburg or Fort Lowther at Carlisle. "Either," said James Young on October 17, 1756, in a letter to the Governor,[66] "take the cannon from thence or station a proper garrison there."

William Denny committed the affair to Colonel John Armstrong, demanding the guns. That commissioner notified Benjamin Chambers of the Government's orders. Chambers demurred; he would not give up[67] his own means of protection for Provincial modes.

Through the Valley went news of his refusal. No Scotch-Irish justice of the peace would act to dispossess the commander and hero of private Fort Chambers; no constable would be appointed to serve that purpose. Frustration of orders from Philadelphia continued. The mood of recalcitrance lasted in the countryside on into 1757.

Mr. Chambers consented only so far as to give recognizance to have his case tried before the law; but he held on to his guns. The Province dropped proceedings. The hero of Kittanning himself had no further acquiescence from the younger son of a former officer of good King William III in Ireland. At most the Scotch-Irish leader John Armstrong could write to Philadelphia of his fellow countryman, scion of the same breed: "Chambers, it is thought, designs to give trouble as he has the brass and malice of the devil."[68]

Apparently both accuser and accused had come well by their parts.

CHAPTER 7

YOUTHFUL EBULLITION

IN 1757 Margery Mitchell, widow from Shippensburg, addressed the Secretary of the Governor's Council in an obvious tone of reproach. Earlier that year she had gone on to Philadelphia, by a "fatiguing and expensive" journey, to deliver an "Indian scalp"[1] to the authorities there, and expectant of compensation. But the "favor of Providence" was not to be so openly revealed to her as it had been to John Armstrong at Kittanning in September, 1756. In fact, she complained spiritedly: "One might think common humanity would influence the Gentlemen to allow me some small matter on that occasion, especially as I have lost my husband and my son";[2] and she left Divine guidance wholly out of her expression of feeling.

Today we do not know whether the Provincial Council eventually rewarded the querulous lady or not; but that Mrs. Mitchell was convinced she had an authentic claim is hardly to be questioned. She was of her era; she had lost husband and son to the Indians; she knew the regulations; she appealed but for fair play from Government; she was both a sign of the times and a woman of her breed. In plight and ambition she shared with her kind; and her kind were the Scotch-Irish.

Burghers in Philadelphia, Provincial leaders and Quakers, would have said that her compatriots out of Ulster and Donegal changed but little between 1757 and 1763; but then their opinions might have betrayed bourgeois and conservative prejudices.

Much really happened during the seven years within Susquehanna country and beyond. The Scotch-Irish themselves won no more battles like Kittanning. Indeed, they had little share in the campaign in 1758 which, by General John Forbes' initiative, gained Fort Pitt for the British Crown. Their participation was as unmarked in the battle fought at Bushy Run on August 5 and 6, 1763, by Colonel Henry Bouquet, as the result of which the stronghold at the Forks of the Ohio was kept in English hands at last fully secure against the French.

Regulars, rather than militia, had been the two distinguished strategists' support on both occasions of contest; and, although numerous back inhabitants had been recruited by the two celebrated officers of the King, the glory of the two feats of war was not given to the frontiersmen. Yet the mood of the Scotch-Irish as a people and a sect crystallized more and more in the period between Kittanning and Bushy Run.

Moreover, during the summer in which Bouquet made history to the west, the Scotch-Irish settlers along Susquehanna were busying themselves with schemes of defense nearer home. The Province had long since reverted to its policy of short-term enlistments for recruits; and in July the Assembly, perennially stalling, granted funds for the pay of officers and men sufficient no further than mid-autumn. Two companies of fifty men each with their complements of commissioned officers were allowed to each of the four counties, Cumberland, Lancaster, Berks, and Northampton.[3] Beyond such recruitments under the command of local township leaders Pennsylvania depended on Colonel James Burd with his men at Fort Augusta and the good offices of the forces of the Crown on the Ohio.

Moreover Burd's companies were seldom in full quota. It was enough for them to provide a bastion of defense at the junction of the North and West Branches of Susquehanna, to maintain some mobility for their officers in care of lesser forts at the gaps of the Blue Ridge, and to ease the responsibility of local protection at Easton, Fort Allen, Hunter's, and Carlisle. They made no distant sallies into Indian Country farther north than Shamokin. Not Colonel Burd, but county justices or natural leaders guided the recruitment of rangers during July and August of 1763.[4] John Armstrong led again at Carlisle. In Lancaster County the Rev. Mr. John Elder, Pastor of Scotch-Irish congregations at Paxton and Derry Old Side Churches, recruited and commanded the two companies provided for by the Assembly.[5] Squires Jonas Seeley and Timothy Horsfield acted similarly in Berks and Northampton.[6]

To these four worthies instructions went with their commissioners in July; and recruiting was promptly, although only transitorily, reinspired.

The provisioning of Fort Augusta was resumed with as much diligence as funds made possible or as agents could practice in the purchase of supplies and in the despatch of bateaux containing supplies up the river.[7] Every boat had to be guarded by an escort of riflemen[8] filing through the dense and rocky edges of the woods along shore from

Hunter's to the Narrows, to the Wiconisco, to the Mahanoy, to Shamokin. So August and September were months of at least comparative
motion.

Yet the air along Susquehanna, from Conestoga on the main river
to Wyoming on the North Branch, remained taut with expectancy.
Every rumor stirred with excitement; every ruse, when attempted, was
attempted with nervous apprehension. Even when the news of Bouquet's success had come, a Scotch-Irishman who had the sense that
much had been achieved in that victory was exceptional. Rather, every
householder had the grim conviction that now only his own cunning
or his own personal force was standing between him and his enemy;
and his enemy he almost universally believed was the Indian.

The Rev. Mr. John Elder raised his two companies, determined at
what loghouses files of them should be stationed; planned the limits of
their ranging for each day on the general line south of Blue Mountain
from Swatara Gap west to the River;[9] and had the general confidence
and esteem of his rangers. But he experienced from them no instinctive
submission either to his counsel or his command. Nor had enlistment
of them been easy.

In fact, two of his letters during July[10] had told of difficulties.
Farmers who had harvests coming on did not wish to leave their fields.
Back inhabitants were skeptical of the three-months' terms of service.
Many doubted whether termination of their duties would be early as
promised; others were afraid they would not only be drawn away from
immediate protection of their own houses and families but be stationed at distant points in the Province and kept there longer than
the papers of enlistment certified to. They might accept command
from their own neighbors; command on Provincial authorization was
suspect. Mr. Elder had to regard his recruits and his official superiors.

With the latter he was blunt enough. His letters to Governor James
Hamilton and Secretary Joseph Shippen made clear the situation south
of Blue Mountain in Lancaster County. Settlers were continuing there
only because of his companies of rangers. As soon as terms of enlistment should expire and these be disbanded, there would be exodus
again; more than that, farms would be laid waste by new incursions of
the foe.[11] And always he had to protest about both the amount and the
quality of the stores of ammunition sent him. No lead came with one
consignment; no buckshot with another. Casks of powder came to
Harris' deficient, broken in carriage from Lancaster, half-empty from
damage done to them in transit, or wanting six pounds of weight when
a cask which was undamaged on arrival had been opened.[12] Such cir-

cumstances tended to discourage enlistment. Terror of the Indian and of his savagery was, indeed, a more certain aid to recruitment; and through the summer of 1763 the Minister of Paxton and Derry Presbyterian Churches kept his two companies of rangers in effective control.

But anticipated expiration of service at the end of September altered the complexion of affairs. It was expected that some of Colonel Armstrong's men would be returning after their discharge to Paxton or Susquehanna country. A number of John Elder's men were hoping, with reinforcement from these, "to scout a little way into the Enemy's Country."[13] They would like to have privileges similar to those previously granted by Governor Hamilton to some of Armstrong's troops on the other side of the River. In fact, the fighting parson's two companies, although not under his leadership on the proposed expedition, wished to adventure upstream to Wyoming.[14] There was talk of an immense quantity of corn left there by the New England men now reportedly fled from their attempted settlements. It ought not to be suffered to become a magazine of supply to the Indians and enable them further to distress the inhabitants of Pennsylvania. Furthermore, a desire was in Elder's men to penetrate, "a little above" Wyoming, as far as Wyalusing. They wished, with Governor Hamilton's "approbation," to "strike" and "root out a nest of Banditti lodged there":[15] Delawares, Nanticokes, and others, "our bitter enemies"—savages who, they believed, had committed the late barbarities in Berks County.

In October the Rev. Mr. Elder's two companies, not troubling to wait for the Governor's approbation, as their chief officer would have had them wait, marched off from Hunter's Fort with the two captains on their errand of precaution. Asher Clayton was at their head. Timothy Green and his ensign Lazarus Stewart were of the great party of scouts, as a letter of the fifth of the month from Captain Green[16] to his "Rev^rd" commander indicated. The latter pair and their rangers from Hanover were to arrive at the fort of rendezvous "on Sabbath Evening,"[17] and they hoped to have the pleasure of seeing there Mr. Elder on Monday before their departure. Green hoped even more; he wished that Jacob Lodwiethe, who was not for the venture, might be cashiered and his lieutenant's commission given by their commander to Ensign Stewart. That subaltern, he was "Shuar, desarved" it.[18]

In brief, the Scotch-Irish of the Susquehanna country had embarked on another emprise. They set off from the point where Thomas McKee and Alexander Armstrong had begun their journey in 1744 to clear up the mystery of Jack Armstrong's disappearance; they followed much of the path which Adam Terrance and John Harris had taken when in 1754 they ascended the River with design to bury the dead massacred in October along Penn's Creek on the west shore. Traveling quite as dangerously, they went farther than the two earlier groups of frontier investigators.

Meantime the Assembly in Philadelphia was maintaining its usual quiescence. Governor Hamilton eloquently addressed the body on October 15. He told of newly well attested "barbarous and shocking murders"[19] performed by Indian enemies upon the inhabitants of Northampton County. He told of homes already deserted, homes about to be deserted, homes closer and closer to Philadelphia. He could not say, he lamented, to what small distance from the Capital the line of the Frontier was to be reduced. He warned of the early expiration of enlistments, of the need for new subsidies. He regretted arrears in the pay of the companies raised during the summer. He called for new funds, new and increased companies.

In peroration he concluded: "I do, therefore, Gentlemen, in the most earnest manner, recommend to your most immediate consideration the distressed state of our unfortunate inhabitants on the frontiers, who are continually exposed to the savage cruelty of a merciless enemy; and request that you will in your present session, grant such a supply as, with God's assistance, may enable us, not only to protect our people, but to take a severe revenge on our perfidious foes, by pursuing them into their own countries, for which purpose there prevails at present a noble ardor among our frontier people, which in my opinion, ought by all means to be cherished and improved."[20]

Six days later the Assembly voted an arrangement for increased allowances to the King's use, providing £24,000 for raising, paying, and victualling eight hundred men and officers.[21] Not a provincial militia was designed, but troops to be recruited by the lieutenants of General Gage.[22] The body, in fact, passed just such a measure as Generals Amherst and Gage had been calling for for many months. But, unfortunately, they framed it with termination six weeks later, on December 1.[23] Then, having done that, they adjourned on October 22 until January 16 of the next year.[24] Quite apparently they wanted no more begging from a Governor for the interim; and quite as apparently they had acted on no new official means of defense along Susquehanna. To satisfy their consciences they endorsed on their last day before adjournment a measure prohibiting "the selling of guns, gunpowder, or other warlike stores to the Indians."[25]

It was not they who looked on the face of horror which John Elder's men, led by Asher Clayton and Timothy Green and Lazarus Stewart, beheld in that month of October in the Wyoming Valley. That sight was reserved for the Scotch-Irish scouts out of Donegal, Derry, and Paxton in Lancaster County.

Mr. Elder had "acquainted his Honor" the Governor on October 17,[26] some ten days after its setting out, of the impossibility of suspending the Wyoming expedition. Eight days later he wrote to James Hamilton of his men's return into Paxton, again acting as scribe for a quota of back inhabitants as he had acted nineteen years before when in his own hand he wrote out the deposition on the murder of Jack Armstrong. This time his quill moved rather less into detail. But his words were graphic enough: The troops of Asher Clayton had looked upon "a most melancholy scene," which had been enacted "not above two days before their arrival."[27] The unhappy people whom they set about burying seemed not so much human settlers who had come hopefully in Wyoming as they were "mangled carcasses"[28]—not so much proper corpses of the dead as the butchered segments of animals. The writer of the letter was willing to let Major Clayton despatch to the authorities more complete information.

But the Scotch-Irish minister and champion of the frontier did not omit either interpretation or warning. The returning men averred their belief that the savages who had destroyed the New England people were the same as those who had just been ravaging Northampton County. Furthermore they were sure that the Indians, after inflicting their atrocity, had gone on to Wyalusing, farther up the North Branch. Their pastor, then, was as sure that, until "that Branch was cleared of the savages, the Frontier settlements would be in no safety."[29] In fact, unless he had new instructions for a new enlistment of men, now that the three months' term between July and the close of September had expired, his troops would disperse; it would be difficult to enlist them again; and, unprotected by their rangers, the frontier settlers along Blue Mountain would once more desert their habitations and evacuate the country on the first fresh alarm from the Indians.

Eloquently, and with statistics, Mr. Elder appealed on that late October date to Deputy Governor Hamilton. Paxton Township needed defense nearer than Fort Augusta. A garrison was necessary at Hunter's, if 18 or 20 men had to be drawn to maintain it from Fort Augusta. A stockade was imperative at that point to cover the men. It could be provided at inconsiderable expense to the Province. If Government would provide for the felling and splitting of timber and carriages for hauling it in, he was confident the folk of the community would be glad to help the garrison set up their structure. He was asking for "a Township of as great consequence to the public, in this time of danger, as any perhaps on the frontiers."[30]

Hamilton, with the Assembly adjourned, could do nothing.

Early in November the apprehensive Presbyterian cleric and military officer had received instructions for new levies of companies. But there were problems for him to write of to Colonel Shippen in Philadelphia. Major Clayton was being transferred elsewhere. He had been very "agreeable" to his superior and "acceptable to the frontier inhabitants."[31] It would be important to replace him with another aide quite as good. Further there was murmuring among the Paxton Scotch-Irish because troops elsewhere had been granted bounties not accorded to them. There was complaint from recruiting officers that they were not allowed sufficient expenses for going from place to place to secure enlistments. They could not afford attendance "at Taverns, without which," Mr. Elder knew that Secretary Shippen knew, "it is impossible to enlist soldiers."[32] In fact, he judged such "saving methods" (on the part of Assembly and Council) "in our present situation . . . very impolitical."[33] Again he made appeal through his secretarial friend to the Legislature, insisting on the importance of a firm barrier against the Indians along Blue Mountain.

But the autumn of 1763, through the August success of Colonel Bouquet, had become for Philadelphia generally a season of immunity from danger. And, as October closed, the city was more attuned to celebration than to the complexities of back inhabitant management.

Indeed, the sympathetic James Hamilton had, for another time, gone out of office as Deputy Governor of the Province.

Mr. John Penn, son of Richard Penn and grandson of the Founder William Penn, was being welcomed as successor to Andrew Hamilton's son. The city was *en fête*. A solemn ceremony at the Court House inducted the youthful Governor into office as Deputy for the Proprietors. The guns of the Battery at Wiccacoa on the Delaware were fired as in a royal salute. The bells of Christ Church, cure of the Rev. Richard Peters, clergyman of the Church of England, rang in welcome. Philadelphians kindly forgot how trivial and embarrassing had been Mr. Penn's conduct in 1755 when he was supposed to be learning the art of government from James Hamilton and Mr. Peters and was rather consuming Proprietary means and carrying on disreputably with an Italian musician and other low company.[34] Nothing was said of the violin he had then been learning to play. Instead, from the wastrel only gravity was expected now.

But that was expected of many another in the Province; and, so far as it matured at all in John Penn, it brought him no glory from his political Indian wards along the Susquehanna. Readier acclaim, in fact, was forwarded to him by the few remaining Susquehannocks at Conestoga Town in Lancaster County.

Those allies of the children of Onas sent particular greetings to him just as his office had become a month old. But history had been made before their letter of welcome—of date November 30[35]—was read in the Provincial Council on Monday, December 19, in Philadelphia; and it was the Scotch-Irish who, for better or worse, had made it.

About the succession of events in the narration was not a little of ironic drama. The address of the Conestogoes, as the remnants of the proud race whom John Smith once described in their splendor were always known to the Penn family, ran cordially. It had been written down by either Andrew Montour or a white-man clerk. It was signed with the marks of three Indians, a Bird, a Horse, and a Tortoise: by Sohays, Cuyanguerrycoea, and Saguyasotha. When John Penn saw the document Sohays was already dead, and his two fellow signatories, the Horse and the Turtle, had both disappeared into oblivion. Strange course of events for the authors of the felicitations and the petitions of an ally!

To the Honourable JOHN PENN, Esquire, Lieutenant Governor and Commander-in-Chief of the Province of Pennsylvania, &ca, &ca

Brother:

We (the Conestogoe Indians) take present opportunity, by Captn Montour, to welcome you into this Country by this String of Wampum, and as/we were settled at this place by an Agreement of Peace and Amity established between your Grandfathers & ours, We now promise ourselves your favour and protection, and as we have always lived in Peace and Quietness with our Brethren & Neighbours round us during the last & present Indian Wars, We hope now, as we are deprived from supporting our Families by hunting, as We formerly did, you will consider our distressed Situation, & grant our Women and Children some Cloathing to cover them this Winter. The Government has always been kind enough to allow us some Provisions, and did formerly appoint People to take care of us, but as there is no person to take that upon him, & some of our Neighbours have encroach'd upon the Tract of Land reserved here for our use, We would now beg our Brother the Governor to appoint our Friend

Captain Thomas M'Kee, who lives near us and understands our Language, to take care, and see Justice done us.

SOHAYS,   his Mark.

INDIAN,   his Mark.
or CUYANGUERRYCOEA

         his
SAGUYASOTHA,   or JOHN
        Mark

But despite the ironic drama, with its reversal from cordiality of welcome and from petition for charity into violence and death, there was another side to the picture of events.

Deep ingrained in the beliefs of the Scotch-Irish families in Lancaster County was an enduring conviction. John Elder had written to Governor Hamilton in September recommending "an immediate removal of the Indians from Conestoga" and the "placing" of "a garrison in their room."[37] To the recommendation he had added his pledge: "In case this is done, I pledge myself for the future security of the frontiers."[38] On the last day of the month he had warned also of a nest of banditti Indians far up the River at Wyalusing. His troops, the people of his two churches in Paxton and Derry, the people of Hanover township believed with him that there should be no overlooking the possibility of collusion between hostile Indians and the so-called friendly Indians at positions or towns protected by the Provincial authorities. Particularly did they mistrust the Conestogoes, who were nearer at hand. To the wigwams there Paxton scouts were sure they had traced marauding Indians;[39] and none found it difficult to believe that those who harbored the foe also were the foe. The channel of resentment flowed very deep. All that the course of it needed was wick, spark, and flame.

Then one night a tense-faced neighbor stopped at Matthew Smith's door. The ranger had a story. Three others and he had discovered a suspiciously moving party of the enemy. From the Big Island at the mouth of Juniata, they had trailed these to Manor Township and to Conestoga. One of the Scotch-Irish scouts left his horse with the others and crawled alone to a place of vantage. From there he saw (or thought he saw) numerous strange Indians arriving. They outnumbered the five Paxton men by dozens.[40] He got back to his fellows bearing such information, and with them he returned to their own settlement.

Now he was saying to Matthew Smith: "We meet tonight; we shall expect you with knife, gun, and ammunition."[41] The hearer of the tale and of the summons complied. To the rendezvous came some forty other young farmers and rangers out of the border townships of Lancaster County. They concerted plans. They ignored a messenger from the Rev. Mr. Elder and Justice Thomas Forster[42] with the appeal that they stay their hands from violence. They let the scout who had discovered the marauding Indians lead them; and, under the cover of night moved on Conestoga.

At that village there occurred a Kittanning-like scene, with slaying unchecked, indiscriminate, and pitiless—although happily, with no mention of Divine Providence. The sudden ultimate, prefaced by months of suspicion and hate-breeding fears, came when the first Indian showed sign that the Paxtonians' presence was detected. He fired toward them and sprang forward brandishing a tomahawk. One scout cried, "Mark him"; and bullets from several rifles felled the Conestogoe, just as a voice called out: "He is the villain who murdered my mother."[43]

After that, there was no stopping vengeance; "necessity," as the Scotch-Irish subsequently argued, "compelled."[44] The forty riders from Paxton and Derry and Hanover wracked ruin and death on the village. They wrought these, they believed, on Indians "housed and fed as the pets of the Province" who had been shown to them "to be our secret foes."[45] Then they mounted their horses and rode off homewards, leaving the Indian town in clamor and confusion, and six Conestoga proteges of the Penns dead: two women and four men. Among them was that old chief Sohays[46] who three weeks before had set down his mark, a hieroglyphical bird, on a message of welcome to the newest Deputy Governor of Pennsylvania.

But only the first act on a stage of terrible irony had ended. The actors, men whose Scottish sires had believed with the pilgrim missionary St. Columba or with the reformer John Knox, whose progenitors had served at Enniskillen and Derry, had not, as it were, finished their parts in a complete performance.

In fact, a good bit was to happen before they fulfilled their roles in entirety. On the morrow there was a coroner's investigation in Manor Township. By Matthias Slough and fourteen aides pronouncement was made "upon their oath and affirmation" that "six Indians were killed by a person or persons to this inquest unknown."[47] Fourteen surviving Conestogoes were gathered together and brought by the magistrates into Lancaster Town for protection as a first letter from Edward Shippen the Mayor, written on December 14, informed the authorities in Philadelphia.[48] On the sixteenth of December John Elder was informing Governor Penn by letter of how his messenger had entreated the Paxtonians to desist from their purpose, but was pleading now that the ill-advised and culpable persons had been such "as suffered much in their relations by the ravages of the late Indian war."[49] By that same date all Philadelphia was talking of the assault: Assemblymen, Councillors, Quakers, Presbyterians, merchants, journeymen, and apprentices.

By the nineteenth the adjourned Assembly was summoned by Governor's writ to attendance. On the same day the Council was issuing a proclamation to all the judges, justices, sheriffs, constables, and officers, civil and military, of Pennsylvania to search out and arrest the perpetrators of the crime. All like performances were "strictly forbidden."[50] Pennsylvanians, officialdom declared, intended to preserve and continue the old friendship with such friendly Indians as were being cared for at public expense on Province Island or elsewhere in the colony. On the twenty-fourth the Assembly—for a change, perhaps, fully responsive to Governor and Council—concurred with the Executive body in attitude and volunteered to provide funds for the maintenance of such friendly Indians as had escaped the fury of their bloody assailants or such as could be gathered together and sheltered in "the interior parts (they meant the coastal parts) of the Province."[51] Sternly the House deplored the "unspeakable cruelties" committed at Conestoga Manor "and all the horrid barbarity."[52]

But the interval of inquiry, resolves, and manifesto did not avail by reason of substance or by either temperateness or sternness of spirit. Rather it served at most as a taunt to the back inhabitants. On December 27 Paxton frontiersmen staged the second part of their drama.

This time they chose not night, but the fullness of day. Matthias Slough the Coroner might not have discovered in the darkness of December 13 the identity of the destroyers of Conestoga. He could see clearly enough the throng of unmasked riders who suddenly appeared, dismounted their horses in his innyard, and sped afoot to the Lancaster Work House, sheltering place of the rescued Conestogoes.

Of the event of their arrival there Mayor Edward Shippen wrote a second letter to the Honorable John Penn, Esquire, Governor:

Lancaster, 27th Decem^r. 1763., P.M.

Honoured Sir:

I am to acquaint your Honour that between two and three of the clock this afternoon, upwards of a hundred armed men, from the Westward, rode very fast into Town, turned their Horses into Mr. Slough's (an Inn-keeper) Yard, and proceeded with the greatest Precipitation to the Work House, stove open the door and killed all the Indians, and then took to their horses and rode off, all their business was done, and they were re-turning to their horses before I could get half way down to the Work House; the Sheriff and Coroner, however, & several others, got down as soon as the Rioters, but could not prevail with them to stop their hands; some people say they heard them declare they would proceed to the Province Island, and destroy the Indians there.

> I am with great Respect, Sir,
> Your Honour's most Obedient humble Servant
> Edwd Shippen

The Honble. Jno. Penn, Esqr., Govr.[53]

Rude pioneer justice had obviously struck a second time. An un-stayable frenzy had come into Scotch-Irish direct action. A day of black memory had been registered in Pennsylvania history.

There was division of opinion, of course. It was the more tense for being near to the crisis of a people. Historians were hardly destined, then, ever to come to one single final and united judgement in respect of it. Which was worse, the inaction of a body of lawmakers, or the direct brute action of a body of men whose children and families had been left unprotected by Government?

Into the initial phases of the long debate came again one now familiar Scotch-Irish voice. On the date of Edward Shippen's letter— on the night, in fact, of the second slaying—the Rev. Mr. John Elder wrote from Paxton to Governor Penn:

> The storm which had been so long gathering has at length exploded. Had Government removed the Indians from Conestoga, which had frequently been urged without success, this painful catastrophe might have been avoided. What could I do with men heated to madness? All that I could do was done; I expostulated; but *life* and *reason* were set at defiance. And yet the men in private life are virtuous and respectable; not cruel, but mild and merciful.
>
> The time will arrive when each palliating circumstance will be calmly weighed. This deed, magnified now into the blackest of crimes, shall be considered one of those youthful ebullitions of wrath caused by momen-tary excitement, to which human infirmity is subjected.[54]

The massacres of Conestoga and Lancaster entered, then, into the record of December, 1763, of American Colonial history. They still stand out lurid in retrospect, not even today fully dispersible into the mists of time. And in this truth there is, perhaps, a certain rightness. For in Provincial Pennsylvania there was something odd not only in popular but in registered official justice of the era. Although generally in abeyance, Robert Hunter Morris' edict of April, 1756,[55] still held as a law of redress upon the Delawares. Indian scalps, however dubious they might be as a political asset in 1763, still had an economic value and bounty-price in the autumn of that year. At any rate on October 29 James English brought three scalps to John Harris, ferryman on the Susquehanna, and collected from that agent of the Province "Five Pounds in full for my share of the Bounty Money."[56] After two centuries the signed acknowledgment of payment to the scalper remains in Harris' Receipt-Book.

From what Indians English and his companion Samuel Murray took their trophies one cannot now learn. But one might hope that the three evidences of achievement against a foe had been fairly taken in some action of defense for the household of a back inhabitant which needed considerably more protection than it was being afforded by the Assembly of the Province.

CHAPTER 8

AFTERMATH OF MASSACRE

OFTEN ENOUGH in history the eminence of a man overshadows the significance of an event. Acts which in their origin have no material relation to his career are dwarfed in the light of a celebrity's opinion. The name of Benjamin Franklin is among the great names of earth. John Hay, Sheriff of Lancaster County in December, 1763, and Felix Donnolly, keeper of Lancaster Jail in the same month, can bear no reputation comparable to that of the famous eighteenth-century scientist, philosopher, man of affairs, politician, statesman, and diplomat. Yet each of these humbler men, in his own way, is worthy of notice; and both were closer to events and to attitudes of mind on the Susquehanna frontier than was the savant.

Hay survives in the minutes of the Provincial Council of Pennsylvania through a report made by him on December 27 to Governor Penn,[1] and in the manuscript text of this, held today among the commonwealth's *Provincial Papers*,[2] Felix Donnolly's name is preserved only in the printed version of the fragment of a deposition[3] made to Mr. Edward Shippen, and originally, question and answer, set down in that gentleman's unmistakable hand. Yet the evidence which may be gleaned from the statements associated with these two names is as worthy of credence as anything ever offered by Franklin on the subject of the incursions of the Paxton Boys upon Conestoga, Lancaster, and the Lancaster Work House.

John Hay's report—by force of event rather than design—was draughted in two installments. The first,[4] written in the morning, offers introductory comments on two lists which he intended then should immediately follow. The second,[5] considerably more graphic in manner, adds new information and throws a baleful and unexpected light on the writer's original enumerations.

A genuine clerkly industry manifested itself in the first. With meticulous care it enumerated the possessions of the Conestoga Indians who

[111

before noon were still being sheltered in the Jail. At the hour of its writing the heirs of the Susquehannocks, it made clear, owned, beyond three horses and two belts of wampum, six several documents, two of them on parchment, four upon paper. Quite objectively, with no merest intrusion of feeling, the sheriff and scribe listed each of the six.

His first two items read:

"A Writing, or Parchment, purporting an article of Peace and Amity concluded between the Governor of Maryland & the Chiefs of the Conestogoe & other Indians.

"A Writing on Parchment, purporting An Article of Agreement between William Penn, Proprietary, &ca, of Pennsylvania, and the King of the Indians inhabiting in or about the River Susquehannah, and other Indian Nations, dated the three & twentieth day of the second month, called April, in the year one thousand, seven hundred and one."[6] The other four embraced directions or agreements with the names of Governor William Keith and Mr. James Logan attached, and dating respectively in 1719 (May 26), 1719 (May 5), 1717, and 1708.[7]

But, wholly unintended, a pathos intruded on December 27, 1763, upon factuality. There, indeed, in John Hay's letter, were detailed all that remained of the last Susquehannocks' charters, of privileges from the white governors in Maryland and Pennsylvania. By mid-afternoon of the day, the last Indian owners of that sheaf of papers guaranteeing them alliance and protection from the leaders of two provinces were themselves dead.

For it was that fact which the second instalment of the Sheriff's letter announced. Indeed, since he had copied down the names of the survivors, gathered together after the fateful raid of December 13-14 by John Miller and Robert Beatty on orders from Richard Hockley and Secretary Richard Peters of Philadelphia, the bearers of the names were neither survivors nor possessors. They had become merely a subject of debate.

On them, and on the behavior at the Lancaster Jail of the Paxton men who slew them, however, Hay's letter had become as authoritative a statement as today can be found. Eye-witness to the event, his version of it is, and should be, as credible as any interpretation set down by Franklin, or by a burgess of Lancaster like Edward Shippen, or furnished by any deponent testifying afterwards before a Lancaster County Justice. Its manner was forthrightly plain:

Since writing the above, the poor Indians whom we imagined were placed in safety are destroyed. A number of Persons to the amount (by their appearance) of fifty or sixty, armed with rifles, tomahawks, &ca., suddenly, about two o'clock, rushed into the town & immediately repaired to the Work House where the Indians were confined, & notwithstanding all opposition of myself and the coroner, with many others, broke open the Work House, and have killed all the Indians there, being the fourteen mentioned in the list to have survived the former affair at their town. After which they in a body left the town without offering any insults to the inhabitants, and without putting it into the power of any one to take or molest any of them without danger of life to the person attempting it; of which both myself and the Coroner by our opposition were in great danger.[8]

No accounts of horrible mutilation, no exaggeration of the number of raiders, no elaboration on the bravado of these. Despatch sudden, relentless, terrible, unvaunting, not even apparently exultant. The perpetrators of it came and went in a body. They offered no insult to the citizens of Lancaster. They molested no man of the town; they suffered no man of the town to molest them. And, quite as obviously, no unofficial townsman offered any molestment. Only Coroner Matthias Slough and Sheriff John Hay, in the dignity of their office, had protested; and other men had objected. But the letter bore no evidence that any one man had offered a form of objection beyond words. In the moment of its enactment, Lancaster had received the affair unperturbed—with something almost of the same incalulable air with which the Paxton and Donegal Boys had conducted themselves.

The calm, however, was only ominous; John Hay's objectivity was but stillness on the eve of storm. Excitement, difference of view, difference of narrative, other posting of information to Philadelphia, and taking of sides—all followed soon enough. There were no Quaker and no Moravian apologists for the Paxton Boys. Markedly there were no Presbyterian and no Scotch-Irish censors of the acts of these either on the frontiers or in Philadelphia. Men's sympathies, men's attestations and proclamations, alike became partisan. Convictions were pretty much a matter of one's politics or of one's creature comforts and group interests.

Governor Penn's Council met with him. A second proclamation against the rioters was issued on January 2, 1764.[9] Duties were once more enjoined upon petty county and borough officials. For apprehending and securing, or causing to be apprehended and secured, any three of the ringleaders in the two affrays at Conestoga and Lancaster, two hundred pounds were offered as public reward. To that sum amnesty was added for any accomplice involved in the riots but innocent of blood shedding who should make discovery to the Provincial authorities of the identity "of any or either of the said ringleaders."[10]

More than that, John Penn, before his proclamation could be printed and posted, was busily addressing both General Thomas Gage, Commander-in-Chief of the King's army in the colonies, and Sir William Johnson, His Majesty's Indian Agent. Of one gentleman[11] he requested the transfer of companies from Carlisle for protection of the Province and of friendly Indians then on Province Island, or being brought to it. He wished the other[12] to use his influence with the Six Nations lest that confederacy retaliate upon Pennsylvania for the slaying of the Conestogoes. Early in January he was bent on having arrangements made to have Captain Robertson of the King's troops at Carlisle escort 140 Indians away from Province Island.[13] They wished to be removed thence,[14] he asseverated, to be put under Johnson's care in New York. To the famous agent of the Crown, and to the Governors of New Jersey and New York, and to General Gage new letters[15] had to be addressed, desiring the interest of all in his project.

Gage, who was glad enough to have a few companies of the regulars in use, was more responsive than the others. He first consented to the use of Captain Robertson's company as a bodyguard for the Indians;[16] then, when the escort toward New York was in motion, reversed orders and had Robertson return the fugitives to Pennsylvania.[17] The two governors, considerably less cordial, had no wish to have a lot of displaced Indians quartered in their two provinces;[18] and Johnson[19] was not the man to appeal for the satisfaction of a request to which Cadwallader Colden of New York lent no gentle ear.

In brief, if Pennsylvania had to be defended from its own frontiersmen, it became incumbent on the Assembly to provide a military through its own subsidies to that effect for the protection of both people and Government. As usual the Quaker legislature was slow to act toward such a consummation; and neither John Penn's helplessness nor his contrivings got him very far. Inaction continued in Philadelphia for a time longer after the proclamation. Gradually, January, 1764, elapsed. On January 24 the Assembly had got no farther with new plans of defense against the back inhabitants toward Susquehanna than a request that the Governor order that the Sheriff and the Coroner of Lancaster County come down to Philadelphia and bring with them information which could be directed toward a proper punishment of the recent "daring disturbers of the Public Peace."[20] It was enough for the legislature of the Province to let General Gage's men take care both of all rescued friendly Indians and the safety of the members and their families and neighbors.

But by that late date in January persistent rumors of plans brewing to the west were coming into Philadelphia. In Lancaster County obvious conferences were occurring. Clusters of men were foregathering at taverns and other rendezvous. Some sort of action was being concerted. Presbyterians and Scotch-Irish settlers were in frequent consultation.

Indeed Benjamin Kendall, Quaker merchant, got back to the city on the morning of Saturday, January 28, from a visit to the frontiers, and came primed in the very latest news. Governor Penn was prompt to have the man make a solemn affirmation before the Council. For the sober Friend Benjamin had a graphic story.[21]

At the "Sign of the Hat," two miles east of the borough of Lancaster, he had met Robert Fulton. Fulton pretended to have learned that Captain Coultas had been appointed to raise five hundred men in Philadelphia to protect the Indians there. The Scotch-Irishman was sorry; he thought it would be well for Coultas to make "his Peace with Heaven."[22] The man, he said, "would not live for two weeks longer."[23] In fact, Fulton averred, fifteen hundred frontiersmen were coming down to the city within a fortnight to kill all the Indians there, Coultas or no Coultas. If fifteen hundred men were not enough to destroy the captain and his *protegés*, five thousand other settlers would join them and help achieve their very definite purpose.

Benjamin Kendall, knowing his informant to be a man of influence, begged Fulton to bend every effort to dissuade them from going on with their planned expedition. Fulton retorted that the angel Gabriel himself coming fresh from Heaven would not be able to induce them to desist from their design. He bade Kendall recall that the people of the settlements along Susquehanna "were of the same spirit with the blood-ran, blood-thirsty Presbyterians, who cut off the head of King Charles I."[24]

Benjamin answered, "I hear you intend to kill the Quakers."[25]

"No, God forbid," answered Robert Fulton, "but they will kill any or all folk who will oppose them." And the Lancaster man added, "If it is true that the Indians in Philadelphia are being distributed in little groups among different families, those families better beware. Their houses will be fired over their heads if they refuse to deliver up their redskin guests."[26]

All this the affirmant dictated gravely; and neither it nor the report with which Mr. Kendall concluded was lost upon the Councillors who listened. They and Philadelphia, they believed, were soon to be confronted with an insurrection—and an equipped one. Their friend, the Quaker, had learned at the "Sign of the Hat" that the intended rebels already had a magazine of three half-barrels of gun powder and one hundred small arms to aid them in their enterprise. So, at the least, had said William Way, a comrade of Robert Fulton.

Governor Penn and the five of his Councillors present, former Deputy Governor James Hamilton, Benjamin Shoemaker, Benjamin Chew, William Logan, and Lynford Lardner,[27] attended diligently every word of affirming Benjamin Kendall; and responded immediately to the extent of their highly impuissant authority. They advised Mr. Penn to give Captain Schlosser, officer in charge of the Barracks where the Indians were now being harbored, instructions to defend that point with full resistance—" to fire upon any body of armed men who should make their appearance in a hostile manner."[28] They were of opinion that the three companies of Highlanders, belonging to his Majesty's forces and now stationed at Carlisle, should be invited to Lancaster to preserve the peace there. Mr. Penn addressed Captain William Murray upon that subject the next morning.[29]

Four days later, on Thursday, February 2, the Council meeting again, with Richard Peters and young Richard Penn now of their number, advised another address to the Assembly. This appealed for a bill to establish a Provincial Militia as being "the most effectual means"[30] of protecting order and suppressing tumults—and was disregarded. All that the Assembly would do in response to the Governor's explanation of the strange footing on which he stood with respect to the troops in Carlisle was to ratify a riot law and let it be enacted by the Executive on the next day.[31] Once that was in effect, the Council could do no more than recommend letters to four justices,[32] Thomas Forster and Adam Reed in Lancaster County, James Reed and Jonas Seeley in Berks, calling for information from them of any riotous parties which they might behold converging on roads to Philadelphia; and the letters were despatched on the Saturday following. Moreover, on that same day—as if as a mere conventional matter of form—the Council again earnestly recommended to the Assembly the framing of a Militia Law.

Inaction, ineptitude, and rumor continued over Sunday. Then, by the new midweek, reports of the nearness and the numbers of the rioters approaching aroused the citizens themselves. Benjamin Franklin afterwards wrote[33] that this was in hearty compliance with a suggestion from himself. *The Pennsylvania Gazette,* in the less vauntful manner of its next issue, remarked that "the inhabitants being called upon by the Governor" entered into "an Association, and took arms for the support of Government."[34] By Wednesday, February 8, the townsmen were at least in a posture of defense. Three companies of regulars were at hand.[35] Eight companies of Associaters[36]—by a happy revival of the organization founded in 1747, frowned on then by the

Penns and long in abeyance—had reconstituted themselves. One battery of artillery[37] was in readiness with eight pieces of cannon planted upon works thrown up around the Barracks. A civilian army, armed with private rifles, was minded to resist a mob of men from the west who were similarly armed with but their own muskets.

Main credit for the affirmative note in the city Franklin was willing to take to himself.[38] He refused command, he said, preferring to carry his weapon under John Penn's instructions and thinking to "strengthen his authority by setting an example of obedience to his order."[39] Yet he did not subsequently omit a statement that in the thick of the midweek alarm, John Penn, "with his Councillors at his heels,"[40] did him the honor of running to his house at midnight, appealing for advice, and making the place his headquarters. Amiably he enjoyed contemplation of the spectacle. For Franklin seldom failed of zest; and now he was without immediate ties in the Assembly. No member of it, he experienced no embarrassment for being connected with a body which again on Saturday, February 11, having done nothing for the protection of Philadelphia and having provided no militia law for the Province, reminded the Governor by formal address that "nothing reposed in them should be left wanting"[41] by them. They objected to the trampling of rioters "on laws divine and human."[42] Beyond that they were content to rely upon the riot act endorsed on February 3. Franklin certainly kept his attention to affairs more lively than these.

Elsewhere, too, folk were on the alert. Couriers were met coming to town, "their horses all of a foam."[43] This one reported an enemy of five hundred seen on the way; that one a throng of a thousand; a third, a force of not less than fifteen hundred.[44] (Although none was ever to see so large a multitude as the sixty-five hundred to which Kendall had totaled the boasts of Robert Fulton!)

It became important to look to the ferries over Schuylkill. Most likely it was that the Paxton men would try to cross upper, or middle.[45]

Men sped to draw the boats employed at that point to the townward side of the river. Others thought of the boats at the Sweed's ford.[46] The stream was in freshet; if the boats there could be kept out of the rioter's hands, those intruders would have to attempt any crossing they made at some distance above the city. A detachment hurried off to save that situation.

While these were away pursuing their mission, a cry went up suddenly, far from the east bank of the Schuylkill and nearer the southward course of the Delaware: "They are coming! They are coming down Second Street—down Second Street!"[47] A band of Associaters seized their firelocks and began to prime; artillerymen threw themselves into order. Passersby scurried out of range; and a troop of young German butchers and porters hove in sight—to be recognized as friends, not enemies, just as one artilleryman got his piece into position and was bringing his match to its touchhole![48] Relief of spirit rather than the discharge of a cannon greeted the amateur cavalry; and the hubbub quieted.

In fact, neither the butchers nor the Associators who in the wetness of the weather abandoned their places under the broad eaves of the Market House to occupy the Friends' Meeting-House[49] had to do any professional military work. Afterwards cartoons might picture them—or even Quakers themselves—leaning rifle in hand from upstairs windows of the sanctuary in attitudes of defense.[50] In reality, they never were to train a single gun on the supposititious foe. Even Captain Coultas, who had ridden into town at the head of a troop,[51] experienced no need of making his peace with Heaven within the time allotted him by Benjamin Kendall on Robert Fulton's predictions at the "Hat" near Lancaster.

Instead, when the frontiersmen in a body of five hundred had finally arrived and encamped on the west side of the Schuylkill beyond Germantown, three peacemakers of advanced years were all that were needed to disarm any will to violence which the Scotch-Irish might have been cherishing. Assembly had failed of having a quorum. Council might have found shelter and safety in their own houses without imposing on Benjamin Franklin's hospitality. John Penn might have risked himself in the Paxton and Donegal men's company with full security had it been consonant with his dignity—the words were his own—as a chief executive to treat in person with rioters. No harm, in brief, befell any one.

The back inhabitants consented to disperse and go home if John Penn's special bevy of commissioners, including Franklin, who had come over the river[52] to meet them, would carry back to Governor and Assembly a petition and manifesto which they had drawn up. By midafternoon, the weather clearing, the Associators of Philadelphia's civilian army could be drawn up near the Court House[53] and a speech be made assuring them that matters on the frontier had been much misrepresented. The "Paxtoneers," it could be said, "were a set of worthy men . . . who labored under great distress."[54] Matthew Smith and James Gibson, who had transmitted their manuscript through three city notables to the Governor, with their fellows had come to Philadelphia intending only to lay certain complaints before the legislature.

As to their bearing arms, they bore them for fear that without them they might be molested or abused.[55] Nothing was implied in the remarks of the commentator from the Court House steps on the subject of Fulton's arithmetic or his threats.

Promptly the townsmen hearers quieted down and disbanded. Few were troubled that they did not have to offer a resistance, although there were certainly among them those who smiled at their nearby visitants' caution of keeping weapons at their sides lest they be molested by the peaceable citizens of Philadelphia. By evening the community was (in general) drawing breaths of relief.

Thursday morning arrived. A cluster of approximately thirty frontiersmen came into town for a brief tour of inspection. Rumor again leaped into being. Mercurial Philadelphians succumbed to new excitement. Word now flew that the "Paxtoneers" had broken their treaty[56] and were moving on the city. With incredible alacrity Associator folk rushed to arms; nearly a thousand of them assembled within a quarter of an hour,[57] so one spectator subsequently asserted.

But no engagement ensued. The thirty visitors from Susquehanna behaved with a sober decency. Their urban hosts suffered them to look about as they chose and offered no opposition. Calm prevailed.

Two days later *The Pennsylvania Gazette* made quiet report of the episode,[58] and printed as well the Act of Assembly of February 3. John Penn could reread if he wished two letters, now a week old, from the Rev. Mr. John Elder of Paxton to himself and Mr. Secretary Joseph Shippen. The Assembly could, if it so wished, take opportunity to study means of redress for the grievances declared by the back inhabitants. Wits in the town, freed from the menace of early destruction by a mob of white savages, could take to lampoons on burghers and rioters. Franklin could put his energy into stern but facile condemnation of the raids on Conestoga and Lancaster. Presbyterian clergymen could spring to the defense of a reviled frontier and to their own censure of incompetent legislators who had let intolerable conditions develop in the back country. The rest of February, 1764, and the spring of that year could make months of polemic literature out of two slayings of Indians and a colonial paradox in which mild men had descended to murder and accused murderers had metamorphosed strangely into modest, though vocal, complainants. Another weird manifestation of Scots breed had, in fact, assumed shape.

The Pennsylvania Gazette of Saturday, February 11, carried the full text of the Assembly's Act of February 3. This embraced many an injunction to county, city, and corporate town officials. Justices, justices of the peace, sheriffs, under-sheriffs, mayors, bailiffs were commanded to let no group of twelve persons or more assemble unlawfully, riotously, tumultuously, or to the disturbance of the public peace. Authorities were to act in the name of George III, then in the fourth year of his reign, and order all suspected gatherings of such number to disperse themselves and depart to their habitations or their lawful business. Persons who so assembled, who persisted in remaining assembled and refused to disband on warning from an official, should be adjudged felons and should suffer death as felons. And they should suffer that death "without Benefit of Clergy."[59]

Such, the Assembly of the Province of Pennsylvania declared, was the King's law. In effect, the legislature said that for the next year men who had assembled as Matthew Smith's and James Gibson's followers had assembled against the protests of Thomas Forster and Mr. Elder in Lancaster County after the date of the Assembly's enactment, might be seized, tried, condemned, and hanged as malefactors beyond even the privileges of grace.

This was in the commonwealth which had been founded by William Penn, which for many years had been governed wholly under the influence of the Society of Friends, which was still legislated for by a body in which the majority were Quakers. It was enacted by a young governor who by 1764, like most of the family to which he belonged, had left the affiliations of his grandfather and become a member of the Anglican Church, and whose nearest associates in the Council were Anglican churchmen. Nothing in the act, or in the conduct of the implementers of it as law, could be construed as any charter of liberties for back countrymen or for Presbyterians who might wish to convene subsequent to it during 1764 and to protest.

Furthermore it was as well that the unregarded voice of John Elder of Paxton sounded out in the days of this austere proclamation.

On January 30 that Presbyterian clergyman wrote to the Governor; and on February 1, before his letter could be posted, he added a second communication to Penn's secretary, Colonel Shippen. He was as direct in both writings as he had been in his letter to John Penn of five weeks earlier. Then he had had no compliments to offer to Government in Philadelphia. He offered none now.

Indeed, he protested frankly to the chief executive of the Province: "The indulgence shown to savages gives a general disgust."[60] Frontiersmen, he warned, thought it hard that so many Indians were taken into protection under the title of friends and were plentifully supplied at the expense of taxpayers. He deplored that in contrast many back inhabitants, "his Majesty's loyal and faithful subjects," were "driven from house and home" by the Indians and "reduced to poverty and want."[61] Sternly in both his capacity as a gentleman and a priest, he repudiated the request which he had received from Mr. Penn to "take all the pains in your power to learn the names of the ringleaders and perpetrators of those barbarities, and acquaint me with everything you can discover concerning them."[62]

"Were it in my power to learn the names of any concerned in the late riots," he remarked, "I should think it advisable, on many accounts, to use silence in that case. The character of an informer is too odious for a gentleman to bear."[63] He referred candidly to the "office I have the honor to be invested with in the Church," and declared his unwillingness to do anything which would tend "to mar my usefulness in that station."[64] Quite obviously he had no intention of being tempted by the lure of the two hundred pounds held out in Penn's proclamation of January 2[65] for causing to be apprehended any three of the participants in the affrays at Conestoga and Lancaster. John Elder had opposed the design of men belonging to his own township, and presumably to his congregation; he had not spied upon them.

His letter to Joseph Shippen was as completely frank. It reported facts as during the last few days he had been perceiving them. Frequent meetings had been occurring. An expedition, he believed, was preparing "against the Indians at Philadelphia."[66] He had been once more objecting, but in vain. "The minds of the inhabitants are so exasperated against the Quakers," he began one sentence; and then excised the words "the Quakers" and substituted the phrase "a particular set of men,"[67] before continuing his statement to the effect that the partiality shown by the group dominating the government in Philadelphia had at length so irritated the men of the frontier counties that no one acting in the interest of the Provincial authorities could any more have a hearing among them. Like his neighbors he lamented, in brief, the heavy burden of cost laid on the Province and its people by its frequent Quaker-influenced Indian treaties. Those ceremonies for trade's sake he could see bringing no advantage to his Majesty or the Province. Plainly John Elder stood for King's law not Quakers'.

On that position in political attitude he wrote with specific clearness. Let there be no more treaties arranged for by men in Philadelphia without the proper legal recourse through King George's Indian Agent for all the colonies; that was the desire of the frontiersmen.

And none of those were there "but what were warmly attached to his Majesty and would cheerfully risk their lives to promote his service."[68] However "furious" their[69] tempers in local affairs, their first allegiance was in 1764 to the Crown.

And just as firmly did Mr. Elder make one other assertion. "The Presbyterians, who are the most numerous, I imagine, of any denomination in the Province, are enraged at their being charged in bulk with these facts, under the name of Scotch-Irish, and other ill-natured titles."[70] They resented having the killing of the Conestoga Indians "compared to the Irish Massacres"[71] (they had in mind the barbarities performed on the Ulster Scots in Ireland in 1641). To have it implied that the slayings in Lancaster County were more barbarous than the slaughters of Protestants which brought General Munro's army to Carrickfergus in the mid-seventeenth century made the Pennsylvania Presbyterians of 1764 the more determined that no more Indian treaties should be held "unless his Majesty's pleasure on those heads is well known."[72] The pastor of Paxton Church, who last summer had commanded two companies of Paxton and Hanover rangers serving in defense of the frontiers, and whose men had many of them been in the Wyoming in the autumn of 1763 witnessing the results of massacre performed by Indians there, when he wrote to officials in Philadelphia was in no mood of appeasement.

Different in tone was Edward Shippen of Lancaster, father to the Secretary of the Province and to the aide of John Penn, whom Mr. Elder was addressing. The older Shippen, who was by this time garnering depositions on the subject of the two massacres, kept himself considerably better attuned to the Anglican heirs of William Penn. He wrote to the Governor at the time; carefully refrained from censure of John Elder and John Harris of Paxton, who were "determined to rely upon the reputation they have so well established";[73] and himself rested in quiet conscience. Sure of the confidence reposed in him by John Penn and the Proprietaries, he was content to "silently remain passive."[74] (What Felix Donnolly, keeper of the Lancaster Jail, would have said of the correspondent's silence and passivity, we have today no way of knowing.)

The man of the day was not the minister of a flock of misreputed Scotch-Irish, not the mayor of a western town of log houses. Nor was he either of the two young men, Matthew Smith and James Gibson, who had brought to Philadelphia in February, 1764, a remarkable document appealing for political, social, and economic rights signed with their two names.[75] The man who captured the stage of the day and figured there brilliantly was Benjamin Franklin.

For Franklin had the gift of narration.

CHAPTER 9

PERVERSITY OF FAME

JOHN PENN kept his word with the back inhabitants. On Wednesday, February 15, 1764, the "Paxtoneers" having really dispersed according to their own promise and gone home, the Governor sent their Remonstrance by Mr. Secretary Shippen to the Assembly.[1]

It was a formal document, and beautifully penned.[2] Nothing in either text or script belied the dignity or the culture of the five frontier counties from which it emanated. James Gibson had copied down the final draft; his signature still stands on it among the Provincial Papers of Pennsylvania, in pattern identical with the script[3] which presents its argument. Quite as firm and clear a hand, although different in conformation, is revealed in the name of Matthew Smith, second signer.[4] Both men wrote as well as could write the best clerks in official or commercial Philadelphia.

Moreover, the wording of the text which they submitted suggested no dearth of culture among the remonstrants from Susquehanna, and from between there and the city. The petition was throughout as fine a piece of prose as could have been shaped by the best scholar or jurist in the capital of the Province. More than that, it was both an able narration of facts and a cogent statement. All that lacked to its force was the popularity of its proponents; and the whirligig of time had to wait a decade and more for its revenges. The salutation was wholly proper: "To the Honorable John Penn, Esq., Governor of the Province of Pennsylvania, and of the Counties of New-Castle, Kent, and Sussex, upon Delaware; and to the Representatives of the Freemen of the said Province, in General Assembly met."[5] Smith and Gibson, in "Behalf of ourselves and his Majesty's faithful and loyal Subjects, the Inhabitants of the Frontier Counties of Lancaster, York, Cumberland, Berks, and Northampton,"[6] humbly begged leave to remonstrate to the legislature and to ask its wisdom in their redress. They made their request to men whose authority they regarded as

[123

delegated to them by the people of Pennsylvania; and they made it as self-respecting subjects of the King. They asked, in brief, only what they esteemed as their native right as English colonials.

Beyond their exordium they presented seven clauses, each framed in a paragraph or a section which led from summary of facts and causes to an appeal.

First they desired equality of privilege with his Majesty's other subjects. That meant to them that if the City of Philadelphia and the Counties of Philadelphia, Chester, and Bucks could elect twenty-six members of the Assembly, and the five frontier counties, which now numbered many more inhabitants than the town and the three interior counties, could elect only ten members to represent them, there should be an immediate reformation in the number of members whom they could name to seats in the body. This initial inequality they pronounced "oppressive, unequal and unjust."[7] They explored it as the cause of many of their grievances, and an infringement of their natural privileges of freedom and equality.

Their second clause ran to greater length and was fully as eloquent. It explained that they understood a bill was then before the Assembly which would provide that any person charged with the killing of any Indians in Lancaster County should not be tried in a court there but in Philadelphia or Chester or Bucks. Such a bill, it insisted, would be an insult to British subjects and their courts in other counties; according to the well-known laws of the British Nation, in a point whereon life, liberty, and security depended, men had the right of trial in their own neighborhood, where their own character and credit, that of their accusers and that of the witnesses, were best known. It frankly objected to having trials conducted by stranger courts, where partiality to Indians was certainly as real as partiality against them was on the frontiers. It was of opinion that the contemplated bill would never have any earnest of passage if the western counties were justly represented in the Assembly. The law which it would seek to establish would take away from "his Majesty's good subjects a privilege so long esteemed sacred by Englishmen."[8] The Legislature of the Province, it was hoped, would never enact a bill of such dangerous tendency.

Longer still, the third clause treated of the horrors of life on the frontiers; charged that barbarities had been frequently performed on men, women, and children without distinction by Indian wards of the Moravians, who had since "under the mask of friendship . . . procured themselves to be taken under the protection of the Government";[9] objected that some of those Indians, "confessedly a part of the

Wyalusing Indians, which tribe is now at war with us,"[10] were being maintained at public expense in the Barracks at Philadelphia. "With sorrow and indignation" the Scotch-Irish authors of the manuscript remonstrated that there should be in Pennsylvania "persons . . . at pains to extenuate the cruelties of the savages";[11] such abettors of barbarity they denounced for a hardness of heart great as that of the perpetrators. They cited instances of the perfidy and the bloody violence of Indians of whom the Moravians were champions; and they challenged the intelligence of authorities who argued that one could be at war with half a tribe and not the whole of it. Obstinately they argued that the Indians then being provisioned in Philadelphia would be succored only to the unhappy effect of being able, after a winter's nourishment, to return to scalp and butcher back inhabitants in the spring. Nearly a thousand families on the frontiers, they insisted, were in the extremes of distress "destitute of the necessaries of life"[12]—and without relief of any sort from the government. As they beheld the situation, while their kinsmen suffered every hardship and fear, their enemies were cordially nurtured. It was enough to make them "mad with rage," enough to tempt to do what only the "most violent necessity could vindicate."[13]

In sum, their third clause demanded that the "enemies of his Majesty should be removed as soon as possible out of the Province."[14]

The fourth clause, more brief than the third but as intransigent, warned first that the entertainment of the Indians was an entertainment of spies in the inhabited parts of the Province; then declared that to the "fatal" intercourse between the pretended friends and the open enemies of the Province were due "the greatest part of the ravages and murders that had been committed"[15] in the long course of the Indian wars. Accordingly the petitioners prayed their "grievance be taken under consideration and remedied."[16]

The fifth clause was brief and blunt. It lamented that the Government of Pennsylvania had made no provision for the care of frontiersmen injured in the defense of the Province. Its appeal was that the lives and liberties of persons so wounded be provided for at public expense, and their wounds cured. It made no mention of sheltered Moravian Indians. But the grievance it indicated was as clear as any; and the redress it asked was for subjects of the King and loyal heroes. Both its logic and its resentment stood for the rights of five counties of free men.

As blunt and direct if not kindly reasoning was the sixth clause, which might as appropriately have been written by Margery Mitchell of Shippensburg as by James Gibson and his fellow commiteemen. This reminded that in the late Indian war Pennsylvania like others of the King's colonies had given reward for Indian scalps. Payment of bounties for such items had of late been discontinued. Lack of such remuneration "had damped the spirits of many brave men, who were willing to venture their lives in parties against the enemy."[17] The solution proposed was restoration of the earlier arrangement. Public rewards for scalps should be made "adequate to the dangers attending enterprises of this nature."[18] No good scouting into Indian territory, the Scotch-Irishmen seemed to infer, unless there were a reward. Scalping for scalps' sake was not in itself the answer.

The seventh clause was both humane and intelligent. It asked for two considerations: a genuine effort on the part of Government to rescue from captivity "among the savage heathen" the prisoner relatives of the back inhabitants, and an embargo on all trade with Indians until "our brethren and relatives are brought home to us."[19]

The eighth clause made vigorous complaint against "a certain Society of People in this Province" which had come to several treaties held by the King's representatives and "openly loaded the Indians with presents."[20] "I.P." (Israel Pemberton, leader of the Friendly Association, organized first by Philadelphia Quakers in 1756) came in for particular denunciation. He, said the frontiersmen, "in defiance of all Government, not only abetted our Indian enemies, but kept up a private intelligence with them."[21] He had gone so far as to receive publicly "from them a belt of wampum, as if he had been our Governor, or been authorized by the King to treat with his enemies."[22] And, in saying that, the Scotch-Irish from Susquehanna knew that if the Councillors gathered around John Penn had wished to corroborate them, many an evidence of the truth of their assertion might have been furnished from official minutes on the ubiquitous behavior of Pemberton at the treaties with the Delaware King Teedyuscung at Lancaster in 1757, at Easton in 1758, and again in Easton in 1761 and 1762. For the so-called King of the Quakers was regularly suspect among all close adherents of the Proprietors of the Province. The frontiersmen may have misconstrued this or that of Israel Pemberton's motives. Other influences than his had contributed to the Indians despising the inhabitants of Pennsylvania "as a weak and disunited people."[23] The activity of his Friendly Association was not unique as a "fatal source"[24] of the calamities under which they groaned. Yet the men from the five remonstrant counties were justified in praying, as humbly they did in the clause, that no private subject be permitted thereafter to carry on a correspondence with any of their Indian enemies.

The ninth and last clause of the petition of grievance was more gently candid. It observed frankly that Fort Augusta, in spite of its expensiveness to the Province, had ameliorated little the condition of the distressed inhabitants. The men stationed there neither helped to save crops from marauders nor made attack upon the Indians in their towns nor patrolled the frontiers. But the writers of the remonstrance disclaimed any wish to reflect on the Commanding Officer at Augusta —Colonel James Burd—whom they left unnamed. He, they understood, was always directed by those from whom he received his orders. Their request, then, was that measures might be taken to make his garrison more serviceable to them in their distress.[25]

Finally, Matthew Smith and James Gibson signed on behalf of their two selves, "and by appointment of a great number of the frontier inhabitants."[26]

But the time of the Scotch-Irish in Pennsylvania had not yet arrived. Their document of February, 1764, had been preceded by acts of violence in the previous December. Their arrival at Germantown the week before had been heralded by a fortnight of rumor. Reputation, rather than justice and understanding, had been negotiating for them during a month-and-a-half. Moreover they were addressing a Governor who was not at all sure of himself and a Legislature which had small confidence in anything beyond its own closed mind. The remonstrance was granted a full reading. More than that it did not have. Indeed, on that mid-February Wednesday the Pennsylvania Assembly "Ordered to lie on the table"[27] the most significant statement of the rights of freemen ever drawn up in the Province since William Penn provided it with his two Frames of Government in 1682 and 1701. From the limbo of the unenacted into which the remonstrance of the frontier was thrust it has never been removed.

Similar was the fate of a second *apologia* at the next meeting of Assembly. On February 17 was read and tabled "The Declaration of the injured Frontier Inhabitants, together with a brief Sketch of Grievances the good Inhabitants of the Province labor under."[28]

This, a more polemical and an even more protestant address than the Smith-Gibson petition, was by the same token more resentful and more vaunting. Flourishes in sentences less orderly in structure signified its quality. Initially it pleaded that the killing of the Indians at Conestoga Manor and Lancaster had been very invidiously misrepresented. It argued, although certainly not successfully, that many folk unacquainted with the true state of affairs had been mischievously inspiring "censure on the authors of those facts."[29] It pretended to openness and frankness: only necessity had induced the conduct of the slayers. In sum, the great purpose of its beginning was to dissipate the appearance of their having flown into the face of authority.

But it was only by begging the question that the second paragraph offered any justification on that score. Here, with an evasiveness seldom characteristic of them and now almost amusing, the Scotch-Irish got behind the English Crown. Their excuse for Conestoga and Lancaster was that they were "loyal subjects to the best of Kings, our rightful Sovereign George the Third."[30] Firmly attached to his Royal Person, his Interest and his Government, they were "equally opposite to the Enemies of his Throne and Dignity."[31] That "Throne and Dignity,"[32] as they saw it, were betrayed by dangerous concealments on the part of the lately slain Indians "under a mask of falsely pretended friendship."[33] To destroy such a mask they believed they must "cheerfully offer their substance and their lives in the King's cause."[34] (Strange championing accorded by men of the breed of Wallace and Bruce, by grandsons of the defenders of Enniskillen and Londonderry!)

On better ground were their arguments when they turned from subterfuge use of a King's name—common enough practice of politicians—to the nature of Indian enemies and the situation and state of the frontier. A legislature more amenable to suggestions than the Pennsylvania Assembly of 1764 might well have given these credit. They protested the caresses accorded to the savages by a minority in the commonwealth, the expense to the Province of the Indian treaties, the servility to the Indians at such functions, easy conditions for traders to the enemy, the inefficacy of measures to recover captives carried away into slavery from frontiersmen's families. They excoriated the lukewarm support which had been yielded during the last summer to Colonel Bouquet and General Amherst. Not one man, they asseverated truthfully enough, had been granted at the cost of the Province to aid Bouquet in the relief of Fort Pitt. "His Majesty's little army, whose valor the whole Frontiers with gratitude acknowledge as the happy means of having saved from ruin great part of the Province"[35] had been left to fend for itself on the charges of the Crown.

Then, in the aftermath of such legislative parsimoniousness, the government had thought to hire the King's troops to protect the King's enemies. (They were referring to the guard sent on from Carlisle to serve at Lancaster in January, and to the companies detailed to escorting the Indian refugees from Province Island and the Philadelphia Barrack across New Jersey.) Such behavior the remonstrants decried with the more vehemence when hundreds of his Majesty's subjects, obliged to abandon their possessions by earlier Indian forays, were still suffered to starve in poverty and neglect. Bitterly, too, they denounced the fact that an expedition of frontiersmen up the Susquehanna last September—it was the expedition of the Paxton scouts drawn by Asher Clayton and Timothy Green out of the Rev. Mr. Elder's companies to march on to Wyoming—had had no recognition from the Assembly for the service which they had rendered. No care had been afforded by the government to their wounded, although recently Philadelphia had been so solicitous for one wounded Seneca at Fort Augusta as to send a doctor on from the city to "cure him, if possible."[36]

Again, as in the petition of Gibson and Smith, it was deplored that premiums for Indian scalps had been impossible to obtain during late months. That fact seemed the worse now, when a liberal reward was being offered by the Government for apprehending the perpetrators of the crime of killing the King's "cloaked enemies."[37] (Thus were the two hundred pounds promised on January 2[38] for the arrest of any three of the ringleaders at Conestoga or Lancaster thrust back into the Legislative teeth!) A vindictive irony had, indeed, gained energy as the Declaration continued. As its force neared consummation, Israel Pemberton, "ancient leader of that Faction which, for so long a time, have found means to enslave the Province,"[39] came in for a scoring.

It had been he, together with other of the Friends, who had persuaded the Indians at Easton that they had been cheated by Onas out of a great deal of land. All Berks County knew, from the days before good Conrad Weiser had died, that Pemberton had convinced the Indians that the sons of William Penn had defrauded them.[40] Everywhere in the frontier counties men believed that Pemberton had instructed the Delawares that "a Rod had been given them to scourge the white people that were settled on the purchased lands."[41] Heatedly, then, the men from Susquehanna delivered their last attack on the Quakers, "a certain faction, that have got the political reins in their hands, and tamely tyrannize over the good people of the Province."[42]

Phrase mounted upon phrase. Finally, as with the poise of a Cicero satisfied that he had said everything well and won all the Roman Senate to his side, the Scotch-Irish concluded that though they were "obliged to adopt a measure not so agreeable as could be desired,"[43] all well-disposed people must entertain charitable sentiments toward them. All must know, they reasoned, that "Extremity"[44] had compelled, that they had been laboring to rescue a land from a weight "oppressive, unreasonable and unjust."[45]

The response of the Assembly indicated clearly that that body had no intention of concurring with their petitioners in such a deliverance. They not only tabled the flamboyant testament. Remembering the stern clauses of their Act of February 3—and not forgetting that the back inhabitants had dispersed from Germantown and gone home— they had their clerk enter the document in their record for February 17 as "The Declaration of the Rioters from the Frontiers."[46]

To brand truculence it seems was more native to the bearing of legislators from Philadelphia, Chester, and Bucks Counties in 1764 than to mitigate conditions of peril and hardship.

Away from the halls of Assembly, however, and in Lancaster County voices kept speaking. No one came forward to claim two hundred pounds of Government for identifying three ringleaders in the December riots. Rather than that, back inhabitants continued deposing through February against the Indians of Conestoga, as Edward Shippen and two justices, Robert Thompson of the Borough and Thomas Forster of Paxton, essayed the gathering of data.[47] Matthew Cowden testified that he had remonstrated with Sheehays for harboring in his village so many strange Indians, savages suspected by frontier families of murdering their neighbors, insisting that the old Conestogoe had retorted: "He was not responsible" for what happened; "let the settlers look out for themselves."[48] Robert Armstrong took oath that in 1762 Sheehays had lived with his nephew Isaac and other Indians near Armstrong's house, and that the party of them had been highly impudent in their talk. They boasted openly that they had been at war with the white people earlier, and that they would be at war with them soon again. The Scotch-Irish Susquehanna River trader maintained they had boasted, according to report to him from two former prisoners, that the same band had sworn they could both go to Philadelphia and get what they wanted and then return and "cut off the back settlements."[49] Furthermore, to add injury to insult, the companions of Sheehays had stolen Armstrong's corn; carried off the fruit of his entire orchard; killed several of his hogs.

Not so definite in his identification of malefactors was Thomas Moore. But that witness, who for six years had been in slavery among the Indians at Salt Lick and other places, had important testimony to offer. His captors often had assured him that messengers—or "carriers," as they called them—came regularly from out of the settlements in which they lived as "Friendly Indians" among white people and gave information "on the motions of the army of the Province."[50] Through such "pretenders" the "advices of the inhabitants of Pennsylvania"[51] were constantly being betrayed to the foe. If Moore could not fix responsibility for such double-dealing upon the Indians of Conestoga Manor, he had small doubt in the matter. But he had no doubt whatever of despatches being carried to the enemy from Bethlehem, seat of Moravian missions.

As emphatic, and more definite about the malice of the Conestogoes, was Alexander Stephen.[52] That Scotch-Irishman testified before Thomas Forster of the treachery of James Cotter, one of the Indians killed in December. The Conestogoe had admitted his share in the slaying of old William Hamilton and the family of another settler on Sherman's Creek; and he had had the effrontery to demand of Stephen a canoe which the several murderers had abandoned after committing their crime. The witness waxed warm, too, as he told Magistrate Forster of Connayak Sally. That Squaw had averred the Indian Jegrea had been killed only because he had stood out against other Conestogoes in their plotting to destroy those "English" who had become the victims of Cotter and his two accomplices.[53]

On the subject of Bill Sock, slain in the Work House at Lancaster on December 27, there were numerous depositions, every one of them denunciatory.

Moses Dickey of Paxton bore interesting witness. During the previous summer he had one day seen the Indian with two others from Conestoga on a march with some strange companions. As the trio took into the direction of the Manada,"[54] he supposed them merely a friendly group. Then next came report from south of Blue Mountain of several houses burned near the creek, and as many families murdered. In the language of his testimony Dickey believed that Bill Sock "done" it.[55]

Other folk, residents of the borough of Lancaster, whose grammar was rather better maintained, were of like mind about the worthlessness of Sock. Anne Mary Le Roy, who had lost her father in the Indian massacre in 1755 at Penn's Creek and herself been carried off in that year to Kittanning, had not only a story of Conestogoes trafficking with the French at that town when she was a prisoner there. She could testify as well that Bill Sock's mother knew her son had "often" been there also, and that the old squaw herself considered Bill "good for nothing."[56]

More precise on the subject of his ill behavior was Mrs. Thompson. By solemn oath on the Holy Evangelists that housewife swore that Bill Sock had two years earlier, during the summer, come to her home and threatened her life. "I kill you," he declared; "all Lancaster can't catch me." Besides, he had boasted, "Lancaster is mine, and I will have it yet."[57]

Abraham Newcomer, by trade a gunsmith but Mennonist in religion—and for that reason not warranted in going beyond "affirmation"[58]—testified that only a few days before he was killed at the Work House, Bill Sock had threatened to scalp him for refusing to "steel" a tomahawk for him. Indeed, the rogue had said: "If you not mend it for me, I'll have it mended to your sorrow."[59] Abraham had afterwards apprehended danger from the fellow.

Colonel John Hambright, formerly an officer at Fort Augusta and now a Lancaster brewer, had no thought of diminishing his own eminence as he offered his testimony[60] before Justice Robert Thompson. In 1757 he had himself detected Bill Sock lurking with a second Indian in ambush near McKee's old trading place. At his challenge of them, both villains had run off; then on the morrow, as Mr. Hambright came down stream to Fort Hunter for provisions, he learned of an old settler's having been murdered the day before. Bill Sock and his comrade were suspect; and, as though to confirm his guilt, the Conestogoe ventured no more on any pretext of trade into the garrison at Fort Augusta.

Quite apparently Bill Sock had no champions among folk in Lancaster or along Susquehanna. Indeed, if any of the dead Conestogoes had aspired to have apologists, they would have had a hard time finding them on the frontier. Not even Felix Donnolly, who of all persons had the nearest view of their final tragedy in the town jail, could be induced to speak whole-heartedly for them. Only a fragment of his deposition[61] before Edward Shippen has survived; and this comes to us in the guise of cross-questioning. The keeper of the Work House could do little, in fact, but answer to interrogatory. To the dead plaintiff's cause he had little support to render.

Summed up, he was reported to say: "The breaking of the door alarmed me; armed men broke in; they demanded the strange Indian to be given up; they ran by me; the Indians guessed their intention; they seized billets of wood from the pile; but the three most active were shot; others came to their assistance; I was stupefied; before I could shake off my surprise, the Indians were killed and their murderers away."[62]

Questions and answers appended to this terse transcript are hardly less factual:

Q. Did the Indians attack the rioters with the billets of wood which they seized?

A. Yes, but the three quickest to seize these were shot down at once. If they hadn't been, they would have killed the intruders, as they were the stronger persons.

Q. Could you have prevented the murder?

A. No, no one here could have prevented it.

Q. What number were the rioters?

A. I should say about fifty.

Q. Did you know any of them?

A. No; they were strangers.

Q. Do you know who was in command?

A. I have been told Lazarus Stewart of Donegal.[63]

So went the questionnaire. Donnolly remained careful. Only on hearsay would he admit the leader of the fray at Lancaster might have been Lazarus Stewart—who, as a matter of fact, was neither of Donegal or Paxton, but of Hanover Township. The keeper would pronounce the actual identity of no one of the raiders.

He was as astute also in response to the next interrogations: "Would the men have fired if the Indians had not resisted?"[64] He could not tell; he did not know.

Q. Do you think or believe the rioters came with the intent to murder?

A. I heard them say, when they broke in, they wanted a strange Indian.

Q. Was it their object to murder him?

A. From what I have heard since, I think they meant to carry him off.

Q. Do you think that was their first purpose?

A. I do not know.[65]

To the last the man was shrewdly non-committal. He parried the final question with the same manifestation of undesigning innocence.

Q. Were the Indians killed all friends of this Province?

A. I have been told they were not. I cannot tell of myself; I do not know.[66]

In fact, it was much easier for Benjamin Franklin to talk than for the humble jailer in Lancaster. For it was Donnolly, not the eminent Philadelphian, who faced a dilemma. In the back country it would not have been well for him to be an accusant; he dared not be a perjurer. His neighbors in Lancaster would have resented accusation. Philadelphia lawyers would have dealt with perjury. To know nothing was safest.

Yet the man's unadorned deposition has proper claim to an accounting. It dilated upon no horror, no mutilation; it purposed no propaganda. It was obviously neither extorted nor suborned. No one gained by attempted third-degree tactics from the deponent; no one was traduced by the purchase of his testimony. The Provincial Government did not break a man in order to work out a punishment on other offenders; frontiersmen on Susquehanna used no money to bribe Donnolly into silence. Could he have spoken, and spoken truly, he might have had two hundred pounds. Unable to speak, or unwilling to speak, he had nothing. No man's innocence, and no man's guilt, is in the last analysis to be demonstrated through him. In the annals of time he is worthy of no marked place.

But that is not to say that it is wholly just that Franklin should have supplanted Felix Donnolly as a witness in the court of history.

Properly enough in the realm of art the great Boston-born Pennsylvanian deserved a measure of fame allowable to neither the jailkeeper nor Sheriff John Hay. For his unsigned pamphlet, *A Narrative of the Late Massacre, in Lancaster County, of a number of Indians, Friends of this Province, by Persons Unknown, with Some Observations on the Same,* First Printed at Philadelphia, in the Year 1764,[67] achieved every grace of clarity, smoothness, and warmth possible to humanitarian exposition and argument. Into it he put all that brand of sensibility which, several decades later, would bring to acclaim the novels of the French Chateaubriand or that masterpiece of sentiment by the German Goethe, *The Sorrows of Werther.* A better example of prose could hardly have been adduced to illustrate that tenderness of feeling by which Romanticism or the Romantic movement in literature is commonly designated. Every word of the story, as Franklin rendered it, was absorbingly interesting and engagingly persuasive.

Briefly he went into older history; into a series of eight characterizations of as many of the Indians slain; into narration of the course of events between December 14 and 27, 1763, including the proclamation of John Penn; into the second proclamation of the Governor on January 2. Having limited the first third of his text to what he called plain facts, he devoted the remaining two thirds to either eloquent denunciation or fervent appeal. When he was not earnest moral essayist, he was burningly passionate rhetorician.

No poet could have been more delicately descriptive than he in his picturing the Conestogoes welcoming the first arrival of the English in Pennsylvania with gifts of "venison, corn, and skins," or entering into a treaty of friendship with William Penn which should last "as long as the sun should shine or waters run in the rivers."[68] No apologist could have been more tender in portraying the several virtues of his massacred Indians. No censor of crime could have selected better examples from among Turks, Saracens, Moors, Popish Spaniards, or pagan negroes to show how degraded in comparison with those notorious races of men the Scotch-Irish back inhabitants on the frontier were. In short, it appeared to Franklin that the Indians "would have been safe in any part of the known world, except in the neighborhood of the *Christian white savages* of Peckstang and Donegall!"[69] "Mercy," he asserted in his peroration, "still swayed the Brave."[70]

For clemency in the human heart, undoubtedly, the great Philadelphian wrote incontrovertible argument. No flaw could be found in his reasoning for humanity of behavior. Everything seemed there in his "Narrative." He had made the very best and most of an occasion.

But one thing he had not done. He had not persuaded any frontiersman of the incontrovertibility of either his intellectual or his moral position. Bigotry or none in them, Presbyterians and back inhabitants failed to be moved by Franklin. Rather they continued their convictions. With the suspected Lazarus Stewart unseized in Lancaster County; with no back inhabitant turning informer on any one probable or actual participant in the two heinous slayings by armed Paxtonians; with James Gibson and Matthew Smith, proponents for a Scotch-Irish bill of rights which should be of the morrow, gone from the city—John Ewing, clergyman of Philadelphia, rose as the challenger of Franklin and as the champion of his fellow Scotch-Irishmen in the west.

Once the Reverend Mr. Ewing met Dr. Samuel Johnson, the literary dictator of eighteenth-century London, at a dinner party. Among the guests being entertained argument rose about America; and the Presbyterian minister offered defense of the colonies. Thereupon Johnson challenged rudely: "Sir, what do *you* know in America? *You* never read. *You* have no books there."

"Pardon me, sir," replied the colonial divine, "*we have read the Rambler.*"[71]

The pastor of the First Presbyterian Church of Philadelphia was no man to quail before either Johnson or the best prose writer of his day on the North American continent. Promptly he produced a blunt retort to Franklin, fortifying it with quotation from the Latin of Lucretius on the differences between truth and falsity, and gathering fire for his patriotic heart from the *Letters* of Cato. Learning, he knew, must vie with learning. He wrote his pamphlet *The Conduct of the Paxton Men Impartially Represented*[72] as one savant and scholar might respond to another.

But Ewing has been recognized more, since 1764, as the author of a candid letter[73] in February to Joseph Reed, then in England, on the

subject of conditions in Pennsylvania. In that missive he deplored the
presence of twenty-two Quakers in the Pennsylvania Assembly, the
unresponsiveness of this majority of the House to the needs of the
King's armies in America, their neglect of frontiersmen's interests, their
lavish squandering of money upon savages who kept on murdering
and scalping back inhabitants. He understood rather than sanctioned
"the desperate young men" who in reprisal for their own murdered
kinsmen and friends had cut off "about twenty Indians that lived near
Lancaster."[74] He made it clear that the advent of James Gibson and
Matthew Smith and their supporters had been no approach of rioters;
and he concurred with them in the justice of their statement of grievances. His summation of the behavior of Indians sheltered at Conestoga squared with the depositions on the subject of these which had
been taken down by the justices of Lancaster County. He denounced
the Assembly for its willingness "to represent this Province in a state
of uproar and riot, when not a man in it has once resisted a single
officer of the Government."[75] For the Assembly's late petition to Whitehall, which Ewing knew had Franklin's whole-hearted backing, to
have Pennsylvania cease to be a Proprietary colony and to come under
the immediate authority of the Crown was thoroughly repugnant to
the eminent Presbyterian.

He saw the unrest in the frontiers being made a political football.
Could the King be persuaded that the Council of Pennsylvania rather
than the legislature was at fault, he knew that Franklin and his ally
in England, Thomas Pownall, would gain the object those two politicians were bent on. Indeed, in 1764, John Ewing, like John Elder
of Paxton, stood with the King. Franklin, he realized as did the frontiersmen, had been very lukewarm about the King's cause in the year
of the Albany Congress. He had been as dilatory as any Quaker as-
semblyman in 1755 to provide Pennsylvania funds for the King's army
until after the defeat of Braddock. He had long fought the Proprietors.
Now, with the newer idea of the Crown colony fixed firm in his brain,
he was nothing loath to take advantage of an uprising in Lancaster
County against Indians and against a pacifist Assembly as if it were
rebellion against the King and made necessary the use of the King's
firm hand in the Province upon the King's subjects rather than against
the King's foes. Fair-minded, John Ewing chose—as did that other famous Philadelphia Presbyterian divine, scholar, and professor, the
Reverend Francis Alison—to adhere to the Proprietary cause of the
Penns. Assembly he continued to blame more than Council. Like

James Hamilton, recently Deputy Governor, he saw that the King's cause in America, as a cause for the growth of England's power against France, as the cause of the power of English Protestantism against French Catholicism, found, and must find, its strength on the frontiers.

So he was as little persuaded by Franklin's rhetoric in the *Narrative* as he was wooed by his politician's statesmanship in 1764. Later both men would serve emphatically in the cause of American Independence in Philadelphia and elsewhere. Paradoxically, in the year when the two clashed over the ineptitudes of government in the Province, when Franklin tried to stand with Assembly and King, and Ewing with back inhabitants, Council, and King, the minor figure had come closer to the main force in the American Revolution, then a dozen years off, than had the ultimately far greater statesman and celebrity. Ewing was, of course, Scotch-Irish. Franklin, never immoderate in behavior whatever the passion of his prose, was in origin English.

But the topic of the town in Philadelphia during February and the spring after the massacres at Conestoga and Lancaster was hardly to be summed up in either Scotch-Irish excess or English urbanity. After Ewing's *Conduct Impartially Represented*, controversy flamed. A third pamphleteer came upon the polemical scene. Ardently his printed words burned to "manifest" the "Ungenerous Spirit" of Ewing's contribution and to strip away from its author his "Spotted Garment."[76] Blasting this third writer's diatribe against the Presbyterian, came *The Quaker Unmasked, or Plain Truth*.[77] The censoriousness of the fourth philippic evoked by way of answer *Remarks on the Quaker Unmasked, or Plain Truth to be Plain Falsehood;*[78] and then from a sixth controversialist came an exposure which enjoyed the florid title *The Author of the Quaker Unmasked Stript Stark Naked, or the Delineated Presbyterian Played Hob with*.[79] A seventh exercise in confutation came as a proffer of *Clothes for a Stark Naked Author;*[80] and an eighth with ironic generosity, as if for a retailored and reappareled verbal adversary, provided *A Looking-Glass for Presbyterians*.[81]

Every Philadelphian was given, as it were, opportunity to see himself as he was seen by others or as mirrored. Pungencies in discourse, spiced with quotations from Cicero, Horace, and Alexander Pope, filled up rhymes on the *"natives of Dunnegal."* The nervously anticipated riot of January, the ebb of hysterically embraced danger from the city in February, the apparition of the men from the back counties faded out of memory; and wags could tread in now where angels would earlier have forborne to enter. Provincial satirists had spurs to their

penning. Pastoral manner or epic manner, in the fashion of the eighteenth-century in England, could be resorted to for travesty. There was,
for the judicious and the alert, plenty to mock.

Accordingly one cartoonist made picture early of the Friends' Meeting House as a fortress of defense, its upstairs windows filled with
Quakers on guard calling for grog to be brought up to them—the whole
having as legend beneath, "Success to the new barracks."[82] A broadside pictured Israel Pemberton, whom its author knew bore no esteem
on the frontiers, embracing an Indian squaw while he shrilled:

> "To arms! to arms! with one accord,
> The sword of Quakers and the Lord."[83]

Agricola—of classical *nom de plume* as should have had one who aped,
although none too fully, Theocritus or Bion—produced in thirteen
stanzas a miniature idyl named "The Squabble; a Pastoral Eclogue."[84]
In it Thyrsis and Corin debated with spirit. But more recognizable to
readers than the brightness of their long-winded and devious speeches
in argument were their two profiles, drawn in crude silhouette and appropriate distortion. Thyrsis, with a Presbyterian proboscis which
would far outdo that of a Cyrano de Bergerac, and with a balding
brow, gazed with scorn on a snub-nosed Corin pursing his Quaker
lips in smug reproof,[85] as the limner would fancy John Ewing doing to
Israel Pemberton.

Best of all, perhaps, as an expression of fun, came the heroic-comical
poem, "The Paxtoniade."[86] Christopher Gymnast, reader of Pope's
satires and of Dryden's *The Dunciad,* admirer and imitator of Samuel
Butler's *Hudibras,* attempted his masterpiece, and cannot be said to
have failed utterly in the attempt. He was wrong in choosing the name
of O'Hara for the chief Scotch-Irish spokesman of his mock epic; and
he was certainly no champion of the Presbyterian at any time in the
course of his portrayal of the character of the marauder during the
last December. But his syncopated couplets have verve and sparkle.
Through his sharp and aspersive wit one can gain clear sense of what
those not Presbyterian and not Scotch-Irish in the era of John Penn
and Benjamin Franklin thought of the man born to the heritage of
Bannockburn and Londonderry, and established, after centuries of
transplantation and wandering, in the western wilderness of Pennsylvania. The picture which Gymnast draws is far from a true one. But,
as a picture of the frontiersman of Scots breed, it cannot be wholly
false. In respects his O'Hara is as much a misnomer as his name. In
respects he is a perfect index to the spirit of anger and hardness out

of which only contention can grow. To understand him is to understand the world of experience which the pioneer of 1764 both thrived in and confronted:

> O'Hara mounted on his Steed,
> (Descendant of that self-same Ass,
> That bore his Grandsire Hudibras,)
> And from that same exalted Station,
> Pronounced an hortory Oration:
> For he was cunning as a Fox,
> Had read o'er Calvin and Dan Nox;
> A man of most profound Discerning,
> Well versed in P————— Learning.
>
> Ye know as how the Indian Rabble,
> With practices unwarrantable,
> Did come upon our quiet Borders,
> And there commit most desperate murders
> Did tomahawk, butcher, wound and cripple
> With cruel Rage, the Lord's own People;
>
> Did war most implacable wage
> With God's own chosen heritage;
> Did from our Brethren take their lives,
> And kill our children, kine and wives.
> Now, Sirs, I ween it is but right,
> That we upon these Canaanites,
> Without delay, should vengeance take,
> Both for our own, and the K——k's sake;
> Should totally destroy the heathen,
> And never till we've killed 'em leave 'em;—
> Destroy them quite frae out the Land;
> And for it we have God's command.
> We should do him a muckle pleasure,
> As ye in your Books may read at leisure."
>
> Is't not, my Brethren, a pretty Story
> That we, who'are the Land's chief Glory,
> Who are i' the number of God's elected,
> Should slighted thus be and neglected?
> That we, who're the only Gospel Church,
> Should thus be left here in the lurch;
> Whilst our most antichristian foes,
> Whose trade is war and hardy blows,
> (At least while some of the same Colour,
> With those who've caused us all this Dolor,)
> In matchcoats warm and blankets drest,
> Are by the Q—————rs much caress'd."

"Seeing then we've such good cause to hate 'em,
What I intend 's to extirpate 'em;
To suffer them no more to thrive,
And leave nor Root nor Branch alive;

I deem therefore the wisest course is,
That those who've beasts should mount their horses,
And those who've none should march on foot,
With as much quickness as will suit,
To where those heathen, nothing fearful,
That we will on their front and rear fall,
Enjoy Sweet Otium in their Cotts,
And dwell securely in their Hutts.
And as they've nothing to defend them,
We'll quickly to their own place send them![87]

Sadly enough neither Benjamin Franklin nor Christopher Gymnast could behold the Scotch-Irishman in his truest worth in 1764. Both men on their instincts for mercy and justice called out against the frontier offender. One in his protest resorted to sentiment and tears. The other applied the scourge of laughter. He who would judge the scion of the Scots best would do well in his appraisal to combine the propensities of both humanitarian and railer.

BACK INHABITANT LAW

THE HERO OF Kittanning sat at breakfast with young Mr. James Cunningham, farmer of Lancaster County and Colonel John Armstrong's guest, in Carlisle on the last Friday of January, 1768.[1] Neither of the two men was unaware of the excitement momentarily stirring in that frontier borough. Six days before, Frederick Stump and John Ironcutter had been jailed there by the offices of Captain William Patterson and nineteen companions, who had made a long march to Penn's Creek mouth on the Susquehanna, taken the two culprits at the house of George Gabriel the trader, and at the end of a third day of fleet journeying turned both over to the civil law of Cumberland County.[2] The will of Governor John Penn, the two breakfasters assumed, was being carried into effect.

Even in the midst of the expedition of his posse comitatus Patterson had planned toward that purpose. From Gabriel's he had posted a messenger off to the Six Nations, the Delawares, and other Indian inhabitants on the West Branch, with a letter.[3] This told of a heart swelling with grief. Patterson, responsible agent of Government, deplored to inform the addressees that Frederick Stump and John Ironcutter had "unadvisedly murdered"[4] ten of their friends. "Sensible of the injury done," he begged the Six Nations not rashly now to "let go the fast hold of our chain of friendship."[5] Warmly he protested the love of Englishmen for the Indians. Sagely he bade the recipients of his message to have recourse to Fort Augusta for any "necessaries"[6] now requisite to them. He gave his pledge that no white man at that Fort would molest any of them whilst they behaved as friends. Eagerly he assured them he would await answer. Messrs. Armstrong and Cunningham knew all these things.

Colonel Armstrong shared fully enough the captain's aim of propitiation. He had known but found no particular pleasure in Indian wars. Yet the Colonel and his friend at their nine o'clock meal were not

[141

too much surprised by the event which was on that January morning shaping to interrupt them. Both realized the facts of the slaying now being everywhere rumored in Susquehanna country. Word of the crime had gone on to Philadelphia. Knowledge of Frederick Stump's offence had become general. Not quite three weeks ago, on Sunday night and Monday morning, January 10 and 11,[7] the trader and his servant had despatched their victims. Drunken conviviality at Stump's house on Middle Creek changed into bickering. The host turned moody. As his guests, four men and two women, drowsed off, he became vindictive; he would show them.

On the morrow six Indians' bodies were being sucked into the currents of the Creek into which they had been cast by the murderer and his nineteen-year-old servant-boy. More than that, Stump and Iron-cutter had gone up creek to the cabin of their victim on the morning which followed and had slain there the survivors of their first crime, another Indian woman, two girls, and a child.[8] The notorious slaughter had become a subject on all tongues in Carlisle.

Side glances from the table at which he was eating suddenly made Armstrong alert. Through a window he saw men gathering with guns on their arms,[9] with more and more every second coming into view. Beyond them was the Carlisle Jail, and their eyes were on that edifice rather than on the coffeehouse window from which the eater beheld them. "They're going to attempt a rescue of Stump," he cried, and was up from his chair and out into the street with James Cunningham following.

But other frontiersmen were more quick than Armstrong. He was at the threshold of the Jail in an instant. But there already were four men just inside the open door, two on each side, and all armed with rifles.[10] Outside, a throng of still others were milling, weapons in hand. John Holmes, Sheriff of Cumberland County,[11] arrived in the same moment with the experienced Colonel. Both arrivals began arguing: "This won't do. What are you boys up to?" And both, police officer and civilian official, attempted entry.

"Not so fast, Colonel," "Not just now, John Holmes," were the rejoinders; "You two aren't wanted in here."

The dignitaries found themselves being thrust back. Both expostulated.[12] They could do nothing more than talk on the Jail steps. The Reverend Mr. John Steel joined them; Robert Miller and Squire William Lyon and other sober and prudent townsmen[13] pressed through to their side.

But it was not the morning for the best folk. "Nay, Colonel"; "Nay,

Parson Steele"; "Nay, Squire Lyon," called dissenting voices; "better keep out of it; we're not for seeing Stump carried to Philadelphia." The throng held the protestants back.[14] Unmoblike, they attempted no jostling. There were no hoots, no cries of civil disrespect, no signs of riot. But neither was there any acceptance of dispersal. The group of men swelled but remained orderly.

Division in their ranks occurred only when a second group of armed men appeared within the Jail door, with two prisoners in their charge.[15] Then there was a neat cleavage, and a passage was formed. Down the steps, through it, and into the street came Frederick Stump and John Ironcutter, attended by a small escort of frontiersmen, tomahawk or rifle in hand.[16]

"Men, you must not," John Armstrong called and pulled himself forward. James Cunningham, Sheriff Holmes, the Reverend John Steel, Robert Miller, and William Lyon tried to identify themselves with the protest of the victor over the Indians at Kittanning.[17]

"Not your day, Colonel," voices called jestingly. The sense of triumph came into the champions of Indian killers, into back inhabitant censors of Proprietary Government and Philadelphia courts. Defiance of the law was the frank unabashed attitude of the Scotch-Irish rescuers of Frederick Stump.

Carlisle hummed with excitement. In the midst of shouts and rejoicing the two slayers were carried out of town to freedom. James Cunningham was left estimating the number of champions of their liberty, "seventy or eighty, all armed with guns and some Tomahawks."[18]

In fact, another exploit had been registered in the light of day in frontier colonial Pennsylvania; and once more, although now with introduction from Colonel John Armstrong, a man could go on to Philadelphia to depose on the matter of a jail delivery. Yet neither the deponent Mr. James Cunningham[19] nor any man of Cumberland County seemed to recognize any participant in the rescuing party. The traces of the captors were as undetected—or, at the least, as unreported—as they would have been had the deliverance they effected been managed in the blackness of night in a community of dumb and blind men.

No one of them was any more inculpated by a witness than had been the Paxton Boys at Conestoga or Lancaster in 1763. Stump, who had founded Fredericksburg in Lancaster (now Lebanon County), fared on in history to give his name to hamlets in Maryland, Virginia, and Kentucky, and to die never tried or sentenced by a Pennsylvania judge. On him time never brought the whirligig of material vengence. The bloody holocaust in which he slew his dazed and inebriated Indian guests and their innocent kinswomen and children remained in the archives of a Province only to serve as an index to the mood of a recalcitrant and an emergent society in Susquehanna country.

The year was 1768. Sheriff John Holmes of Cumberland County did not hand Stump and Ironcutter, whose German name untranslated was Eisenhauer, over to James Webb, Sheriff of Lancaster.[20] Webb had no opportunity to deliver either culprit to John Morton, Sheriff of Chester;[21] nor did Morton ever bear either on to the City of Philadelphia or to its jail or its court house.

Letters of diplomacy on the subject of the crime and of the rescued killers went out to Sir William Johnson, to the Indians, to Crown authorities in England.[22] Verbal pictures of the stature, the countenances, the clothes of the two fugitives when last seen went out to sheriffs and constables.[23] No description of build, visage, apparel availed. Had any physical feature, any halt in speech, any color of cloth coat, any buckskin breeches, any brass-buckled shoes been recognized on the frontiers by a Scotch-Irishman, he would have smiled on them probably as the perquisites of a friend.

Seventeen-sixty-eight was but a prefatory year to other years of unrest. Other jail deliveries were in the offing; there would be other vivid spectacles of defiance of Provincial law and Provincial lawmakers; and men of Scots breed would be connected with them.

Yankee folk of Connecticut had not forgotten the beauty of the Wyoming Valley; Lazarus Stewart—whom men had labored in 1764 to have Felix Donnolly inculpate[24] for a part in the riot at Lancaster in December, 1763,—remembered woods, fields of abandoned corn, burned cabins, and certain scattered and mutilated bodies which he had seen on the North Branch of Susquehanna before folk's minds had begun identifying him with the Lancaster Work House. Legislative action, community enterprise, the fears and the cupidities of men had been playing upon and into the complexity of events and personalities even before Stump's berserker rage had been evoked or been bruited.

The Assembly of Pennsylvania was not willing in early January, 1768, to leave well enough alone. Better to resuscitate a four years' dead ghost was the opinion of that House. On January 13 they despatched a memorandum to Governor Penn. They were of opinion that to punish the offenders at Conestoga and Lancaster would "afford favorable opportunity of restoring the Government to its former power and dignity."[25] "Dread of exemplary punishment, steadily and uniformly inflicted on past delinquents," they declared, "alone can deter the wicked from the perpetration of future offenses. Should crimes of the first rank, of the deepest dye, remain unpunished, wicked men will never be wanting, in any country, to take advantage of the times, to commit the like and other crimes."[26]

Mr. Penn, no more a lover of the Quaker Assembly than he was of Susquehanna rioters, was somewhat dubiously pondering the suggestion of the legislators[27] when "the melancholy tidings" from Middle Creek came to Philadelphia. Those tidings made him for the time being more responsive to arguments for discipline.

❋　❋　❋

But a more stinging goad than the Assembly was necessary to Governor Penn. It came from another quarter as unbeloved as Paxton and Donegal, although not a wholly unexpected one. The autumn of 1768 witnessed the Treaty of Fort Stanwix,[28] at which, in a working out of amenities between King George III and the Six Nations, Mr. Penn's aides, the Reverend Mr. Richard Peters, Benjamin Franklin, and James Tilghman, secured by new purchase from the Indians all those lands along the North Branch of the Susquehanna which the Susquehanna Company of Connecticut were still regarding as theirs through a bargain of 1754. Almost before the wax of their seals was cold on the documents of conveyance, engineers for the Penns were surveying lands on both sides the North Branch at Shamokin, at the point of its juncture with the West Branch.[29] In the February which followed the purchase of November, 1768, Yankees began settling in Wyoming as settlers on what they were convinced was and should be Connecticut territory; but there were Pennsylvanians at the behest of John Penn already there in January, 1769,[30] ensconced upon land of which Connecticut men had been dispossessed by Indians in 1763 and in the struggle for holding which they had met massacre and mutilation.

The Wyoming Valley and the Susquehanna River were not on the eve of peace; and the new year was not to make for the restoration of Government to power and dignity. Amos Ogden, trader, was established, with sanction of Pennsylvania, in a small blockhouse with his goods transferred into it from an earlier post on the river.[31] Connecticut folk, by agreements and instructions from the Susquehanna Company framed in the December just past, planned to come and take possession at the same point in February, 1769.[32]

Plans were definitely set for occupation. Five towns of the New England pattern were projected by the Susquehanna Company, two on one side the river, three on the side opposite.[33] Their breadth would face the stream, their length run back over the valley to the hills. Each was intended to furnish tracts for forty settlers, for men upwards of twenty-one years. Before the spring of 1769 full quotas of settlers were made up in Connecticut, and families were migrating to stake off and develop their lands in Wyoming.

With the Government of Pennsylvania just as avid for pressing settlement, contest between rival clusters of immigrants was inevitable. It grew more tense during the late summer. Then the first crops of the Connecticut men began to need protection. Petitions[34] began going forward that the Assembly of Connecticut erect the settlement on Susquehanna into a county; the assumption of a domain of law grew important. And meantime Governor John Penn, constituted official of a more established legal commonalty, was instructing the Sheriff of Northampton County, Pennsylvania, to dispossess the New Englanders.[35] Direct action between disputants came in November.

Captain Amos Ogden, who had been made a Pennsylvania Justice of the Peace, was confirmed in strength by Sheriff John Jennings and that official's posse comitatus; and was lucky enough on the eleventh to capture a few Yankees with their leader Major John Durkee.[36] More skillful in seizure than were sheriffs in Lancaster and Carlisle, the Northampton County official started his prize prisoner off for Philadelphia immediately. Three days later, in chagrin at the shackling of their champion and weakened by their present loss of him, the Connecticut men were obliged to surrender the fort into which they had gathered and which they had named Fort Durkee (for their commander).[37]

The occasion was momentous: it meant not only papers of capitulation, but promise to abandon their tracts within three days and to await the results of subsequent legal procedure between Pennsylvania and the Susquehanna Company. A party of fourteen men were to be left in six of the closely grouped houses which they had already built, with privilege of gathering their last turnips and corn and of herding their cattle. Beyond that sanctioned care for property, they had only the right to form a company for return to the New England towns from which they had come.[38] For them 1769 was a hard year; and those whom they left behind were to feel its hardness still more before the end of the month.

Amos Ogden broke the terms of their agreement with him and Sheriff Jennings; inspired an indiscriminate plunder of whatever remained behind on their new farmsteads; and drove off to markets on the Delaware horses, cattle, and swine, with the fourteen representatives in Fort Durkee helpless to prevent.[39]

But these things did not happen without their being known to Susquehanna folk downstream, folk of the Province of Pennsylvania who had small affection for Government in Philadelphia.

Indeed, since as early as September, a number of subscribers of Paxton Township, Lancaster County, Pennsylvania, had been angling for an opportunity in the Wyoming countryside. Lazarus Young, John Espy, and William Young went so far on September 11 as to appoint by letter "our trusty friend Jedidiah Elderkin, Esquire, of Windham in the County of Windham[40] in the Colony of Connecticut our lawful attorney." In such capacity he was instructed to apply to the Council and the Representatives of the New England province, as well as to officials of the Susquehanna Company, for "six miles square of lands"[41] sufficient for a township. The memorialists had been living in Pennsylvania, they said, for a long time past "under the great disadvantage of quit rents and the fire of contention respecting the tenure and possession of lands."[42] Unpopular with them was the Penn family's scheme of manors. What they desired were freehold conditions. Manorial tenancy, without privileges of ultimate, bequeathable, ownership of fields which they might bring under cultivation, had no alluring significance for them. To purchase, to own, to till, and to do these things with profit to themselves and without allowances to the lord of a manor or responsibility to a court baron, was their aim.

In a transfer of allegiance the Paxton men—undoubtedly abetted in wish by Susquehanna Company overtures earlier made—beheld opportunity. Welcome to them were thoughts of both land and civil government under a new jurisdiction. The three petitioners requested "quit claim of all right, title, interest, and property"[43] under the Charter of Connecticut.

Moreover Lazarus Young and John Montgomery were ready to go further before the end of November, 1769. Not only migration into territory under another jurisdiction and the boon of six miles square of land engaged their fancy. They deplored the unjust removal of the Yankee settlers which had followed the seizure of Major Durkee. They promised in a letter[44] directed to that gentleman, but intended for the eyes of Connecticut executives and Susquehanna Company authorities, to come with a band of fifty Paxton companions, to accept the six miles when conceded, and to help Connecticut settlers already in Wyoming maintain their possession. Time had grown ripe for exodus for many of the Lancaster County rangers, men out of Paxton and Hanover Townships—indubitably more from the latter community—onward to a new frontier. Both sides of the Susquehanna were now occupied from Juniata to the Chesapeake; Hanover farmsteads were at considerable distance from both the River and Lancaster Town. The soil of Wyoming offered both bounty and a proximity to the great and beautiful waterway which Parson Elder's and Timothy Green's rangers had known far upstream from Shamokin for long years. Ambition tugged in eager, valiant, but not unrebellious Scotch-Irish hearts.

Officials of the Susquehanna Company received the overtures of September and late November, 1769, cordially. In January, 1770, Eliphalet Dyer, Samuel Gray, and Nathaniel Wales, Jun'r, Committee for the Company, responded to Young and Montgomery.[45] They were sending Captain Zebulon Butler and Mr. Ebenezer Backus on to treat further with the applicants and to lay out for them the town which they had asked for. They predicted that Major Durkee would join the Scotch-Irishmen "as soon as his affairs will permit."[46] They were confident of the Colony title to Wyoming. They expected acknowledgment of the validity of it from the Connecticut Assembly in May.

For the twenty-four days' journey[47] of himself and his horse from Lyme, Connecticut, to Hanover Township, Pennsylvania, and from Hanover subsequently to Wyoming, Captain Zebulon Butler forwarded to the Susquehanna Company an account of 240 shillings, plus expenses of 5 shillings and 6 pence a day.[48] The enterprise cost, indeed, in both money and physical energy; and for the price of it no idyllic era in Pennsylvania history was to be the compensation. First fruits of it, however, were early perceptible.

Forty Hanover men and Lazarus Stewart accepted the terms proffered by the Yankee. Lands were to be had by a bargain among free men, at the side of men who had no predilection for manors, no schemes for the enrichment of vast landholders. Lands were to be had in towns governed by townsmen's consent in a prospective New England county. They were to be had by men willing to defy Province-of-Pennsylvania law; and the Scotch-Irish were not novices of defying that. The old friends of Lazarus Stewart and new friends of Zebulon Butler were not unused to risk; they had no esteem for Philadelphia, none for an Assembly which too well remembered the old scores of Conestoga and Lancaster in 1763 and of Frederick Stump's rescue in 1768. Adherents to John Penn had ousted Connecticut settlers from their new farms in the Wyoming; sympathies for the dispossessed were easy and warm. To accept the hazard with another group as little beloved of Government was but to obey instinct and habit; Captain Butler did not have to do any excessive soliciting with the younger men of Paxton and Hanover.

Nor did Stewart himself, always suspect in Philadelphia since Lancaster depositions of 1764, need the prompting of any proscription. Even now there was no official bruiting of his name in any proclamation of the Governor. So all that was necessary to him was challenge; no jeopardy could dampen his spirit.

Word crept about that he and his men were leaving Hanover. The Reverend Mr. Elder wrote regretfully at the time to Colonel James Burd: "Lazarus Stewart is still threatened by the Philadelphia party. He and his friends talk of leaving"[49] The Pastor of Paxton Church, in fact, clung to his faith in the ranger whom he had commanded seven years earlier as an ensign in Timothy Green's Company. "If they leave," he said, "the Province will lose some of its best friends"; and he remained of opinion that the loss was "by the fault of others."[50] It would not be the fault of Stewart. To his friend at Fort Augusta the former fighting parson declared stubbornly: "If any cruelty was practised on the Indians at Conestoga, it was not by his hands or their hands."[51] For Mr. Elder vouched as well for the innocence of Stewart's friends. No one need tell him how the Paxton Boys had mutilated the dead Indians after the slayings of 1763.

Accordingly, on February 11, 1770,[52] on a day which they would have called Sabbath, a company of Scotch-Irishmen joined with Connecticut men in the Wyoming Valley. Their breed were again off on an enterprise, with the old mood of adventure in their hearts. Now at their side were fugitives, victims of the ambush at Fort Durkee in the preceding autumn, pilgrims like themselves in a valley of tribulation.

The fluctuations of border war ensued, contestants being Yankees and Pennamites. Aided by their new allies from Hanover, the former promptly dispossessed the latter's representatives of their hold on Fort Durkee.[53] Then, in Amos Ogden's absence, they broke into his blockhouse on Mill Creek, a mile-and-a-half to the northeast; and from it carried off to their own use all his store of ammunition and a four-pounder which had been furnished from Fort Augusta to that agent for Governor Penn.[54] News of their feat went into New Jersey, and sped Ogden back to his property and stronghold. Before he arrived, Lazarus Stewart and Lazarus Young had begun seizing other Pennamites' houses and ordering their masters out of the Valley.[55] Pennsylvanians, they insisted, had no rights to be there.

Warrants[56] were issued in Easton, county seat of Northampton, for the arrest of the New England men and their allies, roster of named offenders running into some fifty. Affidavits testifying to guilt were made without efficacy. There were no apprehensions. Major Durkee came back into the situation through an intermediary, with promises of support and rewards to the Hanover men.

February became March, and March, April. In the firing between the contestants, Baltzer Stager, German by birth, was killed, first instance of bloodshed in Wyoming in the fighting of white men with each other.[57] The Yankees, of whose party he was, built a new blockhouse for themselves; and late in the month manned in it the Fort Augusta cannon which they had carried off from Ogden. But it was not bombardment from the cannon which reduced the enemy now gathered at that returned Pennamite's establishment. There was a fusilade of three days between the two blockhouses, beginning on April 25.[58]

Then on April 28[59] a sortie from their breastworks took Stewart's and the absent Durkee's men close enough to Ogden's redoubt to fire his main storehouse. Tactics and audacity achieved what steady cannonade had failed to do. A rush of Scotch-Irishmen and Yankees spelled the Pennamites' undoing. Capitulation was forced upon Captain Amos Ogden. Men of the Scotch-Irish element had won their first significant victory over fighting Indians at Kittanning in 1756; here in Wyoming, at the end of April, 1770, others of their stock won a first victory over white opponents.[60]

The summer months seemed also to prosper the Yankee and Hanover Scotch-Irish claimants to the Wyoming lands. John Durkee, brought into court not in Philadelphia but in Northampton County,[61] pleaded his blamelessness there; and regained his freedom to such effect that he could participate in plans of survey and lottery for five town plots. Wilkes-Barre was plotted in June. Settlers won their tracts, and in that town as in the others set to building houses and cultivating their fields. Pettifoggery went on in London at the King's court, in Connecticut, and in Philadelphia. Opposing interests continued effort at Whitehall to gain or to keep the ear of the Sovereign. The situation remained stalemate and for the time being quiescent. John Durkee was characterized by his neighbors as his Majesty's Justice of the Peace for the County of Wilkes-Barre,[62] although not admitted in Philadelphia to be such. More Connecticut men kept arriving.

In August the way seemed clear to Paxton and Hanover men to bring their families on from Lancaster County into the new town which had been awarded them. They were not men to be balked by

John Penn's Proclamation of June 28 against the "intruders"[63] in Wyoming or against any who should join them. That document might denounce and proscribe all who accepted land by other than purchase from the Proprietors of Pennsylvania. They had bought their new Hanover Town at the price of their own action.

The corollary to their visit back home in what they conceded to be Pennsylvania was an escapade of Lazarus Stewart. New notoriety came upon that grandson namesake of an early settler on the Swatara in Lancaster County and leading lay founder of Hanover Presbyterian Church just south of Blue Mountain. Beloved by the Scotch-Irish but renegade to the eyes of all obsequious servitors of the Penns, bearer of a royal Scots name by birth and of a beggar's name by christening, the nonchalant younger Lazarus risked himself in Lebanon Township, ten miles away from the house of his kinsmen.[64] Proper John Phillip de Haas, Justice of the Peace in the community and no respecter of persons however Presbyterian or Scotch-Irish, observed his being there and found in it occasion for delivering to Constable Frederick Buhlman a warrant from the Supreme Court of Pennsylvania.[65] The writ proclaimed that Lazarus Stewart, Lazarus Young, and Zebulon Butler had been guilty of arson and other misdemeanors in the County of Northampton.[66] De Haas looked on—as afterwards his deposition[67] in Philadelphia maintained to Thomas Willing—while Buhlman on September 15, at ten in the morning, served the paper.[68]

But the Justice had not made ready to be a mere spectator. Rather than that, he had three men at immediate hand, each on a promise of five pounds reward, to assist the constable with his prisoner and to help "convey him down the Country."[69]

In perfect form, then, the arrest of Lazarus Stewart took place.

But once more the proof of the pudding was to be in the eating. To have a frontiersman was not to hold him. William Stoy had been as observant on that morrow as John Phillip de Haas; and Stoy had a nephew Matthias Mause at his beck and call.[70] Between uncle and Mause there were nods and words. Suddenly the younger man had supplied Captain Stewart with an axe handle; and suddenly down in a scuffle went Constable Buhlman, beaten, as de Haas testified "in a cruel and unmerciful manner."[71]

The Justice, accordingly, hurried back to the scene, charged bystanders who had been gathering and who had witnessed "the aforesaid outrageous proceeding," to assist himself and Buhlman in "retaking the said Stewart."[72] True to his official code, he emphatically recited to his Lebanon neighbors the crimes of the offender.

But his appeal for aid was unavailing. The interlopers on the spectacle were either afraid or they were friends and abettors. At the least, all remained silent witnesses to the drama of the moment, hearing Lazarus Stewart hardly less well when he stepped forward, "club" in hand, and abused the Justice "in the most opprobrious terms."[73]

So the pillar of province law became aware of the comparative worth of discretion and valor. Indeed, John Phillip de Haas—despite his earlier promise of five pounds[74] each to Buhlman's assistants—encouraged neither the constable nor his aides any further in the performance of their duty. He retired, not willing to inspire riotous proceedings; and an hour later knew that twenty armed men had ridden into Lebanon Town, joined their friend, and with him were parading before the Justice's house.[75]

Intending to get his own pistols, de Haas made for his own door, followed now closely by the Scotch-Irishman. An alert member of his family pulled him inside and drew a bolt just in time to make sure against an unwanted guest.[76] Stewart was left walking back and forth outside calling scurrility and abuse. Pistol on one hand and club—or axe-handle—in the other, he "threatened" the householder "for having procured him to be arrested."[77] Tauntingly he shouted that two hundred pounds had long ago been offered for his apprehension—the immured de Haas believed it was for Lazarus' being one of the persons concerned in murdering the Indians in Lancaster jail. Obstreperously he challenged the Justice to come out and take him. Then the hubbub ceased. Hoofs were heard receding. Not an arrest but a deposition[78] could be made.

It was made in Philadelphia eleven days later. On Wednesday, September 26, 1770, the chief magistrate of Lebanon Town could add to his account the story told him by Nicholas Hausaker, Innkeeper. To that host Lazarus Stewart had said that if ever he should obey de Haas' orders in taking or assisting to take either him or any of his company, he would come and "cut him to pieces, and make a breakfast of his heart."[79] In sum, that fiat having been pronounced, the Hanover company and their hero rode off in triumph. To more the deponent was unable to depose.

Philadelphia law responded promptly in its own kind. On October 3 Governor Penn made formal Proclamation against Stewart,[80] on this occasion first explicitly and individually naming the culprit. He was charged now not only with arson but with resistance to arrest, assault of an officer, and abuse of a justice. Fifty pounds was the prize for securing the criminal in any "of the public jails of the Province."[81]

But the time of eclipse for the scion of Hanover Township, Lancaster County, and of an ancient Scottish clan was not yet.

Instead, Lazarus Stewart's rising star gathered more bizarre lustre unto itself at the close of the next month. On the last Tuesday of October he sought passage for himself and two horses on a ferry over Susquehanna into York County, was recognized and seized and carried into York Town, where he created a problem.

Samuel Johnston the Burgess conferred with the only two justices of the peace whom he could find that night, Robert McPherson and Michael Swoope, and Mr. Wilcocks, the King's Attorney.[82] The four men were prompt to agree they might expect another attempted rescue of the prisoner; there could be no point in trying to hold him in York Jail. Accordingly they sent for the Sheriff of the County and gave instructions. That official should procure assistants, set off in the darkness at once with their captive pinioned and handcuffed, and travel by back roads for Philadelphia.[83]

The beginning was punctual. The Sheriff found three aides, and his party made fifteen miles in the shadows down the road to John Finley's tavern.[84] But, as Burgess Johnston wrote to Governor Penn three days later on November 2, the Sheriff was unwell when he left York, "grew much fatigued with his loss of rest,"[85] and found it best to stop there. The night was very cold. His horses required a feeding. He had himself to have a little sleep. He suffered Lazarus, still handcuffed and tied with a rope, to lie down in a place near the fire with his guards at his side; and in another corner of the room took the opportunity of some repose for himself. When he woke from his sleep he found that his three subalterns had also drowsed off completely.[86]

The fact was that Lazarus Stewart was—or seemed to be—the only unsleepy person at Finley's. But the prisoner made good use of his wakefulness (Johnson's letter, at least, implying no second-party aid); got loose of rope and handcuffs, abandoned his shoes, and was away to freedom.[87]

Discovery came ten minutes later. Diligent search was pressed immediately by the Sheriff, who was "in the greatest trouble at this unhappy affair."[88] Indeed, he grew well enough to keep looking for Stewart until Thursday night; and he offered a reward of ten pounds "for the taking him."[89] It would be superfluous to remark that neither hindsight nor reward availed.

But by Friday night York and York County were buzzing with news. Parties of folk "mostly dressed in blanket coats and hunting shirts,"[90] all armed with rifles and many carrying either one or two cases of pistols, had been dispersed at points about the town. Several eye-witnesses estimated they must have numbered seventy men alto-gether.[91] Few doubted that they had come in some instances out of Hanover Township, Lancaster County. Probably they had come look-ing for Stewart; at any rate both he and they had now disappeared. It was mortifying, in brief, for their Burgess, their Justice, and the King's Attorney to have to send word to Philadelphia of how their endeavors had been "rendered ineffectual by the negligence of the Sheriff's Guard."[92] They hoped, however, to escape censure, their "sincere love of justice and desire to promote the peace and good order of the community"[93] having been guiding principles with them.

As for the historian, he may doubt whether the spirit of frontier York on Friday, November 2, 1770, when Lazarus Stewart was ad-mitted missing, differed from the spirit of frontier Carlisle on Friday, January 29, 1768, when Colonel John Armstrong and the prudent town fathers there saw Frederick Stump being borne off by their unrecog-nized neighbors.

However that might be, the man who had wielded axe-handle with stormy imprecation at Lebanon and plied fingers with surprisingly skillful effect at John Finley's six weeks later, knew the moment of fame had come. It was time for him to issue his own manifesto. His convictions he felt deserved expression, and now, being no illiterate man, Lazarus Stewart declared himself by way of his pen.[94]

The printed words of his declaration constituted neither a model of fine prose nor of invincible argument. Facts mingled with rhetorical outcry and protest. "Let all hear!"[95] was his initial exclamation; and he was prompt to berate the Assembly of Pennsylvania for both its double-dealing and its parsimony. Roundly he scolded its neglect of counsel offered by George Croghan and supported by Benjamin Franklin at a past date. He denounced its willingness to let John Harris pay out of his purse for the stipend for a scouting party which it had endorsed but not provided for.

In contrast he praised the behavior of the frontier Counties of Lancaster, York, Cumberland, Berks, and Northampton. There men had borne the responsibility of protecting themselves. Their volunteer rangers had watched the motions of the Indians, kept intelligence moving from scouting station to station, endured summer's heat and winter's cold, felt the violence of the savage tomahawk—while, in contrast, the inhabitants of Philadelphia, Philadelphia County, Bucks, and Chester "ate, drank, and were merry."[96]

With passion he decried the discrepancy between Province justice for the Indian and Province justice for the white man. Scornfully he pictured the tenderness of the legislature toward aborigine criminals: "If an Indian kill a white man, it was the act of an ignorant heathen, perhaps in liquor; alas, poor innocent. He is sent to the *friendly* Indians that he may be made a Christian."[97]

In his best back inhabitant diction Lazarus averred that one treacherous Indian had murdered a family in Northampton, been promptly taken to Bucks County for trial, been indulged with every necessary there, and saved from punishment by Israel Pemberton. "Who had forgotten Renatus, that Christian Indian?"[98] he demanded, setting his own question mark down with emphasis after his proper adjective.

Worse even than such clemency in Stewart's view was the impolitic attitude toward the slaying of an Indian: "If a white man kills an Indian, it is a murder exceeding any crime upon record; he must not be tried in the county where he lives or where the offense was committed, but in Philadelphia."[99] For always that crux of the argument stuck in the remonstrant's mind: savages were spared for purposes of missionary redemption, frontiersmen were refused the privilege of trial among their own peers.

Stewart harked back to the affairs at Conestoga and Lancaster; reiterated the Scotch-Irish claim of the harborage furnished among the Conestogoes to murderers of the whites, particularly one notoriously barbaric offender; brusquely told of the Paxton scouts tracing that criminal thither, of their being resisted at the town, and of the results: "Conestoga was reduced to ashes. The murderers escaped. The unfriendly and the friendly were placed in the Work House at Lancaster. What could secure them from the vengeance of an exasperated people? The doors were forced and the hapless Indians perished."[100]

If Stewart begged the question and made his rhetoric evasive, still he kept his phrases blunt. He insisted that he and his fellows had been champions of their own people, and could not tamely look on and see their "brethren murdered," their "fairest prospects blasted."[101] If he spoke what John Penn and Israel Pemberton would have called untruth, he did not mince words on the subject of inhabitants of eastern counties who "slept and reaped their grain in safety."[102] And if he was not honest in his own personal defense, the rioter at Conestoga, Lancaster, and in the Wyoming, was a vehement apologist. "These hands," he declared of his own, "never shed human blood."[103] It was unfair that he be "singled out as an object of persecution." "Why are the bloodhounds let loose upon me?"[104]

It is possible that he was thinking of John Phillip de Haas of Lebanon behind the bolt of his house door in September when he wrote: "Let him who wishes to take my life, let him come and take it—I shall not fly."[105] The oratory with which he phrased his long conclusion swayed with fervor. It demanded trial in Lancaster County—rather belatedly, it must be admitted, when he was already the supposed settler on land in another jurisdiction; and it vaunted his intention to protect his followers if they were not accorded similar privileges there. Then it rehearsed his own recent conduct. If he had submitted to the Sheriff of York County, he must not be condemned for escaping from the prospective consequences of that submission. He disdained being "conveyed to Philadelphia like a wild felon, manacled, to die a felon's death."[106] He would otherwise have "scorned to fly York."[107] He "could not bear," he said, "that my name should be marked by ignominy."[108]

Strange, fulsome eloquence if from a liar or from a deranged person! Lazarus Stewart, whether demon or hero, clung to his role of champion with the fanaticism of a perverse Presbyterian saint. What he did, he "had done for the security of hundreds of settlers on the frontiers. The blood of a thousand of my fellow creatures called for vengeance. I shed no Indian's blood. As a ranger I sought the post of danger; and now you ask my life. Let me be tried where prejudice has not prejudged my case."[109]

And his last thoughts in his manifesto were not of himself. They bent on his followers who had "stemmed the blast nobly and never flinched."[110] For them he asked equitable trial. Friends in the hour of danger, "to desert them now were cowardice."[111] Rebellion rang in his ultimate sentence: "What remains is to leave our cause with God and our guns."[112]

For, when Stewart eluded his captors in York County in October, 1770, he had at length crossed the Rubicon of his own career. There was no way any longer for that scion of old Scotland in the midst of dutiful subjects of the Province of Pennsylvania. Early in 1771 he was back in Wyoming, deep in action once more, proscribed again, and charged now not with mere arson or rioting, but with the willful murder of a Pennamite[113]—his Scots name, it would seem, irrevocably stained.

CHAPTER II

BOUNDEN DUTY AND DISTANT RIVERS

On march 22, 1775, Edmund Burke, addressing the House of Commons in English Parliament on the general subject of conciliation with the American Colonies, remarked: "In other countries, the people, more simple, and less of a mercurial cast, judge of an ill principle in government only by an actual grievance; here they anticipate the evil, and judge of the pressure of the grievance by the badness of the principle. They augur misgovernment at a distance, and snuff the approach of tyranny in every tainted breeze."[1]

The distinguished orator was not thinking particularly of the folk of Hanover Township, Lancaster County, Pennsylvania, when he spoke. But he would have understood the temper of the Scotch-Irish who had settled the banks of the Swatara Creek from its mouth on the River Susquehanna eastwards and northwards to the great bow which that stream makes just south of modern Harper's Tavern and two miles below Blue Mountain. Within this north-south bend stretched the rugged hillside farms of the pioneer Stewarts and Youngs, sons of whom had but recently turned into Connecticut men in Wyoming. East and west of it were the homesteads of the members of Hanover Presbyterian Church. Eight miles downstream to the southwest was Dixon's Ford, where men crossed on horseback or with their wagons to follow their way for another eight miles of road and trail to "Old Side" Derry Church. Ten miles due west of the bow was the mill of Timothy Green in Manada Gap. Still three miles farther west, in the forks of Beaver Creek, far above its confluence with the winding Swatara, was the log-house fort of Joseph Barnett. About halfway between the bow and Barnett's, in Hanover Churchyard, were the graves of now venerated first settlers, too many of them hapless victims of Indian raids, others, like Squire Adam Reed, former champions against the redskins.

Twenty miles to the southwest were Paxton Township and Harris'

[157

Ferry; and on the way thither, the farm of Matthew Smith, leader of the Paxton Boys on their expedition of grievance to Philadelphia in 1764. To the northwest, beyond Blue Mountain, was the upstream course of the Susquehanna, along which Hanover men had sped by scouting trails in the French and Indian Wars, and where the quest of new lands for their own had been drawing second and third generations of the Scotch-Irish in Pennsylvania.

The old township, which at the time of its creation in 1737 had taken its name from the royal German house then ruling in England, was a broad one, large almost as a county and destined when new county divisions should come in the next century to be cut into two parts by a line which would leave it half in Dauphin and half in Lebanon. But the spirit of its inhabitants was already one. Considerably before the famous statesman Burke stood out in Parliament as the interpreter of the American Colonial genius, the settlers upon the Swatara and Manada and Beaver Creeks had demonstrated their mettle in a neighborly resoluteness for common defense. It would have been hard to find in 1774 and 1775 ears and minds more sympathetic to the unrest which had stirred in the colonies since the Stamp Act and the year 1765.

We cannot say today how little or how much they knew of the harangues of Samuel Adams inflaming the "Sons of Liberty" to violent defiance in Massachusetts, or of the falling off in trade with the mother country when the collectors under the Stamp Act attempted exercise of their duties in New England. They were not of the temperate blood of such rich Tidewater planters as Richard Bland and George Mason in Virginia, who dominated the Assembly in that royal colony as it drew resolutions protesting the practice of taxation without representation. But the sound of an "alarum bell to the disaffected" always came by nature close to the hearing of Scotch-Irishmen. The male folk of Hanover could not remain unaware of the agitation which continued to shake the spirits of colonists along the Atlantic seaboard between 1765 and the September day in 1774 when the first Continental Congress should meet in Philadelphia.

In the interim had been resistance and repeal of the Stamp Act, imposition and resistance of the Townsend Acts, the speech of many a demagogue and that of many a political seer. Furthermore there had been deeds and events. Eastern merchants had resorted to nonimportation agreements in sturdy refusal to pay duties upon paint, lead, paper, and tea brought to them from England. Colonial homes stayed unpainted; colonial housewives substituted sassafras for tea; men dressed in homespun garb, determined not to wear imported fabrics; students used only colonial-made paper. Customs officials experienced rough handling when they attempted collection of imposts. In the great seaport of Massachusetts a party of rough snowballers, defiant of British redcoats who had been ordered from Halifax at Governor Bernard's behest to protect the Commissioners for the Crown, became so aggressive as to provoke firing on themselves; and suddenly four Bostonians, lying bleeding and dead in the snow on March 5, 1770, had brought into history with little fair cause to justify it the name of the Boston Massacre.

Three years and nine months later, on December 16, 1773, a group of men disguised as Mohawk Indians boarded three tea ships at the same port and dumped their cargoes into the water. Merchants now applauded the offenders, indignant that the East India Tea company should have secured from the British Government a monopoly on all tea exported to the colonies, and that it had so tyrannically brought its vessels to New England with its own agents prepared both to sell their products and to collect duties of three pence a pound upon them. John Adams became exultant enough to declare that many persons wished "that as many dead carcasses were floating in the harbor as there are chests of tea."[2]

And thereupon had come from Parliament the Intolerable Acts of early 1774, with intention to close the Port of Boston until the East India Company's tea was paid for; to change the form of government in Massachusetts; to oblige that colony to transport certain offenders to England for trial.

Little wonder, then, that in Hanover Township during the spring of 1774 normally unquiet Scotch-Irish passions should rise again surfacewards. It was not the fashion of Lancaster County frontiersmen to esteem judgment of any man, guilty or innocent, in a court far from his place of residence. The mood of the times was as active in them as in any colonial of spirit and energy. Indeed, a party of them were in convention before word could arrive that on May 27 a rump assembly in Virginia was sending out from the Raleigh Tavern at Williamsburg a call for a congress of all the American colonies to consult upon their unhappy state. Not they the men to wait until their whole country had made up its mind!

From the four corners they gathered on June 4, more prompt than their kinsmen of Paxton or Derry, requiring no stimulus from the Committees of Correspondence currently forming into a great New England network under the inspiration of Samuel Adams. Captain

Timothy Green came from Manada Gap, hardy warrior in 1763 in the Reverend Mr. John Elder's two companies of rangers, now miller and farmer. From beyond the mountain arrived William Clark, not to be omitted because his acres were close to Susquehanna. Josiah Espy, lately with his brother-in-law Lazarus Stewart in Wyoming, came —as did Lazarus' cousin James Stewart and their friend James Caruthers. Joseph Barnett was accompanied by stalwart sons who would on this day still let their father speak for them. Grave and handsome John Rogers, thirty-six years old, a born organizer and moulded for leadership, took his place in the group. Robert Dixon, twenty-five, joined, keen for participation in any firm conduct. And of the company foregathering was Thomas Koppenheffer, not of Scots breed, but ready to share in the counsel of all Hanover patriots. Other interested men from the township moved quietly in the background.

There were, of course, greetings and jests: "Any news of Lazarus, Josiah?" "Still living at the Ford, Robin?" "So Jemmy Gibson's married to your sister and gone to Cumberland?" "Morning, John Rogers, how'd you get over the Manada?" "Will Barnett should know something of Indians, seeing as he lived seven years among them; but he and his pappy have other things in mind today, mebbe!" "Shouldn't be surprised, brother!" "Just so Cap'n Green's brought his thumb of gold with him."

Eventually there was deliberation in the house where they met. Perhaps it bore the gestures of tattered and excitable yokels much as the intaglio high in the glass front of the Dauphin County Courthouse in Harrisburg suggests today in its picture of the episode. Perhaps it wore only the gravity of austere but unlettered men. Certainly there was no hedging in the results of it when put down in words; and the phrases in which it was ultimately couched, however crude they might be, were comprehensive, intransigent, independent. The five clauses of the Hanover Resolves of June 4, 1774, now famous in Pennsylvania as the earliest open resolutions in the State for independence from England, rang like sterling, keeping the while a Scotch-Irish tone in their sound. The participation of one Pennsylvania German in them had transformed their quality never a whit. They did not call out for a congress as the Virginia lawyers and planters had done a week earlier in Williamsburg; but vigorously they proclaimed opinion, obligation, means, and purpose.

Nine men set their signatures to the document which as a committee they had framed and for themselves and their fellows declared:

1. That the recent action of the Parliament of Great Britain is iniquitous and oppressive.
2. That it is the bounden duty of the people to oppose every measure which tends to deprive them of their just prerogatives.
3. That in a closer union of the Colonies lies the safeguard of the liberties of the people.
4. That in the event of Great Britain attempting to force unjust laws upon us by the strength of arms, our cause we leave to heaven and our rifles.
5. That a committee of nine be appointed, who shall act for us and in our behalf as emergencies may require.[3]

Timothy Green, Joseph Barnett, James Stewart, James Caruthers, Josiah Espy, John Rogers, Thomas Koppenheffer, Robert Dixon, William Clark,[4] had phrased themselves out of experience and persuasion, and for their kind. There was no capital city peering in upon them through noble Georgian windows while they conferred in an architecturally beautiful legislative chamber. At most a log house, a log schoolhouse, or log-built Hanover Presbyterian Church sheltered them as they signed their names to the scribal evidence of their convictions. Moreover, signing was to be for all but prelude to other subsequent acts confirming their acceptance of "bounden duty."

Other men in Lancaster County would follow their example. Patriot men of Paxton Township met at Middletown on June 10.[5] Colonel James Burd of Tinian, Scottish by birth, fifteen years earlier commander at his Majesty's Fort Augusta on the Susquehanna, and—earlier than that—builder of a road for Braddock which that unfortunate British general never had used, presided over the conference. In it joined James Cowden and many another member of Parson John Elder's Paxton Church—determined men, although in their phrasing of resolutions rather more temperate.

They drew up five clauses.[6] In more legal sounding terms they condemned the Acts of Parliament as being unconstitutional and unjust. Aware by now of the Hanover men's resolves and of the recommendations of the Virginia Assembly, they called not only for a close union of the Colonies but also for a general Congress as the most likely means "to procure redress of American grievances."[7] In even tones they added that they would sincerely abide by the measures that such a Congress should adopt. With candor they asserted it would be the duty of those who signed their Middletown Resolves "to oppose with decency and firmness every measure tending to deprive us of our just rights and privileges."[8] Not quite so intransigent as their Hanover fellow patriots, they shaped no phrase mentioning weapons. Some of them must have remembered Lazarus Stewart's Declaration of four years earlier with its final avowal that what remained for the frontiersmen along Susquehanna was "to leave our cause with God and our guns";[9] some of them may have realized that Lazarus' words were echoed in the fourth clause of Chairman Timothy Green and his fellows. As a whole committee, however, they kept a more polite air of tolerance in their resolutions.

But if they acted with greater equanimity, they did not act with less acumen. Indeed, they took one step in advance of the then six-day old Hanover Resolves. In their fifth and last clause they constituted themselves a committee which should expressly act with other committees. The Scotch-Irish of Paxton knew that no group now taking resolves in Pennsylvania could act effectually without cooperation with many other groups; and with them the frontier had grown ready for Associations and Committees of Correspondence. They had begun to be Americans.

That might also be said of the men of Derry Township. Among these, as among all the folk of Lancaster County, a word known earlier in Pennsylvania history came back into use during the summer. A quarter century before, when the Assembly was wholly inactive in measures for defense and the Proprietor asleep to dangers threatening Philadelphia from French and Spanish navies and privateers, townsmen had been inspired by Benjamin Franklin to organize an "Association" to protect themselves. In 1747 a body of "Associators" came into being, unsanctioned by Government, but tolerated and voluntarily trained for a defense which never became actually necessary. This Association had had a fitful career and was most of the time dormant. Philadelphians only thought of it again in 1764, when the Paxton Boys were nearing the Schuylkill. Then, no real danger coming to the city from that source, the organization had lapsed from memories for another decade. Now the name of it was revived in the Scotch-Irish townships; with purpose no longer against mere French and Spanish but against oppression from England herself. By the autumn of 1774, when the first Continental Congress was meeting in the seaport city and when "Committees of Safety" were emerging from everywhere in Pennsylvania, the leading settlers of Derry, Paxton, Hanover, Upper Paxton, and Londonderry had turned into Associators. John Harris, Joseph Sherer, Timothy Green, Castle Byers, William Patton, John Campbell, Robert Clark, and Jacob Cook[10] were all on the alert.

In the spring of 1775, when news of the Battle of Lexington in Massachusetts was still fresh and word of the Battle of Bunker Hill was yet to come from the Bay Colony, "The Association of the Liberty Company in Lancaster County,"[11] met and drew up in Londonderry Township fourteen articles of agreement for itself. Phrases, as they cast them for their muster in May, were grave and stern—proper, in fact, to Associators who were heirs to the linen apprentices of Northern Ireland who in 1688 had saved an older Londonderry for Protestantism and King William III.

Moreover, these heirs accredited themselves with full dignity. They drew the clauses framing their organization as gentlemen. Each stood firm for decorum. Officers were properly designated, and obedience was pledged to them. Every Associator engaged to provide himself with "gun or musket, in good order and repair, with a cartouche-box or shotbag, powder horn, a half pound of powder and two pounds of lead."[12] Each pledged himself to regular attendance at Saturday drills, to meeting upon orders in the County or in Lancaster Town, with a shilling forfeit for every absence. Sobriety and decency of speech were enjoined, every man agreeing that "no person of the company shall appear drunk, or curse or swear whilst under Arms Mustering, or in actual service."[13]

Indeed, the sons of Derry, whether of the "Old Side" flock of the Reverend Mr. John Elder or of the "New Side" flock of the Reverend Mr. John Roan, comported themselves as well might men of the Presbyterian religion. If subsequently they veered from the gentlemanly behavior which they prescribed, at the least they prepared for it with a staunch set of rules. Against drunkenness, profanity, or other forms of misconduct unworthy of the society of soldiers and gentlemen, an ascending scale of fines mounted from three shillings to five.

Yet the Association of Londonderry kept itself democratic. Its members reserved the right not to be employed in service beyond the boundaries of Pennsylvania except on majority consent.[14] But they did not overlook that possibility; and careful clauses authorized their leaders, in the event of need, to combine their company with other companies into battalions, as well as to take initiative in the election of higher officers for these.[15] In brief, during May, 1775, the first band of men in that section of Lancaster County which a decade later would become Dauphin County had organized themselves as a military company to take part in the struggle for American Independence. They could hardly have known that in the same month, far away to the south, another group of Scotch-Irishmen, meeting in convention at

Charlotte, North Carolina, were on May 20 busy drawing up and signing a document which history would later acclaim as the first actual Declaration of Independence in North America. Echoes of Mecklenburg County were at the moment only within their hearts, as they also attuned their minds to the thought of a second Continental Congress.

More directly aware were they, in the year of Concord, Lexington, and Bunker Hill, of men in the next townships. For in Hanover during 1775 another Association was formed and adopted its colors. "Liberty or Death"[16] was its motto; and it adopted a flag showing above those words a ranger in tunic of Lincoln green, with buff breeches and fringed deerskin leggings and a saucy foxtail on his green hat—a fellow of alert face, with powder-horn on his right hip and flintlock gun raised ready to fire.[17] Hanover never did anything halfway; it had no intention of letting Heaven, and not its rifles, take care of its defenses.

Moreover, Paxton Township was as spirited. There Matthew Smith, leader with James Gibson in the Paxton Boys' bivouac on the Schuylkill, eleven years earlier, was stirring in spring and summer; and Smith had no parish reticence about gathering followers to his side from two other sections of Lancaster County, Derry, and Donegal.[18]

The second Continental Congress had convened in Philadelphia in May. On June 23, 1775, George Washington, newly appointed by that Congress general and commander-in-chief of the American forces, had ridden forth from Pennsylvania's capital city on the Delaware to take charge of an army of militia in New England. On his journey couriers kept meeting and telling him breathlessly the story of the Battle of Bunker Hill. It was a year for bold and hazardous strokes. If mischance and tactical folly attended it, effrontery was of its essence. Edmund Burke was not wrong when in March he said that Americans had a faculty for anticipating evil, for judging "the pressure of a grievance by the badness of a principle," for snuffing "the approach of tyranny"[19] and finding taint of it in the breeze.

Continental Congress and General George Washington himself came into one way of thinking on an audacious scheme which Britons themselves would be able to perceive only as an instance of wanton aggression. Indeed, on September 21 Washington wrote from his encampment at Cambridge officially informing the honorable Congress that, "encouraged by the repeated declarations of the Canadians and Indians, and urged by their requests," he had detached "Colonel Arnold, with one thousand men, to penetrate into Canada by way of

Kennebec River, and, if possible, to make himself master of Quebec."[20]

Before the latter had been posted, Matthew Smith of Paxton and a goodly company of some eighty Scotch-Irish lads from Donegal, Derry, Paxton, and Hanover Townships, from farmlands along Chickiesalunga, Swatara, and Paxton Creeks, Lancaster County tributaries of the Susquehanna River, had already set forth with Benedict Arnold's regiment from Prospect Hill, Cambridge, Massachusetts.[21] Four hundred miles from home, days and nights of long marching, and their part in Washington's siege of Boston already behind them, seventy young men in whose temper was the spirit of Maeldun and of St. Columba were again *en voyage* for adventure and a cause.

The story of their part in the expedition to Quebec in the autumn and winter of 1775 was set down in later years by a president judge of a circuit of common pleas courts embracing four Pennsylvania counties. John Joseph Henry had lacked several months of seventeen years when, as a runaway school boy, he enlisted in Matthew Smith's company. His *Account*,[22] written a quarter of a century later for the benefit of his own teen-age children, too often abandoned narrative to run into middle-aged disquisitions on natural history, discourses on morality, encomiums on piety, and prescriptions for etiquette. But, happily, an ex-soldier's pride prevailed enough of the time to lend his tale eloquence and main truth.

The Scotch-Irish blood which he inherited from his father, the gunsmith William Henry of Lancaster and Philadelphia, had been tempered by the son's religious affiliations in childhood with Moravian believers. Yet he fitted in well among those frontiersmen from Paxton and its adjoining townships whom, in a freak of adolescent enthusiasm, he joined in the summer of 1775.

And, when he wrote it down, there still shone in his *Account of Arnold's Campaign against Quebec* a passionate esteem for Scotch-Irish comrades. Accidents, terrors, and feats lived bright in his memory, because he had experienced them shoulder to shoulder with men of Donegal, Derry, Paxton, and Hanover.[23]

Before they left Prospect Hill on September 11[24] for their overland march to Newburyport he and his companions in Smith's company had already known action and trouble. Joined by the companies of Captains Paterson, Lowden, Noggle, and William Hendricks on July 17 in Reading, Pennsylvania,[25] they had made forward with despatch to Swan's Tavern, to Allentown, to Bethlehem, across the Lehigh River into Easton, across the Delaware to Oxford Meeting House, to the Log Jail near that site—where Henry failed to mention Hend-

ricks' Cumberland County riflemen's tarring and feathering a "minis-
terial tool, who refused to comply with the resolves of our Continental
Congress"—,[26] to Sussex Court House, to New Windsor on the North
('or Hudson's') River, across that on to Baker's Tavern, to Litchfield, Hartford, other taverns and meeting-houses, to Farmington, to
Minden, and headquarters at Cambridge.[27] All that march, with only
one stop at New Windsor for the washing of their linens and delay
long enough at Litchfield to witness another tarring and feathering
administered by the company of Captain Price of Maryland,[28] had been
accomplished by August 9. At the end of the long trek they were under the command of Colonel William Thompson of Carlisle, and in
Washington's army.

First fighting came for a detail of them on September 3.[29] It was a
venture in which the Americans gave good account of themselves.
The task was to help erect a battery on Plowed Hill, a quarter of a
mile from the enemy's line on Bunker Hill. Fire from there and from
a floating battery on the Back Bay assailed them constantly as they
labored. Three men were killed; but their companions worked on,
succeeded in sinking the battery in the Bay, forced the marksmen on
Bunker Hill to keep inside their entrenchments, and established their
own position.

In the exchange William Simpson of Smith's company[30] fell. His
foot was shattered by enemy fire. Amputation of the lower leg was
deemed imperative as soon as he had been got to a hospital. Kindly
General Washington himself visited the youthful first casualty from
Paxton Township, and Lieutenant Michael Simpson beheld the Commander-in-Chief and other high ranking officers bowing over the cot
of the injured rifleman.[31] On September 4, a mortification having set
in, death took the younger son of Thomas Simpson, neighbor of the
ferryman John Harris on the Susquehanna. Sorrow had fallen on Matthew Smith's company and on many a man in other detachments.

Then, while grief tugged at hearts, news first came of Washington's
plan to send troops to Quebec; and on September 9 Pennsylvanians
were aware that lots were being cast[32] to determine which three of
eleven companies of riflemen gathered at Cambridge from the several
colonies were to be assigned to that yet more northerly campaign.
None repined at the decision, when it was known that the lot-casting
selected Captain Hendricks' and Smith's Pennsylvania riflemen and
those of Virginia Captain Daniel Morgan. It meant to them that not
only folk of their own blood from the colony to the south but their
neighbors from the west shore of the Susquehanna in Cumberland

County commanded by William Hendricks would be serving with the Lancaster County lads on the expedition. Two days later they set forth, knowing with what men they were banded: Scotch-Irishmen of their own ilk from Winchester and the Valley of Virginia; from Carlisle in their own province and townships along the Yellow Breeches and Conodoguinet Creeks. It was as though all had sprung from Derry, or Paxton, or Hanover. Moreover the riverman, Michael Simpson, third ranking officer in Smith's company, remembered the vows he had made when he had accepted his commission in June and was no man to ask exception for himself in the new hour. Memory of his brother's death pains still vivid in his thoughts, he marched forward to duty unflinching. Superiors, equals in command, and subordinates in the company respected the fortitude with which he continued to smile.

Among his admirers was Private Henry, who, perhaps more than ever he would realize, was of the Scottish breed of his fellows. That youth did not, however, by the same token esteem all the men with whom he was now associated. For on the subject of Captain Matthew Smith he seldom refrained from animus. He "was a good-looking man," he admitted, "and had the air of a soldier; but he was "illiterate and outrageously talkative."[33]

At Newburyport, formed by the waters of the Merrimac River, Arnold's men remained in camp for five days. On the afternoon of the sixth day away from Prospect Hill they embarked on ten transports; on the morning of the seventh they descried the mouth of the Kennebec. Up that river they proceeded as far as Colonel Colborn's shipyard (two miles below Gardiner), where they left their seagoing vessels for bateaux; and then, having ascended again as far as Fort Western, all became interested in the commander-in-chief's tactics.

Arnold decided to despatch an officer and seven men in advance to ascertain and mark the water and forest paths by which his army should follow. Choice for command in that scouting enterprise was Archibald Steele, first lieutenant in Smith's company, a rifleman from Donegal Township. Of "active, courageous, sprightly and hardy disposition,"[34] Steele was complimented with the privilege of naming his companions; and he selected promptly. From the Virginian Morgan's command he chose three: Jesse Wheeler, George Merchant, and James Clifton. From Smith's he took four: Robert Cunningham and Thomas Boyd of Derry, John Todd and John McKonkey of Hanover. Then, indifferent to arithmetic, he added another rifleman, like himself a lad out of Lancaster County and "his messmate and friend,"[35] John

Joseph Henry. A party of nine Scotch-Irishmen, in brief, was to be the vanguard in a wilderness.

The canoes which bore them were so light that a person of common strength could carry one of them unloaded many hundred yards without halting. (Henry added for the benefit of his children that, in the heyday of his youth he could run a hundred yards across a carrying place with a canoe clapped on his back.)[36] Five men rode in Steele's boat with their arms and baggage, "which last was light in quantity and quality, one barrel of pork, one bag of meal, and 200 weight of biscuit."[37] Seven men (for the narrator, with a Falstaffian indifference to number, early increased Arnold's appointed squad to twelve!), similarly and proportionately armed and provisioned, rode in the second birchbark.

By September 23 they were on the way to hospitality, accident, fun, the ardors of inquiry, the pleasures of discovery, the comfort of trustful friendship, disillusionments with their fellows, and the censure of renegades. A week and five days from their breaking of camp before Boston, they were high up on the Kennebec, speeding forward at the rate of fifteen to twenty-five miles a day on the winding bends of a river.

Near ruinous Fort Halifax Archibald Steele's men rested for night at the house of Tory "Captain Harrison, or Huddlestone,"[38] who dilated to them upon the habits of deer, elk, and moose. But, better than that, the morrow showed them that a gentleman could reserve the right of thinking politics in his own way, and yet fairly exchange with them "a barrel of smoked salmon for a barrel of pork, upon honest terms."[39]

After that, for several days they fared on, blithely. Steele's spraining of an ankle at a portage below Norridgewock Falls, while carrying his canoe, seemed a small matter. John Joseph marveled much at a conical rock five feet high which struck his view at a landing, its face of bluish flint scalloped down to the water's edge; and he was pleased to learn from their New England guide Getchel that many an Indian in the past had with rude tools carved spear and arrow points from that unique quarry.[40] A deserted Indian town diverted them.

Then came a perplexing and embarrassing experience for men who believed in good manners. Knowing that they would have to use their stores cautiously, Steele one day indicated, without actual dividing of their rations, what allotment should belong to each man. It was near the end of a stiff morning, and, a surplus occurring after the theoretical distribution had been determined on, the generous lieutenant won approval by deciding this should be the party's fare for their midday meal.

The riflemen sauntered off to have a look at the Falls nearby, leaving to John McKonkey, cook by routine for the day, the simple preparation of their dinner. In due time he called that he was ready. They came back promptly, found their steward seated by a wooden bowl containing the awaited viand, and sat down circlewise around him.

Suddenly McKonkey raised "his vile and dirty hands, struck the meat," with them, and exclaimed, "By G—d this is our last comfortable meal."[41]

At once his gesture, wrote Henry, revolted all. "The indelicacy of his act, its impiety, and the grossness of the expression, deprived the company of appetite."[42]

Whether Arnold's scouts were as sensitive against profanity as the By-laws of the Associators of the Londonderry Liberty's Company or whether the commentator was merely mindful of etiquette for his sons, might be argued. That a cluster of hungry riflemen should so lightly lose zest for a hard-earned dinner in the wilds of Maine maturer readers may incline to doubt. But there, in the *Account,* for acceptance or rejection, stands a naïve apology for the gentle breeding of the Scotch-Irish—with an exception, of course, and this from Hanover Township, to prove the rule.

But recovery from the explorers' astonishment came. In the afternoon they crossed below Norridgewock Falls to the west side of the Kennebec; found the carrying place, although with difficulty; made their portage northwards to good navigation, and on September 27, past rock and stiff current, arrived at the twelve-mile carrying place.[43]

From here, Jeremiah Getchel explained, the riflemen might as well be their own guides. He had hunted east of the spot, never west. The Kennebec was about to become the Dead River, a stream of almost wholly imperceptible current which, although flowing south at the point at which they had stopped, flowed northwards just twelve miles to the west to reach a great bend which would turn it east and then south toward the party. On the portage west they would skirt or voyage in three lakes. Then they would follow the lazy river upstream to the divide between it and the Chaudiere. They would be unwise to attempt the part of the river just above where they had paused; "that part was full of rapids, and impassable to boats, or even canoes."[44]

Steele and his comrades searched for the path at which to begin carrying, blazed its trees with their tomahawks and snagged its bushes, at evening encamped on the margin of a small half-mile wide lake, and there took counsel. It was decided to detail two men to remain where they were with a half of the provisions of the entire scouting party, and wait for the main army to come up to them. For that duty was chosen first James Clifton, oldest man in the group, perceptibly flagging, but good enough as a marksman to fend for himself on game; and then McKonkey, on the nomination of John Joseph Henry, whose youthful motives were hardly those of unmixed kindness. After that, they were ready for further directions from their lieutenant.

Archibald Steele proceeded, accordingly, with distribution of their remaining supplies. But it was not now by a strict counting of pounds or ounces. Rather the leader rose, portioned the food into ten parts equal as he felt he could make them, and bade his men turn their backs. Then he called, "Whose shall be this?"[45] An answer came from Boyd: "Henry's"; another from Cunningham, "Wheeler's"; another from Merchant, "Todd's." As the choices were named the young officer handed his share to each men. When all had been named and all shares had been distributed the Scotch-Irish riflemen, used to the etiquette of honest scouts, accepted what came to each by a fair sportsman's code. It was well that they could do so unrepiningly.

For, on the next day—it was September 28—they resumed the hard labors of portage. Canoes had ever to be unloaded or loaded according as they took to land or back to water alternately. At one point, the two empty canoes mounted on their shoulders, Henry and Boyd ran a race. The Derry rifleman outdistanced his competitor; rejoiced in his victory; and, looking for applause, set his foot, just as he turned, on a bed of moss. The moss yielded; and down went the winner into ten feet of water cold "as was ever touched."[46] Everybody laughed, as Tom scrambled out of the hole; and wet man and comrades carried on to reach a second pond to the west, and camp again. At night there, and by the next evening they had passed a third lake, reached the Dead River, and bivouacked on its farther shore. After that there began ascent of a stream full of perils despite the sluggishness implied in its name. They had bypassed its great north bend; they had now to defy the treacheries of its clear waters.

Many adventures, wettings, and hardships befell during the next long days. "That sensation of the mind called *the horrors*"[47] too often prevailed. But in the midcourse of October reunion with the rest of Arnold's army came, part by part. In the first days of November all had put the Dead River behind, crossed the mountainous divide into Canada, and were keen for descent by the Chaudiere. Captain Morgan had arrived "large, a commanding aspect, and stentorian voice. He wore leggings and a cloth in the Indian style. His thighs, which were exposed to view,"[48] showed lacerations from thorns and bushes. He greeted the scouts "kindly."[49] Lancaster County men found themselves "at home, in the bosom of a society of brave men."[50] More individually Johnny Henry rejoiced to see his company's second lieutenant Michael Simpson again.

Lucky, in fact, he was to have at hand that riverman born and bred on the banks of the Susquehanna back in Pennsylvania. For on October 23 a cluster of men from the Paxton company woke following a night of torrential rain, to find themselves marooned by the sudden high waters on the far side of the stream from the main detachment. Their previous day's advance by land had proved an error in tactics. It was no pleasure, with the perils between, to behold all of the boats on the opposite side of the Dead River, and to see a fall and treacherous eddies at hand. The morning became memorable. What ensued Judge Henry's *Account* narrates admirably:

The pitch of the fall made a dreadful noise, and the current ran with immense velocity. We sat down on the bank sorely pinched by hunger, looking wistfully towards our friends beyond the torrent, who were in possession of all the provisions, tents and camp equipage, convinced however, that the most adventurous boatmen would not dare the passage, for the sake of accommodating any of us. We were mistaken. There were two men, and only two, who had skill and courage to dare it.

Need Lieut. Simpson, on an occasion like this, be named? He, accompanied by John Todd, entered his empty boat. What skill in boatmanship! what aptitude with the paddle was here exhibited! The principal body of the water created a foaming and impetuous torrent. The river was about one hundred and fifty or two hundred yards in breadth, counting on the increase of water by the rains. The force of the central current naturally formed eddies at each side of the river, close under the pitch.

Simpson now disclosed his amazing skill. Though there was an eddy, even that was frightful; he came by its mean nearly under the pitch, and, trying to obtain an exact start, failed. The stream forced his boat down the river, but he recovered and brought it up.

Now we, who were trembling for the fate of our friends, and anxious for our own accommodation, began to fear he might be drawn under the pitch. Quick, almost in a moment, Simpson was with us. He called in his loud voice to Robert Dixon, James Old, and myself to enter the boat. We entered immediately. He pushed off; attempting the start by favor of the hither eddy, which was the main thing—we failed.

Returning to the store, we were assailed by a numerous band of soldiers, hungry, and anxious to be with their companions. Simpson told them he

could not carry more with safety, and would return for them. Henry
M'Anally, a tall Irishman, who could not from experience comprehend the
danger, jumped into the boat; he was followed by three or four other in-
considerate men. The countenance of Simpson changed, his soul and mine
were intimate. "O God," said he, "men we shall all die." They would not
recede.

Again we approached the pitch; it was horrible. The bateau swam deep,
almost ungovernable by the paddle. Attempting again to essay the departure
—we failed.

The third trial was made; it succeeded. As lightning we darted athwart
the river. Simpson with his paddle governed the stern, the worthy Todd in
the bow. The other men sat between the stern and the bow. Simpson called
to the men in the bow to lay hold of the birch bushes; the boat struck the
shore forcibly. They caught hold, M'Anally in particular (this was in the
tail of the eddy); but like children their holds slipped at the only spot where
we could have been saved—for the boat had been judiciously and safely
brought up.

Letting go their holds, the bow came round to the stream; and the stern
struck the shore. Simpson, Dixon, and myself now caught the bushes; but,
being by this time thrown into the current, the strength of the water made
the withes as so many straws in our hands.

The stern again swung round; the bow came again ashore. Old, Todd,
M'Anally, and the rest sprung to the land to save their lives. Doing this,
at our cost, their heels forced the boat across the current. Though we attempted to steady it, the boat swagged. In a moment after, at thirty feet
off shore, it, being broadside to the current, turned; was borne under, in
spite of all our force, by the fury of the stream.

The boat upsetting, an expression, as going into the water, fell from me,
"Simpson, we are going to heaven."

My fall was head foremost. Simpson came after me—his heels, at the
depth of fifteen feet or more, were upon my head and neck; and those
grinding on the gravel. We rose nearly together, your father first—my friend
followed. The art of swimming, in which I thought myself an adept, was
tried; but it was a topsy-turvy business. The force of the water threw me
often heels-over-head. In the course of this voyage, after a few hundred
yards, Simpson was at my side, but the force of the stream prevented the
exertion of swimming; yet the impetuosity of the current kept us up. It
drove us toward the other side of the river, against a long ridge of perpen-
dicular rocks of great extent. Luckily, in the course of some hundred yards,
the current changed, and brought us perforce to the north side of the river.
Floating along with my head just above water—prayers in sincere repentance
having been uttered, a boat's crew of the eastern men handed me a pole.
It was gripped as by the hand of death—but gripped the pole remained to
me. The strength of water was such, that the boat would inevitably have

upset, if the boatman had kept his hold. A glance of the eye informed me that my companion in misfortune had shared the same fate.

Resigned into the bosom of my Savior, my eyes became closed; the death appeared to me a hard one; sensibility in a great degree forsook me. Driving with the current some hundreds of yards more, the most palpable feeling recollected, was the striking of my breast against a root or hard substance. My head came above water. Breathing ensued; at the same moment Simpson raised his head out of the water, his gold laced hat on it, crying "Oh!" Neither of us could have crept out; we should have there died but for the assistance of Edward Cavanaugh, designated in the company by the appellation of Honest Ned. Passing from the lower part of the river, he happened to come to the eddy, at the instant of time my breast struck.

He cried out, "Lord, Johnny! is this you?" and instantly dragged me out of the water. Simpson immediately appearing, he did him the same good office. Lying on the earth perhaps twenty minutes, the water pouring from me, a messenger from the camp came to rouse us. Roused, we went to it.

But all eyes looked out for Dixon; all hearts were wailing for his loss. It was known he could not swim, but none of us could recollect whether he had dropped into the water or had adhered to the boat. In some time we had the inexpressible pleasure of Dixon in our company. He had stuck to the side of the boat, which lodged on a vast pile of driftwood some miles below, and in this way he was saved.

Arriving at the camp, our friends had a large fire prepared, particularly for our accommodation; heat upon such an occurrence is most agreeable.

My two friends in distress, whose clothing was principally woolen, felt none of my private disaster. My leather breeches attached closely and coldly to the skin. Modesty prohibited a disclosure. The sense of pain or inconvenience, which was observed by my seniors, caused an inquiry. Immediately the breeches were off and stuck upon a pole to dry.

Simpson was so much exhilarated by our escape that, seated on a stump, he sung *Plato* in great glee. It became a favorite with us. During all this time, perhaps till one or two o'clock, my breeches were in my hands almost in continued friction.

The laugh of the company was against us, but it was borne stoically.[51]

CHAPTER 12

FEAT WITHOUT LAURELS

SODDEN BREECHES and bared posteriors were not to be Henry's only form of embarrassment as the result of the episode. The youth had stuck his rifle in the railing of the bateau as he and Dixon sat in the stern near the steersman. The rifle was now lost, with his knapsack and his headgear as well.

Lieutenant Nichols of Hendricks' company obliged him later with one of his own two hats. The young rifleman had to draw an order for twelve dollars on William Henry in Lancaster, dated by his son at camp in the Maine wilderness, as payment for a substitute weapon got from a sick man who was being sent back. The draft on his father troubled his conscience. The crude short gun[1] purchased by that means wounded his vanity. But its bore, admitting of a good-sized bullet, and its accuracy of fire were virtues compensating to a soldier's spirit. After all, it provided "armor of defense," a perquisite without which "men and nations are mere automatons, liable to be swayed by the beck of power and subject to the hand of oppression."[2]

Five days later Virginians, Pennsylvanians, Morgan's men and Hendricks' and Smith's, had passed the head of the Dead River and all of them were ready to carry their boats over the Height-of-Land, mountainous barrier into Canada. On October 29 Hendricks' and Smith's companies were encamped on the plain below the source of the Chaudiere, where Morgan's riflemen presently were beside them. In the last two days descent began, with provisions in the scarcest supply, all meat gone, and only five pints of flour left per man.

In the first two weeks of November, if there were to be differences in adventure, there was to be little tempering of hardships. Officers observed that "orders would not be required on the march, each man must put the best foot foremost."[3] Exhausted men of Henry's mess at night crept under each other's blankets, and woke in the morning to find themselves under an additional covering of inches of snow.

[175

The half-blind company drummer went more blind, stumbled his way to the campfire of Henry, and disturbed a second set of nerves by moaning that his cakes had been stolen. Worse even, the poor Shaeffer, as one day the men followed their lithe captain Indian-file through the woods, slipped off a log which the sure-footed Matthew Smith had taken nimbly, and plunged into the abyss of water which it crossed. Hardened men laughed at the Dutchman's confusion; and Henry kept thinking charitably of both the laughers and the laughing-stock.

In the woods icy marshes and bogs were as hard to meet as runnels and slippery bogs. Simpson led the way through these, breaking the ice with foot or gun butt. Often waist deep in freezing water, his men followed. The wife of Sergeant Joseph Greer of Hendricks' company, buxom but virtuous and respectable woman, her clothes gathered up more than waist high, waded in the column as one by one it pressed on. John Joseph Henry, sometimes next in line, was astonished at her sturdy exertions, but would entertain no "disrespectful idea of her."[4]

Ordeals did not cease when a bateau had picked Simpson's men up again and passed them downstream to the upper outlet of the Chaudiere. From its very start that river merited its French name for *cauldron*. Henry could fairly avouch of it that for sixty miles it continued as rapids, without any apparent gap or passage for even a canoe. Smith's men tried launching boats, and lost them. The intrepid Morgan lost still more bateaux and canoes in the same sort of attempt; one member of his company died in that vain endeavor, and the commander with difficulty saved his own life and the company's treasure from a similar risk. Benedict Arnold initiated his own venture by water; but perforce, as he now led the advance, took to the bank, and continued well ahead, Archibald Steele of Donegal acted as marshall with him.

For the private soldier descending into Canada alongside the miry river was a desperate experience. If moccasins wore to shreds, or shoes gave way in the seam of the heel, a man dared not risk losing his position in line. Once out of file, his companions sped on past him; and he must wait, often mending or adjusting his footwear, for a break to open and readmit him to a place far behind in the single column of march. The fear of being left alone became intolerable. Dread of such fate contributed to the exhaustion of McCleland, first lieutenant of Hendricks and friend of Simpson, who loved him and shared his pittances of food with him in his feebleness. The death of that officer saddened long the young rifleman from Lancaster.[5]

Hunger, too, produced wild angers and jealousies. The tired young-ster, on a morning when his shoe had given way again, lurched onto a log, upset a kettle, spilled two-thirds of its contents, and found the owner towering dangerously over him, gun in hand, threatening to shoot. Simpson intervened, made his two subordinates friends again, and laughed as a cup of greenish broth was handed by the conciliated man to his junior. Johnny suspected a Newfoundland dog's meat to be the basis of the food, stopped at a spoonful, and thought morosely on his willingness, after all, to die, with the means of ending his existence actually in his own hands. But "The God of all goodness inspired other thoughts"; and, "under the fostering hand of Providence," to change his sentiments there "was the jovial hilarity of my friend Simpson."[6]

Always, indeed, that riverman from the Susquehanna, son of the Presbyterian Simpsons, brother-in-law of the Reverend Mr. Elder of Paxton Church, was the encouraging influence: "At night, warming our bodies at an immense fire, our compatriots joined promiscuously around—to animate the company, he would sing *Plato;* his sonorous voice gave spirit to my heart, and the morality of the song, consolation to my mind. In truth the music, though not so correct as that of Handel, added strength and vigor to our nerves."[7]

Descent brought scouts on November 3 to their first sight of houses; and, foraging, which would be none too scrupulous, opened cheerful prospects to the fancy. Either in the expectation of plenty or to tease the lad, Captain Smith offered his youngest rifleman a paper packet out of his own hoard of old rations. Henry grasped it eagerly, forgetting his antipathy to his officer, found within an inch-thick hand's breadth and length of bacon-fat, and made greedy luncheon of the greasy morsel.

But no new provisions came into the company larder that day. Simpson ate his evening meal with relish, which consisted of oatmeal warmed in water. His young friend revolted from that slim nourish-ment, and would not take it at all. Nor was his appetite fostered by a trio of Frenchmen who strayed into the night's encampment with stories of how foragers downstream had already stolen their cattle and devoured them to the very entrails.[8]

November 4, Henry's seventeenth birthday, turned out more grati-fyingly. A morning wade through an icy stream for him; then his own first sight of a house in Canada,[9] and better even, the knowledge that Arnold Steele and John Taylor—the accountant and commissary for Arnold's army, now that they were in Canada—had laid in a stock of provisions.[10] There was food; there was gorging; and there was for many subsequent illness. Johnny was prudent and kept to light fare for two more days. But on November 6, with still richer supplies gathered in from a slaughterhouse, the hungry youngster went heavily into a savory meal of bread, potatoes, and beefsteak,[11] and paid the penalty. Next morning he sat ill upon a log at the wayside,[12] powerless to move, while other troops passed toward Point Levis on the St. Lawrence, thirty miles away.

Arnold came along, sized up the situation, beckoned a French householder from across the water, gave the man directions, had another rifleman take Henry's gun and accoutrements into his keeping, and presented the sick seventeen-year-old two silver dollars.[13] Three days of kindness and care followed: to bed with a fever, but fasting there for a day, and then a simple diet of milk, bread, garlic, and salt. On November 10 the patient could be dismissed. His peasant-host refused Arnold's two silver dollars of pay, found a guide for the boy to a ferry on the lower Chaudiere, and generously set him on his way. In the afternoon, in fact, he had found Matthew Smith's company, and near it Morgan's encamped on the bank of the St. Lawrence; and there, after the foreboding and gloom of his own solitary march to that river, it was joy for him to reclaim his gun. He would never part from that again, he vowed, unless "it happened by compulsion of the foe."[14]

On the morrow he was to behold again the mettle of the men to whose breed in spite of his Moravian leanings he belonged—although certainly not revealed with impeccable honor and flawless courtesy.

A rumor came to Morgan's headquarters that the British had discovered the Americans' presence on the south shore of the great river. Captain Morgan, followed by two Indians who had joined his party in the descent of the Chaudiere, darted to a point of advantage. From the brow of a precipice, where he and several men hastily concealed themselves, they could see a frigate downstream and a boat making its way shorewards from that sloop of war. His riflemen opened fire on its crew, just as one young Briton was leaping from the craft to a landing place.

The volley from the men on the bluff failed to reach its target; alarmed, the pilot of the craft pulled off shore rapidly. The youth waded into the river, tried swimming after his receding companions, and came into range of the Scotch-Irish. Almost immediately bullets were circling his head as it moved in the water. Balls played round from the guns of Morgan, of Morgan's lieutenant William Humphreys, of Simpson and Henry. The Briton signaled his wish to surrender and turned back for shore.[15]

Firing stopped. John Joseph Henry had time to repent his own un-sportsmanlike conduct and that of his superiors. Then as he looked at the swimmer nearing shore, he shuddered to see the young Indian Sabatis spring, scalping knife in hand, down the declivity toward an intended victim.[16]

Happily, that spectacle endured for but a flash. Daniel Morgan perceived the intent of his Indian ally, sprang in pursuit of him, out-distanced him, with Humphreys, too, speeding fast after the red heels; and the athletic Virginian saved the young Briton's life.[17] Then that strange affair in the code of honor of warring men turned into anticlimax. As the Americans began escorting their Scottish prisoner McKensie up the cliff side toward their own company, the sloop *Hunter* began pelting the captors with ball and grape shot.[18]

Such was the first meeting with the enemy. The British knew now that there were fighting men hostile to them on the south bank of the St. Lawrence. But they were not to know for three more days that their foes could cross the river.

If his expedition was to achieve any purpose, Arnold, of course, knew he must cross to the north shore. To wait where he was for news or arrival of Montgomery was to admit failure almost before he had begun. With his officers, then, he studied means. The use of canoes was decided on. Lieutenant Archibald Steele, hundreds of miles from the Chickiesalunga in Donegal Township and from the Susquehanna into which that creek emptied and on which he had had his first experiences as a riverman, was assigned command of the twenty-five birch bark craft assembled for the crossing[19]—a new gamble with destiny for a Scotch-Irish boatman.

He rose to his duty with assurance; named the steersman for each of the boats; and directed on the night chosen, November 13, the silent and shadowy embarkations.[20]

Back and forth plied the canoes carrying Arnold's troops. Young Henry was proud to serve as man in the stern of one craft. The first lieutenant of Smith's company himself steered two loads of riflemen over; and then on his third traverse ran into mischance. The load this time was more unwieldy: nervous passengers at the middle of the St. Lawrence proved too much strain for Steele's light birch bark. Suddenly it burst apart.[21]

Other canoes came to the relief of the men floundering in the water and gathered all up except their steersman. The expert from Donegal had to fend for himself. Last of all, he got to the boat which Wheeler of Paxton was guiding. It was too full to take him in. "Cast your arms round the stern," bade the Paxtonian; "clamp your hands tight."[22]

The night was bleak, the water treacherously numbing. Archibald Steele caught and held. Wheeler moved enough to plant his buttocks firmly on the hands of his friend. His crew paddled forward in grim resolution and silence as with dip and twist of his own paddle he directed their course. So it was that their lieutenant, wet belly and half-frozen legs trailing after his friend's boat in the current, was floated to Wolf's Cove.[23]

Yet it was not a really inglorious mode of arrival; and the aftermath brought the upturn of climax. The body of Steele was thoroughly rubbed. A transfer of men which had begun at ten in the evening had brought all but one-hundred-and-fifty of Arnold's army to the north shore. The chief steersman, hero of the crossing, was animated as ever (and ready, as time would tell more than a half-century later, to live to an age of ninety-one years). At dawn, although they must wait for a second night to bring the rest of their fellows to them, Benedict Arnold's troops hardly cared that the British should know where they were.

Indeed, on November 15, having already scaled the heights which General James Wolfe had mastered sixteen years before them, they were safe on the Plains of Abraham to the west of the City of Quebec. At daybreak a reconnoitering party of Morgan's men were reporting that everything towards that walled town was "in a state of perfect quietness."[24] It was rumored even that St. John's Gate, opening toward the Plains, stood not only unbarred but unclosed, with nothing placed there for defense but a single cannon under a drowsy watch. Except that the Americans had now only three-hundred-and-fifty men at their disposal, attack and siege both seemed momentarily easy.[25]

But Arnold and Morgan and Matthew Smith had led their Scotch-Irish followers into a realm of only vainglorious expectations. For the maneuvers before Quebec began with temerity in mid-November of 1775 and ended by an ill-conceived audacity six weeks later.

As Scots had overreached themselves at Neville's Cross, Holmedon Hill, and Flodden, and courted disaster, so again, three and four centuries later, men of their blood had risked themselves far beyond their own borders. Their stamina had been demonstrated in their long march and their stealthy and gallant crossing of the St. Lawrence. But too much they campaigned like men on cattle raids, whether it was with the ancient instincts of the Gaelic Tain Bo Chuailgne or with the more modern bravado of Rob Roy MacGregor. The barns and the stores of quiet Canadians or of absent Britons were to them but rightful provender and provision. With gratitude and without reservation they partook. "Adversity," said Henry, "had destroyed in our minds every decorous or delicate sensation."[26] Cattle-reiving grew into an art with them.

Bizarre experiences succeeded. The careless placing of sentries on the first day outside the city by a young favorite of Arnold's led to the capture of George Merchant of Morgan's men, a rifleman of reputation more than intrepid. Ere he could cock his gun, he was seized out of ambush and carried within the walls. When a thirty-six pounder in the city let loose upon the Americans in the afternoon and the balls from it fell awkwardly. Arnold ordered that there be no form of retort except disdainful huzzas from his troops. That pretense of strength only increased in Sir Guy Carleton, commander of the British garrison, contempt for a Continental General whom well-bred British folk already despised as a horse jockey.[27] Neither that officer nor his aide, Colonel Maclean, would communicate[28] on any terms with their chief adversary and beleaguerer. Moreover, Arnold lost caste with many of his own men for trying to keep rations as thin for them in the land of plenty as they had been of necessity on the stern overland march.[29]

An episode of November 16 seemed requisite, if only to divert newly developing tensions of mind. In it were summed Canadian duplicity, the cupidity of Arnold, the inexplicable mettle of Scotch-Irish men from Pennsylvania. Orders were given to Michael Simpson by his commander to proceed with a guard to the ferry at the mouth of the St. Charles River north of Quebec, cross, and seize certain cattle feeding in a pasture on the far shore. With a "Come on, lads,"[30] Matthew Smith's second lieutenant was prompt to obey. Sergeant Robert Dixon and several other riflemen fell into line.

Complications ensued. At the ferry was a scene of flight. Two carts were there, laden heavy with household stuff and already drawn upon the ferryman's scow. Onto that vessel fugitive women and children were being crowded as the Americans came running in clear view of the city's battlements. There was a sudden hurly-burly of excitement. Overweighted, the long, low boat grounded on the beach.

That was pretty much what Simpson wanted; he was experienced enough to know how to get a scow off shore, and he needed the ferryman's craft for his crossing. In an instant his companions were in the water at its two sides, pushing, pulling, using hand spikes, as he gave commands with his humorous gusto. Evening was advancing; despatch was necessary. The boat was all but clear. Unhappily, however, it had become a target for artillerists on the walls of Quebec;

Robert Dixon stood on the vessel between a cart and its[31] gunwale.

The sound of the first fire was heard. A twelve-pound ball came hurtling, struck with full velocity the nob of a wheel, glanced downward, caught below the knee and tore off the lower leg of the gallant rifleman and forager out of Hanover Township. The man fell, crying, "Oh, Michael, I am gone."[32]

Immediately the purpose of the raid was forgotten and forgone. A shout of jubilation came from the battlements. The scow was let stick. Simpson leaped upon it, gathered his wounded friend into his arms, raised him with his comrades' help, bore him away first to a windmill close at hand, then back to the guard house. More firing and shouting accompanied the withdrawal, mission unaccomplished and abandoned. In the hour of jeopardy not orders but love for a fellow in arms prevailed among the lads of Matthew Smith's company.

Yet, if there was no proper military procedure from a man prescribed a duty by his commander, there was etiquette and spirit in what followed.

A litter was found to carry Dixon away from the camp to the farm of an Englishman whose hospitality, if possibly under duress, was graciously tendered to the bleeding sergeant. In that shelter, to save the man's life a rough amputation was resorted to. The mistress of the house, concerned for the suffering soldier, in the morning set a bowl of tea at his bedside. The feverish casualty, into whose tortured body now had come the pains of tetanus, looked up tense and obstinate. His hand made a feeble gesture of dissent. With a firm quietness his lips murmured, "Tea, madam, is the ruin of my country."[33]

Death came an hour later, with Michael Simpson at the side of his friend, sympathetic to the last recorded remark of Robert Dixon, farmer out of Lancaster County, who like eight other men of Hanover Township had subscribed on June 4, 1774, to resolves which placed their cause with Heaven and their rifles. A year-and-a-half had passed. The brother-in-law of James Gibson, compatriot of the Paxton Boys with Matthew Smith at Philadelphia in 1764, cousin of the distinguished lawyer, grammarian, and loyalist Lindley Murray, himself gentlemen by birth and code, died[34] as might have a Scot at Flodden or an Orangeman in the Battle of the Boyne. His fellows buried him with the best military dignities they could, and afterward boasted his mettle.

Even today Dixon can be thought of almost as a symbol: in his memory a half-impudence seems to vie with a half-impatience, much as in General Richard Montgomery's blood the spectacular competed with the gallant and generous. More than that, the sergeant's pattern of conduct related to the very essence of the campaign for Quebec.

Dixon was certainly not the high-light of that paradoxical enterprise. But all the subsequent trend of the action around the Canadian citadel city was to show the same signs of futility. On November 18, the day after the rifleman's death, Arnold initiated a withdrawal along the north bank; and his men, as they moved southeastwards, suspected they were retreating. Files were slovenly; the rigors of winter opposed; all that cheered were vistas of cultivated acres and neat, handsomely situated farmhouses. At Points aux Trembles,[35] twenty miles upstream, the detachment waited for twelve days, torn between the discomforts of scant clothing and the delights of peasant larders stocked well in beef. On December 1 General Montgomery arrived.[36]

Tall and handsome, though of countenance pock-marked, this hero from victories at Chamblee, St. Johns, and Montreal, made in response to his welcome an "energetic and elegant speech."[37] His praise of the men who had reached Quebec before him, through the wilderness to that rendezvous, was inspiriting. From freezing bodies huzzas of approval resounded. New life seemed to flow into Arnold's corps. Supplies, fortunately, had been brought by Montgomery from his conquests.

On the next day, reinforced by Montgomery's troops, the riflemen retraced their route to Quebec.[38] New positions were taken in the following week, new quarters were occupied, new farmhouses furnished billets and commissary's stores. By December 15 stations of soldiery were set, generally encircling the city: to the west of St. Roque and on approaches to the lower town southwest of Cape Diamond; west and north of St. John's Gate and before the other gates of the upper town; across the St. Charles, near its point of emptying into the St. Lawrence at the northeast; at the southeastern tip of the Isle d'Orleans, downstream and midway in that broad river. Riflemen had been acquiring warmer clothing, gloves, and new moccasins. Generally all were feeding well and expecting an early military success.

High councils on strategy were meeting. Confidence kept rising. Emulation entered. There were differences of opinion, some caustic exchanges in debate. Toward the end of the month tactics were agreed upon; details of action were outlined to the clear understanding of the members of Arnold's, Montgomery's, and Morgan's staffs. All plans made, and to appearance wholly concerted and matured, battle was launched early on the morning of December 31.[39]

Arnold suited his action to strategy already agreed on and moved his forces through St. Roque. Assault, for him to the west and for Montgomery to the south below Cape Diamond, he expected to be made easier by the ruse of an attack before St. John's Gate.

But the American design of drawing the main force of the garrison to a point where only a feint should be practiced, while real power was elsewhere asserted, fared evilly. Stern defense from a battery held the Colonel's men for an hour; and, when it had been taken, it was only after their commander had been grievously shot in the leg and had to be borne from the field. Then news came to Arnold that Montgomery had failed at Cape Diamond. Out of combat himself, the wounded Benedict Arnold learned little of comfort indeed, on the last day of 1775 and the first of 1776.

The brilliant, beloved, and audacious Montgomery had struck too early—although Arnold did not admit *that* in his letters to General David Wooster at Montreal. Montgomery had fallen with his two aides-de-camp, Cheesaman and MacPherson, at his side.[40] All three heroes were dead. Colonel Campbell, Montgomery's adjutant, after the loss of a number of prisoners, among them John Joseph Henry of Matthew Smith's company, had retreated from the second palisade beneath the cliffs with fractions of his general's battalion.[41] Arnold's own force, after gaining the battery which they first attacked and a second barrier nearer the city, had most of them been cut off by a sally of the enemy from the Palace-Gate. Montgomery's premature attack and spectacular failure had not only alerted the garrison but preceded defeat for attacks false or true around the entire circuit of the citadel. Quebec had not been taken. Beleaguering its walls at various distances from them, from the Island of Orleans to St. Roque, was a baffled army of Americans.

For not Arnold alone, but for the rank and file of his forces, it was mid-winter. Daniel Morgan and many another Scotch-Irishman had ventured too far within the open gates of a town, been tricked, resisted, and beaten within the walls. Forty officers and men of his Virginia company had struggled through the long march by the Kennebec, the Dead River, and the Chaudiere to wind up in ironic consummation. Many other men from William Hendricks' and Matthew Smith's companies, both by race and in the field compatriots, were in prison in Quebec to whisper when they met of how Captain Hendricks had fallen, of how Archibald Steele's bleeding hand looked when he was borne back out of action at the palisades, to wonder what had happened to Humphreys of Morgan's, or Dick Steele of Smith's. Sergeant Thomas Boyd and John Joseph Henry wished they could know where their own captain was. And how had Michael Simpson borne himself on the Isle d'Orleans?

The scion of the Boyds of Derry and the son of William Henry, gunsmith of Lancaster, were the guests perforce of General Sir Guy Carleton. In months of imprisonment they would both develop cordial esteem for that military host and attempt escape from his subordinate's custody. For his allowance of burial with military honors and decent interment to Montgomery, Cheeseman, MacPherson, Humphreys, and Hendricks,[42] they would more than respect the deference of the commander to the memory of a defeated foe, who in the happier days of an earlier war had been friend and companion-in-arms. Yet, although they admired the code of *noblesse oblige* in others, they saw no reason for not pushing plots to escape. Failing in the effort at these, they experienced keen disappointment and chagrin. Moreover, despite Carleton's kindliness to prisoners they knew much of want when provisions for their captors had become short enough, too.

Moreover, both Boyd and Henry and others of their fellows experienced another form of embarrassment during their months of confinement before exchange and release of prisoners came in the summer of 1776. They beheld many of their own recent companions-in-arms drawn away or lured away from them "to enlist in the King's service."[43] They thought the more charitably of these because, after all, they had not been born in Lancaster County townships, but overseas in Scotland or Ireland.

Historians, rather than they, might recall that Quebec was not the first occasion when defeated Scots had been transformed into the best fighting men of a British monarch. The Cameronians after the Battle of Killiekrankie and the Black Watch after Colloden Moor, had Thomas Boyd and Johnny Henry thought of it, might have been examples to them of the way men of their breed sometimes behaved.

It is possible, of course, that the lad from Lancaster, recalling how the impetuous leap of Henry McAnally upon it had led to the capsizing of Lieutenant Simpson's boat on the Dead River, did not think of that Irishman as acting unnaturally when he joined the redcoats of George III.[44]

CHAPTER 13

FIRST MONTHS OF LIBERTY

THE FINE FERVOR for liberty which dominated the frontier counties of Pennsylvania in the late spring of 1774, which in the summer of 1775 sent eight companies of riflemen to join Washington in New England, and which in the autumn sent two of them, by the way of the Kennebec into Canada—lasted warmly enough into the summer of 1776 and the anticlimactic autumn which followed. Patriotism continued to stir, although glory tended to show herself far more elusive than brilliant. Failure had come to the men of Paxton, Derry, and Hanover who had marched to Quebec. Many were in prison. Others, after months of harassment by privation, hunger, smallpox, British and Indian attack, were withdrawing with General David Wooster and Colonel Benedict Arnold back into New York State by way of Lake Champlain; in the cup of their bitterness were thoughts of their gallant leader General William Thompson from Carlisle, captured by the enemy at Three Rivers. Death had taken many another of lesser military rank.

But on July 4, 1776, while members of the Continental Congress were affixing their signatures to the Declaration of Independence in Philadelphia, Associators from the entire new Commonwealth of Pennsylvania had gathered into an all important convention of their own at Lancaster.[1] Articles of Association had been passed by the Committee of Safety on August 19, 1775.[2] The Committee of Conference on June 25, 1776, had drawn up an address of exhortation to welcome the patriot soldiery of Pennsylvania when they should arrive for their convention at the county seat.[3] Eloquent words greeted the town's guests from the city and Liberties of Philadelphia, from Philadelphia, Bucks, Chester, Lancaster, York, Berks, Cumberland, Northampton, Northumberland, and Westmoreland Counties.[4] Eleven battalions from Lancaster County, more than from any other, were represented.[5] Captains Joseph Sherer and James Murray were on hand for the Fourth

Battalion,[6] whose commander back at home was Colonel James Burd of Paxton; Colonel Timothy Green and a private, Joseph Barnett's son William,[7] were on hand with two other authorized delegates representing the Eleventh, constituted in Hanover Township. From Cumberland had come Captain John Steel,[8] Carlisle Minister of the Gospel, a man acquainted with action and warfare from the days of the Battle of Kittanning, a representative for the First Battalion of that county. With him were officers and privates from the Second, Third, Fourth, and Fifth, a goodly array of men, all bearing Scotch-Irish names—from Lieutenant-Colonel Frederick Watts and Captain Andrew McFarlane to Privates William Sterrett and James Read.[9] From the Battalion of Colonel Samuel Hunter of Northumberland came Captain Christian Gillespie and Lieutenant George Calhoun.[10] Representing Colonel William Plunkett's and the Second Battalion of the same county was Major John Brady,[11] veteran of Bouquet's expedition in 1763, now occupant of a stockaded house at Muncy on the Susquehanna, always ready to give good account of himself and destined to a less blotted fame among the Associators of 1776 than that of his superior officer. Representing the Battalion of Colonel James Potter, who like Captain Steel of Carlisle had served with Colonel John Armstrong at Kittanning, came Lieutenant Colonel Robert Moody, Esquire; Captain William Gray; Privates James McClenaghan and Benjamin Sterrett.[12] With Colonel Benjamin Weiser, son of the famous old Indian interpreter and treaty-maker Conrad Weiser, only man of German breed to command in Northumberland County, came his Scotch-Irish second, Lieutenant Samuel Maclay,[13] whose sires had done good service for King William in the Battle of the Boyne.

Less distant from their homesteads as they met with the Convention were Lieutenant Colonel Alexander Lowrey and Major James Cunningham of the Sixth Battalion of Lancaster County,[14] the one now become a Donegal esquire after years of eminence as a trader belonging to a family of notable Indian traders, the other a Lancaster townsman already acquainted after a fashion with resolution by the interruption of breakfast with Colonel John Armstrong on a January morning eight years earlier when he watched a cohort of backwoodsmen bear away from the Carlisle jail to freedom a man whose only offence in 1768 was that he murdered a dozen or so of Indians.

Whether farmers from the rich fields about Lancaster City itself, merchants of that town, clerics and burghers of Carlisle, or river gentry and frontiersmen from Paxton, Sunbury, and Muncy, few of the delegates needed to be adjured in the business of the Convention—or by the report of its Committee of Conference.

All would have said, without prompting, that they knew the honor of the Colony was at stake. Any reminder of the glory which they had won "by former exertions of strength and virtue"[15] was a bit superfluous. Rather more they believed that their houses and fields, the legacies of their ancestors and the dear-bought fruits of their own industry urged them to the field. They had no doubt that their aged fathers and mothers, their wives and their children looked to them for aid and hope of salvation, for championship by the instrumentality of their weapons. Having wrestled for the Province of Pennsylvania in the wilderness, they had no difficulty in remembering its name.

Hardly, indeed, did they require prompting from hearing the Declaration of Independence read aloud to them before their temporary dispersal to their homes a few days later. Arming themselves for a cause was familiar to the men of Colonel James Burd's battalion. When Matthew Smith had gone off to Massachusetts and Canada in 1775, eight captains had already mustered companies to serve under the former commander at Fort Augusta in French and Indian War days.[16] When the Declaration had been signed and its glowing sentiments had been disseminated far and wide, men out of every township in Lancaster County, and men from other Susquehanna River counties from York to Northumberland were ready to respond to the summons of the new Congress of the United States.

Away they marched for the Jerseys from July, 1776, to and throughout the autumn.[17] They knew that at Lancaster their Associator representatives had elected Daniel Roberdeau and James Ewing as the first two brigadier generals of Pennsylvania;[18] and their motion was forward, not now reckoning the event. Captain James Cowden's, Captain James Murray's, and Captain Richard Manning's companies had been ready since March 13[19] and Captain Joseph Sherer's since March 25;[20] Jacob Fridley's was ready in May;[21] William Bell's but a little later;[22] John Reed's, made up of men from the Powell's Creek segment of upper Paxton Township on the Susquehanna, was as early as any in readiness.[23]

Nor was the score different for Timothy Green's Battalion. Thomas Koppenheffer's, Richard McQuown's, and William Brown's companies had turned Jersey-wards in August;[24] Captain James Rogers' had been stirring since June;[25] a second Captain John Reed's men were away on July 24.[26] Furthermore, similar promptitude accredited Captain Robert McCallen's company,[27] speeding from Derry Township in Colonel

Bertram Galbraith's Battalion; and Captain John Marshall with a company of men he had raised as early as March 7 in Hanover Township was serving with them and his affable and literary sergeant, James McMichael, in the Pennsylvania Rifle Regiment under Colonel Samuel Miles and Lieutenant-Colonel Daniel Brodhead.[28] Officers and men, they were most of them enlisted for a six months' service and sanguine of a cause to be won for Pennsylvania by making the State of New Jersey, the Delaware River, Philadelphia, and the Delaware Bay safe from the British even if they should have to go with Washington and their own generals as far as New York and New England to do it.

So some marched along overland roads which Matthew Smith and William Hendricks had followed in 1775; others across Lancaster and Chester County to be conveyed by water up the Delaware River, past Philadelphia and on to Bordentown in New Jersey, with destination at Amboy and across New York Bay or the Hudson by whatever port of embarkation or ferry was most relevant and available.

Exactly how particular companies marched is today undiscoverable. Only an occasional soldier's journal blazes the trail for an historian's inquiry. But, luckily, Sergeant (afterwards to be recorded as Lieutenant) McMichael set down in his diary[29] the route of the company of John Marshall. The men of that Hanover Captain formed their ranks at the Cross Roads, Drumore Township, Lancaster County on May 27 and began their march at "3 o'clock P.M."[30], passed through Fagg's Manor the next day, after McMichael had spent the first night in his life in which he "was denied a bed";[31] and at 2:00 P.M. on the 29th, were in Chester, whence they were immediately countermanded back to Prospect Hill, near Marcus Hook. There they encamped that night in tents, which was, said the diarist, "to me very disagreeable."[32] But his spirits lifted on the morrow when the company joined Colonel Samuel Miles's Pennsylvania Rifle Regiment,[33] paraded on orders, went through their maneuvres and evolutions, and won great applause.

After that, the sergeant omitted a day before entering on June 2 his surprise at being awakened on the Sabbath by "the noise of drums and fifes beating the Reveille."[34] Also he deplored in writing that on that date "the soldiers seemed very much intoxicated."[35] What Miles's regiment did in the next eleven days he did not put down, but June 13 brought news warranted to break monotony. An express arrived with word that a number of Tories were mustering at Lewestown, and Captain Marshall's men made ready with others to speed south and disperse the enemy, which they meant "to do at the hazard of our lives."[36]

Ripening of experience but no great participation in a campaign came out of that fond resolution. They marched to Wilmington, only to be ordered back to Prospect Hill on June 14. At noon on the 15th they filed onto vessels at Marcus Hook, were transported by the succeeding dawn to Port Penn, then were disembarked to encamp inland and on the 17th proceeded on foot to Dover. Fatigued at the end of that march, they were pressed on in the two following days to Lewes. There they paused for a week without incident to themselves. They learned that a British man-of-war, the *Roebuck*, besides the *Liverpool* and three tenders, had come into the Day,[37] but took no action because of that information. More satisfying was it to be told on the 27th that the Tories, having learned of the presence of the riflemen outside the Town, had evacuated it; and on the 28th James McMichael had the pleasure of recording that scouting parties had been sent out, had captured the officers of the Tories, sworn them to be true to Congress, and dismissed them. All that, indeed, was but a modest beginning for the men of Hanover, whose neighbors and townsmen two years earlier had resolved to trust Heaven and their rifles.

Unscarred by battle, Colonel Samuel Miles's battalion re-embarked for Marcus Hook on June 29; landed there in the morning of July 1; and three days later marched through Chester and Derby, over the Schuylkill and into Philadelphia. In that city they arrived at two o'clock on the first Independence Day of the United States of America. Yet Captain Marshall's sergeant inserted no comment on the Declaration in his journal—resolutions had become an old story to Lancaster County men; one more could be taken in stride. More worthy of notice in a diary was the record of disembarkation from Stamper's Wharf on the afternoon of July 6. Not Philadelphia, but movement forward to Bordentown and New Jersey interested McMichael.

At sunrise on the 7th they landed in the upstream village; and at 2:00 P.M. they were marching again, now in the Jerseys. Near to Allentown an officer's gun went off accidentally and shot a common soldier. No further point for dismay or for approval met them in the next few days. They passed through Cranberry one noon and reached Brunswick at dusk—to be no more impressed by that town, apparently, than they had been by Philadelphia. Perth Amboy, where they arrived on July 11, was more inspiriting. The inhabitants seemed friendly to the cause of America and the riflemen; across Raritan Bay on Staten Island, it was rumored, enemy were stationed. In the air was promise.

But nothing happened for six more days. Reveille on the 17th alerted them for a march to Elizabethtown, where it was said the

British were making landings. Arrival showed that they had been falsely alarmed. Men and officers grumbled in chagrin. To hearten themselves a number of them entertained the thought of crossing the water that night "to visit the troops of General Howe"[38] on Staten. A hurricane rose and tempered their rash ambition; and in the morning they were relieved to know that they had not been cut off, as they would surely have been had they indulged their whim.

On the 18th they shuttled back to Perth Amboy; became a part of General Hugh Mercer's brigade in the Continental Line, although they had enlisted for the defense of Pennsylvania; and repined not at that change. On July 23 they were aware that one thousand other militiamen from their home State had arrived to become like them a part of General Washington's army. Confidence prevailed. A rifleman, shot by an enemy on a boat for Staten Island, was an affront rather than a matter of moment; on the next day another boat, deserted by the enemy after being hailed by American sentries, occasioned no excitement; on July 25 cannonade between an American battery at Amboy and a British battery at Billop's Point on Staten Island, as a schooner passed down the river refusing to salute, caused more furore—and rejoicing that the silent vessel, if it had to get off, got off much damaged. Only when July, 1776, turned into August, did it seem that crisis was at hand or that scales hung in the balance.

The new month became charged with expectancy. Emotion and the minor play of tactics alternated. Men listened with interest to orders, or followed with zest the details of employment. On the 3rd McMichael was busied with a detail of 120 men assembling all the small craft from Amboy to Red Boot Creek. On the 9th Colonel Miles had a letter from Washington "requesting"[39] the riflemen to come to Headquarters in New York; and John Marshall's Pennsylvanians agreed *"nemine contra dicente"*[40] to march on the next day. No honorable patriot dissenting, the regiment proceeded to Elizabethtown, encamped on the Plains, and on the 11th after general reveille at sun-up, paraded, marched through Newark, boarded ferries at Passaic, Hackensack, and Paulus Hook. At four o'clock they were in the city, on their way to encampment at Pleasant Hill, one mile out; and after joining Lord Stirling's brigade of Pennsylvanians, Virginians, and Marylanders there, they beheld down the river a formidable English Fleet of 100 sail maneuvering along Staten Island.

But neither that nor information on August 12 that the large reinforcements were swelling the ranks of the enemy and so presaging sudden attack caused the riflemen any concern. Rather they waited "impatiently" for British assault of the town, said McMichael, "as we only act in our own defense."[41] Indeed, they received the experiences of the next two weeks with considerable sang-froid.

General Washington, expecting attack, ordered all women, children, and infirm people to be evacuated from the city until after the prospective engagement. Two men-of-war with their tenders on the river were given hot fire from American shore batteries. The enemy struck their tents as if readying for movement on the 19th. The American troops were inspected that day for arms and ammunition, paraded, received orders to rest on their arms all night, and went into bivouac pleased to learn that the man-of-war *Phoenix* had been seriously hit by the battery-fire on the 18th. A severe storm of thunder and lightning on August 21 killed three officers in the detachment encamped next to Captain Marshall's men. On the day following, that company knew that the British had landed on Long Island; were ordered to parade; then, having seen the rest of the First Battalion together with their musketry and the Delaware Blues embarking to meet the foe, accepted modified orders for themselves to return to their tents. That fact did not disturb them, for with the command came the instruction that they should be ready to follow at a moment's notice.

Spirits undampened, they received the anticipated orders two days later; and on August 24 marched from Pleasant Hill, crossed by St. George's Ferry, and joined their brigade.

Welcome came from not only their companions-in-arms. A cannonade from small arms greeted them; there was hard rain in the night as they lay tentless in the woods amid a constant firing of sentries. At dawn there was bruit of an immediate attack. They formed ranks and marched to meet the enemy. None appeared, and they returned to their camp in the woods. On the 26th a scouting party of 120 men, properly officered, found no discoverable enemy lurking.

But it was on Tuesday, August 27, 1776, that the Battle of Long Island was lost by Washington's army. General Sir William Howe, who historians tell us played no long game with constancy and persevering effect, for the time being had been playing skillfully and had taken every advantage of the British Fleet and his own superior ground forces. Military analysts later have told the full story of his strategy.

Contemporaneously James McMichael could only narrate the tale of the day as it affected his own company and regiment in the American army. His description of the day's events, and of the two days which succeeded, offers as good an account as may be had of what happened to Lancaster County and Susquehanna River riflemen and

Associators in an action which in its whole import will always embarrass Americans. Yet none need be ashamed of the share which Scotch-Irishmen had in the defeat:

August 27—At sunrise we were ordered to march easterly from near Flatbush a few miles, when we discovered the enemy coming against us with 5,000 foot and 500 horse. We numbered just 400. We at first thought it prudent to retire to a neighboring thicket, where we formed and gave battle. Here my right hand man fell, shot through the head. We were attacked by the enemy's left wing, while their right endeavoured to surround us. Their superior numbers forced us to retire for a short distance, when we again formed and fought with fortitude until we were nearly surrounded.

Having by this time lost a great number of men, we were again forced to retreat, when we found that the enemy had got between us and the fort. Then despairing of making good our retreat we resolved to die rather than be taken prisoners, and thus we were drove from place to place 'till 3 o'clock P.M., when we agreed to attempt crossing the mill-pond, that being the only way left for our escape. Here numbers were drowned, but it was the will of Providence that I should escape, and at half past three, we reached the lines, being much fatigued.

The enemy advanced rapidly and endeavoured to force our lines, but were repulsed with considerable loss. They afterwards marched towards the Narrows, where they found our First Battalion and the Delaware Blues under command of Colonel Hazlet. These battalions were chiefly cut off, we were ordered to cover their retreat, which exposed us in open field to a heavy fire from the enemy 'till evening—the remainder of our troops brought us 23 prisoners. At dark we were relieved and ordered to St. George's Ferry to take refreshments. Thus happened the memorable action on Long Island, where the enemy attacked and defeated Lord Stirling's brigade, consisting of the following regiments: Colonels Miles, Atlee, Smallwood, and Hazlet. Major General Sullivan, Brigadier General Lord Stirling were taken prisoners, also Colonels Miles and Atlee; Lieutenant Colonel Piper—all of our regiment, also 19 commissioned officers, 23 sergeants, and 310 rank and file.

My preservation I only attribute to the indulgent Providence of God, for tho' the bullets went around me in every direction, yet I received not a wound.[42]

All the events and all the implications of the Battle of Long Island were not presented, of course, by James McMichael. The exact share which the Scotch-Irish soldiery of inland Pennsylvania had in that action remains today about as immeasureable as it was in August, 1776.

To an extent the ageless saying about the Gaels held true of them. "They went forth to battle," and they came perilously near to fulfilling the second prophetic part of the proverb: "and they always fell."[43]

They gave of themselves whole-heartedly, in nothing shrinking from the odds of the contest. But certain it is that they won no lasting celebrity for the part which they performed during the first two months of national independence. Besides McMichael's witness, little survives in documents to indicate just how the Associators and militia of the Scotch-Irish counties of Pennsylvania were distributed or where on Long Island they were stationed: also what survives is somewhat clouded.

What best we know of their participation comes from the hindsight truncated journals of two of their battalion commanders, Colonel Samuel Miles of Philadelphia and Colonel Samuel J. Atlee of Lancaster.[44] Miles blamed his superior, General John Sullivan, for having assigned him a position directly in front of the village of Flatbush, and then, despite relays of information from his subordinate on British approaches, neglecting to provide him with support on his left. From that neglect sprang several evil consequences; and on maneuvering his battalion, the Pennsylvania officer had presently the chagrin of discovering himself and his men cut off from the lines of General Sullivan and Lord Stirling by the main British army in full march.

Realizing their predicament, after a conference with his staff he made the hardest of three choices, and failed of success in it. A few of his men cut through the British to safety; 159 of them were taken prisoner; he himself and several devoted companions concealed themselves for a time in woods and brush. Their hope to elude captors at nightfall was disappointed when a party of Hessians found and picked them up in midafternoon.[45]

Colonel Atlee experienced fortune equally ill. The great landing of General Grant's British in thousands at Gravesend Cove on the southwest caught Lord Stirling suddenly on the 27th. That titled nobleman and Continental general ordered the man from Lancaster to take a position of defense in marshy ground at the foot of the heights which he first sought to hold. When the ebb and flow of the day of battle in that quarter had ended and Stirling had withdrawn, Colonel Atlee and forty of his men, ammunition spent and retreat cut off, surrendered.

In the journal in which after two years' waiting to be exchanged he set down his discomfiture, he wrote: "The World may judge my surprise when, coming to the ground where our Brigade had been drawn up to find they had gone off without my receiving the least intelligence or orders what to do."[46]

It might have been more relevant for him to say that William

Alexander, Lord Stirling, and General John Sullivan had learned on the unhappy day that out-maneuvered and defeated officers are not always in a position to issue instructions. And how George Washington rescued the broken remains of their forces from Long Island is, after all, part of a more famous man's story.

In the sequence of history Sullivan was exchanged early for the British General Richard Prescott, and, three months later, was ready to supersede Charles Lee in command of his division of troops, participate in heroic actions of Washington at Trenton and Princeton, and earn an undying name for himself in the story of the year 1779 in the War for Independence. Lord Stirling was as early exchanged, entrusted to new commands by Washington, aided in the retreat from New York and New Jersey, protected the rear guard at Princeton and Trenton as the army retired from New Jersey into Pennsylvania, and significantly helped keep its position west of the Delaware secure until its leaders ventured to strike again with their forces. And he himself eventually won notable fame for help in a victory.

Colonel Atlee's subordinate, the prisoner Major Edward Burd, was received with courtesies among British officers, "used with great civility by General Grant," and "admitted to his parole"[47] within a week of his capture. On September 3, he could write from Long Island to his brother-in-law Jasper Yeates appealing for funds. By December 12 he was in Philadelphia, exchanged—as he put it in a letter to his father at Tinian, as "the first Major"—and, in his epistle, obviously not pleased that General Washington "was surprised to see"[48] him. In fact, he wrote to James Burd : "However, he [Washington] was so polite as to tell me, from the character I bore he was satisfied with my being the person, though he did not like the mode, especially as I was in a standing regiment."[49] Nor did the young Major know "What he could mean by that, as the time of our regiment will expire by the first of June next, and I am sure the men will not stay a day longer."[50] Like his sire, distinguished veteran of the Provincial Wars of Pennsylvania and latterly Colonel of the Fourth Battalion of Lancaster County, after December, 1776, Edward Burd was wholly out of military service. But that somewhat negative qualification would not debar him from subsequent eminence as a Philadelphia attorney, first cousin to Peggy Shippen, and nephew to that lady's father, Edward Shippen, who later became Chief Justice in the Pennsylvania Supreme Court.

If, however, two generals and subaltern Major Burd were to win no undying honor from the Battle of Long Island, that is not to say that back-county Scotch-Irish Pennsylvania militiamen deserved no credit for their part in that chequered engagement. Atlee's men had rallied to his side after a demoralizing break brought into their ranks by the panic of two Delaware companies; had recovered their position with him; and a second time had repelled the foe under heavy fire, before the final exhaustion of their supplies. Miles's men had been farther in advance in Washington's army than any other company except Samuel Wyllys' Continentals.[51] Both groups had been given untenable and futile positions, while greater armies formed into a wedge and left them at the base of an otherwise empty triangle. When they went forth to battle, they did so without the guarding control of other tacticians.

Yet it was only an occasional person like McMichael—who got undrowned through his mill-pond and on to Brooklyn by the Providence of God[52]—who could write of them without apology.

Luckily, too, for the American cause, a greater man than that young Hanover gentleman took advantage of the three bitter wet days which followed August 27 of 1776. General Washington, by dint of Howe's failure to consummate his victory by immediate renewal of arms and by the miracle of his own quiet poise during adversity, got the shattered divisions of his army back across the East River into New York. General Putnam, who had designed the great crescent of the American army for a defence on Long Island, which had failed, helped his commander in swift, early September measures either to hold the town on Manhattan Island or safely retreat from it. Generally, apart from the fortifications at the Battery and on the two sides of the city, further movement of the American forces was northwards.

Such concentrations of the companies of the Pennsylvania Flying Camp as were made led them to Fort Washington overlooking the Hudson River on the west, to King's Bridge beyond the Harlem River and Harlem Heights, on to Morrisania and points on the east of the Hudson in West Chester County. On October 9 General James Potter, from Northumberland County, Pennsylvania, and Colonel Edward Hand of Lancaster, in conference at Delancey's Mills,[53] were contemplating the organization of battalions for a march to Ticonderoga. Hand had got together 700 of the Scotch-Irish militia rescued from Long Island, and was seeking to enlist them for a new mission despite General Ewing's reminder that the expiration of the term of their six months' enlistment for the Flying Camp was still several months off.[54] Potter busily directed a letter to the Committee of Safety upon the subject, told of the eagerness of the men for the new arrangement, and added—as if to gainsay his declaration—a picture of sick and shelterless men in Pennsylvania battalions, "lying on the bare earth without boards, without blankets, and no conveniency of making fires,"[55] and surgeons wholly unprovided with medicines to relieve them. Then a heavy cannonading to the southwest interrupted the clerk as he was putting the officer's words down; and Potter, Hand, and John Morris, Jun'r, mounted posthaste to ride to King's Bridge.[56] They stopped there to close the letter with a postscript which told they had arrived in time to see the last of four tenders following three British frigates as, unharmed by American battery fire, they passed up the Hudson.[57] Indeed, the fact was that Pennsylvanians were needed more for stay-ing action near at hand in mid-October than for the remote possibility of saving Ticonderoga. An American army which could not restrain the movements of enemy men-of-war on its chief river had already wisely been abandoning the city of New York. Washington aided by Putnam—and Putnam aided by a lucky suggestion of young Aaron Burr— had got his main force upwards to Fort Washington and be-yond, after rescuing it a month earlier from entrapment by a sudden British landing in strength at Kips Bay on the east side of the town, and saving it by its own gallantry a day later on Harlem heights.

Now Fort Washington, slightly to the northwest of that last point, must be held—if possible, permanently, if not permanently, at least until the Commander-in-Chief could remarshal his strength for control of the Hudson higher up, preserve communications with New En-gland, and prevent a south-north division of the new United States. Deep into November, General Washington adhered to the purpose of holding it as well as Fort Lee on the opposite shore. He watched Howe and chose new positions for his own divisions. The fortunes of war fluctuated. The Battle of White Plains, on October 28, was in effect a draw. General Charles Lee, when he was instructed to bring his men from Fort Lee to the east of the Hudson, disobeyed and kept them where they were. General Nathaniel Greene when he was in-structed on discretion to remove his 2,000 men to Fort Lee on the west bank, acted with indecision. Congress had given positive orders that the North River be held.

On November 16 the British stormed and reduced the ill-fated re-doubt which bore the name of the General of the American Army. Among its defenders at the last were three companies of men from Lancaster County, officered by three Scotch-Irish captains.[58] No nar-rative survives today to tell us how they behaved on the occasion. Only three factual inventories of material losses of these remain in the archives of the Commonwealth of Pennsylvania to avouch for their participation in the engagement.

The Colonel of the Fourth Battalion was back at his home "Tinian." His confirmation could be added only to subordinates' testimony. But interesting is the witness of Captains John Reed, James Murray, and James Cowden, officers of the depleted Flying Camp faraway from their homes in Susquehanna townships when they fought—lost, or were aware of their men's loss of guns, pouches and powder horns, blankets, and knapsacks.[59] Their reports give strange insight into how riflemen from the frontier gathered their weapons and equipment together.

They had been supplied, not by Congress, but by their neighbors and themselves. James Burd had lent rifles to three men of Captain Cowden's company. Robert Elder, who would succeed James Burd next year as commander of the Battalion, had lent—and indirectly lost—another. A dozen other men from Paxton Township had furnished guns which could not be brought back from Fort Washington.[60] Blankets gathered from Robert Chambers and Thomas Sturgeon for John Reed's men had fallen into the enemy's hands; and Reed entered into his companies' expense for them an item of £4.[61] The generosity of still other patriot benefactors netted an even bigger claim for the same sort of loss by Cowden, through whose company's service one John Rutherford now lacked all four of gun, powder horns, blankets, and knapsacks.[62] Moreover, similar scores held for Captain Murray's men, whose loss in muskets and rifles was in cost heaviest of all.[63]

If the men of Colonel Miles on Long Island had been without bayonets when the British charged on them, and if at the end of a day's fighting Colonel Atlee's circle of defenders found all their ammunition gone, it was as true that for a month before and another month after the fall of Fort Washington, the Scotch-Irish militiamen from Paxton, the Paxton Narrows, and the neighborhood of Reed's Ferry at Fort Halifax in the Susquehanna were in many an unfortunate predicament. From mid-October they had to face for two months the reforming of ranks, companies, battalions, and regiments; the studied and cautious retreats of Washington and his generals; the long marches, the ferryings, the brief encampments, the resumed marches by which a reduced, cold, hungry, and often uncomprehending army were got up the Hudson to Peekskill and across the river, down the west side through treacherous and untenable positions, from New York State into New Jersey, and from New Jersey across the Delaware into Pennsylvania.[64]

Various experiences befell them. At White Plains, mistaking each other for the British enemy, a party of the battalion to which Mc-Michael belonged and a company of Delaware Blues exchanged fire which resulted tragically in the death of six Pennsylvania riflemen and nine of their friends, the Blues.[65] To offset the discouraging effect of that error, odd captures of one British regular and 34 Tories on one day and 13 Waldecks and 3 regulars on another were not full comfort.[66] The withdrawal from White Plains on October 28 led to encampment that night on a hill without baggage and cooking utensils, to a bivouac on November 1 without tents in the severe frost and cold. From North Castle they proceeded on November 8 through Philips', Van Cortlandt's, the Livingston's Manors to Peekskill. On the next day they sailed five miles down the river to Lamb's Landing on the west shore and marched southwards five miles. Eight more days, with march and change of quarters on each, made the companies and battalions from the Susquehanna River counties more than deserving of their name, the Pennsylvania Flying Camp. Through Haverstraw to Clarkstown, to Tappan, Hackensack, Newark, Elizabethtown, Beamantown (where on November 16 they could hear the cannonading at Fort Washington), to New Brunswick, they sped.[67]

Arriving there at 2 P.M. on November 17, they took freely, as McMichael's diary confessed, to spiritous liquors; and their four days' sojourn was, as a result, given color by the so-called "Barrel Fever, which differs in its effects from any other fever—its concomitants were black eyes and bloody noses."[68] After the fracas came, on the 21st, news of the American evacuation of Fort Lee and of a landing of 16,000 British at Dobb's Ferry above that redoubt on the Hudson;[69] and, as in the following days sobering up ensued, the riflemen of Pennsylvania comprehended again their situation. It became unwise to try holding Newark first, then New Brunswick.[70]

A heavy cannonading between 1 and 2 o'clock on December 1 hastened their departure from New Brunswick. Nightfall found them encamping near Kingston. The next morning took them into quarters at Princeton, where five days' pause satisfied McMichael that the town was "chiefly inhabited by Tories."[71] Breath, however, the Pennsylvania Scotch-Irishmen could take; and on the appearance of the British on December 7 they were in condition to evacuate the town of the College of New Jersey and march to Trenton. There they took quarters from 10 P.M. until 4 A.M. of the next morning. At that early hour they paraded, and at dawn on December 8 began crossing the Ferry into Pennsylvania.[72]

On that day they greeted the Hessians' arrival at 4 P.M. at Trenton with salvos from an eighteen-pounder on the west shore of the Delaware, and enjoyed seeing the Germans dispersing. But the exhilaration of that pleasure was not the immediate preliminary to comfort. Their first night back in the State where their Independence had been declared five months earlier was spent in the woods without either tents or blankets.[73] Moreover, on the next day the riflemen of the Flying Camp were marched on to Thompson's Mill near Coryell's Ferry, which as modern cartographers would explain to us is a distance of seventeen miles. There they began a sixteen days'[74] encampment on a forest bank overlooking the river, in a terrain then scarce more than a wilderness.

CHAPTER 14

OUT FROM A SETBACK

To GEORGE WASHINGTON rather than to Pennsylvania or to Pennsylvanians belong such distinctions of fame as emerge from the annals of the United States and Americans during the last week of December, 1776, and the first few days of January, 1777. The military victories of Trenton on December 26 and of Princeton on January 3 accredit the Commander of the Army rather than either any other general or any one contingent of fighting men. Apart from the comparatively modest share of its soldiers in those two achievements of the great Virginian, few laurels of praise were netted to the Keystone State. It would not be accurate to say that many Scotch-Irish folk shone during December in a marked and constant glow before the Battle of Trenton, or that in the first week after that engagement they retrieved their reputation with a unique glory. Since Long Island, in fact, a considerable dubiety with respect to the ruggedness of the American cause and of its leaders and leadership had come upon them as it had come upon citizens and militia generally.

In anger or chagrin officers recoiled from an earlier fervor for the new nation; and Associators—weaponless, blanketless, tentless, too often shoeless and ragged—recoiled from their service. If for officers like Colonel James Burd of the Fourth Battalion of Lancaster County[1] and Major Ennion Williams of the Pennsylvania Rifle Regiment[2] it was a period for resignation from duties in which they no longer felt themselves dignified, for lesser men it was time for fluctuation, mistrust, and return—if distances, and winter, and the hardships of travel on foot did not prevent—to homesteads in the back counties. New enlistment, or for seven-months'-men, reenlistment, was not universal.

The situation, if one had to go farther west than Philadelphia to note it, was clear enough in York County. Distressful was the letter addressed from there by William Leas, local chairman, to the Pennsylvania Council of Safety in Philadelphia, on December 27.[3] That good patriot acknowledged several communications from the Council received by his committee; replied that "several men friendly to the cause of Liberty are on their march to the metropolis";[4] and then added his fellow-committeemen's regrets that "many, too many are so lost to virtue and love of liberty as to refuse marching, notwithstanding all the persuasions and admonitions that have been used to them."[5] No men would volunteer for the first battalion of Associators; no militia would march, lured by the promise that they should be substituted for "in a month or six weeks."[6] A meeting of the York Associators was called; few attended. Five gentlemen were elected to choose the Associators who should march; they fixed on their choices, notified them to prepare themselves, only to find "that they still absolutely refuse to move."[7]

But, happily, York Countians did not remain obdurate in their recusancy. On the last day of December Chairman Leas wrote with greater cheerfulness. This time he reported that several companies of militia were marching from York. A number of gentlemen had exerted themselves much "in the Grand Cause."[8] Especially public-spirited had been David Jameson, Hugh Denwoody, Charles Lukens, and George Eichelberger. The York Committee recommended them cordially for field officerships: colonel, lieutenant colonel, major, and quarter master. The sponsors were willing to rest their merits with the Philadelphia Board. Most important point, however, in their chairman's letter was congratulation "on the success of the American Arms at Trenton":[9] York was willing to fight when Washington was winning.

More rugged would appear the attitude of the patriots of Northumberland, of whom Colonel Samuel Hunter wrote on December 24. Men in that county knew more of reverses on Long Island and about New York, and could not know of the still unfought victory of Trenton. A company of his battalion of Associators, indeed, had set forward to join General Washington just before their colonel sat down to his letter.[10] Heading this detachment were Captain Major John Lee, Lieutenants Hugh White and Thomas Gaskins, and Ensign Gustavus Ross, all elected by their men. They had begun the march to Philadelphia, a number without blankets and not all supplied with guns, despite Hunter's diligence to borrow or impress those necessaries for them.[11] Lee's was a group which would be heard from; they had been undeterred by a crisis.

Redeeming also to the credit of back inhabitant Pennsylvanians was the comment from Carlisle of Colonel John Armstrong addressed to the Council of Safety at Philadelphia on January 5 before he could learn of the successful issue of the Battle of Princeton:

I'm but a few hours got to this place, and hope it will give you some pleasure to know that I have not travelled in vain; for notwithstanding the culpable stupor and timidity which had seized the minds of many in this State and partly arising from that temporary cloud which the wisdom and goodness of God thought proper to throw over our troops on their passage through the Jerseys—and partly from the spurious doctrines of dastardly and ill principled men, I think there is good reason to believe that a number of the Americans—the generality of the Irish, and part of the Germans will stand firm in the common cause.[12]

To his words of confidence in that breed of men with which he had won at Kittanning in 1756 the pious correspondent could add inspiriting information both that Colonel McCoy's Battalion of Cumberland County was on that day coming into town "not quite so destitute of clothing"[13] as had been rumored, and that despite winter snow and the difficulties of crossing the Susquehanna between Carlisle and Lancaster five or six companies of militia were now on the march or getting ready to march.

Truth is, however, that contingents twice prompted from York; companies inspirited in Cumberland County by John Armstrong's return; John Lee's men from Northumberland, for whose comfort mothers and wives had culled out the last of the family blankets, were not with Washington at Trenton. Rather it was the officers and men of Scotch-Irish blood who had been with him on Long Island or in the arduous retreat through New York and New Jersey and then paused for sixteen days in the forest above Thompson's Mill on the western cliff shore of the Delaware who shared in that action and won for Pennsylvania whatever meed of honor the State deserved in it.

The story of the victory is commonly known. General Washington recrossed the river on the night of December 25. On the morning after Christmas day he attacked, and by the evening of the 26th had withdrawn again to the Delaware's west shore with the bulk of his army, 900 or more Hessian prisoners, a thousand fine muskets, a full set of German band instruments, and six field guns of high calibre and in prime condition.[14]

It was a great bag of military capture, and the course of history had been turned. Partaking in the feat, to make it more representative of a whole nation, were field officers and regiments out of states from New Hampshire and Massachusetts to Pennsylvania, Maryland, and Virginia. Generals Henry Knox of Massachusetts, John Sullivan of New

Hampshire, Adam Stephen of Virginia, Nathaniel Greene of Rhode Island, Hugh Mercer, now of Virginia, Arthur St. Clair of Pennsylvania, all took part.[15] Lesser luminaries as regimental commanders were there: colonels like John Stark, a veteran of Rogers' Rangers and of the Battle of Bunker Hill; or like John Hazlet of Delaware, who had led his men with conspicuous gallantry through a thousand reverses since the defeat on Long Island.[16]

Leading his Pennsylvania riflemen was Colonel Edward Hand of Lancaster County. With them he had gone through the discomfitures of four bitter months. Still clear in his memory in December was an incident of the retreat on August 29. He had been then an officer in one of four *corps de reserve,* under commands to cover the withdrawal from the Island. First Thomas Mifflin had reprimanded him as he halted with his men to take up camp equipment.

"Damn your pot and kettles!" swore the general; "I wish the Devil had them! March on."[17]

He had obeyed, only to be halted presently by the commander-in-chief. Washington was astounded by his march; he said bluntly that he would not have expected Colonel Hand to abandon his post. Firmly the Lancaster Irishman retorted that he was following orders from his immediate superior, whom he named. Mifflin appeared and drew on himself prompt rebuke from Washington.

Two generals, as Edward Hand remembered, had thereupon sworn at each other. "General Mifflin," cried Washington with an oath, "I am afraid you have ruined us by so unseasonably withdrawing your troops from the lines."[18] With responding imprecation Mifflin answered that in what he had done he had followed precise orders communicated to him by the commander's aide-de-camp of the day, Alexander Scammell.

The troubled Washington pronounced the miscarriage of instructions all a mistake.[19] ("God," James McMichael, had he known of the episode, would have said, "had in his Providence determined that ruin of the American army should not grow out of the mischance, and chosen to overlook the profanity of commanders.")

But, as for Edward Hand, he was pleased now both that Washington was showing trust in him and that there was no Mifflin close by on that day to counter the orders of a superior by either error or authorized instruction.

At sunset on December 25 Hand's Lancaster County men marched with him from their encampment down the west bank of the Delaware to McKonkey's Ferry.[20] Four hours later, "in weather uncommonly inclement,"[21] they were moving eastward across the river, defiant of whirling currents and blocks of ice floating amidstream. At dawn on the 26th, with James McMichael in their number, they were attacking, fighting, firing, wounding, slaying, and capturing; on the afternoon of that second day they were busy recrossing the river at McKonkey's; diligently transporting their prisoners thence to Newtown, Bucks County, into Lord Stirling's charge;[22] and then marching doggedly back to camp beyond Coryell's. It was a day of elation, and of grinding energy. No wonder that when McMichael had got back to his billet he should find "Morpheus had got possession of him."[23] Little wonder that young officer of John Marshall's company of Hanover Associators, any one of his fellow marksmen, or Colonel Hand himself then lacked condition of mind or body to realize how his labor would loom on history's page.

So far at least as the diarist was concerned, the romance of the American cause—"common" or "Grand"—was hardly more than prosaic matter of entry on the turn of the year 1776 into 1777.[24] The story of Washington's achievement at that ebb of time has often later been told, and glowingly. The tale of the end of gallant General Hugh Mercer at Princeton is common knowledge to readers of history. Once he had fought on Drummossie Moor in Bonnie Prince Charles' cause at Culloden. He had been a captain in the ranks of the Pennsylvania Scotch-Irish of the back counties fighting under Colonel John Armstrong at Kittanning against the savagery of the Indians during the French and Indian War. Latterly he had left his office of medicine and surgery in Fredericksburg, Virginia, to drill soldiers and earn a colonelcy in the third regiment of Virginia. Unhorsed by the shattering of the foreleg of his gray charger, closed in upon by the enemy at a position in advance of his men, he played his sword against adversaries, until a gun butt savagely struck him to his knees, and he fell wounded, stunned, half feeling and half feigning death. Rescued by a sally and carried by his men from the field broken in body, he died nine days later at Thomas Clark's house in the landscape of victory, mourned by commander-in-chief and army.

All this, with the deaths of Colonel John Hazlet of Delaware, of Captain John Fleming of Virginia, of artillery Captain Daniel Neil of New Jersey, was subject appropriate for epic. But it would be hard to find a better yeoman account of what the victory of January 3 meant to the soldier participating than the version which reveals itself in James McMichael's diary. Three brisk entries there present it with vigor:

December 30.—Left Yardley's at 8 A.M. and reached Trenton at 10 A.M., where we had the pleasure of seeing seven prisoners brought in by our light horse, from whom we learned that the enemy are at Princeton 7,000 strong, and intend to attack us at Trenton in a few days.

January 2, 1777.—At 10 A.M. we received news that the enemy were advancing when the drums beat to arms and we were all paraded on the south side of the bridge [over Assunpink Creek]. General Sullivan with 1,000 men were detached to bring on the attack, which they did and reached town at 5 P.M., but our artillery fire was so severe, that the enemy retreated out of town and encamped on an adjacent hill. We continued firing bombs up to seven o'clock P.M., when we were ordered to rest, which we very commodiously did upon a number of rails for a bed. Thus my friend Capt. Marshall and I passed the night until two after twelve o'clock.

January 3.—At 1 A.M. we all paraded and marched to within 25 yards of them, and then commenced the attack, which was very hot. We kept up an incessant fire until it came to pushing bayonets when we were ordered to retreat. Here Gen. Mercer was mortally wounded, Col. Hazlet and Major Fleming both killed, with 19 rank and file, and 60 wounded. Having retreated a short distance, we were reinforced, when we immediately rallied, and with the utmost precipitation put our foes to retreat. We killed 60, wounded 75, and took 215 prisoners. We evacuated Princeton and marched for Somerset Court House, where we arrived at 8 P.M.[25]

The advance after the battle could only be matched for endurance and distance with the hardihood of Hand's riflemen on the day of the capture of Trenton. From Stony Brook to Princeton, to Kingston, along roads paralleling the Millstone to Somerset was but repetition in exploit of the march from Trenton to McKonkey's Ferry, to Newtown, and back to camp on December 26; and now, as then, it was achieved by a preceding all night's march. No deathless fame was won by the fleeting detachment, but the mettle of the men involved suffered by the same token no stigma. In the next few days, too, the battalion in which McMichael served kept maintaining its record. By midafternoon on January 4 they were at Pluckamin; by five P.M. on the 6th they were at Morristown, "encamped in the woods, the snow covering the ground."[26]

Well that on the morrow they found comfortable lodgings and agreeable people. If the diarist had to admit that the town was "devoid of beauty, both in form and location," he experienced one deep satisfaction. The inhabitants were not only hospitable; they were "all professors of the Presbyterian religion"[27]—a circumstance which more than commended them to him.

Yet, as Washington's commands kept the divisions of his army moving in order to follow up his victory and confine the retreated British to New Brunswick and Amboy, and Hand's men had to leave Morristown and advance again on January 12 to Chatham, the subalterns were not too much troubled. Chatham may have had fewer strict Calvinists among its Christians; but, happily, the young ladies were "very fond of the soldiers, but much more so of officers"[28]—a solace which Scotch-Irish Pennsylvanians during an eleven days' encampment were not likely to scorn. So long as their general was succeeding in his strategy of confronting Howe's or Cornwallis' position at the mouth of the Raritan and on Staten Island, and shifting camps of his own to keep the enemy hemmed in by lines to the south and east supplementing the lines which they held to north and east as far as Elizabethtown, they bore him no grievance. Bivouacs back and forth between Chatham and points on the Bay, after all, did not spell exceeding hardship in the January which followed Trenton and Princeton.

Besides, the Pennsylvania riflemen had the stimulation of a triumph over the British at Quibbletown (modern New Market) on the 24th. Themselves numbering 350, in the absence of their own officer of the day, Colonel Buckner, they routed an enemy force of 600. Out of the contest they came with but 4 of their own men slightly wounded, as opposed to casualties inflicted on the foe to the number of 70 killed and wounded.[29] When in February, 1777, McMichael obtained furlough to visit with his friends in Pennsylvania, he had plenty to tell them and the bride whom he married before he returned to the army in April.

Elsewhere, too, men from Lancaster County had demonstrated their spirit after Washington's two successes.

A letter written by Adam Hubley, Jr., to his brother from Bordentown on January 4th told a good story.[30] A party of 120 Associators' had sped forward south of the main battle lines for the engagement at Princeton, got deep into Monmouth County on lands sloping toward the Atlantic, and turned a detachment of 200 British under Colonel Morris into flight for Middletown and coastwards. So hard did they press the foe across the virtual width of New Jersey that they captured 23 prisoners, 7 wagon loads of stores, and 12 horses.[31]

It is not surprising, then, that the writer should set down considerable jubilation and indulge a great deal of wishful thinking.

For Washington did not take the stores of the British at New Brunswick, as Hubley declared he had; nor did General Howe with his main body fall into the hands of the American general, as the enthusiast predicted he would. But the rejoicing of Hubley served well enough as an index to the first month of 1777. Neither Scotch-Irish nor any patriots generally knew then the full import of the two victories. Bitter years, and Valley Forge, were yet ahead for the American cause. It is true that the pair of brilliant military feats meant the saving of Philadelphia for another season, the protection of Pennsylvania, and prevention of Howe's cutting of the United States into two parts north and south. The history of the world would have been different if in the winter and spring of 1777 Howe had possessed New York City, the State of New Jersey, and Philadelphia. But such points were not common knowledge when young officers wrote to friends or put down records in their journals. Only a quiet, patient, and undeluded Washington could have the clearest and undeceived understanding of what their significance was and could be. And, luckily, now more occasion had risen for attracting the aid of France to the cause he wished to triumph.

NORTHUMBERLAND

NOTHING IN Pennsylvania history is more true than that from their first settlements along Chickiesalunga Creek in the 1720's the Scotch-Irish kept on subduing for their farmsteads and their trading posts the shores of the great river into which the creek on the west boundaries of Donegal Township emptied. Creek mouth by creek mouth, before 1772 they had ascended the Susquehanna northwards: on the west bank to Sherman's Creek, to the Little Juniata, to the Juniata, to Penn's Creek, to Buffalo Creek; on the east to the Conewago, to the Swatara, to Paxton, to Clark's, to Powel's, to Mahoney, to the Mahantango Creek, to the meeting of the West and North Branches at Shamokin, and, beyond that point of confluence, by the eastern and northern shore of the West Branch, onwards as far as Muncy, and even farther to Loyalsock Creek. Throughout the decade which followed the erection of Fort Augusta and the French and Indian War they were busy on the west shore of the West Branch turning the forested valleys of White Deer and White Deer Hole Creeks into arable lands. Philadelphia authorities were not loath to have colonization proceeding at "the Point," as the Forks of the Susquehanna were locally termed, or along lesser streams tributary either to branch or main trunk of the river. The more occupation by settlers with the consent of the Penn proprietaries, the firmer political and legal resistance to the Connecticut intruders in the Wyoming Valley. Upstream on the North Branch, Lazarus Stewart still lived unhanged. Conrad Weiser's numerous past missions to the Six Nations Indians, and the establishment of Fort Augusta with the King's aid had, of course, made migrations easier for the Scotch-Irish. But it was those pathfinders of destiny rather than the scant clusters of Germans setting up their farms on Penn's and Middle Creek, on the west shore of the Susquehanna twelve miles below the Forks, who conquered with axe and plough upland and valley for the white man.

The warrant and the patent books of the Land Office of the Province confirmed settlement not first made by squatter sovereignty. In fact, there was no long demurring in Philadelphia on the subject of the petition "from a number of the inhabitants on the East [North] and the West Branches of the River Susquehanna" presented to the Assembly on January 14, 1772.[1] That document very much resembled in spirit the appeal of numerous Scotch-Irish settlers of Chester County in 1728 for erection into a new county, aspiring to convenience of legal jurisdiction, to security, and to civic order. It pointed out clearly the advantage of having courts of law, a magistracy, a county town, a court house, and a jail. It argued frankly that, where these exist, reputable "men of property"[2] can settle, confident that they will be maintained peacefully in their possessions. Every benefit of proper local government was touched on. Relevantly enough the Assembly in Philadelphia could respond to suggestion. Presently they had drawn a Bill to carry out the purpose of the petitioners, and in March they were ready to offer it to Deputy Governor Richard Penn, representative of his family.[3]

So, on January 21 a new county was erected, with parings from Northampton, Berks, Lancaster, Cumberland, and Bedford Counties included in it (any one of the five almost as large as a province) and embracing beyond those parings a westerly and northwesterly territory which spread its jurisdiction over a tract of country reaching in one direction as far as the Allegheny River, in another to the Lehigh, and northwards to New York[4]—larger, indeed, than many an European principality or kingdom. The grandson of William Penn and his Council intended that the Proprietaries and their Province, not the Colony of Connecticut, should rule there. But the fact was that most of the land occupied by white men during the year when Northumberland County was constructed had been settled upon by Scotch-Irish farmers. The lots of the county town which William Maclay, as assistant to Surveyor General Lukens, forthwith set to work laying out in 1772[5] were to be taken up promptly by the same kind of men. Seeds were sowing for the eventual control of the vast region of promise of which Philadelphia legislators recked little. The jurisdiction founded on the eve of the American Revolution was not only to secure in the passage of time the geographic mother of twenty-eight counties, it was to be pivotal in a new civic and political order. Family names like Barnett, Brown, Clark, Crawford, Gray, Hunter, Lowden, Maclay, Moody, Potter, and Wallis were to become familiar ones in the new county.

Matters moved briskly as declarations of independence loomed nearer. Sunbury was surveyed on the east shore of the river to the south of the Point; the Shamokin of Shickellamy's time and the Fort Augusta of Major James Burd's became mere area for town lots and out-lots; more houses were planned; court house and jail were provided for: officials were chosen.

At the first court, on April 9, 1772, a private session of the peace, with William Plunket presiding and James Potter and John Lowden assisting, Northumberland was divided into eight townships.[6] In May the first court of common pleas was held to hear commissions read and swear in members of the bar; William Maclay became prothonotary; men chiefly of his ilk constituted the fraternity of barristers and the grand jurors.[7] In August the first criminal case was tried, with two emigrants from Derry Township, Robert Fruit and Robert Clark, concurring in the jury on a sentence of twenty-one lashes on a bare back and a fine of £5 as punishment for a larceny.[8] During the same term Thomas Hartley, Andrew Ross, and James Whitehead were sworn in as attorneys.[9] In October, Colonel William Cooke was commissioned as county sheriff.[10] In that same month plans were reported for carrying a new road, continuing the old road from the head of the Schuylkill River to Sunbury, across the North Branch, and then along the upper shore of the West Branch as far as Loyalsock Creek.[11] By the mid-summer of 1773, when John Penn had succeeded his brother Richard as Deputy Governor, the leadership of the vast county at the Susquehanna Forks and beyond was in the hands of Samuel Hunter, member of the Assembly, Presiding Justice William Plunket, Prothonotary William Maclay, Sheriff William Cooke, Coroner James Murray, and County Commissioner Casper Reed.[12]

Nor were the rosters of officialdom in 1774 and 1775 to lose their Scotch-Irish color. By May in the latter year James Potter was returned as a second member of Assembly for Northumberland, indicating growth of recognition for the county at Philadelphia;[13] and in July Captain John Lowden, with a company of 97 riflemen drawn from Sunbury from the hamlet of Northumberland now begun at the Point, and from the West Branch, was marching away[14] to join other Pennsylvania riflemen under the command of Matthew Smith of Paxton and William Hendricks of Cumberland County and to speed on with them to Washington's army before Boston. Indeed, Northumberland men, like their fellows from down the river, were earlier in the Revolution in 1776 than many a legislator of Continental Congress.

Not slow, however, to follow their example were other men of the three-year old county. On July 4 proxies from four battalions of Associators were in Lancaster[15] helping to elect generals to lead them in their cause. It was a day when the name of many a Scotch-Irishman from the county entered into the military records of the War for Independence: Brady, Calhoun, Gillespie, Gray, Maclay, McClenaghan, Moody, and Sterrett.[16] And as true was it that throughout the year the spirit of liberty was no more vivid anywhere than among the men of Northumberland.

John Lowden's men had not been chosen by the chance lot-casting of September, 1775, to proceed to Quebec with the other two Pennsylvania companies of riflemen from Cumberland and Lancaster Counties on the march at Morgan's and Arnold's side. But other service was not denied them. They were across both the Delaware and the Hudson by August 20.[17] On the 30th they were encamped at Dudley, Massachusetts; and on the last day of the month at Cambridge.[18] There they were promptly employed as the picket guard for the entrenchments of Ploughed Hill.[19]

Various duties came to them in September and October: Parr with thirty of his men detailed at times under Edward Hand's orders, Captain Lowden with others directed as a constituent part of Colonel William Thompson's Battalion of Riflemen.[20] With a detachment of the command of that Carlisle gentleman they served vigorously on November 9 in the exploit at Lechmere's Point, one mile and a half from Cambridge.[21]

The British, covered by fire from their batteries on Bunker, Breed, and Capp's hills and from a frigate lying some three hundred yards off Lechmere's and minded on forage, made a quick landing. A high tide covered the causeway leading to the farmsteads which they had already begun plundering. Thompson's men could see the raiders shooting cows and horses, making ready to drag their spoil of carcasses to the boats. They waited impatiently for orders.

Despite the firing from batteries and frigate, command came. Lechmere's Point must be taken as though it were an island.

John Lowden dashed with his men into the tide. Up to their arm pits they waded, receiving fire and firing.[22] First on the shore was their captain. He looked as he drew himself out of the water, and saw Samuel Brady at his side, second to emerge.

"You were told to stay in reserve," he reproached his subordinate.

"Look at them, sir," rejoined that marksman; "Let's let them have it."[23]

Forward the sharpshooters from Northumberland sped, first to rout the foe from behind stone walls, then to hurry them fleeing to their boats. Providence—if it was not sheer audacity and agility—was on their side. They could advance as securely under fire as their enemies could run. Darting forward, dodging, bending, firing as they charged, they carried the Point.[24] When the British marauders had fled, they numbered an English loss of seventeen killed and one wounded.[25] Of their own men one was dead and three wounded. Against odds, a band of provincials from the back counties of Pennsylvania had triumphed.

Little wonder that men of their mettle should, on the expiration of their earlier terms of enlistment, become a company serving in the First Regiment of the United Colonies in January, 1776, prepared to serve in that year with Colonel Edward Hand, when their earlier commander General Thompson had been delegated other duties of relief to the Americans of Arnold's army struggling along the St. Lawrence in Canada.[26]

Still in Washington's army, they fought early in March in the battle for Dorchester Heights.[27] From that position, when it had been taken, they had sight of British preparations to evacuate Boston. Then on January 14th[28] they posted away from the scene of General Howe's discomfiture, James Parr now commanding them in the place of John Lowden, designated with five regiments under General John Sullivan to prevent British landings at New York.[29]

In Hartford, Connecticut, on the 21st, at New York on the 28th, they were stationed three months later on Long Island.[30] When in July their compatriots of Northumberland were meeting with other Associators at Lancaster and Continental Congress was approving the Declaration of Independence, they were picketing the roads and beaches of the sound or watching beyond the Lower Bay the shores of Staten Island.

Late in August they partook unhappily in the disaster of Washington's army, and in the next two months in the long retreat northwards from New York and southwards again on the west of the Hudson. But it was not ignominiously that they shared in the succession of Washington's reverses; and their part in the battle of Fort Washington on November 16th, although it lost them four men by capture, made them not the less ready to be telling marksmen under Hand at the victories of Trenton and Princeton.[31] Indeed, by January 1777 many of them had become veterans of every engagement since the Battle of Bunker Hill.[32]

Less notable were the laurels of the company of Northumberland and patriots headed by Captain Casper Weitzel and Lieutenants William Gray, John Robb, and George Grant.[33] These rendezvoused, as did John Marshall's Company of Hanover Associators and riflemen, at Marcus Hook in June, 1776.[34] Ordered on to Philadelphia in July, they marched thence to Bordentown and Amboy. In August they were on Long Island; and there, in the battle, they shared the chagrin of Colonel Samuel Miles, and eighteen men and Lieutenant William Gray were captured.[35] Badly broken by their losses, and their term of enlistment either nearing completion or at an end, men of the company consolidated with other organizations, while William Gray, exchanged on December 8, 1776, and his brother Lieutenants Robb and Grant were all three promoted into captaincies in other regiments.[36]

Less brilliant, too, in comparison with James Parr's riflemen, were other companies from Northumberland mustered into service in the autumn of 1776. Guns, clothes, and blankets wanting, early in December—when Washington's army had taken shelter west of the Delaware above Trenton—Colonel William Cooke, aided by two thousand dollars from the Board of War, got a battalion of recruits together from the West Branch.[37] These set forth from Sunbury by boat on the 18th,[38] destined for service in New Jersey and Pennsylvania during the next year from spring to autumn, but too late now to have honor in the triumphs of December 26 and January 3. Be it remembered, however, that the Scotch-Irish in the four companies of Hawkins Boone, John Brady, John Harris, and Nicholas Miller were hastening forward when the fighting men of Washington's army had for three-and-a-half months known nothing but displacement and retreat. Like the detachment of Major John Lee,[39] which marched away from Fort Augusta six days later than they, all were loyal to a cause which, although at the time in eclipse, still held for them honor.

Fortunately the year 1777 was to accredit them as it would generally accredit Northumberland. Busily Cooke's Twelfth Pennsylvania Regiment, whose commanding officer had joined his men before March, participated in Washington's Jersey campaign from April to June. They fought in skirmish after skirmish: at Bound Brook on April 12; at Piscataway on May 10; at Bonhamtown, Ash Swamp, and Metuchen Meeting House; at Brunswick on June 15; at Short Hills on June 26.[40] When Howe's fleet gave up action off Amboy and sailed for the south thinking to let New Jersey go and take Philadelphia instead, Colonel William Cooke's men moved back into Pennsylvania to serve Washington and their country there as they might.

Meantime, however, compatriots of theirs from the great county on the two Branches of the Susquehanna were giving good accounts of themselves on other fields.

In early March, 1777, before Washington had moved from his winter quarters at Morristown, he determined on a new corps of riflemen to serve with Daniel Morgan,[41] happily returned as a paroled prisoner of war to New York harbor on Sepember 11, 1776, released from parole and exchanged early in 1777. That Virginia veteran of Quebec, rested from a six months' sojourn at his home at Winchester, promptly began recruiting his "Partisan Corps."[42] Of it promptly were Captain James Parr[43] and many of his followers, heroes now not only of Dorchester Heights and Long Island but of Trenton and Princeton, soldiers of the First Pennsylvania. Not much later the riflemen out of Captain Hawkins Boone's Company,[44] newer heroes of Cooke's Twelfth Pennsylvania, were numbering themselves with "Morgan's." At the close of June they were among the chosen peers of Washington's army, Parr, Brady, and others, jubilant at seeing the British retreating from New Brunswick[45]—but with their riflemen honors still ahead.

In mid-August they knew that their colonel had been commanded to lead them to join the army in New York then forming to check the further progress of General Sir John Burgoyne, already down Lake Champlain and possessed since June of Crown Point and since early July of Fort Ticonderoga. Off they marched, devoted to their hero and leader from Virginia, as had been John Joseph Henry of Lancaster, knowing that stalwart in his hardihood in the waters of the Kennebec and the Chaudière. Sharpshooters in the band told stories of the prowess of their companions; of Timothy Murphy, originally of John Lowden's Company,[46] not lucky enough to be sent to Quebec but already reputed among many for being the finest shot in the whole army; of James Parr who had himself killed four men by the deadliness of his aim in the New Jersey summer.

"So," went the tale, "Major Miller said, 'Can you pick off yon Highlander for me, captain?' "

" 'Aye, I can,' he answered, and raised his gun; and, quicker than you can say Jack Robinson, he added, 'Do you see the mon falling, Major?'

"Then, as the lad lay sprawled there in the field, it would have made you smile to hear Jern Parr, who would tell you 'he and his shot couldn't be separated one from the other,' remark of his bullet 'By God, Sandy, it's myself that is in you.' "[47]

They were alert men, Northumberland scions of King James I's Plantation in seventeenth-century Ireland, grandsons of Scotch-Irish sires who remembered Enneskillen and Londonderry, sons and brothers of women on whose minds was still being stamped the stern experience of making homes for husbands and children in the vast wilderness of the Susquehanna country. Recent history elsewhere in America, too, had been paving the way for them. Much had occurred and much had been contemplated before the path of pilgrimage should carry them on to the great valley of the Hudson.

By dint of the prowess of Ethan Allen, Fort Ticonderoga at the head of Lake Champlain had been won for the Americans in May, 1775, and held for two years. Arnold, who had helped Allen take that fort, had later become the outstanding figure in the Expedition to Quebec in the autumn and winter of that same year, and then, on the failure of it, the most oddly memorable figure in the long retreat up the St. Lawrence and down into New York. Among English statesmen and military strategists had persisted the conviction that if the Colonies could not take Canada, the English, at least, could marshal from Canada expeditions which should cut off New England from the rest of America. The Americans had held Massachusetts and Boston since the spring of 1776. But Washington had lost New York City; and New York State—or the Colony of New York, as King George's advisers still thought of it—was vulnerable from both North and West. Routes would be long from them; but the Great Lakes, Toronto, and Erie, and the St. Lawrence River were British possessions. From outposts on or along these, armies might make their campaigns. A secondary operation from the west, and a primary one from the north— the Province of New York would fall, and with New York the Americans' scheme of independence.

Preparations became major in the early months of 1777, and instructions from the Court of St. James's were elaborate.

Colonel Barry St. Leger, entrusted with the minor but fully designed and generously equipped operation from the west, ascended the St. Lawrence and Lake Ontario, ascended the Oswego and Oneida Rivers, crossed by land from Lake Oneida to a point near Fort Stanwix and the head waters of the Mohawk River,[48] and planned to proceed eastwards in its valley to join in course of time with a British army moving south along the Hudson. But his plans and the Ministry behind them did not succeed. He began investment of Fort Schuyler in July, was in early August outwitted by a sortie from that garrison while concerting tactics of his own to dissipate militia coming from the east to its assistance, and found his camp plundered—even to his own desk and papers—by the Americans.[49] Before his own men had set up the entrenchments from which they were to ward off the forces advancing to raise the siege, the blow had fallen. Several days later his Indian aides ambuscaded a march of General Nicholas Herkimer near Oriskany, did great slaughter upon that warrior's army, and wounded Herkimer himself severely; but, in what became a drawn issue St. Leger now lost eighty Indians, and netted nothing more than the abandonment of the field by the assailants.[50]

On August 7, St. Leger sent word forward to Burgoyne that he was sure of Fort Schuyler. Yet, within another week he was frightened by information of new battalions coming to relieve the garrison and alarmed by rumors of disaster to Burgoyne. In mid-August he precipitately abandoned his entrenchments and fled back to Oswego.[51] On the field he deserted a liberal portion of his artillery, baggage, and camp equipage. Far from supply lines, arrogance and panic alternated in him. He let "I dare not" wait upon "I would"; and both what he dared and what he would not venture spelled eclipse. History, in brief, despite an initial abundance of provisions and a numerous army at his disposal, was to make him no herald of another commander's success.

More famous, of course, is the story of Sir John Burgoyne, commander of the major operation of the British in New York State in 1777. That general, too, had to depend upon long supply lines and distant points of provision. Of paramount importance was support from St. Leger to the west and from Howe to the south in New York. Howe, with Washington still safely ensconced in northern New Jersey and still in secure communication with his regiments along the upper Hudson, dared venture no loss to the Americans in either position, if he was to take Philadelphia, as that year he designed doing. So the officer campaigning from Canada moved problematically like St. Leger, although certainly with a more complete and a more balanced self-assurance. Neither anticipating a trap nor hastening impetuously into one, Burgoyne moved inevitably in the direction of disaster.

With superiority of numbers, a staff of spirited officers, and skillful campaigning he made his way southwards throughout the month of July. His victory at Ticonderoga was behind him. Stiff resistance and considerable gallantry by officers and men in the forces of General Schuyler checked but could not stem his advance. Fort George and Fort Edward fell. Eastwards of him in Vermont and Massachusetts he knew were enemies; but he did not expect strength from that direction, and waited for news of St. Leger to his west, expecting his own strength to grow even stronger. Then in mid-August, when General John Stark outplayed and out-fought two of the British colonels in the Battle of Bennington and destroyed an army of 1,000 men with a corresponding small loss to the Americans,[52] hazards became more serious.

American Congress, more to his content than Burgoyne could have realized, supplanted Major General Philip Schuyler, true soldier and doughty officer, with General Horatio Gates as a commander of the Northern Department. But Burgoyne was not to win either of the two engagements, by fleet-minded historians commonly reduced into one as the Battle of Saratoga. Gates planned positions and gave orders; Benedict Arnold put them into command at Stillwater, or Freeman's Farm, on September 19, on the field; and no men fought harder on that day than Daniel Morgan's Partisans.[53]

The riflemen with Major Henry Dearborn's light infantry opposed the advance of the British right, succeeded temporarily, and then were turned into a repulse, falling back before Major Forbes and the Earl Balcarres. Morgan admitted afterwards that he thought them "ruined,"[54] with twenty of his men lost and others disorganized. Burgoyne, in a report of their action, wrote that they had "counter-marched"[55]—as it were allowing the Devil his due.

Yet the day was not lost to the Americans or to the men of Northumberland. General Arnold, authentic but inglorious veteran of the Campaign for Quebec whose laurels were yet to wear a certain tarnish, became the hero of the first battle of Saratoga. General Simon Fraser with his grenadiers and light infantry had resisted firmly. To thrust that first chieftain of Burgoyne back Arnold had to bring his own whole division into action.

The fight of Morgan's men had been but a preface. Now began a dreadful conflict. For four hours fire was constant. Each army seemed determined on death or victory. At the end of the exchange the British were unable to resume the fight; until further supplies of ammunition should arrive, the army of Gates, now dominated by the spirit of Benedict Arnold—and, for the time being, by his caution—dared attempt no new advance. The day was an apparent draw. Its consequences would have to wait until the next month to be seen, although future nineteenth century historians would one day declare that only Daniel Morgan, among American officers on Gates' staff, could compete[56] with the hero of September 19, 1777, and particularly of October 7, for the honors of the Saratoga victory.

For General Burgoyne's eventual surrender of his army was assured from the September day when he failed to defeat Gates and Arnold. There was withdrawal by the British for two weeks, establishment of new positions, and—unhappily for them—diminution of stores. For the

Americans had taken both opportunities of advance and of scouting parties to cut into the lines to the rear of the enemy's forces. The Battle of Bemus' Heights came. A second time Benedict Arnold proved a meteoric hero. He rode forward with the dash of his charger and the staylessness of a whirlwind. Troops cheered and fell into line after him. His wounds did not stop him; his spirit was infectious to the army of General Gates. Here he took the lead of one brigade, there of another. Repulsed at the entrenchments of the Earl Balcarres, he met General Learned's brigade, took the lead, cleared two stock redoubts of the enemy supporting the Scottish peer's position, and so broke it. Through the fire of the lines he sped repeatedly unhurt. Then, when the left was broken he turned to the right, and, as it was breaking for flight, in the very moment of victory his horse was killed beneath him and his own leg broken.

But the honors of that day which preluded the defeated Burgoyne's forced surrender on October 17 of an army of 5,791 men, cut off north and south and stripped of munitions, provisions, and supply line far more truly than ever a St. Leger could dream, belonged not all to the officer who had lost at Quebec and who later would lose credit infinitely more ignominiously.

Morgan was in the second battle, the Virginian of whose riflemen Washington had predicted great service when he detailed him as an aide to Gates. The commander-in-chief had written: "These are all chosen men, selected from the army at large, well acquainted with the rifle and with that mode of fighting which is necessary to make them a good counterpoise to the savages."[57] With Morgan were Captain James Parr and Lieutenants Samuel Brady and Benjamin Lyon of Northumberland.[58] With these was Lieutenant Thomas Boyd[59] of Derry in Lancaster County, whose valor John Joseph Henry had revered during the campaign for Canada, and who had promptly enlisted after his release from imprisonment and parole.

And in James Parr's company was Timothy Murphy, veteran of all the exploits of Captain John Lowden's company in 1775 and 1776, a celebrity for deliberateness and certitude of aim. Morgan was near. Two hundred yards away he recognized Simon Fraser, heroic figure of the September encounter, long experienced officer, once a soldier of Wolfe at that English general's taking of Quebec, now a favorite second to General John Burgoyne, and a Scot known as "the charm and the inspiration of the British army."[60]

"There's a good man to pick off," ordered Daniel Morgan.[61]

Murphy heard. From his perch in the fork of a tree he sighted his double-barrelled Pennsylvania rifle; and he shot. Simon Fraser fell from his horse, mortally wounded.[62]

On the morrow at dawn the only British general known to have been killed by an American private during the War of the Revolution was given burial.[63] A leader whose loss was critical to an enemy army had been brought down by a man whose reputation for marksmanship was still in the making. Two years and three months before, Murphy had begun his march to the front from Northumberland County and the shores of the Susquehanna. Since then he had been in three distant campaigns.

But it was not in the summer of 1775 that the sharpshooter's life-story began. Two decades earlier than that, indeed, it had been given first propulsion towards danger and legendry.

He was three years old in 1756, the infant son in a family of four. With his mother and a six-year old sister, his father took him back to Duncan's Island from the shelter of Hunter's Fort in the month for reaping. Grain must be cut in the tiny fields about their log cabin near the mouth of Juniata, across the Susquehanna from the Paxton Narrows. His father ran the risk; an Indian raid followed—as in that year it might have been anticipated—unerringly.

When it was over, William Baskins was dead and scalped. Into captivity was carried his wife and two children of this river man who in 1744 had gone up the Juniata scouting with other Paxton settlers to discover the body of Trader Jack Armstrong. And for the time being the frontiers of Pennsylvania and the wilds of Ohio and Canada swallowed the remnants of another Scotch-Irishman's family. Mrs. Baskins escaped and remarried. The daughter was recovered in 1764 and brought back by Bouquet, grew up, and married a Juniata River pioneer. The son became Irish-named Timothy Murphy, child of the forests and of fantastic abductions, wanderer, warrior, good companion.[64]

At Saratoga it was Murphy's destiny to bring sudden death to another Scot almost as myth-creating as himself. General Fraser fell in a battle, still seeking to redeem his own name from the attainder which had come upon his clan by the treason of his kinsman, Simon Fraser Lord Lovatt in 1745. Murphy fired the destroying shot, unconcerned by any name worn by him apart from being a patriot soldier enlisted out of Northumberland and now with Jim Parr's riflemen serving under an American officer out of Virginia, like himself a sprig of the back country.

CHAPTER 16

NO SHINING GLORY

Neither Timothy Murphy nor Benedict Arnold drew the plaudits of the autumn of 1777 for the victory of Saratoga. Major General Horatio Gates reached the heyday of his fame, and for some time held it to the detriment of a commander infinitely more worthy and able than himself. The months in which George Washington lost the Battle of the Brandywine and, in the crisis which followed was obliged to make the blunder and know the defeat of the Battle of Germantown, were not months in which either Continental politicians or military leaders attained impeccable honor.

Congress demanded that Philadelphia be saved from the army of Sir William Howe, who in the British-directed campaign of the late summer, came up the Chesapeake Bay rather than the Delaware Bay and the river; and Congress, which had left Washington no choice in the matter, fled the city during the interval between Washington's two battles and acquitted themselves with but little dignity elsewhere in the winter which followed. Washington, aided unintentionally but no less certainly by General Sullivan on a day of confusion and indecision, was outwitted strategically by Howe along the Brandywine on September 11. On October 4 he saved a diminished and ragged army in an eleventh hour, withdrawing in the nick of time out of the onset at Germantown. Then, thanks first to the inevitable, when the British struck a vigorous and effectual counterblow to the arms of America, and second to General Sir William Howe's negligence of the moment and overconfidence of the morrow—Washington's paths took him inescapably toward the winter of 1777-1778 in Valley Forge.*

---

* "Washington impressed the world with his initiative, his skill in keeping the army intact, and in preserving his communications with the South. That he dared attack the British at Germantown did as much as Saratoga to convince France the United States was worth backing," *Paul A. Wallace.*

[223

A season of diminution had come. Gate's star shone in a time out-of-joint and before the event was at hand for setting it right. In fact, both in New Jersey and in Pennsylvania, after Washington's victories of the winter before at Trenton and at Princeton, the succession of nine months had been anticlimactic and the slough of despond unbroken. Moreover, what was true of the attitude of the two States before the news of Saratoga came, was the same in the back counties of Pennsylvania. There too, the summer of 1777 was lacklustre.

At the least, Lancaster County officers found their neighbors none too easily managed. President Thomas Wharton of the Executive Council of Pennsylvania addressed them in the late April through Bertram Galbraith, Esquire, Lieutenant of the County, forwarding with his missive copies of the resolves of Congress designed to alert the colonels of the county's several battalions.[1] The enemy, Mr. Wharton said, were preparing to make an immediate attack on Pennsylvania. Six hundred men must march immediately to Chester with as many arms and accoutrements as could be had for them locally. Blankets, which should remain the property of Pennsylvania, were to be sought for them out of funds which President Wharton would be sending. So burdens began for Colonel Galbraith and Sub-Lieutenant Colonel Joshua Elder and their colleagues, Colonels John Rogers, Timothy Green, and Robert Elder, brother of Joshua Elder. Letters passed back and forth offering suggestions, reciting objections, retailing grievances.

In Paxton County, Sub-Lieutenant Elder reported matters as going "tolerably" well on May 11;[2] but, although three of the companies from there met and chose their officers agreeably, "the Germans chiefly all stood aloof"[3] and two other companies demurred emphatically. One of these wanted all its members to be officers; the second wanted all its men to be privates. To meet that paradox of equalitarianism during a revolution for liberty, Colonel Elder was constrained to inform Colonel Rogers that the Lieutenants would have to choose the officers without the men's votes.[4] By June, marching orders for men in the first and second classes had come and men were looking for substitutes in the third or fourth classes. Elder repined that none of these could be found among the Germans, and complained to Rogers: "O their clay cold heads and lukewarm hearts."[5]

In the midst of such variances Colonel Galbraith wrote warningly of new British penetrations into New Jersey as far as "Rockey run five miles from Princeton," relaying to Rogers orders from the Pennsylvania Generals Mifflin, Armstrong, and Potter to have the first class get into readiness "agreeable to former orders."[6] No substitutes from the second class should be allowed for the first; the second class should "hold themselves in readiness."[7] On their way to Chester, at Lancaster Town or in camp, they would be provided with everything except blankets. As an example of patriotism the letter called attention to the citizens of Philadelphia. Those heroic folk had "made up all variances and marched yesterday morning unanimously in defense of their country."[8] That was on June 16.

Four days later, however, the march of the first class was countermanded. From Wharton to Galbraith to Rogers came instructions.[9] Howe's army had been seen retreating from Somerset, Brunswick, and Amboy to Staten Island. Suspicion was entertained that he was meditating an attempt upon our Capes.

But Galbraith clung to his optimism.[10] He did that, too, although when he had been absent from Donegal and in the district of Rogers, a riot had occurred back home. Evenly he stated the facts: "When I was in your country, our people had a brush with a number of rioters in which one of our people was killed by the stroke of the coulter of a plough and three of the others wounded, which I hope will put a stop to other insurrections of the like kind."[11] Well that a patriot who the year before as a representative from Lancaster County had helped frame the Pennsylvania Constitution of 1776 and its famous Bill of Rights, could in the summer of 1777 believe that the example of disaster in a riot would be deterrent to other rebellion! His serenity spoke well for a grandson of the Reverend Mr. William Bertram of Derry and a great-great-grandson of that rock of Presbyterianism, the Reverend Mr. George Gillespie of Scotland and the Westminster Confession of Faith. But if County Lieutenant-Colonel Galbraith was poised in hope, he was not soft. June passed into July and from Donegal he sent firm instructions. "Drudge,"[12] he called himself in respect of the Pennsylvania Assembly, and he sent stern orders that the colonels of the several Lancaster County battalions have their captains read to their men the rules by which the Continental Army was governed and inform them that they must abide by these same rules of discipline. He had made up his mind that the mute Assembly must endow him with the liberty to judge and act for them. He hoped the substitutes, who were ordered to behave quite as those for whom they substituted would be expected to behave, would manifest conduct "becoming men of candor and probity."[13] As for their wages, he was "their mark"[14] for the payment of them.

Three weeks later, on August 3, he had other commands to transmit. President Wharton had now sent him the "alarming intelligence of the enemy's near approach to our Metropolis."[15] Philadelphia was being threatened. "By all the ties of virtue, honor, and love of your country; as freemen, determined to defend and protect your inestimable and just rights and privileges,"[16] the battalions of Lancaster County were to march without loss of time to Chester and Delaware. Without standing on their order of going, let first, second, and now even third class proceed at once. Their harvests were in. Let there be no more argument about substitutes; and let all—apparently whether or not they had any—carry their blankets along.

As an afterthought, on August 10, he sent word through Mr. Joseph Barnett, signer of the Hanover Resolves in 1774, to Colonel Rogers, a cosigner of the Hanover Resolves, that the men of Paxton and Hanover should provide their own rations until they arrived in Lancaster:[17] the public houses on the way to that town had entirely run out of provisions. Then, on August 24, Colonel Joshua Elder had information from Colonel Galbraith that the enemy's fleet had come far up the Chesapeake Bay and were landing their army above Baltimore. The men of his district must march with "such arms as could be procured";[18] and let those who had no arms march without them in the expectation of being supplied at Lancaster. Furthermore, as the son of the Reverend Mr. John Elder of Paxton Church read the instructions from the County Lieutenant, not any particular classes, but the whole of the militia were to set forth. One duty further he relayed for Colonel Galbraith to John Rogers. He was to collect all the Hessian prisners among the Mennonites in his part of the county and transfer them to Lebanon.[19] Clearly it would not do to have the Scotch-Irish leave behind them when they marched the parolees captured at Trenton and billeted as aides to German farmers in Pennsylvania; best get them away from temptations to rejoin the army of King George.

All these points had an oblique eloquence of their own. Much in the quality of them also was a terse letter of September 2 from Colonel Timothy Green of Hanover to Colonel Rogers. Nine days before the Battle of Brandywine was to be fought, that veteran of the French and Indian Wars and organizer of the Associators of his district in 1775, wrote importunately to his friend; "With all speed you must provide fifty or sixty blankets for your militia, for they are in great need."[20]

But the lack-lustre and equivocal midyear and late summer of 1777 in inland Pennsylvania was so not only for patriot arbiters in Lancaster County. York and Cumberland Counties, just across the Susquehanna, provided situations as challenging to county Lieutenants there.

In York, Colonel Richard McAlester found circumstances trying month after month. He was, his letter of August 28[21] to President Wharton indicated, suspected of lukewarmness. At home he was misrepresented and plotted against by neighbors. Early embarked on principle in the unhappy dispute between America and Britain—Pennsylvania Archives record that he saw military service in 1776—he believed his conduct as firm and unshaken as that of any one in the State; he was confident that he was as well attached as any to the defense of Pennsylvania and of "the States in general."[22] It grieved him considerably that censors should doubt his constancy. He was not resigning office when he wrote; if President Wharton could find a better man to replace him and some other to get out more militia to serve in the cause, he would be glad as any patriot to behold a more effectual County Lieutenant in charge. When he wrote, five companies had gone forward; three more, he and his colleagues were striving to march[23] in a few days—and the tally then would be one company proceeded for the front from each battalion in York.

Hardly, however, did those facts seem to be compensation for the cup of bitterness which Colonel McAlester was having to drink. For he plied his pen even more eloquently when he wrote of the obstructing Germans in the county than when he gave statistics of patriotism or pleaded his own virtue.

Two hundred malcontents had recently met not more than a mile from his home. They had bound themselves to each other: they would not muster in the militia, would not go with it in any way, would not suffer any of their effects to be sold to pay fines for them. They would "kill any man who would distress them."[24] As for McAlester himself, they had resolved to be troubled no more by him; either by killing or beating him they would be done with his activities. Several Germans, in fact, he said, came into Hanover Town with that purpose in mind. But his neighbors of twenty years past did not find him at home on the day they had chosen to seize him. He had gone to York Town to attend a meeting of his battalion. Such being the conditions, he could not see why he should be censured for inability to turn the hearts of those people, "which none but God that made them can do."[25]

In brief, the Germans and their disputing bothered Richard McAlester greatly. He conceded some force in their argument that, having been naturalized in Pennsylvania because of their oath of allegiance to the King, they dared not abjure to take oath to Pennsylvania.[26] It was awkward, he admitted, to have the clause of abjuration prefixed to new vows of loyalty to the State. But he found few Germans refusing to take the new oath when it became necessary to swear in a land transaction,[27] especially if a bargain were to be had in a conveyance which was made more legal by ready compliance. Implicitly he continued to reason, that if a Pennsylvanian could abjure the King for a title to a tract of soil, he might as honorably abjure him in the cause of freedom. Colonel McAlester's letter was possibly based upon several misconceptions and framed out of a patriot's prejudices. But the smoke in it was not without genuine sparks at its base. Historians have lamented the Tory environment in Delaware and Chester Counties in which Washington was constrained to fight the Battle of the Brandywine. They might have found York County in August, 1777, no more propitious a site for the unhappy issue of the engagement. The reluctance of abjurers fitted in definitely with anti-Whig politics.

Nor was the ill-omened season of expectancy more repugnant to men's minds south of the Yellow Breeches and Codorus Creeks than to the minds of Scotch-Irish folk in the county above York on the Susquehanna.

Cumberland had known abundance of perils during the French and Indian War. John Armstrong had led men from its county seat Carlisle to help win his victory of Kittanning in 1756. Colonel Henry Bouquet had brought back to that town the white prisoners, women and children whom he had recovered in 1764 from their French and Indian abductors. The community was not one of unsuspecting or incautious folk. Danger was always high; and, as latterly they were seeing it, it was danger to the new State they had been helping to make. Ears and eyes were kept open alike to overt and covert acts.

So, five days before the Battle of Brandywine two loyal guardians of the Commonwealth of Pennsylvania had a story to swear to before the notaries of Carlisle.[28]

What had happened did not so much afford encouragement as it provided index to fears and beliefs in a community. William Beckworth and Adam Laughlin had shared in refreshments with David Copeland at Prunk's Tavern on the west shore of the Susquehanna, opposite to Daniel Shelly's Island in that river. David had guided the two Carlisle men forward from a night's lodging in John Rankin's Tavern at Lisburn; and at the riverside his whisky had inspired rather than allayed the mood for revelation, he ventured to confess.

Conspirators were ranging the country from Croghan's Gap in

Cumberland as far east as Lancaster County. Shelly's Island, midway, was a place for rendezvous and transmission of messages. To the east of that point of exchange was Sheriff of Lancaster County John Farree, who could raise 800 men; to the southwest of it the miller and distiller James Rankin of near York Town could not only raise another 500, but was ready with 2,000 bushels of wheat and rye "laid in his mill for Howe's army."[29] In the vicinity of Prunk's a "principal man,"[30] William Willis, had taken a subscription of 50 men who had sworn to be true to one another. A person named Batwell was sure he could gather 350 more men friendly to the British general. A Scotch commander, McDonald of Croghan's, had declared he could raise 100 men to surprise Carlisle by night.

Give those enemies of the Whigs head, and Howe would have only to send 1,000 of his men or a few light horse to seize with them and to control Little York and the whole of York County! As a matter of fact, Copeland himself was now keeping a herd of fourteen cattle in a byplace in his woods, for a Lancaster County farmer who intended them for Howe's army.[31] Shelly had five more on his island.[32] Other folk were in covenant with Copeland's friends not merely in Middletown, but even in Carlisle.[33] The ringleaders were under direction to meet at Shelly's. James Rankin and Batwell had been forewarned of the meeting; Copeland was on his way now to summon Willis.[34]

The narrative of Beckworth and Laughlin wore, perhaps, something less than verisimilitude. A few drinks too many may have done for their faculties of exaggeration somewhat as it did for Copeland's enlargement of numbers and his increasing confidence.

But assurance was made doubly sure at Carlisle. Shelly was seized; the deposition of the two informants was made full enough to inform the Supreme Executive Council in Philadelphia of his arrest before it went forward on September 10.[35] Ironically instructions went back to officers John Creigh and George Stevenson on September 16, five days after Washington's bewildering reverse.[36] Shelly was promised eventual pardon from Council if he would "candidly become a public witness"[37] and lead to the arrest of Rankin and the other conspirators. But let John Creigh and his associate John Agnew take the man's examination and oath in writing, and send it signed by the culprit to the Council. So, in the bleak hour of national crisis, the Dogberrys of the frontier counties were to be constrained to their functions! Thomas Wharton and his colleagues at the administrative head of Pennsylvania's new government had not interpreted a lost battle as a lost cause. Moreover, another county official kept vigilance in Carlisle. County Lieutenant John Carothers added his name to George Stevenson's in a letter of September 25 to William Henry of Lancaster;[38] informed his vigorous compatriot that the Reverend Mr. Thomas Barton had been charged by a witness with complicity in a plot to destroy the public magazines at all three towns, Carlisle, Lancaster, and York; and recommended that the clergyman be "secured" as "prudence should direct."[39]

Such, then, was the spirit of the inland counties whose militia participated in Washington's actions on September 11. The position chosen for the companies which had been sent forward by the three County Lieutenants Carothers, McAlester, and Galbraith was an honorable one for Pennsylvania. Under the command of General John Armstrong and on the left of the army, they were so placed as to be the prospective defenders of the roads from Wilmington and Chester toward Philadelphia, as though Howe would attempt his way in the most direct beeline for the city. It seemed they were to have the prime opportunity of defense for their own State; and no American officer on the eve of the day anticipated Howe's striking farther west than Chadd's Ford.

But as the battle went, Howe got the main force of his army far to their right by an unanticipated fishhook movement, employed a minor force against the American center, played his feints successfully there first against General Maxwell's light troops and then more heavily at Chadd's without advancing against Anthony Wayne; and, outwitting and outnumbering Sullivan on the far right of Washington's planned battlefield, turned the flank of the American forces. A hot morning with persistent fog served more than well Sir William's beginning of the day. After that, the change in position to which Sullivan was compelled by a long and difficult sudden march to the right not only demonstrated the British general's superiority in tactics but brought desperate confusion upon Washington's center, and forced his immediate retreat far from the Brandywine to Dilworth Village in the northeast and his prompt withdrawal within the next three days from his position at Chester. Then the way to Philadelphia was open to Howe; and the Scotch-Irish farmers and militia from Cumberland, York, and Lancaster Counties, in main number drawn safely from a part of the front where they had no enemy to fight, had nothing more to be proud of than that they had shared with George Washington an eclipse of his military reputation.

The Battle of Germantown, fought three weeks later, added no particular distinctions to their score. Indeed, on October 4 they were by another irony of circumstances at some distance from the main action. From Chestnut Hill they marched with Armstrong far to the south on the Manatawny Road, closer to the British Camp than any other detachment of Wayne, Sullivan, Maxwell, or Greene—only to have the brunt of the day's action contested along other roads to the northeast. On that autumn day of dense fog, they experienced no opportunity to rival the fortitude of their kinsmen who had marched with Arnold to Quebec in 1775, or the gallantry of the others who had won with Washington in the winter at Trenton and Princeton. Their best luck was to have survived a battle with General Washington still at the head of an army, and to learn within the next fortnight of how the British Burgoyne had lost. For the Battle of Saratoga had been won only three days after Germantown had been lost.

Happily, furthermore, awareness of the ordeal the winter of 1777-1778 would mean for the army and its commander was not known in September, or even October. Although both the Council of Pennsylvania and the Continental Congress had to remove from Philadelphia into the interior, men who saw the full import of Washington's defeats were not a majority—and as little as any to understand it were the politician friends of Gates. Before and after the disaster optimism prevailed among numbers of men of good sense.

Certainly General Armstrong had no prevision of catastrophe. As he wrote to President Wharton from Chester on September 1,[40] planning the distribution of as many blankets as could be collected and appealing that the Philadelphia Troop of Light Horse be given opportunity appropriate to their ambition to act in the field, he was comfortable in all points. The one matter on which he insisted most upon that date was that rum be purchased and provided for the militia just as sufficiently as for the Continental Line.[41] He wanted no risk of disturbance from the Pennsylvanians of the new classes coming to field service because they were without liquors "when on fatigue and in bad weather."[42]

On the 8th he was as sanguine. Then he believed Howe intended to reembark on the Delaware, cross with his forces to New Jersey, and move up the Bay to attack Philadelphia from the east side of the river. But that belief did not disturb him: "the army generally were in good spirits and looked for action."[43] Attack upon Howe's camp, under the conditions which Armstrong thought he foresaw, would be easy. The British general's rear could be pressed hard, while he was waiting for his ships to move from the Chesapeake and come to his support in Delaware Bay. (Obviously Howe's tactics remained anybody's guess among Americans as late as three days before the Battle of the Brandywine, as they remained for Washington up to the day of action.) Cheerful, too, was Colonel Galbraith in Lancaster at the end of October. The Battle of Germantown had been fought to its bitter conclusion. Washington had called upon Council "in the most pressing terms for a more effectual aid of men and arms"[44] from Pennsylvania. Council had called for the immediate marching to camp of classes 6th and 7th of the Lancaster County battalions. The County Lieutenant was transmitting instructions to Colonel John Rogers for the men of the last classes in Hanover Township: "Let us then follow the example of the eastern militia and serve Howe and his army as they have served Burgoyne and his . . . which, if we turn out, is in our power positively—unless kind Providence has otherwise determined."[45] The grandson of a Presbyterian clergyman had, of course, to allow for possible other foreordination. But he was too jubilant "on the late success of our American arms" in New York—"beyond everything to be looked for"—to think that the men of Hanover and of Lancaster County would not march "to a man, as called for, and wipe away the stigma now at our doors."[46] Thomas Barton might have gone over to the cause of Britain, not Bertram Galbraith.

Yet more able to look at the situation with good humor and wit than either of his fellow Pennsylvanians (Armstrong and the Lancaster County official) was General James Potter. That stalwart from Northumberland County was not one to despair easily. He had been at Kittanning as a subaltern in 1756, and had known other experience in the French and Indian Wars. From Cumberland County he had moved on the eve of the Revolution into the new county up the Susquehanna; and, pioneer in spirit, had ventured thirty miles or more upstream on Penn's Creek west of the river to break forest lands for a new habitation. The summer of 1776 had found him a leader in Northumberland County and once more a soldier. He had acquitted himself with dignity on Long Island in the long retreat through New York and New Jersey which followed, and led a contingent of Northumberland militia at Trenton and Princeton. He had been tried and respected. Representative of the Scotch-Irishman at his best, he blended intelligence with his drollery. A month before Washington had led his depleted army into Valley Forge, Potter was still keeping himself conversant with all that happened around Chester, and with much that happened in British-occupied Philadelphia. So he could write with aplomb on November 12 to President Wharton,[47] then snug with the Supreme Executive Council in Lancaster Town.

He reported neatly the latest military and naval news: what firing there had been in the three days just past, how many enemy ships were in the river, where two brigs and a sloop had stolen past one American fort, how certain militiamen had seized a group of Tories loading enemy boats with fresh provisions and destroyed six of their vessels. But interspersed with his account was his waggish mirth. There were 38 British sails on the Delaware; but "what number of troops on Board is secret to me."[48] "Howe is the best Whig maker in the United States; he has converted many from the evil of their ways and turned them unto their Country. Distress and want is likely to abound in the City; I am told the poor would have suffered before this time if General Washington had not allowed them to get flour at the Frankford Mills."

"Friend Howe is not a partial man; he uses Whig and Tory alike— which is the best thing I can say of him. . . . My men brought in this day five British soldiers prisoners; we catch them nappin'."[49] One month after he wrote this, his stout opposition to Cornwallis drew praise from Washington, and made the commander-in-chief's retirement into Valley Forge a successful military maneuver.

It would have been well, in fact, if James Potter's sense for the laughable had been ingrained likewise in the minds of the Congress which, in the months now ahead, was to doubt Washington, play to the conceited Horatio Gates, accredit the adventurer Thomas Conway, and make smooth the way for a cabal which should presently add to the bleak misery of Valley Forge the still colder spectacle of a designing consent to rob a great man of his rightful meed of praise.

CHAPTER 17

"AND DEVIL TAKE THE HINDMOST!"

THE YEAR 1777 closed without shining glory for Pennsylvania, and the year which followed opened with no particular brightening rays. Bleak December changed into chill January; hope and understanding continued frostbitten. Spirits easily numbed among Pennsylvanians defaulted—some morally only, some both politically and morally. The most honest and courageous citizens and patriots saw their duty clearly as ever. But not all, even among the Scotch-Irish, were courageous and honest. Farmers who put in and harvested crops of wheat by indurate habit of mind expected gain from their labor and prudence. Millers who converted wheat into flour expected compensation for their skill and for use of mill-wheel, mill-stone, and hopper. Wagoners who transported wheat or flour looked for monetary reward for their service. And wagon masters who gathered wagoners together and directed their routes of delivery anticipated at least a modicum of prosperity for their superintendence.

A government or an army which sought to do business with farmer, miller, wagoner, or wagon master, had to deal always with the human equation; and the human equation demanded a return in the soundest form of money obtainable. Of that, little kind was on hand which commanded unwavering respect. As buyers, Continental Congress, the Supreme Executive Council of Pennsylvania, and the Commander-in-Chief of the American Army carried no great impressiveness with either Continental bills or State-issued script. In a period of need, in brief, the purchaser had little weight with the producer; and the producer, whether he had much or little left in his storehouse, had grown dubious of why he should produce any more than food for himself and family; a roof over his and their heads; shelter for his live stock; oats, hay, or corn to be put into the feed troughs of his farm animals. Provisions for the camp at Valley Forge, under the circumstances, were

[235

bound to come, if they could be induced to come at all, from a reluctant market.

In the popular version of the history of the American Revolution contrasts are always made vivid between the snug comfort of Howe's army in Philadelphia and the ordeal of cold and hunger facing Washington's men in their winter camp. In fact, contrasts might be made quite as sharp between the enduring patience of the common soldier in his chill bivouac of 1777-1778 and the paralyzing blend of parsimony and timidity in the civilians of the Pennsylvania counties from the Schuylkill River to the Susquehanna and beyond. One did not have to go very far west to find the farmer who feared trouble from the Indian quite as much as—if not more than—he feared a possible campaign of Howe westward in the spring. As generally as they could do so, the militia of the State had disbanded and sought their own homes during the winter of Valley Forge. Commonly they resisted either lures to new enlistment or orders to their particular class to proceed to camp; few wished to belong to an unpaid army, or to an army paid in a medium possessed of little or no buying power. From Westmoreland County eastwards to Bedford and York and northeastwards to Cumberland and Northumberland Counties depredations were perennially anticipated from the redskins on the borders.

As back inhabitants too frequently saw the situation, theirs was the choice between serving unremunerated in an army or serving with their neighbors in scouting parties locally organized to defend their families and farmsteads. The easier decision to remain near home seemed to them, honestly enough, the one more relevant. Their inertia during the winter of suffering for Washington and his men certainly manifested no quality of heroism, but it had causes altogether human. To keep household and children safe seemed first civic duty, and the best reward was immediate security for them.

Liberty for the realist has always inhered in tangible privileges and commodities. With him the thought of home comes before the thought of country; the thought of property-rights precedes constitutional law. By definition the individual thinks for himself before he thinks for society. It was both the strength and the weakness of the pioneer that he thought for himself first. Unselfishness was not the prime trait of the colonial settler of Pennsylvania: English, Scotch-Irish, or German.

There were, of course, different sides to the picture in that winter of crisis. As early as December 22 General John Armstrong saw the conditions as they faced him personally. With diligence he had set about the duties which Washington assigned to him on the outposts of the encampment "at what was called the Forge or Valley Hill."[1] Nine stations of sentinels had been arranged for on nine "Capitol roads."[2] The men detailed there were to prevent marketers from carrying produce into Philadelphia; and by their patrols and a few light horse to see that the enemy made no forages into the country.

But that plan called for frequent movement and constant change of lodgement for the officers who administered it. Armstrong felt his physical unfitness for the task. His lodgings, he pleaded in a letter to President Wharton, had grown "too hard" for him, and "severer weather must be at hand."[3] His compeer General Potter, he declared by way of example, "says he can by no means tarry the winter."[4] What Potter could not do, he implied, Pennsylvania ought not to expect of a man four years Potter's senior. Yet "some *Head*," he continued, "these people must certainly have very suddenly, else all will go to confusion."[5] Obviously he wished himself to be clear of the responsibility; and, as he wrote, he "flattered" himself "that from my letter by Doctor Duffield a new appointment would have been made, and the person ready for duty."[6]

The Supreme Executive Council took the hint offered by Armstrong; reasoned on the subject of the major general's "advanced age" (He was then not quite fifty-three) which was obliging him "to quit the field during the severity of the season";[7] and, on December 31 from Lancaster, they wrote to General Potter somewhat apologetically. That officer Wharton requested to be the head in Armstrong's place —could Potter remain longer? "Council" were "aware of the peculiar hardship"[8] on their addressee in being kept so long from his family and his private affairs; but could he remain so long as through the winter?

Nine days later, however, the consent of Council had been granted to both John Armstrong and James Potter to go home. Brigadier General John Lacey had been appointed[9] to the service for which Armstrong had reported an administrator was needed, and to which Potter, his friend and one time aide at Kittanning, did not wish to succeed. The illness of his wife had made the forty-nine-year-old Potter return to Northumberland immediately. In brief, the age of one Scotch-Irish general took him away from the side of George Washington at Valley Forge, and a family indisposition took another. Happily both officers left names for valiant service back at camp, and Potter at least was missed by the commander-in-chief not as a slack friend but as one honored and regarded as unavoidably absent.

Other persons, not so old as the Scotch-Irish generals, likewise found it impracticable to help Washington's army that winter. If Congress directed 12,000 barrels of flour to be deposited at or near Reading, 6,000 barrels at or near Bethlehem, 2,000 at Downing's Town, and 2,000 at Pottsgrove,[10] commissaries promptly found farmers and millers reluctant to part with their products for forms of payment unsatisfactory to them, and wagoners or wagon owners just as skeptical of the form of compensation purporting to reward them for their haulage. If salt were needed and expected from the Pennsylvania Salt Works, an organization near Egg Harbor, New Jersey, with which contract had been made by the Pennsylvania Council, it was found by Thomas Savadge, the manager there, that he had not enough pans for the boiling of the salt brine available, not enough smiths and carpenters to set up new pans, not enough militiamen to transport salt when he could turn it out at the rate of twenty bushels a day.[11] The militia near by did not enjoy making salt; their officers accepted any excuse to draw them off to other duties; furthermore, before salt could be made, barracks were needed for officers and salt-workers, and the winter was not a seasonable time for building new barracks.

In supplying the flour, similar obstacles arose. Wagon Master General James Young learned of Mr. Leonard Reed, Wagon Master for Berks County, that his problems there were many: he lived in the extreme west of Berks on Tulpehocken, his wife was in a bad state of health, he neither read nor wrote English.[12] General Young suggested that he resign and let another be appointed in his stead, but the man demurred at that and refused to give to his adviser the list of wagons he had been making up in the countryside. So the work of enlisting wagons had to begin all over. Then, when lists were ready, came new problems. A new regulation by Act of Assembly affecting commissioners and the magazines of flour being gathered together was seized on for pretext, and new interruptions in the loading of wagons were immediate.[13] Expresses came from Head Quarters to Reading in February urging immediate supply, only to find wagoners quarreling about clauses in the Act.

So bad was the situation on February 12, 1778, that Ephraim Blaine of the Pennsylvania Line, a deputy commissary general, wrote from Valley Forge his inability to render support to the army; "not one brigade of wagons had come from Lancaster or the Back Counties"[14] in the past three weeks to aid in hauling from the magazines of flour.

His quartermasters were complaining that they had no power to press or procure a single team. Three days later General Washington himself was writing to Congress, constrained to inform them of the critical and alarming state of the army "for want of provisions of the meat kind."[15] Many of the troops for four days, and some longer have not drawn the smallest supplies of this article." He warned: "This being the case, it is needless to add, to convince you of their distress, they have been on the point of dispersing; and, without the earliest relief, no address or authority will be sufficient to keep them long together."[16] In a postscript he added that as it was with provisions for his men, so it was with forage for his horses; supply was materially wanted. "Without it, and very speedily, we shall not have a horse left."[17]

Ultimately, in fact, Washington had to abandon deference to civil authority; correspondence with an ineffectual or—so far as he was personally concerned—double-dealing Congress; respect for the measures of the Pennsylvania Council and Assembly; regard for the property-rights of the Pennsylvania householders and farmers. He felt compelled to concert schemes with his best friend in camp, General Nathaniel Greene. That aide and he threshed out matters. Greene accepted a repugnant task.[18] The army was now the imperative; without it there was no solution for the American cause. Not Congress, not citizenry must first be served if the cause was in the end to prevail.

A stern work was begun. Ardent young officers, generals like Mad Anthony Wayne and Lighthorse Harry Lee, became raiders plundering the whole surrounding region to feed the men and keep their few regiments and battalions intact. As Greene saw it and instructed a subordinate, "You must forage the country naked"; to prevent complaints of other officers that there was no forage for their horses, "we must take all their cattle, sheep, and horses fit for the use of the army."[19]

The will of the commander-in-chief and of his adjutant in the winter of distress became, in brief, the deed of the season. Food came into Valley Forge; by main force the American army was preserved through stripping the stores of Pennsylvania; treasures of the field, the granary, the mill, and the larder. Counties like Chester, Berks, and Lancaster had no choice but to render tribute to imperious military necessity.

Almost as informally, meantime, the stage was being set in frontier counties. There men thought as obstinately of the defense of their homes as generals at Valley Forge thought of the preservation of an army's potential.

From Northumberland County, in a petition to the Supreme Executive Council of Pennsylvania, came a clue to back inhabitant attitudes and sympathies of the period.[20] The petitioners frankly admitted themselves to be settled on unpurchased lands. Their necessities had driven them to find homes for themselves and their families. But they were satisfied that they had been good citizens of the State: they had submitted to the militia law of Pennsylvania, they had taken the recent oath of allegiance, many of them had already undergone "the hardships of a severe winter's campaign in New Jersey," they had "early encouraged a number of their brethren into Continental Service."[21] Furthermore they were confident that their presence in the county was a deterrent to the New England settlers up the North Branch in Wyoming on the Connecticut Claim.

Yet two other things were equally obvious: they mistrusted the wisdom of having a few large land owners in Northumberland; they saw that any displacement of the Wyoming settlers would be a displacement of small settlers like themselves in favor of the great owners under Pennsylvania title.

In fact, they saw no more harm in Wyoming people settled by Connecticut title on small lands not their own than they saw in themselves. Also they testified in their petition that people in the Wyoming were like themselves supporting "the present contest," the latter point meaning "not only against the British army but also against a cruel and savage enemy on our frontiers."[22]

Vouching for such sentiments by their signatures were men who had served in the battlefields of the past two years. The name of Matthew Smith was there, who had campaigned with Arnold before Quebec but who had now become a settler in Northumberland; that of Captain William Gray, veteran of Long Island; of Colonel Samuel Hunter, old mentor in Susquehanna River affairs; of Major James Crawford of the Twelfth Pennsylvania Regiment in the Continental Line, who had been wounded in the Battle of Brandywine; of Colonel William Cooke, commander of that same regiment even then wintering with General Washington in the bitter camp of adversity. All spoke for what in the twentieth century would be called "the little man," propertyless, exposed to danger, prone to think first of offspring and mate.

Fitting to much the same key was a letter from Samuel Hunter at Fort Augusta on January 14.[23] This deferred properly to President Wharton, and in conclusion informed that dignitary that his earlier instructions ordering out the fifth class of the militia were being attended to and that the men had been commanded to be ready to march on the 20th. But in other details it was more definite. The Indians had been striking at several points in the county. Two settlers had been killed and scalped near the Great Island on the West Branch; a third had been slain near the mouth of Pine Creek. The inhabitants were experiencing considerable confusion. Rumors were speeding about of Indians seen: a party here, a group there, all suspected of hostility. Mr. Hunter had ordered out three classes of Colonel Cookson Long's battalion; they had scouted diligently along the West Branch; yet on January 1 they found another inhabitant dead and scalped two miles above the Great Island. That discovery had quickened pursuit again; and two Indians, whom snow had enabled the scouts to track, were killed in reprisal. Long's men, however, had now returned to their families, which were "suffering at this inclement season of the year, as they are afraid to live in their own houses."[24]

In sum, wrote the squire from Fort Augusta, "The generality of the inhabitants does not think it prudent to let any out of the county at this present call for the militia, when the frontiers is like to suffer by a cruel savage enemy."[25] Five days later, Thomas Wharton and the Council in Lancaster framed and forwarded instructions. They remarked that if the militia of Philadelphia and Bucks Counties were kept out to protect the inhabitants there from the British, it was as relevant for the Northumberland militia to be held for similar purpose in their own county against "the insults and murders of the savage tribe."[26] Let the militia of the fifth class stay in their own country and be usefully employed in protecting settlers along the Susquehanna.

In distant Bedford County the same apprehensiveness obtained. County Lieutenant John Piper addressed the Supreme Council on January 20,[27] making both report and appeal to that body in Lancaster Town. He and the Sub-Lieutenants of Bedford had been laboring on measures to keep the countryside from being evacuated by all its inhabitants. In the old pattern of protection exemplified by the Paxton and Hanover Rangers in Lancaster County during the French and Indian War they had raised men and established stations of scouts, thirty for the settlement "called the Gleads,"[28] forty for the center at Bedford, thirty for Frankstown, thirty for Sinking Valley, thirty for Harts Log Settlement and Shavers Creek. From Maryland to far north and northeastwards into the valley of the Juniata, the passes of vast domain of forests and mountains had to be guarded, and, unhappily, provisions for the rangers were scarce and prices exorbitant. Colonel Piper had been obliged to offer his scouts pay for five pounds monthly, and had to enlist them for a service of nine months. Bluntly he presented his opinion that Council would have to find funds to meet the expense, provide stores at each scouting post, and raise supplementary troops. If Council would not support the measures which he proposed, he predicted "that on the first alarm from Indians, a great part of our country will be left desolate."[29]

Six days later a petition to Council was being framed—as if to corroborate John Piper—at Standing Stone Valley,[30] far from Bedford Town. Twenty-eight men of Scotch-Irish name reported in this that all had faithfully taken the oath of allegiance to Pennsylvania, and argued accordingly their rights of protection from the Indians as elsewhere other citizens were defended from the British. To illustrate the dangers which they confronted they told of their nearness to Kishacoquillas Creek in Cumberland County, and of the nearness of that neighborhood to Bald Eagle Creek in Northumberland from which the settlers were "drove in"[31] a month earlier by the Indian murder of Anthony Saltzman; and tersely they requested that Council ratify their raising a company for their defense. More than that, having reminded the authorities that to date their scouts had had to be reimbursed out of the private pockets of their wealthier citizens, they urged two terms: first, payment in advance of the first month's five pounds compensation; second, equal recognition with the Continental Line in claims for "bounty and clothing."[32] Liberty, quite apparently, if it was worth fighting for, was worth being paid for. Scotch-Irish rangers on the frontiers did not hesitate to put an economic value on their guardianship.

Something of their truculence manifested itself, too, as far west as Westmoreland County, beyond both Bedford and the Allegheny Mountains. To Brigadier-General Edward Hand, promoted in April, 1777, after his feats with his riflemen at Trenton and Princeton and sent into Western Pennsylvania to mobilize militia there against Indian and Tory, came the doleful response of a dweller on Ten Mile Creek. "Would to God," wrote Daniel McFarland on February 5, 1778, "I could inform your Honor of anything relating this county but disobedience and the greatest contempt of all authority."[33] Out of 150 privates, he protested, only 70 would consent to serve at the several stations in Westmoreland. To the writer it seemed ludicrous that men of the "interior parts of the country"—by which he meant the counties to the east—were "railing because they are called to guard the frontiers."[34] The absurdity was the greater, in fact, because "the frontiers are making preparations to remove, being afraid of the danger."[35] So, although he had stored six month's provisions for the rangers of the county, McFarland was angry that men adhered more punctually to cabin and family than to army and scouting. All he could do was to hope for the counsel of General Hand, when his field officers and men should meet on February 10. Householders, it was quite apparent, were designing generally to remain close to their chattels and farmsteads. When they moved, many undoubtedly kept thinking, it would be with their families, eastwards or southwards out of the nearer pathways of the Indians.

Not different was the discontent in York County during the winter of Valley Forge. Not of Washington, and not of the dangers at far points like Ten Mile or Bald Eagle Creeks, but of pay was the thought there. County Lieutenant Richard McAlester fretted now not by reason of George III's recent German subjects refusing to take oaths of allegiance to the American cause. A new cause of irritation had come. The Supreme Council had not met the payments due the militia who had marched, the official for York reminded the body in a letter of January 22. The classes which had not marched knew that, and no one cared to march under the circumstances. It was impossible to get a Constable to do his duty in the militia.[36] No one was willing to undertake collection of money to procure readier service of the recalcitrants. The men would "rather go to prison."[37] The "great part" of their excuse was "the militia not being paid," and the "supposes" that they never will be."[38]

The spirit of inland Pennsylvania, indeed, had become nugatory. Scotch-Irish county lieutenants and militia field officers in the back counties did all they could to maintain or to restore morale. Among farmers, small traders, and woodmen an economic crisis and a fear of Indians dampened the ardor for far adventure in a high cause. The pinch of poverty played in with remoteness and isolation. The winter of suspense bred one common and desolating conclusion: it was every man for himself, and devil take the hindmost! Desperation, cunning, terror, and cowardice had become bedfellows. Small men cringed before an irony of circumstance which they read as necessity.

But theirs was plight rather than envy or contempt or malice. It was not the frontiersmen who in the sad winter after Brandywine and Germantown schemed against Washington. Not they, but Continental Congress, complacent to the maneuverings of Thomas Conway and Horatio Gates, and those two ill assorted generals themselves properly bear the odium in American history which comes into the record of the encampment at Valley Forge. The charlatan military adventurer from Europe, whom Congress in affront to the commander-in-chief honored with an inspector generalship, and the conceited American major general who flaunted the laurels really won by another officer at Saratoga, strutted and conspired. Politicians during the winter of 1778 conceded to them the privilege of attempting an expedition which, it was vaingloriously promised, should wrest Canada from Britain; consummate every possible advantage out of Burgoyne's defeat of the previous autumn; and, incidentally, eternize the fame of the two conspirators.

But before March the bubble of Gates and Conway was pricked. Congress became better aware of the incompetence of the Board of War which had countenanced the exploit. Divulgence of the cabal against Washington came to that general through James Wilkinson. There were scenes of recrimination, tears, *opéra bouffe*, reconciliations among the doubters and the enemies of the one great enduring hero of Valley Forge. Chagrin, if not shame, came upon Gates; disgrace upon Conway.

Happier for Washington than those experiences, with their acrid and smoky tang spoiling the freshening winds of spring, was the arrival at Valley Forge of Baron Frederick William Von Steuben.[39] He came in February, almost in time to be a birthday gift to the commander. History, however, had a more exalted purpose for him than that.

Born a petty German noble, trained in the school of King Frederick the Great, he came now on a service for France. Charles Gravier, Comte de Vergennes, Foreign Minister of Louis XVI, had sent him. That French statesman had no love for England; he had thought Washington a remarkable general in having so trained a broken army in a year that he could attack General Howe with it at Germantown; he had learned of the success of the Americans against the British at Freeman's Farm and Bemus Heights. He wanted Washington to be able to keep his army longer. He regarded Von Steuben as a disciplinarian who might well help the American general.

The Baron was, in fact, the godsend of early 1778 not only to Washington but to the cause of liberty in the United States. He entered the American scene with no pretentious dazzle, as Conway had. He was a drillmaster, but undeniably he brought something like the increasing warmth of a late winter sun, and an assuring power of its penetrating and livening rays.

When he arrived he saw men literally naked;[40] he saw officers who had coats, but coats of every color and make; he beheld men of rank, even at a grand parade, wearing old dressing gowns, old blankets, old woolen bed covers for coats as they mounted guard.[41] Washington made him acting inspector general—Conway still having the inspector generalship from Congress, not from the general.

Von Steuben set to remaking a bleak contingent of tatterdemalions into a disciplined and competent army. Day after day, from early morning until late at night, he drilled. Vociferous in his command, he shook now with rage, now roared with laughter. He swore much, but for want of English words had to keep his worst words in German.[42] When he could not make these tell as he wished, he called aides to him and made them swear at their soldiers in their own native tongue. To the men he imparted new spirit, to the officers, mirth.

Merriment became the mood among his subalterns. If they had to club rations when he had them to dinner with him, their vaunt was that no guest dared appear unless he came in torn clothes and ready to eat tough steak and potatoes as sumptuous food, topping it off with hickory nuts for desert.[43] As for the wine, they boasted that the best substitute for it was liquor of flame in their glasses, which they drank fire and all. And none minded that their host called them his "sans culottes."[44] What mattered a fleer in a French tongue or the lack of a whole pair of breeches, if Steuben was entertaining!

Strange quirk in the romance of time and seasons that a stocky German, of temperament oscillating between the phlegmatic and the violent, should have been in 1778 the harbinger of better months ahead. The fatality of men escaping for themselves or the devil taking the hindmost could not endure permanently among men of military age of Valley Forge or elsewhere, once Steuben had been allied with George Washington.

CHAPTER 18

WYOMING

BUT, AS SUMMER BEGAN that year, the lessons of discipline did not everywhere ripen into fair fruit. Certainly into two sectors of the contest for liberty came instances of behavior gainsaying the perfectibility of military science. Tactics, in the last analysis, are dependent upon persons; and persons, for causes however dissimilar, act differently from expectations. The Battle of Monmouth in New Jersey at the end of June and the Massacre of Wyoming in Pennsylvania—or, as many settlers then thought of it, in Westmoreland County, Connecticut—five days later on July 3 are events not commonly associated in the annals of history. Yet from each there survives a clouded name, remembered by the historian because of a man's refusal to be dominated by the wisdom of a military superior.

Major General Charles Lee by his disobedience robbed Washington and the American army of the fruits of a victory which Washington's intelligence and his men's valor had rightly earned. A Scotch-Irish farmer among the men of Wyoming is the bizarre example of a leader elevated to his position by a mutiny and then moving forward, trusted and trusting, to die with his men and his compeers, out-generaled and out-numbered, on a forefront of horror.

The outward course of events, American and European, in the spring of 1778 was all but panoramic. The Conway cabal declined into nothing. Congress diffidently but gradually made amends to Washington. France played a politic game, continued to enjoy the advantages of commerce with America, for a time longer spared herself the expense of a war. Britain accepted the resignation of Sir William Howe, determined to replace him in his Philadelphia station with Sir Henry Clinton, and issued instructions to Clinton. The Tory families of the city founded by William Penn joined with British officers to accord Howe a gala farewell, and the Mischianza, fantastic combination of dress ball, water race, tournament, wining and dining, was contrived to allay as it could the sorrows of parting. To Valley Forge came a courier from the east with valid news of a French frigate arrived in New England bringing a treaty of alliance between France and the United States. Vergennes had wielded his influence; in Paris the court had chosen to act with the American side. French generals and admirals were talking maneuvers and campaigns. Capitals like Berlin and St. Petersburg, whose armed neutrality had worked to the interest of America, smiled as a world war loomed, projected with definite odds against England. Moreover, General Clinton matured plans for carrying out the instructions he had received; and mid June, to the surprise of American generals and civilians, witnessed the spectacle of the British army withdrawing from Philadelphia in a north-east diagonal across New Jersey. In its wake thronged a miscellany of aristocratic refugees, Tories who dared not remain in the city, and the usual nondescript camp followers and loose women.

Everything suddenly constituted for Washington and his country a magnificent opportunity. With his army refashioned, he moved promptly, shrewdly, effectually. After two weeks of the most skillful maneuvering, he had the chagrin of knowing that, through his insistence on courtesy to a rival, his unperturbed confidence in a fellow Virginian, and the latter's misbehavior on the field, he had been cheated of a triumph. Lee "had not put his whole soul into the discharge of a trust"; and on June 28, 1778, Washington had lost in what is sometimes called "the greatest tragedy of the Revolutionary War."[1]

Court-martial, suspension from his command, eventual discharge from the Army, disgrace, and obloquy followed for Lee. By the ignominy of Lee the War for Independence was prolonged for the United States.

In the days when the stage was being set for the failure of the Battle of Monmouth in New Jersey, much was shaping along the shores of the Susquehanna also to an unforeseen end.

Seven-and-a-half years had elapsed since Lazarus Stewart had been charged with the murder of Nathan Ogden through a loop hole in the fort which that "rioter" and his New England companions were holding against Pennsylvania law. Nearly eight years had receded since his escape was made good from Pennsylvania sheriffs at Lebanon and York. There had been in the interim no clearing of his reputation among Philadelphia authorities; and oppositely there had been no impugning of it among his immediate Scotch-Irish fellows or among the Connecticut men who with his aid had prevailed against the Pennamites in 1770, lost with him in January, 1771, and won again in August of the latter year. Since that month the Yankee settlers of Wyoming and their allies out of old Paxton and Hanover, Pennsylvania, had maintained their effectual power on the river shores which they occupied in Westmoreland County, in the jurisdiction of the New England Colony which in 1776 had become a State.

Depositions carried to Philadelphia in February, 1771, pictured Lazarus' treachery. He had, they declared, invited Nathan Ogden to a friendly conference before the walls of Fort Durkee, then wantonly shot him dead as he began parleying, while other men in the redoubt kept firing from all corners. But the sponsors of the Susquehanna Company of Connecticut had persisted in accrediting him. At the Proprietors' Meeting in Wilkes-Barre, in October, 1772, with Captain Zebulon Butler moderating, it was voted that Captain Lazarus Stewart and William Stewart were deserving of "the Town of Hanover."[2] In the same year that great tract of land, on a southwest fraction of which stands today the famous town of Nanticoke, was divided among him and his followers. Six out of its thirty-one lots were assigned to him, one other lot was reserved for a parsonage, and two more for public purposes. None of his Scotch-Irish fellows but expected presently to have a Presbyterian minister among them, a cleric who would respect their captain as did the Reverend Mr. Elder in Lancaster County, Pennsylvania. On Stewart's honor as a frontiersman no Robinson, Graham, Espy, or Young among them beheld any blot. He was as worthy of respect as his grandsire Ruling Elder Lazarus Stewart, founder of the Presbyterian Church in Hanover back home; and he and his companions-in-arms were as ready to become farmers on new lands as their sires had been down the River forty years earlier. The man who had cried out against Israel Pemberton and defied the government of John Penn built a house for his wife Martha Espy and their growing family on a rising plot which overlooked the Susquehanna.[3] Days became more peaceful. He was turning forty; let younger men assume responsibility as leaders. As for him, let him be a freeholder on a limited acreage of land settled to the pattern of Connecticut policy and get possessions together for his two sons and parcel of daughters.

But more than private wishes kept shaping Stewart's destiny. The cause of Independence, not from Pennsylvania but from Britain, was in men's talk. News of resolves down the river in Lancaster County came to the expatriate's ears. Josiah Espy and James Stewart and other folk in old Hanover were declaring for liberty. In 1776 men of Westmoreland County were as ready to support Connecticut against

England as were folk in Lancaster and Northumberland Counties in the old Province to defend Pennsylvania. The American Revolution added its excitements on the frontier to the old excitements of the Pennamite War; and, since the Indians too commonly were joining the foe, the excitements of Indian war became only a recurrent proof of the indispensableness of freedom. While Washington was at Valley Forge in the winter of 1777-1778 and Continental Congress was in Lancaster and York, old hatreds, resentments, expressions of consciousness of right brooded menacingly. The Indian resented the presence of the white settler in the Valley of Wyoming, long reserved to him by sacred agreement; the Pennsylvanian resented the New England man there; the Yankee resented the pretension of the Pennsylvanian to have any privilege in the Valley unearned by collaboration with himself. Loyalists out of neighboring counties in Pennsylvania or New Jersey or New York deplored any men in the Valley having a grievance against Britain, or wanting to separate from it.

Complexity of motive waxed and prevailed. Ears remained alert as in York, Bedford, Westmoreland, Cumberland, and Northumberland Counties, Pennsylvania. As rumors of Indian maraudings flowed to Thomas Wharton in Lancaster or York Town, so in the first months of 1778 did memorials speed from the Wyoming settlements to the Connecticut Assembly.[4] Dangers were anticipated from Tioga, the point at which the Chemung empties into the North Branch of the Susquehanna.[5] Tories were suspected to be operating among Indians there; and more than confirmation of the soundness of that suspicion was the capture of a band of Tories by a scouting party of Westmoreland militia in January. The menace was more near in February when Parshall Terry, Westmorelander member of John Butler's Rangers, with a party of fifty Indians and Tories plundered the household and family of New Englander Amos York at Wyalusing, and carried him away with his meat and his grain, his own and his family's bedding and wearing apparel, and his faithful neighbor Lemuel Fitch into the bargain.[6]

Despite a march next month by Colonel Dorrance with 150 men of the 24th Regiment of Connecticut to a successful rescue of the man's wife and children from their consequent destitution, there were by May other maraudings and expulsions of New England families reported to the authorities in Connecticut.[7] Petitions for protection and appeals for the payment of companies of militia with the duty of protecting the settlements went forward. Anxiety continued, the pitch of it rising higher as May turned into June.

By the middle of June clusters of scouts knew that Indians and Tories were lurking on the river above Tunkhannock and that their friend William Crooks of Kingston, Westmoreland County, had been shot dead by a redskin assassin at the abandoned house of John Secord in that vicinity.[8] On the 17th a party of six Connecticut men from Jenkins' Fort in the Valley had encountered a band of Indians six miles below Tunkhannock and had seen with them no less a person than Elijah Phelps of Butler's Rangers, brother-in-law of Miner Robbins.[9] On their canoe had come suddenly a fusillade of Indian bullets; and, although they escaped as a party, it was only to gaze on helpless next morning as their friend Robbins died of his wounds, and then to hasten word to the settlement of treacherous fire on the River.

Reports from Colonel Dorrance went forward to the Board of War at York, Pennsylvania, and to Connecticut officialdom in New England[10] where Colonel Nathan Denison was attending the Assembly as representative from Westmoreland. Continental Congress was informed of impending danger in the Wyoming.[11] Lieutenant Colonel Zebulon Butler was designated to remain in that area and to direct the operations of a military force to be collected there. Two independent companies from Westmoreland, whose numbers had been diminishing for various causes, were ordered to be reduced to one company[12] detailed to service on their own frontier under the new command of Captain Simon Spalding. Officers of the former dual muster resigned from the detachment[13] and set off for their homes to the aid of their threatened people. Simon Spalding marched away from Lancaster, Pennsylvania, with the Westmoreland Independent Company on June 28, having a distance of over 125 miles by road to cover between Lancaster and Wilkes-Barre.[14] Zebulon Butler, his errands at York accomplished, hurried back to the scene of apprehension;[15] Colonel Denison turned thither from the Connecticut capital, Hartford. Families from outlying farmsteads began flocking to the stockades and block-houses in the Valley—greater numbers of them gathering at Forty Fort for protection. Scouts penetrated less far up the River, and none more distant than Wyalusing.

Every man, young or old, who had a gun or could procure one, began training. Companies were ordered to be ready to act at a moment's warning. The one and only cannon in the settlement, a four-pounder at Fort Wilkes-Barre,[16] for which no shot was on hand but which could be charged with powder was put into readiness to serve as an alarm.

On June 30 a group of Yankees from the lower end of Exeter Town, who had proceeded upstream on a harvesting errand to Stephen Harding's cornfield on the flats above the mouth of Sutton's Creek and had set to work, found themselves early victims of duplicity.[17] As a kinsman of Harding stood sentinel, Michael Showers and Frederick Anger, known to him as recent settlers of Fort Wintermute, appeared and volunteered to relieve him at his post if he wished to join the other harvesters in their work. The wary guard accepted their offer, but promptly looked for his horse, intending to warn his fellows against possible ambush. He reached them just as they had quit reaping and were readying to pass southwards again. Path changed, they started through a narrow ravine for the riverside; and, suddenly, not more than five miles from home, they found themselves fired on from a thicket. Indians rushed out upon four men and a boy, shooting spears, wielding tomahaws. Benjamin and Stukely Harding returned fire as long as they could; then, as their enemies closed on them, clubbed their guns and fought furiously.[18] But numbers overpowered the two; and, hacked and cut to pieces, they fell to be scalped, while their weaponless companion John Gardner was taken prisoner and the two younger members of their groups escaped into the woods. After a night of wandering and exposure, on July 1 Stephen Harding, Jr., and the boy Rogers got to Jenkins' Fort with their news of violence and alarm.

Unhappily, corroboration had already come. At the tanyard of James Hadsall at the mouth of Sutton's Creek there was another raid on the last day of June. The tanner, his son-in-law Daniel Carr, and his Negro Quocko were carried off prisoners. James Hadsall, Jr., was killed. Ebenezer Reynolds was wounded, but escaped with David Wallen to wander one path through the woods, while a third refugee, young John Hadsall, wandered other paths, until they could severally report their experience at Jenkins'.[19] Word of the two attacks coursed down the Valley, to Wilkes-Barre, fourteen miles below Sutton's, and Forty Fort, twelve miles distant. In brief, although it was not known on that first day of July, 1778, that the elder Hadsall and his Negro had died of horrible tortures in the night,[20] it was realized throughout Wyoming that a malign and formidable enemy had come to the very threshold of the Connecticut settlement. No man knew the number of the foe. Consternation threatened.

It did not dominate, however, for order and procedure were prompt. Four hundred men, fully armed and equipped, assembled during the morning of July 1 at Forty Fort.[21] Early on hand, Nathan Denison, Representative of the County and now returned from Hartford, advised that their most experienced leader would be Colonel Zebulon Butler of the Continental Army, who was fortunately then in Wilkes-Barre. Sent for, that gentleman came at once and accepted the proferred command. Then, stern and silent, without music and with no waving of banners, the force of 400 Westmorelanders set forth, resolved to meet the suspected enemy before attackers in any main body could descend on the settlements. Up the Valley for ten miles on the right bank of the River they marched without any encounter; in midafternoon they halted at the mouth of Sutton's Creek and sent a squad of men under Lieutenant Rosewell Franklin forward to the scene of the slaying of the two Hardings, which the young officer and his comrades reached without being detected. Suddenly they found themselves looking from behind the green brush at two mutilated bodies, with two Indians, curiously enough, guarding them.[22]

Impulsively Franklin's men fired. One Indian fell dead. The other, slightly wounded, made for the water, thinking to escape by swimming. But Rosewell Franklin and another Westmorelander were as swift. Their canoe sped after the fugitive; and with their setting-poles the two despatched the young sachem, elated with their success but not knowing that the brave whom they killed was a son of Esther Montour.[23]

No other Indians appeared; and the scouting party reverently lifted the dead Benjamin and Stukely Harding and bore them downstream. On the return of this detail, Colonels Butler and Denison, deceived by the nonappearance of Indians in any number,[24] considered it best to march their main army back to Forty Fort. Arrangements were made for the burial on the morrow of the two murdered men at Jenkins' Fort. The Westmorelanders thought of their families and of having all more secure in the settlements should a hostile army strike at them in force later. By evening of the long summer day they had fatefully retraced their ten miles to Forty Fort.

That was the first mistake in their tactics. They had reckoned without adequate knowledge of the number of their foe, and they had allowed for no treachery from white men living within their own Wyoming towns upstream. While the men of Zebulon Butler's and Nathan Denison's army banded their families into places of greater security at or below Forty Fort, traitors at Wintermute's Fort five miles up the Valley moved stealthily. Elisha Scovel, Lieutenant of the Exeter Company of the 24th Regiment of Connecticut Militia, who had been left in command at that stockade, had a surprise. Two men of the Wintermute family slipped away in the early evening. When they returned on the deepening of twilight and called for admission at the gate they had with them a third figure.[25] Indeed, Lieutenant John Turney of Major John Butler's Rangers entered, and in a moment was demanding, in the name of King George, the surrender of the Fort.

There was immediate protest. Daniel Ingersoll seized his gun; Mrs. Ingersoll seized a pitchfork to aid her husband. But the Wintermutes and their kin stolidly announced that Major Butler would be welcome in their establishment. His detachment being both divided and outnumbered, Lieutenant Scovell could only execute Articles of Capitulation. By the terms of those, stores, arms, and ammunition in the Fort passed to a commander of the enemy who were secretly bivouacked in force at the Gap of Mount Lookout, hardly a mile and a quarter away. Toward that point, in fact, Butler's 700 Rangers and Indians had been guided by the two cravens. With a vast hostile power in hiding, the Lieutenant of the Exeter Company became a prisoner. More than that, he had been obliged to sign pledges that he would not bear arms further against the King; and he had to see Major Butler enter within another half hour and put him and his handful of men under heavier guard. Moreover, in the morning which followed he saw the British commander send a captain off with a white flag to demand the surrender of Jenkins' Fort, next stronghold downstream.[26]

In brief, on July 2, realization was to come to Nathan Denison at Forty Fort that an army, undiscoverable the day before, now possessed Wintermute's Fort and was encamped in considerable strength somewhere in the woods and the Valley above. The paths, the forests, the banks, the windings, the very currents of the Susquehanna had all grown ominously threatening. But it was not in the nature of the pioneer Connecticut Yankee to despair without reason or action. Mystery dared not master the event without resistance or advance into its domain.

There was brisk resummoning of the captains of the Wyoming Valley and their companies. Trios of scouts were sent in the direction of Wintermute's. Officers waited for reports which did not come of contacts with scouting parties sent from that Fort by the invaders. Captain Hewitt and two companies ranging for the Westmorelanders remained unheard from, one of them shot and scalped by Indian scouts, one wounded, one captured. What of news the day told was that Jenkins' Fort had been taken. Strangely uninformed of the progress of destiny, the companies gathered; and there was for them, plus mystery, debate.

Both these continued on the morning of the next day, when they still did not know that Major Butler and his Indian ally the Seneca Sayenqueraghta had months earlier begun assembling Rangers, Indians, and Tories at Fort Niagara; moving across New York down to Tioga Point, where the Chemung and the North Branch of the Susquehanna met and where two rival states temporarily were not pushing their claims of jurisdiction; down the river by Wyalusing, by Tunkhannock; and on July 1, with the aid of a treacherous family, into the very heart of Wyoming. Decades would elapse before the whole story of the slow, gradual, stealthy, insistent invasion could be clearly recounted by historians. But on July 3, 1778, the last chapter began its shaping at Forty Fort; and into the debate, on the brink of catastrophe, came a Scotch-Irishman.

Four of the nine regular companies of the 24th Connecticut could not report in quota to the muster.[27] The 9th, or "Up the River" Company had for some time been dispersed through the loss of both officers and privates. The 8th was far away, defending the Lackawanna settlement. The 7th was virtually *hors de combat;* its officers, the wounded Captain Stephen Harding and Lieutenant Elisha Scovell, had been seized by Major Butler's men at Jenkins' and Wintermute's Forts. The Pittston Company, or the 4th, did not dare leave its families unprotected when the enemy had seized all the watercraft at Jenkins' Ferry on the river just opposite their stockade. The five other companies convened promptly as circumstances permitted. The 2nd, the Kingston Company, was already stationed in home territory at Forty Fort. From first rendezvous at their stockade, "Garrison Hill" in Plymouth Town, the 3rd arrived as the morning grew late. The 6th, or upper Wilkes-Barre Company, had not only to march some distance but also to cross the river to the right bank. The 10th, or the Salem and Huntingdon, was delayed by a necessary change of its order for the day when Colonel Denison's summons reached its captain, John Franklin. The 5th, or Hanover Company, previously stationed at Fort Wilkes-Barre, likewise must cross the Susquehanna.

By noon, however, although it was with muster rolls irregularly completed, the active man power of the 24th had reassembled, and supplemented by two "Alarm List" companies,[28] variously domiciled older men or boys in their early teens. While they were gathering, the situation, although it lost nothing of suspense, had gained new definiteness.

In the early morning came an overture. Daniel Ingersoll arrived, bearing a flag of truce in his hand, with a set of terms from Major

Butler, presently holding Wintermute's Fort up the Valley.[29] The Major demanded unconditional surrender not only of Forty Fort but of all the forts in Wyoming with all their public stores, and the surrender of all Continental officers and soldiers on the ground. He promised, in the event of compliance with those first conditions, he would extend lenient terms of capitulation. If his overture was rejected, he would move upon Forty Fort at once.

Strange confrontation for the army of Westmoreland County, whose latest detachments were even then reporting for duty. Convene, stack arms, open the gates of Forty Fort, march out carrying flags of surrender! Such could not be conduct for wise and brave men. Daniel Ingersoll was sent back to John Butler with a refusal. Colonel Zebulon Butler was sent a despatch for more posthaste from Wilkes-Barre.

Council of war was pressed. Captains closed in conference with their superiors. For the 2nd company stood James Bidlack, Jr.; for the 3rd Asaph Whittlesey; for the 6th Rezin Geer; for the 10th Lieutenant Stoddard Bowen in the absence of Captain Franklin. For the 1st "Alarm Company" stood James Bidlack, Sr.; for the 2nd stood Captain Dr. William Hooker Smith. The 5th, or Hanover Company, of the 24th Connecticut was represented not by its long official leader. Indeed, that company, enlisted two-thirds of Scotch-Irishmen, had just experienced an internal problem all its own. Its men wanted to fight; but in the crisis they wanted not to fight under their good schoolteacher friend and captain, William McKerachan. They loved him; he was fine for drills, parades, and reviews. In an action they preferred the leadership of their former captain, Lazarus Stewart, Sr. They had mutinied in order to have that private become their commander again.[30] The scholarly McKerachan had bowed to their will; he would be glad to be a lieutenant to their old hero. So, at noon on July 3, 1778, there acted for Hanover Town the man who with Lazarus Young had founded it, a recusant from the old Provincial law of Pennsylvania.

The question was, should the Westmorelanders attack or wait to be attacked? Colonel Zebulon Butler presided over the council. Separately two flags of truce were sent forward, ostensibly to request better terms of Major Butler, really to delay the enemy until more militia of the 24th Regiment might be gathered. Both flags were fired upon and their bearers forced to return to Forty Fort. Captain Robert Durkee and Lieutenant Phineas Peirce of Captain Simon Spalding's Independent Company arrived to announce that that detachment was nearing home, must join their fellow-Westmorelanders in two more days[31]—an argument for waiting for increase of strength. But word now was coming in of depredations upstream. The Tories and Indians were burning all settlements and collecting all cattle. They were not yet ready to attack Kingston; but Lackawanna, or Pittston, on the bank opposite Jenkins' was in an exposed position and might soon fall. It would not do to let John Butler's incalculable force gain increasing and obvious strength. If he was not going really to advance farther down, they ought not to let the man's Indians loot and slay their neighbors above and then withdraw scot free. Yet Colonel Nathan thought it more prudent to wait and have the army at Forty Fort be further recruited. John Franklin would be coming soon with more of the Salem and Huntingdon Company. Spalding might get his company on to the end of its long march from Lancaster in a day or two. Denison was no coward.

But Lazarus Stewart was in the circle of conference, and the Scotch-Irishman talked warmly. A century later men would say he talked turbulently, insultingly, mutinously—that he had to be ordered under arrest;[32] that, when he was arrested the 5th Company mutinied and declared they would fight under no other officer; that perforce Colonel Denison must yield to them and to him, and march.[33] No contemporary document told any such tale. But history has it that at two o'clock on the afternoon of Friday, July 3, 1778, under a hot sun, the meager army of Colonels Denison and Zebulon Butler marched out of Forty Fort in column formation. After the two mounted leaders moved a stalwart color-bearer, carrying the new national flag of America.[34] Fifers and drummers played "St. Patrick's Day in the Morning," and the several companies turned northeast.[35]

At the bridge over Abraham's Creek, one mile upwards, they paused. Another flag of truce was sent forward. Then they reformed and made ready to resist an attack from the enemy. None came; but while they waited for the return of scouts and of their messenger to Major Butler, two officers and a Negro servant from Simon Spalding's company, almost exhausted from their long march and hunger, appeared and joined them. When they made forward again, Dethick Hewitt's Company of Continentals was on the extreme right; abreast with it were the Lower and the Upper Wilkes-Barre Companies and the Hanover Company with Lazarus Stewart;[36] and on the extreme left Asaph Whittlesey's Plymouth Company with Lieutenant Bowen's Salem and Huntingdon men interspersed in it, as the men from the two "Alarm List" Companies were generally intermingled now within their main fraction of the 24th Regiment.

But the enemy kept his tactical advantages still secret from them. Zebulon Butler sent ahead a reconnoitering party, who moved effectually enough to discover numbers of the enemy in station at Wintermute's but not effectually enough to prevent two Indian scouts whom they met from escape back to join the enemy. It was four o'clock when that news was reported. Colonel Butler decided to move on the enemy, and addressed his men: "They knew from the fate of the Hardings what fortune would be theirs if they did not succeed; they must save their homes from destruction, their wives and children from the savage."[37] He ordered advance; and the thin, unwavering line of defenders marched forward for another mile. Near the end of that distance Hewlitt's men on the right beheld Wintermute's, not encircled with a great and hostile guard, but in furious conflagration.

It was nearing five o'clock. Two-and-a-half hours more of day remained. Colonel Butler grew easier in mind. He ordered his men onwards again. Enemy skirmishers, singly or in couples, emerged from field and thicket ahead, fired at the advancing column and fled into hiding. Always they darted into retreat; but the wary Yankee officer perceived them disappearing into either a swamp some distance ahead or behind a long fence nearer on his right. So, as his line approached the latter barrier, he ordered an immediate volley against it. Fire was prompt, but it brought no response from the suspected concealed enemy. It was repeated with a second volley, and with a third, with no answer coming.

A fourth time the Americans, now moved up at closer range, raised their muskets to fire. Then, ere triggers were pulled, suddenly Major Butler's Rangers leaped from behind their log fence, fired, and fell back. "The enemy retreat!" cried Zebulon Butler. "Stand fast, men; and the day is ours."[38] The five Connecticut companies cheered their commander and sprang forward. The Rangers retorted with a yell of defiance. Firing from both sides grew general. Steadily, left and right, the Americans advanced; Captain Hewitt's men made a gain of thirty yards against firm, but not unstayable opposition; victory seemed offering, with companies on the left still scarce untouched. The log fence lost its fears for the army from Forty Fort. On they drove.

But as tacticians they had not won. They had made too much of present fears, not foreseeing all possibilities. Out of the morass on their left Sayenqueraghta's men began leaping, firing as they charged on Asaph Whittlesey's Company. Colonel Denison ordered that body and the Hanover Company next to it to fall back, wheel into a line at right angles with the main line, and flank off to the left.[39] The order came too late. In six waves, six bands of Indians, yelling fiendishly with each successive surge, hurled themselves on Whittlesey's and Lazarus Stewart's men. The left wing of the 24th Regiment crumpled and was borne back by a rush of savages upon Zebulon Butler's right. In a nexus of disaster, officers and men fought off the tomahawks of Indians with the butts of their guns, their arms, or their hands, as long as they could; fell; and died—or, worse fate, were seized and pinioned. The Battle of Wyoming was lost in a rout. The honors of war, such as they were, were with Major John Butler.

In the heat of the engagement, during the last hours of a long July day, catastrophe was repeated for many a man. Death ended for many all the woe which the Valley had known since the first unseating of the Indians there before Teedyuscung's death; for Lazarus Stewart and many a Scotch-Irishman in his Hanover Company it concluded all memory of the Paxton Boys at Conestoga, and Lancaster, or at Philadelphia. For Lazarus, too, it broke off all possibility of knowing what future generations might say of him as a rioter, or of how, through a mutiny, his fiery persuasion became the evil genius propelling an army of patriots to doom. He died in the battle as did every other captain leading a Connecticut company into action that day.[40]

At the back of each captive stood an Indian guard. Around the circle moved the daughter of French Margaret, this inheritress of the mixed seed of races, female chief in her own right among Indians, mother and fiend. Rhythmic, fantastic, demoniac she moved, her lips chanting weird cadences. Her arms were strong and her hands steady. They clutched firmly the hasp of her death-maul; and, as one of her warriors held each prisoner, she struck that ever bloodier and bloodier weapon into the unfortunate's brain. Never had Moloch been served by a more awesome priestess. Fourteen of the captives perished under her blows.

Yet, truth it is that once surrender of the Wyoming forts had been made on July 4 to Major John Butler, multiple butchery of white men was not again enacted in the Valley. In the two months which followed, panic rather than horror characterized settlers on the banks and the course of the Susquehanna, while a new punctuality of purpose redounded to the credit of the Supreme Executive Council of Pennsylvania. But the "Great Runaway" and the commitments of military duty to Colonel Thomas Hartley began during the first half of July, 1778. Battle, horror, and surrender occasioned flight; but, for once, they inspired officialdom.

Robert Fleming, born in Argyleshire, Scotland, in 1716, had found a bride in Ulster in 1745, and in 1746 had emigrated to Pennsylvania. After fourteen years in Chester County the two[3] Flemings and their children settled in Cecil County, Maryland. The 1770's found them at a far cry from there, living on the Big Island on the West Branch of the Susquehanna below the mouth of distant Bald Eagle Creek. In 1776 Robert and his son Robert, Jr., served in Captain Cookson Long's company[4] of militia on the frontiers in Northumberland County. They had heard stories of this raid or that for two years and more. In January, 1778, almost within earshot of Long's garrison, Anthony Saltzman had been tomahawked and scalped. Six months later came the news of Wyoming. At once Lieutenant Robert Fleming, Senior, and Ensign Robert Fleming, Junior, thought less of military duties and more of family;[5] safety was better than a new farm on the Big Island; down the Branch and down the river they fled with their women and children and such few chattels as they could carry along —to Hunter's Fort, to shelter among Scotch-Irish folk in Hanover Township, Lancaster County.

As with the Flemings, so with the Clarks who have given their name to a famous valley in Dauphin County. First they had taken up land in Chester County, where the second William Clark was born. That enterprising Scotch-Irishman, on his father's death, struck for the frontier. Presently he held land among other Presbyterians in the Narrows of Paxton. But immigration was in his blood, and the river called him upwards into Northumberland County.⁶ On the eve of the War of Independence he was breaking new acres to the plough. The tale came of the massacre on the night of July 3, 1778, and again William Clark moved, militia duties foregone. Time enough to bury their farm implements, and his family were in flight. Down the Susquehanna they made their fugitive way, with two canoes lashed together,⁷ and in the holds of those two shallow vessels children and what of extra wearing apparel they had bundled together. Beating in their minds, as they fled, was the question: Would the farm they had earlier in Paxton shelter them now?

Westmoreland families who could be gathered together by a surviving father or a widowed but spirited pioneer mother fled by rough and almost impenetrable ways to the Delaware River and New Jersey or New York, determined on ultimate refuge in Connecticut. Long journeys took them on upward paths along the Lackawanna Creek, then over a divide and down the Lackawaxen, and so onwards. Some chose a nearer asylum, descending the Lehigh River to find what succor they might among their late Pennamite foes at Easton in Northampton County. Others in their desperation decided to escape down the North Branch of the Susquehanna itself and then by the main trunk of that river; and these, as they fled, imparted their fears to the Northumberland folk whose settlements they passed through. Their mood seized on settlers at the Point and at Sunbury, quickly spread from the North Branch to the West Branch, sped along that great arm of the river as far as the Big Island, and deep into its valleys.

For a year back-inhabitants had been anticipating Indian forays; now, more than a foray, an invasion was being bruited—and a massacre had come with it as aftermath. Incalculably savage violence was everywhere believed to be immediately at hand, while Congress and Council, to the skeptical mind ineffectual bodies of politicians, seemed far away. Flight was the only logic; escape was the first law of self-preservation. Again many a Scotch-Irishman became a pilgrim of adversity.

Within nine days of the defeat and the atrocities at Wyoming, the spectacle of misery had reached Harris' Ferry. There on July 12 Matthew Smith beheld "the greatest scenes of distress I ever saw";⁸ and that former captain with Benedict Arnold in the forests of Maine and at Quebec wrote of what he had seen and heard to Vice President George Bryan of the Pennsylvania Council. The numerous poor had run away from their habitations, leaving all their goods. Families still more unfortunate had left behind members of their own circle killed and scalped. The "most cruel butcheries ever known," said Smith, had been practiced; "wounded and others thrown into fires while yet living."[9] To him fugitives had reported that Major John Butler's force had numbered 199 Regular, 100 Tories, 700 Indians.[10]

For Peter de Haven, gunsmith of Hummelstown, nine miles east of Harris', that same July Sabbath offered a twofold spectacle of interest. Through the streets of the village he saw twenty or thirty families passing, "some from Buffalo Valley and from Sunbury, and some families from this side of Peters Mountain."[11] "Wyoming," they said, "was taken"; "most of our people have left Sunbury, and are coming down—200 wagons will be coming in a day or two."[12] But that part of the troubled scene did not keep the armorer from attending sermon at Mr. Elder's Derry Presbyterian Meeting four miles away. And at that church, when preaching closed, he witnessed new activity. Colonels Robert Clark and John Rogers "made a Particular to the inhabitants for them to turn out about 100 men as volunteers"[13] and called the Battalion to meet on Tuesday. Moreover, that done, they assured de Haven they would have to have arms for 50 or 60 men.[14] Indeed, the Hummelstown gunmaker admitted to Colonel Timothy Matlack, to whom he was writing, that without his Philadelphia superior's "consent"[15] he had promised the guns. Then he who had seen the Scotch-Irish fugitives scattering into Derry Township and the serious-faced worshippers at Derry Church on the same day recommended to Secretary Matlack that the Council be informed of his conduct and asked that "directions how I shall act"[16] be sent up.

From a more eminent man than Peter de Haven came a momentous report to the Secretary in Philadelphia. The surveyor, William Maclay, son-in-law of Ferryman John Harris, soldier of Northumberland County, officer and veteran of the campaign of 1776, was among the fugitives from Sunbury. Five days after the catastrophe of Wyoming, on Wednesday, July 8, 1778, he had left the frontier county seat with "almost my whole property."[17] He chose not to trouble Colonel Matlack with any recital "of the inconveniences I suffered, while I brought my family by water to this place."[18] But never in his life had he seen such distress: "The river and the roads leading down it were covered with men, women, and children, flying for their lives, many without any property at all, and none who had not left the greatest part behind."[19] "Northumberland County," Maclay wrote, "is broken up";[20] Colonel Hunter there had fewer than a hundred men on whom to depend for defense of it. Wyoming was totally abandoned; "scarce a single family remained between that place and Sunbury, when I left."[21]

For nine days the "Great Runaway" on Susquehanna continued. William Maclay had served the Penns in the laying out of their manors on that great river; he had resented the presence of Connecticut settlers upon it; now, unless aid could be got in time to Colonel Hunter, there was the fearful possibility that all that great tract of Susquehanna country should be recovered to British control and exposed to the barbarities of England's Indian allies. From such a condition his mind recoiled. His tender heart thought no longer politically. Wyoming people had come down "absolutely naked";[22] the sight of them had precipitated the abandonment of Sunbury by its Scotch-Irish townsmen. "Something in the way of Charity ought to be done for the many miserable objects that crowd the banks of this river, especially those who fled from Wyoming; they are a people, you know, I did not use to love, but I now most sincerely pity their distress."[23]

It was from Paxton he wrote—from the community, indeed, which had given its name to the frontiersmen who raided Lancaster in December, 1763, and frightened Philadelphia with their presence on the Schuylkill at Germantown in February, 1764. With her kinsmen, the Espys of that Scotch-Irish haven, Martha Espy Stewart, widowed on July 3, 1778, by the death of her husband in the Wyoming Battle, had in the same days been finding refuge for herself and Lazarus Stewart's six children. So did stroke and counterstroke continue to work themselves out in the history of Susquehanna settlers.

Yet not all in the summer of 1778 was panic or futility. Colonel Thomas Hartley had for five months been preparing for his quiet entrance upon the stage of history. Two competent and foresighted distinguished veteran generals were at their homes in the frontier counties of Pennsylvania: John Armstrong of Carlisle and James Potter of Penn's Valley were not men to lose their heads in a crisis.

To Berks County Hartley, commander of the brigade under Anthony Wayne in the Battles of Brandywine and of Germantown, the Board of War had committed the recruitment of a new regiment.[24] He had responded prudently, advising of proper bounties to be paid to recruits, warning that a Continental officer "must be allowed to give the same bounty with the State in which he beats up or he will get no men," sagely counselling "not to advance the whole bounty at once to every loose fellow";[25] and he had undertaken his mission for Congress, expecting funds for his purpose from the Council of Pennsylvania. In May his officers had built up a roster of 46 men.

Nine days after the Defeat of Wyoming a letter[26] was despatched by General Armstrong to Vice-President George Bryan of the Pennsylvania Council with outcry in it upon "the savage villains of the north"[27] but with a reminder that the harvests along the upper Susquehanna stood in the fields ripe for the reaper. It was up to civil and military authorities, he made it clear, not only to move to the defense of the fugitive settlers from Northumberland County but also to the rescue of their crops. Men needed food, and armies needed provision. From County Lieutenant Samuel Hunter of Sunbury came in the same season to Council the appeal, "If we are assisted to stand and save our crops, we will have enough and to spare."[28]

Answers to these and other advices from the frontiers were orders issued by the Board of War that Colonel Daniel Brodhead, instead of continuing the march of his battalion for Pittsburgh, march for the Standing Stone in Northumberland County, and that Colonel Hartley's regiment, on July 16 numbering about one hundred men, proceed for Sunbury by way of Lancaster and Harris' Ferry, there to be joined by two companies lately raised at Wyoming.[29] These were supplemented by Secretary Timothy Matlack's assurance that the Council had ordered to Sunbury four hundred Lancaster County militiamen,[30] besides another detachment of eighty men of Hartley's regiment proceeding by way of Easton in Northampton County.

Yet it was more through intelligence than through officialdom that Daniel Brodhead and Thomas Hartley served Pennsylvania in the summer and autumn of 1778. The two marched to their destinations with meager forces, either depleted or uncompleted companies. Their best fortune was that they had the support of John Armstrong, experienced veteran of Indian warfare, and in Penn's Valley they had James Potter.

Colonel Brodhead was the first to arrive in Northumberland County. That veteran soldier, who had seen action on Long Island and hardship at Valley Forge, had on July 24 already reached Sunbury[31] and passed onwards up the West Branch to Muncy. Prompt strategist and familiar with frontier tactics, he fixed at once upon two principal posts and disposed his scouts to watch the Indian paths. One detachment of them, a major, two captains, a subaltern, and eighty men including sergeants, were stationed at Briar Creek, below Nescopeck on the North Branch forty miles distant. Another twenty-five men he sped with a captain to General Potter's to cover the harvesters, few in number, returning to Penn's. He kept one hundred and twenty men with him at Muncy. His scouts, sent out regularly from there, came back with accounts of Indian encampments, of slaughtering of deserted live stock, burning of houses, of savages who ran off when they found themselves discovered. He rejoiced to see settlers returning to Muncy, on his approach there, to gather in their crops. In that fourth week of July, 1778, he doubted his power to hold the valleys of the Susquehanna for Pennsylvania without further help. But General James Potter rejoiced that Brodhead had arrived;[32] he saw now the prospect of saving grain in the county which might be well worth £40,000.

Hardly had letters of report left for Philadelphia from Potter and Brodhead before Colonel Thomas Hartley was on the scene at Sunbury.[33] There he found upwards of 200 Pennsylvania militiamen awaiting him, to be added to his companies of regulars, and there, on August 1, he waited for two independent companies from Northampton County, instructed by the Board of War to serve with him[34]—they were really two clusters of Connecticut men assembled by Colonel Zebulon Butler and Captain Simon Spalding, who would themselves have declared their followers mustered from Westmoreland County. With that mixture of experienced and inexperienced warriors, and one other company of his own Continental regiment coming from New Jersey by way of Easton to unite with their fellows-in-arms, the Berks County officer designee of the War Board Hartley worked out a rerallying of the frontier, a timely warning to the now absconded Tories and Indians of Major John Butler, and a preliminary to the destruction of Indian power in the seaboard states of the Union.

A heavy task confronted him. Four-fifths of the settlers had fled from the West Branch. He would need to set up and support four or five posts between the Great Island and Fishing Creek if the inhabitants were to be induced to return.[35] He feared few of the women would be willing to come back to their former homes. The Wyoming settlement was almost entirely destroyed; most of its surviving inhabitants had fled to Connecticut and to pauperdom. There was no prospect at all of resettlement on the North Branch in the autumn ahead. Yet much, he thought, might be done in favor of Northumberland County; and, resolved that "Nothing shall be wanting on my part,"[36] he set to work.

Within a week he supplemented Colonel Brodhead's activities with posting of scouts and laying out a fort at Muncy, and Samuel Wallis wrote from there to Timothy Matlack of the recovery of spirit among people who noted Hartley's behavior and that of his Continental troops.[37]

But for a time new horrors were mingled with new hope. A corporal and four men of Colonel Hartley's regiment had been detailed with three militiamen to guard fourteen reapers and cradlers cutting the grain on Peter Smith's farm above Loyalsock Creek.[38] The wife and four children of the owner had been murdered by Indians, omen enough to dissuade harvesting—except that no chance of provisioning must in dire times be forgone. In the early morning of August 8 treachery lurked in the fog. An hour after the scarcely perceptible sunrise, one sentry discovered a band of Indians creeping up on the reapers. He gave warning, and the circle of harvesters drew back cautiously. Young James Brady paused stubbornly to fetch his rifle, previously set down a small distance off, and drew pursuit and attack. He ran after his companions, fell wounded by a shot, was tomahawked, scalped, and left for dead by his assailants. The sentry fired, but he too was shot down. One militiaman died near him in the skirmish, another was lost in it. The cradlers, hearing the firing, took a position on rising ground, and with their guardsman corporal and his three men beheld the unhappy attack and the retreat of the marauders.[39]

At the close of the bloody episode, Brady rose and made his way to Smith's farmhouse where he found a friend to staunch his wounds. Presently he was borne on a litter to the camp of Thomas Hartley at Muncy. That kindly officer admired the fortitude of the "exceeding fine young fellow,"[40] but doubted the possibility of his recovery. "Bravery and steadiness," he commented, "were of use."[41] He praised Mr. Jerome Veness for succoring the injured youth. But the thirty Mingoes involved in the raid and its unhappy outcome prompted him to reflect that "too much caution cannot be used in a war with these savages";[42] and the death next morning of Captain John Brady's son only confirmed him in the soundness of his conclusion.

With a valiant prudence, however, Hartley continued his campaign. Wisely he maintained a conservative defensive, studying not only practicable positions, provisions, and medical stores, but also the mettle of his men. Not before September 1 would he report to Council of the near completion of his fort at Muncy, earth and fascine works and stockade, and of the placing of his one four-pounder in position.[43] He had still to lament the lack of swivels for his four bastions, the lack of medicine for his sickly militia, and the raggedness of his detachment out of Northampton County. But he had displayed good sense by inducing settlers to put in fall crops, and he frankly admitted that to date his scouting parties had killed no single Indian.

Then, positions to his rear properly established, at the end of three more weeks he was ready to set off from Fort Muncy with three-hundred-and-odd men for an incursion on Indian towns upstream on the North Branch and its tributaries.[44] Fifteen days after his egress from that new West Branch stronghold, he was back at Fort Augusta and Sunbury with laurels cautiously won. Samuel Hunter wrote praises of him to Vice-President Bryan of the Council: His loss was only seven killed and eight wounded, including those killed among Zebulon Butler's men operating around Wyoming; yet he had taken his army far enough to destroy the Indian village at Tioga and nearer Sheshequin, both places far beyond Wyalusing. From the enemy he had recovered fifty head of horned cattle and a number of pack-horses, besides other articles in his soldier's canoes.[45]

On October 8 Colonel Hartley himself addressed Council and Congress.[46] A long report to Congress detailed or described every stage of the route of his forces: rains, swamps, mountains, defiles, and rocks mastered on their expedition; huts seen in Indian villages where the scalps of helpless white women and children hung dressed and dried; minor encounters with the foe; rumors of the retreat of Major John Butler with his 300 green-clad Tories; the burning of Queen Esther's Palace and Town at Tioga.[47] The account of every maneuver and of every subaltern officer's service or feat was meticulous. But the veritable summary of Hartley's achievement was rendered modestly at one point in his communication to the Pennsylvania Council: "Considering our numbers, we pushed our good fortune as far as we dared, we gave a present relief to the frontiers, and turned back the Barbarians from deluging our country with the blood of helpless mothers and infants."[48]

He had wisely refrained from tempting Providence. The town at Chemung was only a few miles above Tioga on the tributary; but it was in Indian country, where he knew that the savages would fight more bravely than they would fight "when among us."[49] And like John Armstrong he saw what must be made the pattern of things in another campaign. It was too late for another expedition this fall; "we must only secure our posts for the winter, and early in the spring a body must march against their towns on this river."[50] Hartley was of English descent. It was the Scotch-Irish General Armstrong who on August 6, 1778, had the vision of what would occur in 1779. The northern expedition which that gentleman had then at heart was to come of a union of two forces, one moving by way of Cherry Valley, New York, the other from rendezvous at Wyoming or at Tioga; and their direct route, once the two had joined, was to be to the Seneca Towns "as the first mark."[51] The hero of Kittanning was "for leaving inferior tribes to be subdued by traverse marches."[52] He anticipated peace by the destruction of their towns. His recommendation was made to Vice-President George Bryan, prime sponsor for the campaign of Hartley.

John Brady,[53] son of Hugh and Hannah Brady, sprang well from Scottish breed. Born in 1733 in Delaware, he was guided by his parents into a sound and competent education, and himself had presided at the schoolmaster's desk before he left Delaware for Pennsylvania and found there his bride, Mary Quigley. Twenty-two at the time of his marriage, he was a handsome man, six feet tall, athletically proportioned, dark, black-haired, hazel-eyed. More than that he was a man in whom traits of character were emphatic. Impulsive and generous, he inspired no mere neutral responses from other persons. Men either hated him or loved him. Among his own kind of honorable gentlemen he was beloved and a leader; and for the frontiersman's life he was fitted superbly by nature. Moreover he was destined to meet with poise and grace every experience of life and death which came to him.

Not that he was a stay-at-home. Far from that, he was ever the pilgrim by choice. Always beyond the closed horizon another vista was to be sought. The French and Indian War challenged his mettle; in 1763 he served as a captain under Lieutenant Colonel Asher Clayton on the frontiers, and in 1764 with Colonel Henry Bouquet on the expedition beyond the Ohio. In 1766 he was among the officers petitioning the Proprietaries for the founding of a compact and defensible town at Bedford; in 1768 he removed his family to land at Standing Stone, which in the course of time would be Huntingdon. In 1769 he moved household again, and settled on the West Branch opposite to the mouth of Buffalo Creek. In 1772, on the founding of Northumberland County, he was appointed foreman of its first grand jury. Four years later he had proceeded farther upstream to the confluence of Muncy Creek with the river. For wife and children he built there a fortified loghouse, and then in the summer of 1776, with grown sons able to fend for farm and family, he was off with other Northumberland County men to advance the cause of Independence. On July 4, as Major of Colonel William Plunkett's Battalion of Associators, he was attending the great convention of military patriots at Lancaster. After the campaigns on Long Island and in the Jerseys, he was a captain in the Twelfth Regiment of the Continental Line serving with Colonel William Cooke. Wounded in the Battle of the Brandywine, he could take no part in the Battle of Germantown. But after spending the winter of 1777-1778 with Cooke's men at Valley Forge, at the end of June he was in the field at the Battle of Monmouth.[54] The Massacre of Wyoming in July and the death of his son James on August 9 at Muncy brought him back to Susquehanna country for a brief sojourn; and his family were with him in Sunbury for some weeks. Then duty called Brady back to the Continental Army, and on September 1, 1778, he started for Philadelphia with a letter from Commandant Thomas Hartley for the Pennsylvania Council.[55]

When Fort Muncy had been built and garrisoned by Hartley's men, Mary Quigley Brady returned with her younger children to their farm and stockaded fort for the winter. The spring of 1779 brought Captain Brady again to the county, on orders to serve now with Colonel Hartley; and, although omens still impended from river and forests, signs looked fair to the Brady family circle. Much with them now was Peter Smith, widowed and childless, on whose farm James Brady had served with such ill success. Smith and Captain Brady were bringing provisions for the household on April 11, 1779, as the two paused at Wolf Run, three miles away from Fort Brady, to wait for a wagon to come up to them.

"A good place for Indians to hide," said John Brady, alert suddenly to the silence of a thicket.

"Yes," Smith nodded in affirmation; and as he began speaking was aware of the blasts of three rifles in paralyzing succession. Then, there upon the earth at his feet, he saw Brady fall dead. In terror the man leaped on the captain's horse, and fled to the settlement.

The searching party who sped at once to the point of the attack, found John Brady's body unscarred except for two bullets which had cut between his shoulders into his heart. His head was unscalped, his gold watch untouched, his money in his purse. In a pouch suspended from his neck over his chest was his Twelfth Regiment commission, dearest of his earthly chattels, proud badge of a gentleman who had been teacher, surveyor, and soldier—however slight comfort it could bring to a Scotch-Irish wife whose son had died at Indian hands only eight months before his father did.

There would be in 1779 other slayings, stealthy or savage, out of the forests along the Susquehanna. But the Lord was not always to chide his Presbyterian saints, and his anger was not to be kept forever with them only.

Seven weeks after the death of John Brady, George Washington issued instructions to General John Sullivan to lead an army deep into the country of the Six Nations and establish a central post there from which parties could be detached to lay waste all the settlements around. Orders were not merely to overrun but to destroy. The lands of the Indians were not to be left as a reservoir providing food for British troops in Canada; the Iroquois allies of Britain were to be put out of the game. The month of May terminated apparent inaction. In June two forces fell into march, distant from each other as far as Schoharie Valley, New York, is from Easton, Pennsylvania. More than two months passed before their converging paths brought them to meeting; but in their eventual union was nemesis.

In the overland Odyssey from the northeast, as part of Brigadier General George Clinton's army, the Fourth Pennsylvania Regiment and Major James Parr's Rifle Corps proceeded, the latter contingent including veterans of the Battle of Saratoga. Among them were two heroes who had once served with Arnold in Canada: Michael Simpson of Paxton, who had risen from his lieutenancy to a captaincy, and his fellow rifleman, Sergeant Thomas Boyd of Derry, who three years earlier had shared imprisonment at Quebec with Captain Daniel Morgan, General William Thompson, Private John Joseph Henry, and a bevy of other Scotch-Irish patriots. Boyd was in arms again, intrepid as ever; and with him was that non-pareil marksman Timothy Murphy. To preserve the record[56] of the part to be played in the expedition by Parr's men, Lieutenant Erkuries Beatty, Pennsylvanian like the others, marched in the column.

The forces destined to ascend first from Easton by way of Blue Mountain and the Wind Gap into the Wyoming Valley, and then by way of the North Branch to Tioga and onwards into New York State, were a far more numerous aggregation. Gathered from many points came the brigades of Generals Poor and Maxwell and Colonel Proctor. Leading them in position were the light troops of General Edward Hand, back now as an officer in Washington's army after duties of 1777-1778 in western Pennsylvania. On June 18 they marched away from the town at the junction of the Delaware and the Lehigh Rivers, pack-horses carrying stores, other animals drawing their artillery, cavalrymen riding in guard over this.[57] A great and goodly division, indeed, was commanded by Sullivan, who had bungled on Staten Island three years earlier, hardly redeemed himself in the Battle of the Brandywine in 1777, yet maintaining himself always as one of Washington's most loyal supporters and loved by officers and men for his delightful and gallant demeanor. In his army mechanics, smith, gunsmiths, wagoners, quartermasters, physicians, surgeons, and chaplains were in full and competent array. Every stage of the expedition was realized with a fine military prudence. There was no indiscreet marching ahead of provisions; no failure to secure and place stores to fit strategic needs.

Moreover, the procedure of the campaign, especially that part taken in it by Edward Hand's men, came under the eye of the affectionate Reverend Dr. William Rogers, Baptist chaplain. Faithfully for two months that divine set down in his journal[58] the story of the upstream Odyssey along river, over mountain, and through forest.

Now Dr. Rogers wrote of what he saw with a gentle piety, now with the fidelity of a clerk, now with almost the romantic eye for landscape of a poet. Into his diary went much of the anniversary sermon which he preached on July 4 to Hand's brigade and Proctor's artillerymen. His text was Psalm 32: 10, "But he that trusteth in the Lord, mercy shall compass him about."[59] He reviewed the blessings for America since 1776. He urged the importance of cheer, and of remembering Jehovah "who is great and terrible."[60] He spoke of fathers who had trusted and found God delivering them; he prayed that it might be so with them "for the sake of Christ Jesus, who came to give Freedom to the world."[61] He recorded seventeen days later the joy[62] which Sullivan's men felt when news came by express of General Anthony Wayne's capturing the British garrison of Stony Point with all its stores, and only four or five Americans lost in the action. He rejoiced in Sullivan's generous pardoning of twenty-nine German troops who had deserted and been court-martialed. He had found the culprits attentive when he tried to administer religious instruction to them, and he pitied their ignorance.[63] Their petition for lenity he respected. He was glad to see them returning to their duties: five not shot, as earlier judgment had decreed; twenty-two spared from running the gauntlet through Hand's and Maxwell's brigades. In contrast, on August 6, when he had learned of Joseph Brant's appeal to the Canadian Indians to join 450 British troops coming from Canada, he indulged in scathing irony upon that "devoted servant of the man who bears the title of the 'Defender of the Faith.'"[64]

On other days he described the progress of the army, its line and order of march, its difficulties, its discovery of dead unburied at Wyoming twelve months after the massacre,[65] and of a grave in which seventy-five hapless victims lay. He met the Connecticut officer Colonel Zebulon Butler and heard from him the story of the fourteen murdered men found lying "in an exact circle"[66] after the witch-like atrocity of Queen Esther, and many another account of horror and treachery. But he maintained with dignity his tenderness of heart. Tears came into the eyes of marching patriots as they passed two boards fixed in the earth over the graves of two tortured Westmoreland County officers. Chaplain Rogers was glad that Colonel Proctor, "out of respect for the deceased, ordered the music to play the tune 'Roslin Castle,' the soft and moving notes of which tended greatly to fill our breasts with pity."[67] Into his mind came solemn verses from Young's *Night Thoughts:*

> Life's little stage is a small eminence,
> Inch high above the grave, that home of man
> Where dwells the multitude.[68]

Of natural scenery, of flora and fauna, he was, however, as observant as he was of man's life and its brief passage. On the second day of the great march, "on a mountain between Sullivan's stores and Pokono," he admired "a fine prospect of nature's works . . . the water gap of the Blue Mountains, and hill upon hill surrounding us."[69] On the third, which was Sunday, June 20th, he pitied the exhausting labors of the horses drawing the artillery over the hills, and he refrained from preaching to men sorely fatigued. And he noted the timber along or through which they passed: pine, poplar, and oak, and "a quantity of the largest laurel."[70] The Great Swamp, eleven or twelve miles through and called on maps "the shades of death," impressed him with the "amazing height"[71] of its trees: hemlock, birch, pine, sugar maple, ash, and locust. To his eyes, when they left Wyoming on the last day of July, the fleet of one hundred and twenty bateaux carrying Proctor's stores and guns up the North Branch was beautiful on the river.[72] The plain above the mouth of Lackawanna Creek, where they encamped that night was beautiful. When on August 1st the army must pass in Indian file along the narrows between mountain and stream, and two thousand pack horses must move in the same fashion in a train six miles in length,[73] he found the array a grand spectacle. At one point a cascade, "or falling spring," of eighty foot height (they had come to what later generations would call Buttermilk Falls), inspired him with awe; and his "ear was agreeably stricken by the constant sound created by the descending water."[74]

The long progress took them on and across other "beautiful purling streams or creeks";[75] through herbage with "a most fragrant smell,[76] flowers of various hues, hazelnut forests, wilds abounding "with other things delicious to the taste."[72] They passed Tunkhannock Creek, Meshoppen, and Black Walnut Bottom, at which latter point the Reverend Mr. Rogers was moved—on a fisherman's return from a flanking maneuver with a good string of fish to add gusto to the evening camp meal—to quote four lines of gratitude to the universal bounteous Lord.[78] Then next day Wyalusing Mountain aroused marvel in him, its gradual ascent beginning with thickets of sycamores, many nine to twelve feet in diameter, twenty to thirty feet in circumference, numerous sugar maples on the bottom slopes, and the forest floor filled with sweet Sicily, a root of anise taste.[79] Ten miles beyond Wyalusing were the Standing Stone Flats, "plenty of good land, fit for meadow and for raising wheat and other grain."[80]

On August 11th, one mile and a half above Sheshequin, "overalls" removed and tied round their necks, the light troops forded the North Branch, keeping strict platoon formation, each soldier grasping the hand of the soldier next to him for support, while the fleet covered their march, and General Edward Hand, dismounted, struck boldly through the water in front of them.[81] Mr. Rogers doubted whether any army of Alexander the Great had ever endured an ordeal "with as much good humor as ours has evinced."[82] Soon, drums beating, fifes playing, colors flying, Sullivan's men paused at the mouth of the Tioga, or Chemung, River. To their rear stretched verdant plains; on their right flowed the Susquehanna. Before them was that fine neck of land which modern Pennsylvanians know as Tioga Point, opposite which Hartley's men had destroyed Esther Montour's palace and village last September. Encircling them on that day were mountain prospects which "afforded pleasant reflections, though separated from friends and in an enemy's country."[83] It seemed a prosperous August 11th.

Five days later Generals Poor and Hand, with 900 picked men, a suitable number of commissioned and of non-commissioned officers, two pieces of artillery, and provisions for eight days, marched[84] up the North Branch to meet the troops and boats of General George Clinton, descending toward them from Lake Otsego, whence that second army had been instructed to march on the 9th. On Friday, August 20th, early in the morning, Mr. Rogers had the pleasure of seeing Lieutenant Thomas Boyd of Parr's Rifle Corps, arrive at Sullivan's camp. That swift-moving courier, whose legs had lost no agility from long marches three years earlier up the Kennebec River and down the Chaudiere in Canada, came with a letter to Sullivan from his now approaching chief adjutant. The latter's army and the Major General's detachment had met on the preceding day, eight miles this side of Chenango. Boyd had left them at Owego at eleven P.M., and traveled through the night to bring word of the successful rendezvous. He predicted their joint arrival at Tioga before another nightfall.[85] But bad weather intervened and there were two days of waiting.

Then on Sunday came the grand union of forces. The majority of

Clinton's men descended in two hundred seven bateaux "of the small kind";[86] thirteen rounds from two six-pounders gave them salvoes of greeting; Hand's brigade came on foot bearing their arms; the band played airs of welcome; drums and fifes alternated with each other in martial tunes. The only thing to regret was that the provisions which the second army brought were small; the long wait at Otsego for Sullivan's forces to get to Tioga before moving southwest had cut sadly into its stores.[87] But a power of no insignificant strength had marshaled now to bring punishment to the foe.

It had not been unified, however, to bring a singular glory to the annals of war, or to deliver the conqueror from new sorrow. General Sullivan's marches in the six weeks which followed bore doom, westward and ever westward, to Indian village and lurking, skulking, hidden bands of Senecas. Reprisal was taken. Hut and settlement perished in fire after fire.

But Thomas Boyd was not to reap joy for himself out of the great vengeance. At nightfall on the 12th of September, detailed to his duty on instructions from General Sullivan, he set off from camp near Lake Conesus with twenty-five picked riflemen and the friendly Oneida Chief Han-Jost to reconnoitre another Indian town.[88] A village on Lake Canandaigua had just been destroyed, the enemy were moving in flight northwestward, one stray band of them had fired on a surveying party, tempted a skirmish, and fled. It was for Thomas Boyd to scout warily.

Accounts vary. But Erkuries Beatty had from Timothy Murphy, who was of the detail, what he believed was a very straight story. The captain lieutenant got to his destined town at daybreak, found it evacuated, drew back into the woods to catch any Indian who might come prowling, and despatched a report by two couriers to his General.[89] Presently he saw four redskins ride horseback into the empty village. He sent five riflemen to take or kill them, and again sent runners to warn the main army. His squad returned after killing and scalping one enemy, and seizing one horse and bridle. His second pair of runners returned with information that they had seen five Indians on the road.

Thereupon Boyd thought it proper to bend back with his own men to the army. As he deployed he saw a second time the Indians whom his men had fired on, this time fleeing precipitately.[90] Neither premonition nor previous experience in forest warfare availed him. He began pursuit, he pressed it with energy, he heard the drums of Sullivan's army at what seemed no distance, and he ran into ambush. A large party of Indians had tricked him.[91]

He formed his men for action immediately, and they gave such account of themselves as they could. Two men of the detail of riflemen escaped, as did the Oneida, who afterwards maintained that he had warned Lieutenant Boyd not to pursue. Timothy Murphy told only that he feared his officer had been taken prisoner.[92] It was an unlucky 13th of the month, and the night of it ended in horror.

What Clinton's and Parr's men perceived at the close of their advance on the 14th at Genessee Town in a crook of the Genessee River was more than "extraordinary land and seventy houses very compact and very well built."[93] Here was a community to be destroyed; but here, too, were the signs of savage orgy on the day and night preceding. That other good rifleman, Captain Michael Simpson of Paxton, and Timothy Murphy of Northumberland looked on the naked, mangled, and headless bodies of Thomas Boyd and Michael Parker.[94] Marks of hideous torture upon the two men while they yet lived showed the full grimness of their last physical agony.[95] In a cabin not far off, the riverman from Harris' Ferry, who in the wilderness of Maine had sung *Plato* to hearten his comrades in 1775, found the flayed head of his friend, and looped above it the scalp, recognized as the token of a savage's triumph by "its long brown and silky hair."[96]

Thomas Boyd, veteran of the March to Quebec, was not suffered, either in dying or after death, to retain that dignity in the mortal flesh which the mystery of the Indian killing had allowed to Captain John Brady. Rather what came upon him was a consummation of the phantasmagoric and the macabre. Long, indeed, the story of Cornelia Becker and Thomas Boyd[97] was to survive in the Schoharie Valley. Orders came in June, 1778, for Colonel William Butler's and Major James Parr's troops to march. Dalliance with Schoharie sweethearts must end; girls of the community must bid goodbye to their soldier lovers. As riflemen were falling into line for departure, Bartholemew Becker's daughter came in tears to Lieutenant Boyd, clung to him, and begged him to marry her before leaving. The gallant drew loose from her grasp, made promises of returning, was embarrassed as his superior officer William Butler first regarded the scene and then reprimanded him for unsoldierly delay. Cornelia's appeals increased frantically. She shrilled: "If you go off without marrying me, I hope you will be cut to pieces by the Indians!" Thomas' rebuff was luridly melodramatic; he drew his sword and threatened to stab her if she did not release her hold. She let go his arm and implored Heaven's vengeance upon him. Shamefaced, the young man left her and made forward with his company. The episode[98] was not one pleasant to remember—and it had reverberations.

In the course of time all Schoharie believed that Cornelia's child born out of wedlock was Thomas Boyd's daughter; and those of the community who cherished faith in the ways of retribution testified to the completeness of fulfillment with which the deserted mother's prayer for punishment had come on her seducer.[99] The tale of grandsires for children on the ways of the evil doer recurred ever and anon in the countryside. In the middle of the twentieth century there is little way of gainsaying it.

Certainly Thomas Boyd belonged to the race which was still to claim a bizarre distinction, like Robert Burns and George Noel Gordon Lord Byron, in the not too ethical annals of lovemaking. Special pleading to clear his memory would be superfluous. But that there was taint upon it seems not to have appeared to Erkuries Beatty or Michael Simpson. Those two were at hand on September 14, 1778, when the pitiable members of heroes Boyd and Parker were "immediately buried with the honors of war."[100]

It will always be interesting, too, to read the entry[101] in Lieutenant Beatty's journal some time later, when news arrived at camp of Spain's declaring war on Great Britain. General Sullivan in response ordered a *feu de joie*[102] to be fired, and delivered the evening over to celebration. To the officers of each brigade five gallons of spirits and a choice ox were presented. There were roast beef and rum aplenty. Thirteen pine knots illuminated a great bower. Bread, knife, and plate in hand, captains and lieutenants sat in a circle on the ground, General Hand at their head and Colonel Proctor at their foot. "They spent the evening very agreeable."[103] They supped "very hearty" on Sullivan's munificence, and went—it may be presumed as heartily—to drinking their spirits.

The toasts were offered by the General. First of these were "the Thirteen Sisters and their Sponsors," and there followed:

> "The Honorable the American Congress"
> "Gen'l Washington and the American Army"
> "The Commander-in-Chief of the Western Expedition"
> "The Allies of America, and the United House of
>   Bourbon"
> "The Memory of Lieutenant Boyd and the Brave Soldiers
>   under his command who were unhumanly massacred on
>   the 13th Inst."[104]

Little doubt may be entertained of the sincerity of the sixth tribute. It preceded cups for the hoped-for wisdom of Congress and Legislatures, for unanimity in support of American liberty, for the expulsion of discord and fraud from America's shores, for the friendship of Ireland, for honorable peace. Humorously the last toast wished that the enemies of America might "be metamorphosed into pack-horses and sent on a Western Expedition."[105] Then came frolic—two or three Indian dances "led down by General Hand and performed by the rest middling well."[106]

Something of mirth was needed at the mouth of Spring Creek on the Susquehanna, a little above Newtown, by men in camp remembering how Thomas Boyd and his friends had died twelve days earlier.

CHAPTER 20

TRUE TO HERITAGE

WHATEVER ELSE they had gained for the cause of the United States between the summer of 1775 and the autumn of 1779, the Scotch-Irish of the Susquehanna region of Pennsylvania had been active on the far-flung battle fronts of the War for Independence. At widely different points they had demonstrated their mettle: Robert Dixon, Edward Hand, James Potter, John Armstrong, William Thompson, James Parr, Thomas Boyd, and many another. Boston, Quebec, Long Island, Fort Washington, Trenton, Princeton, Brandywine, Saratoga, Wyoming, Hartley's Expedition and Sullivan's—all had been the scene of their heroism.

Yet to say that the motives of the Scotch-Irish for serving the new nation as its soldiers were altogether undivided would hardly be true. At least no loyal daughter of Derry Township would have subscribed oath to the one-mindedness of these champions of liberty.

Frontier ladies, indeed, had codes to accredit their sex. When on June 11, 1778, William Clingan of Donegal was married to Mistress Jenny Roan, daughter of the late Reverend Mr. John Roan of Derry, the occasion was turned into a genuine "Whig" wedding. Proud feminine guests were aware that not a man attended the ceremony "but had been out in the service of his Country."[1] The groom himself had several battles and skirmishes to his record; and he had been an Associator. He was worthy of his Jenny, maidens reasoned. Banter and mirth marked the festivity. If Associations of men, why not Associations of women? The daughters of Donegal and Derry found themselves framing a new organization. Before the gaiety broke up they had drawn the by-laws for "The Whig Association of the Unmarried Young Ladies of America."[2] One first rule dominated. Each and every female who accepted membership must pledge herself "never to give her hand in marriage to any gentleman until he had first proved himself a patriot in readily turning out when called to defend his country from slavery, by a spirited and brave conduct, as they would not wish to be the mothers of a race of slaves and cowards."[3]

One month before the news of the Massacre of Wyoming came down the river to Lancaster County, Scotch-Irishmen there knew the challenge which shone in the eyes of Scotch-Irish women. Like the poet Lovelace, patriots must admit that service to country comes before love; love would not be offered to the sons of Derry and Donegal unless first they served honor. Regard for woman, not as for mother or daughter but as for mistress and mate, as for wife and "help meet," mingled deep in the Scotch-Irishman's passion for country. Wayfarers and warriors though they were, they wanted a home also. They could win it for happiness only by first being valiant. No courage, no paying suit!

So, after Long Island, Princeton, Brandywine, and Valley Forge they were ready for campaigns on the northern and western frontiers of Pennsylvania in 1778 and with Sullivan in 1779. Men of Paxton, Derry, and Donegal stayed "out."

Moreover, when campaigns shifted from east, north, and northwest, to south and southeast, Scotch-Irishmen were not so active. Hand, Armstrong, Potter, and Thompson did not play leading parts in warfare in Virginia. Other generals became more eminent than they in the closing battles of the American Revolution. But the way to the victory at Yorktown was for many another man of their kindred in the First Pennsylvania Regiment of the Continental Line the lasting way of pilgrimage. Their fellow Lieutenant William McDowell of York, Pennsylvania, traced it for them in his journal in 1781.[4]

Under the command of General Anthony Wayne on May 26, the eight hundred men of the First fell into line at York and marched off for the south. Eleven miles toward Frederick Town, Maryland, they paused for encampment. The second day they went 14 more miles to Peter Little's Town; the third, an equal distance to Taney Town and Pipe Creek. On the 29th of the month they arrived on the northwest bank of Monocacy Creek, where the soldiers could "wash themselves," scour their arms and accoutrements, and make ready for a review by their general early next morning. On the 31st they marched through Frederick Town, where British officer prisoners could see them as they passed, "making a very respectable appearance." Then, after that soul-satisfying parade before the captured foe, they crossed the Potomac at Nowland's Ferry, where boats were, and one of them loaded with artillery sank and a sergeant and three privates were drowned.

South of the river in Virginia all should have been well; and officers could smile at having taverns become, in the southern phrase, "Ordinaries." But the night was so bad on May 31 that tents could not be pitched; and, to dampen enthusiasm for the new State into which they had marched, the first two days of June were wet and disagreeable. Leesburg, which they reached on the 3rd, moved no hearty response in the First Regiment of Pennsylvania; it was "a small town and not built regular."[5]

Poor roads, miry from the rains, delayed them and their heavy baggage for two more days. On June 5th, in Prince William County, they had to bivouac without any shelter; and next day, although they marched at 6:00 A.M., they did but nine miles into Fauquier County, where they had to remain in camp for another sodden day.[6] When again they marched on, Culpepper County and the two branches of the Rappahannock afforded no thrills: the country was poor and buildings very small. In fact, the men of Wayne's regiment needed the stimulation of joining the Marquis de la Fayette's Troops on June 10th, and with that corps, passing a body of 1800 Virginia Militiamen. Their march was lengthened from fifteen to twenty-three miles, and they got into Orange County at last.

On the 12th, starting early in the morning, William McDowell had to lead his men by a footpath through a pine forest. Nine miles of that made him long hungrily for the road which at the end of five more miles led the First Pennsylvania into Louisa County. Next day they had to stay in camp to rest up. But on the 14th they marched at 5:00 A.M., earlier than ever, through a poor unwatered country; and esteem for it was not enhanced for the Lieutenant from York County, Pennsylvania, when he saw a number of negroes, most of them entirely naked. Sight of human creatures in that condition offended his sense of a decent society.

Farther on Hanover County was better. The fatiguing march which brought them into it terminated pleasantly in an orchard where the Marquis, General Wayne, and Colonel Thomas Robinson had refreshment and "took a bite" with the staff. Two days of the country, and McDowell was willing, when they encamped at Dandridge's, to call it the best country they had seen in Virginia. Had he been a James McMichael, he might have explained that that was true because Hanover had been settled largely by Scotch-Irishmen and Presbyterians! But he omitted such an overture, greeted a fine morning on the 18th, and became absorbed in the events of the day.[7]

Monotony, at least temporarily, was dissipated. The enemy advanced on them; and, ready for action, the First Pennsylvania struck tents and marched, hoping to bag a party of Tarleton's Horse. All night they moved, only to find at daybreak on June 19th that they had been played the fox. The foe had evaporated. Boredom became disappointment instead.[8] In disgust they back-tracked four miles; and in Henrico County lay for the next night "destitute of refreshments, bedding, or covering."[9]

On the 20th they marched early, presently paused for a review by General Wayne, then lay again on their arms. Two more days of fatigue, delighted with neither Simm's Mills nor Burrell's Ordinary, got them into "a well inhabited country."[10] But no hospitality was accorded them by residents; and the female sex piqued McDowell. Young women would take a look at the troops passing on the roadside, yet themselves could not be seen, for, to protect their complexions from the sun, they kept their faces muffled with linen, nose and eyes only showing through apertures. The Scotch-Irish lieutenant could recognize little cause for such delicate feminine etiquette, in view of the fact that naked Negroes were everywhere around. Indeed, all the satisfaction which June 22d accorded him was that the British had evacuated Richmond and struck into retreat.[11]

On the 23rd Wayne's Pennsylvanians pressed after the foe. Success seemed near; the men kept their arms at hand, hourly expecting action. But again "intelligence"[12] was bad; the alarm had been false; and a heavy rain at midnight once more dampened their spirits. Next day the regiment had the chagrin of seeing a deserter from the Fourth Pennsylvania shot.[13] Then, to consummate their recurring boredom, Tarleton's Horse were a second time reported near, and a second time vanished. They found no relish in arriving in Charles City County.[14]

The next two days in Tidewater Virginia had more interest. The First Pennsylvania kept on the heels of Colonel Jones's Horse, rear guard of the retreating British but bearing away with them cattle and other plunder.[15] McDowell detested the spectacle of a Negro with smallpox left lying on the road by the enemy to deter the American's advance.[16] So much for June 25. Then on the 26th, one month after they had left York, Wayne's men saw action. The diarist was obviously pleased; but he wrote modestly of the skirmish, although it netted a capture of horse and cattle and the killing of forty British infantrymen.[17]

After that, the First Regiment, united with numerous other contingents, participated in a summer of maneuvering. Back and forth McDowell moved with his company in the peninsula country between the James and the York Rivers, in intermittent heat and wet. The

Fourth of July was celebrated below Byrd's Ordinary, troops worn out with the weather but happy. Wayne's Regiment paraded. LaFayette spoke his thanks to the troops. A *feu de joie* was run with fire from right to left of the army. McDowell, not adept in French, spelled it "Fude of Joy."[18] On the 5th they marched for Williamsburg, which the diarist longed much to see. On the 6th they were repulsed below Chickahominy Church, and had to retire.[19] On the 11th McDowell was ordered to march with a party of men and four wagons for Hanover Court House "to press spirits for the army."[20]

That mission required four days, spirits proving about as elusive in Hanover County as Tarleton's Horse had been in the Tidewater. But when on the 15th McDowell was returning through Richmond with three of his wagons loaded, good news came to him. In the Capital of Virginia Lieutenant Campbell had word of an "Incorporation"[21] about to occur in the army; a number of men, including himself and his friend, were to go home. The informant happily shared with the recipient of his cheerful message a second bottle of wine, taken out of the precious supply which McDowell's three wagons were transporting. Together, indeed, they drank to the opportunity "of leaving the Ancient Dominion, which few of us were fond of."[22] Then the temporary quartermaster reported to Anthony Wayne: delivered his load to the Commissary, 700 gallons of it;[23] and, glad to have been praised for his vigilance by his general and happy in his possession of leave, posted away at once for Little York.

His holiday got him back into Pennsylvania in sixteen days,[24] as he was now not traveling with an army. But within a week he was ordered by General St. Clair to repair to Philadelphia,[25] where he remained for two months while history was being made in Virginia. In brief, via Christiana Bridge, the Head of Elk, Baltimore, and a sailing vessel, he got back to the York River on October 18, 1781, just one day before the surrender of Cornwallis.[26] His own chief distinction had been in successful foraging of liquor for an army, or in recording events for us to read.

On the morrow he wrote down factually a brief account of an event which was to change continents. "We landed at 12 o'clock. At one o'clock this day Maj'r Hamilton with a detachment marched into town and took possession of the Batteries, and hoisted the American Flag— The British Army marched out and grounded their arms in front of our Line. Our whole army drew up for them to march through. The French Army on their right and the Americans on their left. The British Prisoners appeared to be much in liquor. After they grounded their arms, they returned to town again."[27]

Quite apparently the diarist took the great victory in his stride. He visited Yorktown and its military works next day and admired them for being "something strong."[28] On the twentieth he copied the words of General Washington's congratulations to all his French allies, his generals, and all their officers and men on the glorious event; and his heart was warm toward the commander-in-chief.[29]

But to William McDowell the grand occasion was preliminary only to another fourteen months' marching with the First Pennsylvania Regiment. Until December 21, 1782, he was moving, his total travel from May 26th, 1781, totaling 2,755 miles, and the last 22 of them bringing him from Hagerstown, Maryland, home to York.[30]

The lieutenant's total itinerary led him to Richmond again, over the James River on to Petersburg, past Dinwiddie Court House, across Brunswick and Mecklenburg Counties to the Virginia line, then first westwards and presently southwards through seven North Carolina Counties, to Twelve Mile Creek and the Camden district of South Carolina, and eventually south and southeast across the third State to participate in Greene's army's equivocal desultory operations about Charleston for the better part of ten months. On November 5, 1782, he recorded that the General was still obstinate about letting retiring officers go home before the eighteen months' men.[31]

But Greene became accommodating three days later; and on Tuesday, the 12th, provided with new clothes, a wagon, horses and the privilege of forage for them, three half-joes for army pay, and spare cash in hard money, McDowell started for home;[32] other officers accompanied him northwards.

His own route bore through generally the same counties in the two Carolinas, then guided him by new roads in Virginia until he reached Louisa County and could again proceed direct for Frederick and Hagerstown, Maryland, and his Pennsylvania destination.[33]

Experienced marching or wayfaring were everything from tedious to rigorous, and bitter and painful to zestful and amusing. Wildernesses, heat, rain, thunder, lightning and hurricane, owls and mosquitoes in wildernesses, heat, rain, the swamps, autumn dews, winter fog and snow were trying. Food was too often poor, again and again inadequate. Rice as a substitute for potatoes had little appeal. (A milk cow and her calf[34] turned into mess one day were better than poor beef and rice, but none too succulent.) Pay was irregular, and in an ever depreciating currency. Clothing was seldom in supply; it entertained McDowell one day that a deserter to the British army had deserted back again to the American provided with a new suit of clothes.[35] Desertions in either direction he seldom recorded without mention of apparel carried off or brought into camp.

Shelter was unsatisfactory; now without a tent he was forced to contrive a hut of bark to keep the rain off; now with one, he had to contrive a bower of foliage[36] to keep the burning sun off its canvas.

Yet there were occasions of hospitality: from patriot citizens or kindly housewives, from the great General Greene and other high ranking officers. When rum was in supply, a lieutenant got a quart of it to a common soldier's gill.[37]

May 20, 1782, was a sort of red letter day. On the morning of it, when Lieutenant McDowell happened to have had the duty of mounting the advanced guard, there was an exchange of visits with flags of truce. General Lessly of the enemy conversed affably with him, hoping that soon there would be a footing of peace, that they then could have a glass of wine together; and the young York County officer had a drink of porter from the Briton as a pledge of happier subsequent indulgence. Indeed, on the score of it, McDowell gave the visitor privilege of refreshment at Mr. Izard's until General Greene should come.[38]

As a rule, in brief, the subaltern endured his hardships with patience or good grace. To the amenities he rose like a gentleman. When he was mounting guard near her house and Mrs. Middleton was kind enough to send him a bottle of port wine, he divided it among the sick of his company.[39] A vomit, which he felt perforce he must take, might almost kill him;[40] but, if a lady made him a good dish of tea, (unlike Robert Dixon of Hanover) he drank it—even if his toothache were to be worse afterwards.[41] Frankly he did not enjoy a day when his whole diet was corn and watermelons.[42]

But there was an adventure now and then to keep him interested: hunting for deer or wild turkey, and shooting only one squirrel for a day's bag; or better, killing single-handed a seven-foot long alligator.[43] He always got zest out of occasions when deserters from the British got into the American lines with good clothing on their backs and fine accoutrements to sell to American officers.[44] All in all, he fitted well into his Scotch-Irish inheritance.

In his humor he did not manifest the insouciance of a French gallant or the contented aplomb of a British peer; but often his wit revealed sharpness as of a dry, clean, wholly unrusty blade. (He would have been at home among New England Yankees of the next century.) His contempt for a wealthy North Carolina landholder who owned 85,000 acres and lived "very poor" summed itself in one incisive phrase: "his mother, while alive, was obliged to lay on a bed of straw on account of his contracted heart."[45] In Orangeburgh District, South Carolina, where detachments of both American foot and horses had to keep the inhabitants in, he remarked crisply: "The Germans, like the greater part of this country, are all Tories."[46]

When on March 17, 1782, Widow Izard, "for the honor of St. Patrick," gave each soldier of his guard that day "a gill of spirits" he characterized her candidly as "a lady of the first fortune and taste in these parts."[47] Eight days later, "quartered in an elegant house," he remarked dryly of an absent hostess: "But our landlady was in Charlestown, and no appearance of anything to eat."[48]

He was not impressed with practice maneuvers of the North Carolina Brigade in May: even with blank cartridges they fired amazingly bad.[49] On one occasion he almost condoned desertions; what can we expect of common soldiers, he queried, "without clothes and pay for two years"?[50] Then, with something near the camp philosophy of a modern G.I., he added: "Every person must allow there is still virtue in the army when *we* have any left."[51] He had been in the Pennsylvania Line for four years and three months when he made that remark.

❋   ❋   ❋

But, what modern historians rather than participating riflemen and artillerists have recognized as the triumph of Yorktown, was not all the boredom of young officers in the Southern Campaign.

For Michael Simpson, veteran of Arnold's march into Canada and of action around Quebec, of the battles of White Plains, Trenton, Princeton, and the Brandywine, and of Sullivan's Campaign, life still retained in 1782 the zest of new horizons. Ready for action with Captain Simpson were two other rivermen of Paxton and the Susquehanna. His younger cousin Nathan Simpson, like himself, had grown up on the river; his nephew William Kelso was the son of the ferryman who plied his boats from the west shore opposite John Harris' Ferry. Uncle and kinsmen were all three boatmen *par excellence.* Together they enjoyed high emprise while William McDowell waited for the evacuation of Charlestown or gave up witnessing it for the joy of getting home.

Friday, May 10, 1782, the three Paxton men were at Fort Pitt. Behind them was a journey with wagons laden with flour from Kelso's Ferry on Susquehanna. Their lading had been for sale; but they had not come upon a purchaser ready to buy it for hard coin—not at Carlisle or the Big Spring or Shade Gap or Dry Run or Fort Littleton or Bedford or Ligonier; nowhere on the Forbes Road; not even at the Forks of the Ohio. To the Fort they had brought their flour unsold; General William Irvine was willing that three wagoners be allowed the hospitality of the Fort; but he could not authorize his commissary to buy their stock in the only monetary form of exchange which the owners would accept. Nor was there at hand a more solvent purchaser than the army. They must bear their product farther if they insisted on payment in anything else than Continental or Pennsylvania paper.

So it was down the river for Captain Simpson and his two colleagues. To their friends at the garrison they announced that they were making New Orleans the destination of their flour; and blithely they "sailed"[52] off on a fair May day. Two boats, 60 by 12 feet in dimensions[53]—in structure they must have been much like what later generations would call Durhams—carried their cargo. Accompanying the proprietors to their launching came General Irvine and his officers; and, as the Susquehanna rivermen pulled out from shore, the staff of Fort Pitt gave them three cheers. From the water the merchant adventurers responded with a salute of one rifle shot from each boat.[54] The army men were left to the tedium of life at their military post, and the Paxtonians began the excitement of descending a thousand-mile waterway.

In the evening of the first day—for to the three Scotch-Irishmen *evening* was, as it still is to the modern Southerner, any hour after noon—they were nearing Fort Mackintosh on the east bank when a sentry's hail stopped them. That meant drawing ashore and showing their pass, which was satisfactory, and then a stop for some hours. But it was far too early in their voyage for any flagging of spirits. At 10 o'clock, after nightfall, but still evening to them, again, they took to their boats.

Sharp, contrary winds greeted them in the morning of their second day; but these abated presently and they floated on to Wheeling. At that point mischance awaited. In the darkness Kelso ran aground with his craft. All had to halt until morning, when they had "some trouble to get off."[55]

The third day offered fine sailing. The afternoon was sultry. It rained for an hour at about dusk. But nothing deterred their floating all night, as William Kelso's log put it.

Morning on the fourth day began for them at 3 o'clock, when for the second time they ran aground. Once more, however, despite the shadows, they were equal to the event. By discharging casks of their precious lading on an island they first lightened their vessel. Then they waded into the water up to their oxters, shoved off the shore again, recovered the casks which they had discharged, and were glad for daybreak. In fact, they seemed never to admit that they had begun a day other than auspiciously. Life wore for them always something of the freshness of primordial dawn. Simpson, whether or no he continued to sing *Plato*, remained the man of good cheer.

Various experiences befell as they kept descending. High and contrary winds assailed them. Clouds and rain alternated. Passing the mouth of the Muskingum they grew wary, ran ashore, and placed sentries to watch as they rested in the darkness and waited for the wind to abate. At 10 o'clock again they proceeded, and another time grounded themselves. As next day their maps told them they were passing the Kanawha they remembered that it was there that Colonel Lewis had the battle with the Indians "the last war."[56] But on they fared past the Big Sandy Creek and the Scioto River. Below the latter they caught sight of two canoes, and so "looked for"[57] savages. More than that, they lashed their two boats together for defense.

None was necessary, however, and suspicious canoes forgotten, they had the sport of killing a bear as he crossed the water. Then easy voyaging took them past the Little Miami, the Licking, the Big Miami, and Big Bone Lick. It was almost like travelling on the Susquehanna from creek mouth to creek mouth. On their eleventh day they landed at the Falls of the Ohio, and—instead of floating—found it wise to bivouac all night at Bear Grass. Indeed, on the morrow they were conservative enough to let Captain Peate of that community pilot them as they ran the Falls.

On May 22, which was their thirteenth day and should have been unlucky, they experienced no adversity beyond a blustering wind and the view of an empty boat drifting downstream stripped of everything except its frame. (As they had themselves already ridden the rapids successfully no warning seemed intended.) Two days later they passed the Wabash "on the west shore"[58] of the Ohio. On the 25th of May they were hailed by a party of hunters, one of whom came aboard and visited with them for an "evening" hour; and on the 26th, without any recorded marvel at it, they joined the Mississippi and descended it 13 miles below the mouth of the Ohio. Before daybreak they were again on their boats.

But, as it were for novelty's sake, they halted at a French hunter's camp long enough to barter some of their flour for a pack of beaver skins. Then, having passed a "swirl pool,"[59] they deemed it wise to spend the next night on an island rather than on the water.

Nine days later they reached so "remarkable"[60] a part of the river that they supposed it to be the Gulf. What were the first highlands they had seen since leaving the Ohio, however, deceived them; and not too much disappointed, they next saw and rejoiced to see a small frame house on the east side of the Mississippi with a plantation road leading to the river. Satisfying also was it to land at Mount Pleasant and see apple and peach trees, before, trade in mind, they floated on for thirty-three miles of the swift river to within one league of Natchez. Then at sunrise, twenty-nine days after their departure from Fort Pitt, the voyagers reached that old French and Spanish centre and were willing to pause for the afternoon and night.

It was well that they lingered. For, following their brief sojourn came hospitality. Mr. James Truby, a gentleman of name Scottish as their own patronymics, waited on them with horses. Would they go to spend the evening at his house? That invitation they accepted without hesitating; and soon they had the pleasure of being introduced to Miss Patsy Truby. She in turn presented them to the Misses Polly Birch, and Tabby, Polly, and Betty Pain. So with five Louisiana belles the rivermen from Pennsylvania passed the evening. Kelso's log characterized them "as ladies of the first rate of that place."[61] More than that, they breakfasted with the same ladies next morning, before Mr. Truby, perfect host, accompanied them with horses back to the Mississippi.

The idyl of gracious entertainment was succeeded, however, by more rigorous experience. On the second night after leaving Natchez, having passed the Cut-Off by five o'clock, the voyagers decided to try floating.

It was a mistake, and they did not right it by their attempt to get back to shore. Instead, Michael Simpson, his hands and his boat all fell into the Chaffillia; and when William Kelso reached the bank again with his own craft, it was a quarter mile down from his uncle's unlucky landing. Three days passed before the two crews and their vessels could be reunited.

They got them into a French settlement and devoted a pleasant mid-June day to efforts to dispose of flour. Not too successful in that endeavor, they compensated themselves by finding some cordial French ladies with whom they made up "a merry collection to dance."[62] Whether their new companions were of the "first rate," the diarist did not volunteer. But they stayed all night among the inhabitants; and, then after two more days of alternate floating and offering of their cargo for sale, a French gentleman, Monsieur Gillard, extended them the courtesy of horses and his house. With him they breakfasted, and with his servant and mounts they were sent back to the river. There for a day they rested. Then, before they set off again, M. Gillard reappeared. For a parting gift he had brought them two bottles of spirits.

More pleasant days followed. They arrived at Baton Rouge, showed their pass, and were accepted as friends to Louisiana; a Dr. Flowers invited them to his house at Manshac. After visiting with him they waited in Baton Rouge to see the Governor, whose arrival was early expected. On June 22 that grave Spaniard, Bernardo de Galvez, received them politely and granted them "every satisfaction and liberty as far as his authority would extend."[63] They remained for June 23, when the dignitary departed for Natchez. Next morning they continued voyaging.

At the mouth of the Plaquemine they entered the river with a barge of flour, and rowed on it for fifteen miles until it joined the Ackafalaya. This they also entered. Then for eight days they rowed about the bayous of the former Attakapa Indians' Country, aiming to sell their cargo among the exiled Acadian folk now settled there. But the first excursion proved monetarily profitless; and they returned to Manshac to reassemble crews and stock provisions before trying sales in other parts of the same region. A second time they maneuvered their boats to Attakapas.

July passed. Business remained dull. The keeper of the log of their long voyage stopped making daily entries.

Mid-August came. The French "bought but slowly."[64]

On the 25th of July Captain Simpson and William Kelso were at last willing to read the handwriting on the wall. Hard money was not to be had from people who had only paper. The solution was barter. The two Pennsylvanians admitted they were "under the necessity of selling their flour for cattle."[65] They traded their cargo for a herd; and that they resolved to drive to New Orleans. There they would "turn their cattle to money."[66]

On September 27 they left the Attakapas; drovers now rather than boatmen, they headed back for the main Mississippi current through lowlands and along bayous. That fairly indeterminate destination kept them walking with their cattle for five days and the forepart of a morning. Then for seven days they followed the main bank down to New Orleans. On October 9, five months after they sailed from Fort

Pitt they reached the capital city. The voyage and trek had been long.

But alas, it did not bring them to a good hard money market. Their flour was now only beef on the hoof. Sale was dull. Again necessity constrained. There was nothing else to do but to have their animals killed, salted, and barreled.

That procedure the gentlemen adventurers adopted. But anticlimax persisted in dogging William Kelso and his two Simpson kinsmen. With undaunted spirit they attempted the new measure, but it was not to lead to fortune. On December 11, with their casks of salt beef in the hold, the three men sailed from New Orleans for Havana, Cuba, on the brig *Russia*. On December 22 they left the Delta of the Mississippi and entered the Gulf of Mexico. For six days they voyaged serenely. Then came mischance in the form of a British man-of-war.

H.M.S. Ulysses, mounting 44 guns, crossed their path. Captain Elia Boothe of the brig found his vessel boarded by Lieutenant Murray on the orders of Captain Thomas Spry. The course of the *Russia* was changed, on command of that officer, for Jamaica. Its American passengers were made prisoners. Moreover, the rivermen from Susquehanna were without their casks of beef. Those, as part of a prize, were being carried to a separate West Indian destination. The luckless proprietors could only look on while the *Ulysses* added other prizes to its score: two Spanish men-of-war, one of 20 and one of 9 guns. With these Captain Spry headed also for Jamaica.

Then came a happier experience. The brig *Turk's Island* crossed, bound for Saint Thomas. The two British vessels exchanged greetings and courtesy. The three Pennsylvanians applied to be let go on the brig to the Lesser Antilles port, and their request was granted. On February 10, 1783, they arrived at Saint Thomas, prisoners no more.

For seventeen days they visited on the Danish West Indian island, meeting their own expenses. Then came the schooner *Hope*—Captain Conner and owner and supercargo Mr. Earl Hart, two gentlemen who were not averse to accepting three passengers on their voyage out next day. On March 1 with a fair wind the *Hope* stood to sea.

The new cruise kept the two Simpsons and Kelso on the water for eighteen days. But not all was anticlimax now. As on the night of the 8th the schooner lay to under head of square sail, a violent storm struck suddenly. Two six-pounders (for the *Hope's* cruise was not altogether pacific) had to be thrown over before the craft would right itself —and, after near foundering, race on before the wind. That adventure was fine excitement for water dogs. On March 15 the *Hope* made land, and by the 22nd it had sailed up the Potomac to disembark three cheerful passengers at Alexandria. From that river port in Virginia they were not long in making their way back to Paxton in old Lancaster County, Pennsylvania.

And, after that, they belonged to the Susquehanna if men ever did. Back to ferrying went William Kelso; and into the same sort of enterprise two years later went his uncle. Indeed, Michael Simpson purchased a ferry for himself in 1785, and operated it for twenty-five years or more. In October, 1794, he entertained as a guest President George Washington at his house on the west shore of the Susquehanna, when that Commander-in-Chief was returning from his expedition to check the Whiskey Rebellion. In May, 1800, he became a Brigadier General in the Pennsylvania Militia; and, when the old riverman died in 1813, his name stayed in the Simpson's Ferry Road, famous old Cumberland County highway from opposite Middletown on the Susquehanna to the illustrious frontier post and beautiful city of Carlisle.

CHAPTER 21

LAWMAKERS AND FOUNDERS

THE CONSTITUTION of the commonwealth of Pennsylvania of the year 1776 was remarkable, if not unique. It developed during ten weeks of deliberation, between July 15 and September 28, and had the advantage of following the *Declaration of Rights* of the Stamp Act Congress, the *Declaration of Rights* of 1774, the Virginia *Declaration of Rights* drawn by George Mason of May, 1776, and the *Declaration of Independence* of the United States of America of July 4, 1776. Largely it emanated from the newly shaping political attitudes of these; and with all of them in its own preamble, "A declaration of the rights of the habitants of the commonweath or State of Pennsylvania,"[1] in one respect or another, it conformed. In phrasing it had every aspect of law and government. In appearance it was candid and democratic. In its assertion of the individual rights and privileges of freemen and in its provisions for the protection of these in a society of men who would build a State out of their liberties and then accord to it responsible duty and allegiance, it seemed an instrument of truth and wisdom.

Yet it stemmed from neither unanimity of opinion nor completely legal procedure. It was a revolutionary paper; and, although it had notable friends, it was due to have enemies. Not springing from the time-honored Assembly of Pennsylvania, established almost a century before by William Penn's *Frame of Government,* it was, of course, anathema to many a sober-minded Quaker. In the eastern counties conservative Philadelphia Episcopalians and friends of the English Crown and Parliament did not like it. For too many moderate thinkers it smacked of Presbyterian hot-heads plus David Rittenhouse and Benjamin Franklin. It had been drawn in a Convention of representatives from eleven counties; but generally people knew that the seventy-five members of it had been chosen out of Associators and Committees of Safety rather than by county elections. Those who sat

[295

in it for Philadelphia City and for Philadelphia and Bucks Counties enjoyed the esteem of only a minority of their neighbors. Only two men attended for York County. With seven members Bucks outnumbered the six of Chester, the six of Berks, and the five of Lancaster, but Bucks was equaled or outnumbered by the five frontier counties of Northampton, Cumberland, Bedford, Northumberland, and Westmoreland. Representation from there was obviously disparate. Indeed, anyone who had been privileged to examine the signatures appended to the Constitution of 1776 would have recognized forty out of the seventy-five as those of Scotch-Irishmen. In the list from Northampton were two; from Lancaster three; from Cumberland all eight; from Bedford six; from Northumberland seven; and from Westmoreland six.[2]

The disparity, in brief, was on the side of the back inhabitants. It was they who filled up the Convention. Even that good clerical friend of back county folk, the Rev. Dr. Francis Alison of Philadelphia, regarded them dubiously: "They were mostly honest well meaning country men," he said; "but entirely unacquainted with such high matters . . . hardly equal to the task of forming a new plan of Government."[3] Peter Grubb of Lancaster was far less complimentary; he called the members of the group "numskulls."[4] Not so blunt but more bitingly ironic were opponents in the *Pennsylvania Evening Post*. One critic in that newspaper scoffed that other states lacked "such *leading* men—in their Conventions, as we have in ours." Forming "a frame of Government"—elsewhere in the world a task for the greatest efforts of the human mind—becomes "mere Play to *our* statesmen."[5]

And "Orator Puff," over a bottle of Madeira, responded: "*This damned simplicity* of theirs will make us simple freemen—It all arose from so many plain country folks being in the Convention."[6]

Such comment was not fully relevant in the year when John Adams of Massachusetts had just published his *Thoughts on Government* and Tom Paine his *Common Sense,* or in the summer when Benjamin Franklin was presiding over the Convention itself. Countrymen capable of thinking at all had been for some time having abundant opportunity of schooling in politics. Nor were the Scotch-Irish inexperienced in the drawing up of grievances or demands for their rights. Frontiersmen though they were, Matthew Smith and James Gibson had framed their *Petition of Remonstrance* for the Paxton Boys in 1764, Lazarus Stewart had issued his *Declaration* in 1770, the *Resolves* of Hanover and of Middletown in Lancaster County had been drawn in June, 1774. For a decade men of the Susquehanna country and the west had been alerted in concepts of their rights, liberties, and independence. For them it was no great transition in mood to pass under the influence of Tom Paine, to follow the leadership of Franklin when he had turned his back on England, to align themselves with Continental Congress when that body had not only signed the declaration of national independence but made it clear that the best aid to resisting the power of Parliament and Crown was to have each one of the new thirteen independent colonies form a new constitution of its own.

Nothing loath were Bertram Galbraith and Alexander Lowrey of Lancaster, eight Scotch-Irish gentlemen from Cumberland County, five from Bedford, seven from Northumberland, and six from Westmoreland to collaborate with a handful of intransigents from Philadelphia, City and County, and from Bucks, or even to make common cause with four Pennsylvania Germans from Berks and five from Northampton, if in new alliance with City men and their too long despised country neighbors they could demonstrate the soundness of the principle that men are born free and equal. Not they, who for centuries had known the hand of the oppressor and evinced the mood of the ever-moving rebel, the folk to hesitate at the mere charge of being called revolutionaries.

In September they set down their names[7] to a charter of laws and liberties which, whether or not it was constructed with the consent of the heirs of William Penn and of the Assembly—which still in 1776 recognized John Penn as the legal Lieutenant Governor of Pennsylvania—declared to their own satisfaction that in the people of the State lay the sole, exclusive, and inherent right of governing and regulating the internal police of the same; that all power inhered in, and consequently derived from the people; that therefore all officers of government, whether legislative or executive, were their trustees and servants, and at all times accountable to them. In their signing they understood that they were founding nothing less than a sovereign political entity.

If they did not fully comprehend all the implications of the document, at the least, they believed it guaranteed them a protection of certain "unalienable" rights, freedom of person, freedom of speech and religion, freedom to hold property, freedom of the press, freedom of assembly, freedom of conscience; and what it guaranteed to them they believed it guaranteed to others. One after another of the Declarations of their Bill of Rights they witnessed; one after another of the chapters of the Frame of Government they ratified as ensuing from and crystallizing the intent of these. By their action they constituted a unicameral legislative body (not unably persuaded to that by Tom Paine); a supreme executive power vested in a president and council with one representative in it from each county; a judiciary providing a court in every county and a supreme court of judicature, both on appointment of the executive council; other officers of state similarly appointed; and a council of censors whose duty it should be to see that no servant of the State should fall derelict in his duty or be after his derelictions retained in office. Confidence in the wisdom of the constitution was in them as they affixed their signatures; in Franklin and Paine and Thomas McKean; in their purpose of severing all political ties with Britain.

It was not the first time that some of them had the sense of breaking chains. Fifty-year-old Alexander Lowrey of Donegal, now trader turned delegate, had been a man of affairs for many years. He knew the routes of packhorse commerce deep into Ohio, the language of Indian tribes, the subtle ties of bargaining with George Croghan and with Lancaster and Philadelphia merchants. Always mobile, he had maintained trading posts at Carlisle, Logstown, and the Forks of the Ohio. For the map maker Lewis Evans he had been two decades earlier as good as a guide. He was not a man to be pinned down, and would yet give account of himself as an officer in the battles of the Revolution. On instinct he was a pilgrim, and a forerunner of freedom.

Less hard schooled in the forests, his fellow member of the Convention from Lancaster County, Bertram Galbraith, knew from what stock he himself came. His grandmother had been Elizabeth Gillespie, wife to the Reverend Mr. William Bertram of Derry, and granddaughter of George Gillespie of Scotland. In the family life remained stories of the insult done to that worthy Scottish divine by the violent Anglican adherents of King Charles II in 1661, tearing his tombstone out of Kirkaldy Church and thinking to disgrace the good Calvinist by having the common hangman shatter it in the market place. There was a tale remembered, too, of a son of that collaborator in the shaping of the *Westminster Confession of Faith.* Robert Gillespie, Covenanting minister, had suffered more than mutilation of a memorial. For his faith that great-uncle of Bertram Galbraith had endured imprisonment during Stuart days in the murky dungeons of the Bass Rock, island prison circled by the cold waters of the Firth of Forth and the tides of the North Sea. After his death the royal mercy of King William III to his widow and children had come tragically late. Furthermore, Alexander Lowrey's companion had been a boy in a Lancaster County township on the Swatara where memories lingered of the siege of Londonderry. It was not the first time for a man of his breed to be cancelling ties with a British monarch. In a firm hand Galbraith set his name to the Constitution.

As bold were the signatures of the four descendants of Ulster Scots out of Chester County; of the eight from Cumberland: John Harris, Jonathan Hoge, William Clarke, Robert Whitehill, William Duffield, James Brown, Hugh Alexander, James McClean; of the two from Northampton, who felt no embarrassment in enrolling now with the good Germans Samuel Driesbach, Jacob Arndt, Peter Burkholder, and Abraham Miller; of the six from Bedford who felt honored in having among them John Cessna, descendant of the Huguenots; of the six from Westmoreland, who did not hold back at having a French surname added to theirs; of the seven from Northumberland, who rejoiced at having Teutonic John Weitzell among them.

Of those last doughty figures from up Susquehanna were James Potter, destined soon to be sharing distinctions among Washington's generals; James Crawford, who in the next year fell wounded at the head of his men in the Battle of the Brandywine; William Cooke, who officered the Twelfth Pennsylvania Regiment in the Continental Line in the hard winter at Valley Forge; Matthew Brown, forty-four-year-old committeeman from White Deer Creek, zealot for liberty and disciple of the Reverend John Cuthbertson, Reformed Presbytery of Scotland. The latter's older brother was William Brown of Paxton, leading elder to that tireless itinerant preacher to the American remnants of old Scottish Covenanting families, and like himself a grandson of the Scottish martyr John Brown of Priesthill.

Both brothers would have said unhesitatingly that they owed more to God than to any British allegiance; and both believed like Tom Paine in the natural and unalienable rights of man. Like their parents they had known wandering and exile. In them was no diminution of the spirit of their grandmother Isabel Brown. If they revered the name of their grandsire whom John Graham of Claverhouse, Viscount Dundee, in 1685 had his dragoons shoot down in the roadway because the Christian carrier refused to recant from his loyalty to the Covenant, they well remembered the words of the Scottish wife of the slaughtered victim of monarchical and ecclesiastic tyranny:

"Now what do you think of your man?" demanded the proud military agent and judge of James II.

"I ever did think well of him," answered the simple and loyal spouse; "and now I think more."[8]

Well they knew the story how Isabel Weir had bowed over the body of her dead husband and drawn his plaid about him as Claverhouse rode off cursing. Indeed, it was not in the nature of the Browns to truckle to either bully or despot.

Rather it was their tradition to consider what they could do for a right cause or to advance the Kingdom of God. True Calvinists, kings were to them as to Andrew Melville only God's "silly vassals."[9] Both believed implicitly, as the second clause of the Bill of Rights in the Constitution of 1776 declared, "that no authority can, or ought to be vested in, or assumed by any power whatever, that shall in any case interfere with, or in any manner control the right of conscience in the free exercise of religious worship."[10] They did not oppose giving the franchise to Catholic or Jew. It was enough for them to accept in the new Constitution, which Matthew Brown helped draw, the clause which required of members of the prospective assembly declaration of his belief in "one God, the creator and governor of the universe, the rewarder of the good and punisher of the wicked."[11] They were satisfied to have the future representative "acknowledge the scriptures of the Old and New Testament to be given by Divine Inspiration."[12]

So did the frame of government which would govern Pennsylvania for a decade and a half come into being by an action of revolution, a shaping of convictions and sentiments, a fusing of claims of privilege with asseverations of unequivocal and natural liberties. Like most charters of law and of principles which generously offer emancipation, it would meet rebuff and challenge rancor. But the faith of good men was in it, and at the least, a basic integrity which could never be wholly destroyed. To the Scotch-Irish it spelled light.

Matthew Brown, after signing it in September, 1776, joined the "Flying Camp"[13] in New Jersey as a soldier, contracted a fever in the service which brought on his death seven months later. William Brown became guardian and foster father to his brother's two infant sons and reared them in the tradition of their forbears. That godly pillar of strength in Dr. John Cuthbertson's Reformed Presbyterian Church saw in the 1776 *Constitution of the Commonwealth or State of Pennsylvania,* as in the victories won at Princeton and Saratoga and York Town, only the proper cause for the extension of comparable liberties to others who at the end of the Revolution still did not own them.

He approved the ringing phrases of the last two sections of the Pennsylvania Declaration of Rights:

> XV   That all men have a natural inherent right to emigrate from one state to another that will receive them, or to form a new state in vacant countries, or in such countries as they can purchase, whenever they think that thereby they may promote their own happiness.

XVI   That the people have the right to assemble together to consult for
their common good, to instruct their representatives, and to apply to
the legislature for redress of grievances by address, petition or remonstrance.[14]

They upheld what he believed God intended to be the liberties
of men while they had mortal being, free movement from place to
place, privilege of petition, remonstrance, and redress. The more he
trusted in them the more he deplored chattel slavery; for the condition
of the black bondsman in Pennsylvania and in the other new States
was to him the very negation of those principles which he avowed.

Other Scotch-Irishmen in Paxton, Derry, and Hanover Townships
owned slaves or were buying them from time to time. Heroes of the
Revolution, signers of the local resolves on independence, took no discredit to themselves for holding men, women, and children in bondage.
Valiant old Timothy Green, worthy William Kelso, wealthy James
Crouch, John Harris of the Ferry, Joshua Elder, James Cowden, Cor-
nelius Cox, John Cochran, William and Patrick Hay—these and three
score other folk, including a number of widows, owned one to ten of
the unfortunates.[15] William Brown did not regard them as hard
masters; but a hundred black-skinned children on the farms of the
three townships destined to lives of servitude gave him pause for
thought.

Quietly then he prepared the draught for a legislative act[16] which
should in due course of time set all slaves free in Pennsylvania, and
patiently he bided his time. If the Assembly of 1776 was not ready
for his suggestions, he could wait.

Three years elapsed. Then in the Assembly under the new Constitution the celebrated George Bryan, statesman and recently Vice-
President of the Supreme Executive Council, urged the passage of
William Brown's bill.[17] From November of 1779 to March 1, 1780, it
challenged debate or sought decision. Then a session passed it by a
vote of 34 yeas to 21 nays.[18]

The "Act for the Gradual Abolition of Slavery," as its title implied,
did not bring about immediate or complete freedom in the year of its
engrossment into the laws. Its clauses and provisions were many, and
most scrupulously couched. The property of men—and slaves were
property in Pennsylvania until 1780—could not be wrested autocrati-
cally from citizens at once. But the effects of the new law were simple.
No child born of a slave in the State thereafter could be deemed and
considered a servant for life. Slaves could not be held for a period
longer than 28 years. Offspring born to a Negro or mulatto bond-

servant in 1780 had to be manumitted not later than 1808. Other black and mulatto bondservants, whose owners did not register them before the November 1 next appointed, became free at the age of thirty-one. By 1811 those born before March 1, 1780, had all to be released from their bondage.

These effects did not, of course, amount to universal emancipation. Within them it would be possible for a child to be born into a time-limited slavery in 1799, or even 1810, and continue in bondage to 1827 or 1838. But a beginning had been made. Exactly drawn clauses determined the conditions of more limited ownership of the holders of slave property, the rights of masters against absconding bond servants, the rights of manumitted and free Negroes, the responsibilities to the law of Negroes and mulattos whether free or still unenfranchised. William Brown, George Bryan, and the Pennsylvania Assembly could not end slavery in a single stroke. For a century it had endured in the Province, unchecked by either Parliamentary or Proprietary law. Anglicans, Quakers, Presbyterians, Lutherans had none of them attempted effectually to discountenance it. It had persisted unabashed as a legal institution.

Early abolitionists like the 34 yeas in the Assembly and George Bryan and William Brown had to face the inertia and the material privilege of ancient custom. But there had been fellows to Brown in his thoughts. Others had reflected like him on the cause for which they had been fighting Britain in five bitter years of war. These, as the first two clauses of the Act for Gradual Abolition made clear, had abhorred the condition of subjection which Britain sought to impose upon them enough to deplore a state of being more reduced than that which they had successfully, they believed, thrust off from themselves. By variety of danger they had gained deliverance. They had attained, by the grace "of that Being from whom every good and perfect gift cometh," to a "serious and grateful sense" of their "manifold blessings."[19] They could not look with content now upon the thraldom of other less fortunate men. "It was sufficient" for them "to know that all are the work of an Almighty hand."[20]

It would be a privilege, then, "to add one more step to universal civilization."[21] Weaned themselves by a long course of experience "from narrow prejudices and impartialities"[22] which they had earlier imbibed, they were eager to transmit to others the freedom which they had been finding. Negro and mulatto slaves had been deprived "of the common blessings that they were by nature entitled to."[23] The natural rights for which the American War for Independence had been waging belonged to Negroes and mulattos as intrinsically as to themselves. Unhappy circumstances had long prevented them from sharing in their native right. It was for William Brown and his fellow-believers to restore, as best and earliest they could, justice to the enslaved who, "having no prospect before them whereon they may rest their sorrows and hopes, have no reasonable inducement to render their services to society, which they otherwise might."[24] This the Abolitionists of the Scotch-Irish brood and of that Pennsylvania Assembly constituted by the action of a Scotch-Irish dominated Convention of 1776 would do "in grateful commemoration of our own happy deliverance from that state of unconditional submission to which we were doomed by the tyranny of Britain."[25]

There was something very human and kindly in the spirit of the men who framed laws and statutes between 1776 and 1780 for the Commonwealth of Pennsylvania. What they had received, they wished to give. The liberty of faith and person which a Covenanting family out of Scotland had for a century been desiring for themselves, one scion of them was laboring now to extend to the humblest of all mankind. And in that wish, be it said to the credit of Revolutionary Pennsylvania, William Brown had many a compeer.

But be it said frankly that he and his fellows in Paxton Township were interested in other matters besides liberal statutes. Like their friend and intimate John Harris, they were more than well disposed to having civic centres in their own midst. For some years before 1785 the ferryman had had a neighbor in his son-in-law William Maclay, that former surveyor to the heirs of William Penn having acquired by purchase the farm land of old Thomas Simpson, first tract to the north of his father-in-law's. Since the Massacre of Wyoming Maclay had made his residence near by.

Laying out manors and towns had been with him a familiar experience. So he could enter both professionally and obligingly into a new promotive scheme. Without any demur, indeed, he prepared the plot for a borough on Mr. Harris' land[26] while other friends of that projected enterprise worked for it with legislators in Philadelphia.

Among those particularly interested were Jacob Awl, Joshua Elder, Andrew Stewart, James Cowden, and William Brown—every man of them, besides his other qualifications, as Scotch-Irish as the surveyor, their record as Presbyterian—and, in the War for Independence, as patriotic. Too old for military service in the Revolution, the tanner Jacob Awl had earlier accredited himself among Paxton rangers during years of French and Indian warfare; esteem for him in the vicinity of the Ferry was general. He was accepted as a prudent man, wise and foreseeing.[27]

Joshua Elder was less eminent with transit and level than Mr. Maclay, but he added to his score of services as a Sub-Lieutenant of Lancaster County during the Revolution a skill in surveying. Son of the Reverend Mr. Elder of Paxton Church, he had been provided with an excellent education. He could enter naturally into leadership, and could ply his quill in an effectual and right clerkly manner. He wrote his opinions down with energy during the war. As firmly he saw to it that men of Paxton Township took their oaths before him as notary in 1777 and 1778,[28] renouncing all allegiance to King George and swearing loyalty to the Commonwealth of Pennsylvania. No hesitant man was the second son of the "Fighting Parson."

Andrew Stewart was by birth and mien as outstanding. His father was old Andrew Stewart, the Covenanter, husband of Mary Dinwiddie,[29] sister of the famous Scottish governor of Virginia who had given that royal colony a dauntless leadership when George Washington was still a subaltern officer in its militia. The father had settled early in Paxton. In boyhood the younger Andrew had listened to the preachings of Dr. John Cuthbertson in his parent's house in Paxton.[30] As a young man he had felt the mortification of the family circle when his older brother John had become a priest in the Church of England and turned missionary to the Mohawks in New York under the sponsorship of Sir William Johnson.[31] Not too happily had he followed the career of the Reverend John Stewart in later refusing to swear allegiance to America and departing as a Loyalist four years ago into Canada. More true to the tenets of the ancient Scottish "Solemn League and Covenant," Andrew found himself at home with James Cowden.

That son of Matthew Cowden of Paxton, Scotch-Irishman descended from an old Borderer family of the Cowden-Knowes of Tweedside Berwick in Scotland, had had only a frontiersman's education. But he had been solidly taught in the clauses of the *Westminster Confession of Faith*,[32] and could measure both piety and patriotism with his friend. Among his memories were the gathering of patriots to shape with Colonel James Burd the *Resolves* of Middletown in June, 1774;[33] the campaigns of the Flying Camp in 1776; the battles of Long Island, Fort Washington, the Brandywine, and Germantown; the debates in the Pennsylvania Assembly during two years of membership there in 1780 and 1781.[34]

More experienced, of course, in that unicameral hall of legislation was William Brown, Esquire, grandson of Claverhouse's victim at Priesthill, advocate of emancipation for Pennsylvania's slaves. Four terms of office in 1776, 1777, 1778 and 1784[35] had fitted him for the drafting of acts as family tradition had equipped him in courage and insight.

Indeed, no ill chosen group met with John Harris on July 6, 1785,[36] at his stone house facing the Susquehanna. They came with full legal powers; and back of the five Scotch-Irishmen was now the authority of the Commonwealth.

In March, action in the Assembly had been prompted by the old ferryman. His letter of the 3rd to that body frankly proposed laying out a town on his land, a town designed to be a county seat—if not to have ultimately other civic advantages. He proposed a community of two hundred lots, with a large street to be left for public landings along the river side.[37] Lanes, alleys, and streets he offered to arrange to the approval of appointed commissioners. To those same representatives for the Commonwealth, when they had been chosen by the Assembly, he promised to convey a lot for a court house and jail "and a square of four acres to the State of Pennsylvania, for such purposes as the Government may apply."[38] Prudently he left for the moment unsaid the more ulterior motive which he had in the last offer; better get a county before asking for a capitol!

On the next day, however, the Assembly responded with broad and detailed official effect. An Act for creating Dauphin County was passed on March 4.[39] In the preamble to this were echoes both of the wishes of the petitioners for the erection of Lancaster County in 1729 and of the sentiments of the farmers of the Susquehanna river townships in 1784. Not forgotten were the old protests against having truculent back inhabitants like Lazarus Stewart carried to distant points for trial. Their first petition for being made into a county was not verbally a protest against having to ride far to pay taxes. What they wanted most was a seat of law in their own midst. They wanted a new county because they deplored their distance from courts; and that was the difficulty which the preamble solved for them, for first of all they were accorded a "seat of judicature"[40] at a centre of their own choosing.

After that, clause after clause planned boundaries; named the new creation, named offices in it; designated electoral procedure for these; allowed four representatives from Dauphin County seats in the Assembly; provided for courts "near Harris' Ferry";[41] appointed and instructed Messrs. Jacob Awl, Joshua Elder, Andrew Stewart, James

Cowden, and William Brown, of Paxton to secure a "lot or piece of ground"[42] for a court house and jail and to arrange for the building of those structures at a cost not exceeding fifteen hundred pounds; took all due procedure for the completion of law cases in Lancaster County begun before April 1 and for the handling of law cases newly begun after that within the territory of Dauphin at the new seat. The final section of the Act of March 4 named five good men and true to run the new county lines, all of them by descent Scotch-Irish and Revolutionary patriots: Joshua Elder, Bertram Galbraith, Thomas Clark, John Glendillor, and James Cunningham.[43]

By these men the groundwork for Dauphin County had been done during the spring, while draftsman Maclay was employing himself on the prospective county seat plot. And during that season, on the third Tuesday of May, before Justices Timothy Green, Samuel Jones, and Jonathan McClure, the first Court of Quarter Sessions in the county was held. As Scotch-Irish as were the three men on the bench were some jurymen that day: James Cowden, the foreman, John Gilchrist, Rowen M'Clure, Archibald McAllister, Richard Dixon, James Rogers, Andrew and Samuel Stewart, John Carson, John Wilson, and Alexander Berryhill.[44] John Harris might have sprung from English Yorkshire stock; there was to be no mistaking now who expected to lead the new county, its courts, and its county seats. Bench and jury box were packed with the heirs of St. Columba, Sir William Wallace, and John Knox.

In fact, it was with men of their like that John Harris met on July 6, when Messrs. Awl, Elder, Cowden, Stewart, and Brown accepted of him legal conveyance drawn up by Mr. Maclay for sundry parcels of land. All was in accordance with the Act of Assembly of March 4. For a first five shillings legally paid and legally acknowledged the streets of the ferryman's new town were conveyed into the trust of the five commissioners, their heirs and assigns. For another five shillings went into like trust lots nos. 120, 121, 142 and 143 for the court house and jail which were to be built for fifteen hundred pounds by the appointees of the Assembly. For a third five paid to John and Mary Harris similarly went the ferry lot "together with all and singular the rights, liberties, privileges, hereditaments and appurtenances whatsoever thereunto belonging."[45] For a fourth five went "in trust for public use, and such purpose as the Legislature shall hereafter direct, a certain lot or piece of ground, situated in the said town of Harrisburg (now explicitly so named), in the said County of Dauphin, marked on the general plan of the said town Public Ground."[46] Moreover, as the five commissioners received it, their shillings paid into trust, they knew that John Harris was passionately hoping to bring the Capitol of Pennsylvania to the very heart of old Paxton Townhip. It may be doubted, too, that anyone of them felt other than the self-same wish.

Three weeks later on the 28th occurred another scene at the founder's house, when charge was put into the care of Jacob Awl, Joshua Elder, Andrew Stewart, James Cowden, and William Brown, with five shillings now paid by John Harris' hands into theirs. For that emolument they committed themselves, their heirs and assigns again. This time it was to the trust of protecting forever the fifteen-foot square lot "beginning at a mulberry tree on the southwest side of Mr. Harris' stone dwelling-house"[47] in which rested the body of the late John Harris, Senior, pioneer settler on the river front of Susquehanna in 1718. Theoretically, at the least, when the conference broke up each of the five commissioners was four shillings less in the pocket.

The late July occasion, perhaps, was less abiding. The trust assumed what has not, in the whole and constant course of time, been always faithfully adhered to by the heirs and the assigns of the five middle-aged and elderly commissioners and patriots of 1785. About the burial lot of John Harris, the early riverman, would come change, now by the force of nature, now by the wilfulness of vagrant, now by the negligence of citizen or city official. Yet year after year his grave remains on the green bank of the Susquehanna, in mute testimony to an era of fortitude and simplicity. Nothing on the gravestone bespeaks the material splendor or shame of a modern American metropolis. Rather it says with the seven Presbyterian men whose legal procedure together gave being to the Town of Harrisburg one hundred and sixty-five years ago: *A CRUCE SALUS*. There, on a back inhabitant's tomb, the Latin words remain today, proclaiming that out of patient suffering and the Cross must be had the redemption of men and of cities.

CHAPTER 22

ILK OF DOUBTING THOMAS

IT IS NOTABLY to the credit of men of Scottish race that, when the convention met in 1787 to draft a constitution for the United States, Mr. James Wilson of Philadelphia was a member of the body convening. Even more to their honor is the part which that scion of Carskerdo, St. Andrews, Scottish-born statesman, played in the framing of the document which ensued from what an eminent latter day historian has called "the Great Rehearsal."[1] No lawmaker in American history outshines the colleague of James Madison and John Dickinson in the shaping of the statement of principles which Americans of the twentieth century accept as the foundation of their liberties and the pledge of their security in them. No orator deserves greater praise for influencing fellow members of the Constitutional Convention at Philadelphia to adopt the several clauses of the form in which they voted finally on September 28 to present the Constitution to the States for ratification. Wilson left a Caledonian name to be remembered for all time.

But that is not to say that Scotch-Irishmen from inland Pennsylvania without exception and enduringly accredited themselves when two months later they met in Philadelphia to deliberate on the acceptability of the new federal frame of government to the commonwealth of which they were now citizens.

The convention assembled on November 21 and continued in session until December 15. Members of it had been elected from their several counties; and they were not long in knowing that they were to function very much as a mere debating society. From the start they realized that two-thirds of their number were for Pennsylvania's ratification, that only one-third was opposed to such action. Yet the die-hards among them saw no point in voting one way or another before their views could be aired with all others. For three weeks they adhered to their convictions. When, on December 12, last roll calls were taken on action to ratify, twenty-three men out of sixty-nine voting stood against adoption.

Pennsylvania cast forty-six votes in favor of the Constitution,[2] and became through those ballots the record State to embrace a position in the Federal Union. The men whose convictions kept them from voting approval came four from Cumberland County; five from Berks; two from Northumberland; three from Dauphin; two from Fayette; and three from Westmoreland.[3] York County had sent six representatives, all of whom—rather surprisingly for back countians—stood for the Constitution.[4] Lancaster County also sent six, of whom—perhaps less surprisingly, as that county had lost its radical elements to Dauphin in 1785—five voted for the new instrument, as did Philadelphia City and such eastern counties as Philadelphia, Bucks, Northampton, and Chester.[5] In the solid front of opposition, in brief—taking sides for a change with the Germans of Berks—stood the Scotch-Irish Pennsylvanians, every elected representative of them, from Cumberland, Northumberland, Westmoreland, Fayette, and Dauphin.[6] The fellow-patriots of the men who had adopted the Pennsylvania Constitution of 1776, with its unicameral assembly and its studiously planned check-on the executive for the Commonwealth, were not ready for new-fangled bicameral legislation in a federal government or for an executive control which had not been designed to their liking. Some of them, like William Findley of Westmoreland, had fought the battles of the Revolution for their conceptions of independence and democratic liberties. They could not see that these were guaranteed to the measure they desired by the Federal Constitution. Some of them, like John Harris and Jonathan Hoge of Cumberland County, had participated in the convention which framed the Pennsylvania Constitution of 1776 and had set their names to that document.[7] They thought that they knew the form democratic government had best take. Captain William Brown of Dauphin County, who had gone to the front from Hanover Township in 1776, voted against ratification. Probably his cousin William Brown, Esquire, of Paxton, a gentleman who had died one month before the Convention met, or William's brother Matthew, who had signed the Constitution of 1776 and then gone to the field as a soldier would have so voted, too. William Findley, the man to be cajoled by a majority from eastern counties, cast his ballot in opposition, as did Abraham Lincoln of Berks, the German Nicholas Lutz, and Robert and John Whitehill, John Smilie of Fayette, and William Todd.[8]

Indeed, a goodly number of Scotch-Irish Americans, when the Constitution of the United States had been ratified by Pennsylvania in December, 1787, went back home to their constituencies unashamed. They had gone into the War for Independence after signing oaths of allegiance to Pennsylvania only. Farther than that prime loyalty they had not yet reached. They doubted the infallibility of federalism. Their instinctive Calvinism had always disposed them to respect Divine Law more than it had taught them to admire formalized modes of political government.

Something of their intransigence inhered in William Maclay of Dauphin County, who a year and four months later took his seat in the first Senate of the United States under the Federal Constitution. He came to New York in April, 1789, a man from the back provinces. But he came neither ill-born, inexperienced, nor uneducated. Although he was born in a pioneer family first settled in Chester County and later in Cumberland, he traced his lineage to aristocratic antecedents in Great Britain. In Antrim County, Ulster, his Scottish forbears out of ancient Rosshire Clan Laigh had acquired both lands and a title. His great-grandfather had been made Baron Fingal of Lurgan,[9] and the name Lurgan had been adopted for the township in Cumberland where his parents had established themselves near Middle Spring Presbyterian Church. Two of the Baron's sons fought on the side of James II in the Battle of the Boyne.[10] One gave his life for the king in that engagement. Another followed the defeated monarch into exile. A third died duelling with a French officer in Dublin during the bizarre era of the Stuarts in Ireland. From such a betokening William Maclay should have derived patrician impulse and pride.

But better than pedigree was the respect for education which Charles Maclay and his brother John brought with them from their Irish background; and the back inhabitant fathers were prompt to enter their sons as pupils with the Rev. Mr. John Blair when that distinguished classical scholar became the pastor of Middle Spring. Tutelage from him lacked nothing of the solidity and dignity of training which other Presbyterian boys were getting from Dr. Samuel Blair at New Garden Academy or from Dr. Francis Allison at the New London Academy in Chester County, where the elder Maclays had first lived after coming to America. It gave William conversancy with language, literature, and mathematics from his boyhood years and equipped him to take up both surveying and law by the time he had reached his majority. To postpone his development as a civilian cultured man of affairs the French and Indian Wars had intervened, and as an ensign he had served in the campaigns both of Forbes and Bouquet. Then at twenty-three he had been accepted for practice of the law in the York County Courts and was ready for a busy career in civil life on the frontiers.

Marriage to John Harris' daughter Mary and service as a surveyor for Proprietors Thomas and Richard Penn brought him to the Susquehanna in his early thirties, and the course of that stream thereafter was home for him. From scenes and duties along its shores he parted for military services during the Revolution in the Flying Camp and at the Battle of Princeton, for representative services in the Pennsylvania Assembly and the Supreme Executive Council, for professional aid to the Penns in their claims on a commonwealth which they had once owned as a province. Before he went, at age fifty-five, to serve in New York in the first Congress of the United States, he had belonged to four Pennsylvania Counties, Cumberland, York, Northumberland, and Dauphin; and frontier blood was in his veins. He had long followed forest and river paths, surveying for warrants, Penn manors, town lots. He knew the lay of fertile land, the barrenness of mountain soil, the course of creeks. He had laid out Sunbury for the Penns, had resented the intrusion of the Connecticut men into the Wyoming, had witnessed the terrors of the Great Runaway in 1778, had welcomed the news of Yorktown three years later, and had helped his father-in-law plan Harrisburg in 1785. A year later than that, in the autumn, he again left the river, this time to represent Northumberland County in the Pennsylvania Council; and under the presidency of Benjamin Franklin in that perfunctory body, to approve orders on the Treasury, resolutions of the Assembly, appeals of criminals for pardon, sentences of banishment for conspirators against the commonwealth, pardons to erstwhile subjects of King George III who at length were admitted not to have been traitors, and divers other measures.

In four months of such services, until February, 1787, he was punctuality itself. Then, with forty-nine pounds and fifteen shillings as reward for attendance in his pockets, he journeyed westwards for the Susquehanna—to stay away until his wheat had been harvested in Northumberland and on his Maclaysburgh farm above Mr. Harris' town, and until his last child had been born, a second William to bear his name. At the end of July he left once more for Philadelphia, and remained there active in the fairly nondescript activities of his peers on the Council until the last week of September. Then threat of new intestine war in the Wyoming Valley called for his presence on the North Branch of Susquehanna, and a second time he departed from the capital city of Pennsylvania in which the Federal Convention for drawing a constitution for the United States had been meeting since

May 14. More than that, he departed from it just on the brink of the resolution of the Convention on September 28 to transmit the new organ of government to the States.

Historians have not told us whether on the occasion he considered the document of minimum importance. But it is true that he returned to two counties whose representatives two-and-a-half months later voted against ratification of it by Pennsylvania.

On December 10 he would probably have applauded John Smilie when the man from Fayette objurgated, "No, Sir, this is not the voice of the people of Pennsylvania."[11] It is certain that he was not in Philadelphia, although he was by right still of the Executive Council, on December 13, to participate in or look upon the procession when officialdom celebrated the entrance of the State into the new national pact. The Constables with their staves, the Judges of the Admiralty and Wardens of the Port, the Secretary of the Supreme Council, his Excellency the President, the President of the Convention for Ratification, the Delegates of Congress, the Provost of the University, the Officers of the Militia—all paraded without him. Had he witnessed their march, he would no doubt have reflected on the vanity of pomp.

But it is one thing to scorn procedure in law making, and quite another to refuse conformity to laws which have been made. William Maclay had not critically lost caste with the Pennsylvania Assembly when it met in early September, 1788. If he was not wholly loved by them, and if for three weeks many members were loath to give him consistent support, he commanded an unquestionable respect. Moderates among the Anti-Federalists forces had hoped to team the venerable Franklin with General William Irvine for membership in the prospective Federal Senate; but age militated with them against the old standard bearer, and Irvine's appointment by the old Congress to settle accounts in the Treasury Department.[12] There were informal partisan conferences and complots. Other possible candidates were considered, studied, withdrawn, presented on September 30, when 134 votes were eventually cast, 67 of them were for William Maclay, 37 for Robert Morris, and 31 for the former commandant at old Fort Pitt; and Maclay and Morris were declared "duly elected."[13] On Friday, October 3, in the morning session the speaker read their letter of acceptance. In it they expressed the hope that the "high station" to which they were chosen would afford them[14] "the opportunities of meriting the approbation of the General Assembly and of all our fellow-citizens." The text of the communication, as it stands recorded in the minutes, looks very much like the composition of William Maclay; and his signature to it stood first.[15]

But, whatever the fact in that small matter, the now delegated representative out of Northumberland County intended sincerely to avail himself of his own opportunity "by a faithful discharge"[16] of his duty. No one who reads the *Journal*[17] of the three sessions of the First Congress which William Maclay set down in 1789, 1790, and early 1791, can doubt for a moment the diarist's integrity of purpose. From the first days of his arrival in New York in the April of 1789 to his last day of attendance in the Senate at the close of its third session on March 3, 1791, in Philadelphia, he was the same man, earnest champion of what he believed right, watch-dog of incontrovertibly democratic principles.

Unfortunately, however, to his own peace of mind, the tall, handsome, cultivated, and energetic fifty-five year old Maclay added to his gifts too quick a penetration into the motives of fellow statesmen and a strange combination of sensitiveness and caustic wit. Always he was ready with a wry smile; too often back of his laugh was disappointment in leaders, measures, and Senatorial decisions. Too ready was he to realize "how from the drift of dust and feathers you see the wind blow."[18] Too quickly for his own comfort did he feel the "profane muscles"[19] of his face betraying his awareness of the absurd.

The Scotch-Irish son-in-law of John Harris came to the Senate neither to mock nor to pray; he remained resolute to effect all that he might in the cause of the people; if he achieved little by his part in legislation, he dwindled not at all in his capacity as an observer, or in his stature as a thinking individual. He continued belonging to country rather than to clique or to party. From the first he was both amused and tried.

Used as he was to the distributed authority of the Executive Council of Pennsylvania, he smiled at the ubiquitousness of his fellow Senators on April 24. On the 23rd it had been understood that they should meet on the morrow at the Hall, then proceed in a body to pay their respects to General Washington. At the appointed hour for their rendezvous he found they had already gone in clusters to wait upon that gentleman; and in his diary he pronounced their behavior "a perfidious custom."[20] In some dudgeon he joined the Speaker Frederick Muhlenberg of the House and several other Pennsylvanians and moved off to concur in that informal formality. Then he reminded himself in his notes that he had done so "not to resent it," but to keep himself[21] more out of the new President's power. For he was resolved to offer

nothing of adulation to any one official; and the morrow was to demonstrate his fidelity to democratic independence.

John Adams fluttered on the 25th. From the Chair as Vice-President
nervously he pondered the question: When Washington was received
in the Senate Chamber preliminarily to being accompanied by the
Senators to the House Chamber to be sworn there, just how should
he be first seated? Had the framers of the Constitution thought of the
two kings of Sparta or the two consuls of Rome when they designed
an arrangement by which on one day there would be in Senate Chamber two Presidents, one the presiding officer of the body, the other the
President of the United States? Indeed Mr. Adams wished the gentlemen to think "what he should be."²²

William Maclay sat smiling. But his was not a smile of pleasure, nor
did it alter in quality on the next four days before the Inauguration.

In that interval, on the 28th, General Washington paid William Maclay a visit; he was paying calls upon other Senators. With the Pennsylvanian at the moment was Henry Wynkoop of the Lower House;
and punctually they asked the President to sit down. He explained
that he could not stay: he was making a number of visits. Maclay and
Wynkoop accompanied the President back to the door. In the street
he made them two complaisant bows: one before he mounted, the
other as he started away on horseback. The experience prompted the
diarist, Maclay, to praise the "plainness and sincere openness of behavior in Pennsylvania"; and to discount the conduct of folk farther
east with "their readiness to stand on punctilio and ceremony."²³ If a
little learning was a dangerous thing "Might not the same be said of
breeding?"²⁴

When the Inaugural was over that idle and innocuous query was
to prove but an unconscious preface to days of debate. For, instead of
attacking industriously all the political problems of a new government, the Senate fell to discussion of the etiquette proper in addressing the new chief executive or in making reference to him. Should the
President be called His "Elective Majesty," His "Excellency," His "Electoral Highness the President of the United States of America and Pro-
tector of the Rights of the Same?"²⁵ From the beginning, while other
Senators racked their brains for an answer or argued for a choice, William Maclay protested against all forms of title. On May 1, when the
minute of the Inaugural was read, it stood *His most gracious speech;*
and the Pennsylvanian sprang at once to his feet, interrupting the Secretary and addressing John Adams. "Mr. President," he said, "we have
lately had a hard struggle for our liberty against kingly authority. The

minds of men are still heated: everything related to that species of government is odious to the people. The words prefixed to the President's speech are the same that are usually placed before the speech of his Britannic Majesty. They will give offense. . . . I . . . move they be struck out, and that it stand simply 'address' or 'speech,' as may be judged suitable."[26]

The new Vice-President of the United States was astounded, and in his capacity of speaker spoke his surprise. He reminded the Senate that he had drawn his sword early in the Revolution; he was, he meant to imply, the same man now when he was for "a dignified and respectable government."[27] But the man on the floor did not quail. Painful though it was, he chose to contend with the Chair. Argument grew tense between the men. Other Senators began taking sides on "most gracious."[28]

Richard Henry Lee came in, little aware of the subject at issue, and seconded the sentiment of Mr. Maclay—only to be reminded by Vice-President Adams that the discussion was upon words taken from the late comer himself. That fact troubled the Viriginian not at all; the question went to vote; erasure of the debated words was decided without a division. The Pennsylvanian won his first motion, and one of the few motions he ever would win in the Senate. The subject of how to address President Washington remained on the floor for another week; after that the chief executive became permanently, *Mr. President.* Such titles as maintained in Senatorial usage in New York became only satiric ones; Maclay enjoyed thinking of John Adams as his "Rotundity,"[29] appellation fastened on the Vice-President by Mr. Izard. At the least, it seemed to fit in with what he himself thought of the person of the man, his dimpled visage, his "silly kind of half smile," his way of moving his head, as he sat in the chair with downward glance now at this knee, now at that, like "a monkey just put into breeches."[30]

Quite obviously the Scotch-Irishman from Sunbury and Harrisburg was not endowed by nature to be a serene figure in political circles. He was not skeptical of everything, and he did not fight everything, but he was uncomfortably mistrustful again and again throughout the three first sessions of Congress, and he fought hard and often. He never gave up fully his doubt of the danger inhering in highly centralized authority, or in an executive who could legislate as well as be the agent of legislative action. Washington showed him courtesies on a number of occasions; Maclay never made himself comfortable with Washington, the master of quiet poise. He was frequently a dinner guest in the most eminent society of political New York or political

Philadelphia; he never relaxed from his fixation of democracy when he met with the elite in either capital. Yet men sought his company, and isolation was never forced on him. If he lacked sympathizers, he had friends always on cordial terms. None of his strictures upon good breeding separated him from his kind. Unparaded courtesy, what he designated Pennsylvania plainness, was innate in him. Yet he never failed to be a patrician.

Unfolded at length, the story of his unequivocal and yet paradoxical statesmanship would register his impatience with the placid and too often indolent conformity of his colleague Robert Morris to every Federalist measure. It would reveal with greater extension his consistent and vigorous opposition to everything proposed and everything supported and finally endorsed in the program of Alexander Hamilton. Suspicious of the Constitution—the clauses of which no man in the first Congress knew better than he—he watched narrowly all efforts of the Senate to establish a working judiciary under it, fighting to see that in the administration of the courts there be no leaning to chancery, no formulation of practices which should favor the lawyer rather than a property-holder or his heirs. Idealistically he clung to the democratic conviction that "the jury were more proper chancellors"[31] to assess damages than was a judge. He wanted courts neither to supersede the rights of people nor the powers of the people's government. A judge he knew to be of "like passions and resentments with other men"; he desired no such construction of juridical procedure as would enable judges "to be both witnesses and judges, accusers and all."[32] But he did not have his way at the end of long debate. The bill passed over his negative on July 17, 1789,[33] leaving him still with his fear that it would be "the gunpowder plot of the Constitution."[34]

No less apprehensive was he on the subject of the Military Establishment Bill, read for the first time on March 26, 1790, and calling for augmentation of the force by 1,600 men.[35] The proposal seemed to him a mere ruse, now that the country had a Secretary of War when it was at peace,[36] to find troops for him lest his office run out of employment. It was "an egg from which a standing army would be hatched, the smallness of the number did not diminish the principle."[37] When it was concurred in a month later, he found it strange that not a Pennsylvanian objected, although "it flatly contradicts the Constitution of Pennsylvania, old and new."[38]

Still more determined was he in his opposition to the Hamiltonian program for having the debts of the several States funded, and obligation for payment of them assumed by the new Federal Government.

That meant to Maclay the advantage of the rich Easterner—or worse, of the speculator. Every lately worthless State security or paper pound or dollar would appreciate and acquire definite monetary value; its face denomination would be guaranteed by the privilege of the United States to levy taxes on all Americans. More than that, while the rich who had hoarded the old certificates or the speculators who had recently been buying them up would find themselves possessed of a new negotiable currency, Maclay believed that the levies which made their funds enormously valuable would be imposed on the farmers and small landholders. Entirely lost upon him was the point that making the old money effective as a means of exchange would restore the National credit and give America opportunity of becoming a solvent political and economic power. Too much was his thought that the Hamilton-encouraged Acts were but class legislation directed against the frontiers. But if his view was short-sighted, he clung to it with integrity.

Certainly he had not foregone it when in July, 1790, the Funding and the Assumption Bills were finally consolidated into one and approved in the Senate.[39] To the last he spoke against it; but as he confided to his journal on the 16th, he "might as well have poured out speech on senseless stocks or stones."[40] Then he went downstairs from the Hall in New York, to see "all the speculators, both those of the Representatives from the Lower House and the city . . . about the iron rails."[41] Hamilton and "his gladiators,"[42] the latter inspired by the six dollars a day which they were paid as legislators, were triumphant. Ardently the aristocrat from the Pennsylvania frontier wished to go home.

One slight satisfaction, however, he had before he left New York some days later. Residence for the Federal Government had been determined for the Potomac. He would have liked to have the Capital on the Susquehanna, which would have been a better location—as he believed with Mr. John Harris. But at the least it was to go to an area which might give "a preponderance to the agricultural interest."[43]

The third session of the First Congress met not in New York but in Philadelphia,[44] then the capital of Pennsylvania. William Maclay arrived on December 1, 1790. Three days later his mind was perplexed with problems of etiquette. "Jacta est alea,"[45] recorded his journal; he knew that, unless he should be reelected, he would attend in the third his last session among the Senators of the United States. The short term for one of the pair of Senators from a State called for by the new Federal Constitution had fallen to him at the casting of lots. Robert Morris, voted into office with him by a much smaller count of votes in 1788, had drawn the long term of six years. The gentleman from Susquehanna did not like that. Moreover, under the circumstances, he thought it would have been proper for his fellow representatives in Senate and House to wait upon him.[46] But it was he who in the end adjusted the amenities and visited a number of them. And, while he did so, he studied signs.

He was met by affability, had chats with Morris, George Clymer, Thomas Fitzsimmons, and William Bingham. Speaker Muhlenberg assured him that Dr. Rush had said they "would all be re-elected";[47] but he did not find Dr. Rush at home, though he called twice, and he became skeptical. Unhappily, a month of small vanity came on him.

Self-conceit made him crave reelection. Insight into others' motives revealed to him clearly enough that rivals were aspiring to succeed him. He watched his associates jealously, listened more furtively than was customary with him to the comments of his fellows, realized more and more sensitively just by what minor cabal that one or this was intriguing to capture his seat through interests in the Pennsylvania Assembly. Comfort left his mind for what should have been to a Presbyterian saint a mere peccadillo. Discontentment clearly registers in his journal.

But Maclay had both stamina and character. On December 31, 1790, he took himself in hand. He reread his minutes of the month; and then wrote a new entry: "It is with shame and contrition I find the subject of my re-election has engaged so much or any of my thoughts. Blessed with affluence, domestic in my habits and manners, rather rigid and uncomplying in my temper, generally opposed in sentiments to the prevailing politics of the times; no placeman, speculator, pensioner, or courtier—it is equally absurd for me to wish a continuance in Congress as to desire to walk among briars and thorns rather than on the beaten road."[48] It was a thorough self-castigation he set down. He did not, however, let it rest with that. On the eve of the annual day of good resolutions he put down several resolves. The first of them was that he would "avoid with the utmost care the subject of senatorial election and everything connected with it."[49] The others were on courteous and amenable personal behavior.

If, like other folk, he did not keep all his moral promises, he kept in his minutes, at the least, the first one. On the subject of his self-forbidden ambition he never made another entry, although he served in his position for two more months and maintained his journal to the end of them.

Beyond that respect he remained quite himself. He supped and dined with the best and the most eminent. He attended Washington's levees, and "did the duty"[50] of them. He chatted, he argued, he drew verbal portraits with his old alacrity. To his earlier pictures of bonny Johnny Adams and of Thomas Jefferson with his "loose, shackling air" and his "rambling vacant look,"[51] he added a word-picture of Washington much of which some Maclay of a later generation would tear out of the diary lest it bring the ancestral writer into disrepute for scurrility. He fought a bill for pensioning Baron Steuben. As he had opposed funding and assumption, he battled against the bill for creating the United States Bank, and once more lost. To the Excise Bill he objected vehemently, persuaded that defeat of it was essential to guarantees of political liberty; and he objected in vain.

That Bill carried. He read the signs of the times and entered record of them: "The ministry forsee opposition, and are preparing to resist it by a band, nay, a host of revenue officers. . . . War and bloodshed are the most likely consequence."[52] The passing of the Act seemed to William Maclay the final proof that Alexander Hamilton had grown all-powerful; he failed in nothing he attempted. "Congress may go home";[53] autocracy could get on without them.

The date of the passing of the Act and his comment was February 9. Little wonder that a man who had such accurate presage in 1791 of the Whiskey Rebellion three years away should be able twenty-two days later to leave the Hall of the Senate for the last time with a sense of satisfaction. On March 3 he had no more to feel like a culprit serving in pain and mortification at a wheelbarrow for two years. Indeed, his "honorable station"[54] no more interested him.

In the course of time he would come into eminence. Historians would turn to him for his frank wording of all that occurred in the three first, secretly held, sessions of the United States Senate, his diary a substitute for minutes which by later Congresses would be printed. Exponents of Jeffersonian Democracy would resort to the same text to read the thoughts and arguments of Jefferson's predecessor. Maclay would become known as the precursor of the great Virginian's policies as President. Hamiltonians among scholars would decry both his shortness of political wisdom and his aspersiveness of tongue. But whatever exponent's or censor's estimate of him, the Scotch-Irish Maclay had drawn his spirit from the Pennsylvania frontier and had become earnest of the impact of that spirit upon American history.

Perhaps he was neither a great man nor a complete gentleman. But artist he was. No American of his century wrote a more racy and incisive prose. There was something Chaucerian about his interest in the brands of men, and in his discernment of details he had the acute powers of a Dante. A page which the Pennsylvanian set down in irony on a day (April 12, 1790) when assumption lost in the House of Representatives reads like the Italian poet's *Inferno*. Fiery and darting lines, crude and smoky shadows burned their way out of the mind of the one-time pupil of John Blair to portray the bewildered discomfiture of William Maclay's political opponents on the occasion:

Sedgwick, from Boston, pronounced a funeral oration over it. He was called to order; some confusion ensued; he took his hat and went out. When he returned, his visage, to me, bore the visible marks of weeping. Fitzsimons reddened like scarlet; his eyes were brimful. Clymer's color, always pale, now verged to a deadly white; his lips quivered, and his nether jaw shook with convulsive motions; his head, neck, and breast contracted with gesticulations resembling those of a turkey or goose nearly strangled in the act of deglutition. Benson bungled like a shoemaker who had lost his end. Ames's aspect was truly hippocratic—a total change of face and features; he sat torpid, as if his faculties had been benumbed. Gerry exhibited the advantages of a cadaverous appearance, at all times placid and far from pleasing; he ran no risk of deterioration. Through an interruption of hectic lines and consumptive coughs he delivered himself of a declaration that the delegates of Massachusetts would proceed no further, but send to their State for instructions.

Happy impudence sat enthroned on Lawrence's brow. He rose in puffing pomp and moved that the committee should rise, and assigned the agitation of the House as a reason. Wadsworth hid his grief under the rim of a round hat. Boudinot's wrinkles rose in ridges, and the angles of his mouth were depressed and assumed a curve resembling a horse's shoe.[55]

James Wilson, who rendered no mean part in drafting the Constitution of the United States, might properly have more honor from ancient Caledonia today. He could hardly have illustrated better the penetration of men and of pretext which belonged to the Pennsylvania back inhabitant Senator in whose veins flowed the blood of Calvin Laigh of Ross, and the steel of whose temper had been set in the fire of the 1776 Constitution of Pennsylvania.

CHAPTER 23

EXCISE AND FRENCH REVOLUTION

THE FOUNDER of Harrisburg, unfortunately, died too soon to become a reader of the first newspaper printed in that borough; but within a year and a few months of his death the small reading public of his town, most of them Scotch-Irish folk, were having the fun, fancy, and excitement of perusing weekly Mr. John Wyeth's *Oracle of Dauphin*. The editor of that four-page sheet had come out of New England, and was destined in succeeding years to become a Federalist in politics. But early issues from his press were not calculated to fly into the faces of his new fellow-townsmen. Burghers in the little community on the Susquehanna and residents on outlying farmlands in the county were most of them not in the camp which the printer would eventually join. To them the *Oracle of Dauphin* remained distinctly an open press from 1792 to 1794.

It was an interesting paper; mirrored the times comprehensively; and in its inclusions was no mean index to the culture of Pennsylvania's now eastern-most frontier. The first two numbers of it have been lost; but the third, of Saturday, November 3, 1792, suggests its circumference. Of its four three-columned pages not more than one-and-a-half columns were devoted to advertising. As much as nine-tenths of its space was dedicated to news, foreign and domestic, gathered at home or culled out of Boston, New York, and Philadelphia journals; to political and legal notices; to education, moral counsel, literature, poetry, anecdotes, announcements of marriages and of deaths.

Its advertisements were but miniature squares: the sort of thing which proposed Wyeth and his partner George Allen for printing "with accuracy and despatch" handbills and circular letters; announced the readiness of dealers in dry goods and groceries to sell for cash or "in exchange for country produce"; proffered a reward for detecting a thief; informed the freeman of Dauphin County of a coming election of "Fifteen Electors of a President and Vice-President of the United

States"; gave Postmaster General Timothy Pickering's notice as to the modes of conveyance to be allowed to newspapers in the mails; offered the schedule of William Coleman's Stages for Reading and Philadelphia; or listed Stacy Potts' offerings in leather, calfskins, boot-legs, men's strong winter shoes, and his "few barrels of excellent salted shad."

Within the frame of a less obviously materialist culture the *Oracle* struck its stride early. Its third[1] issue offered initially an essay on "Printing," by Wilmot; followed that with an aphorism on "Fortitude"; and pressed forward to an anecdote distilled from the Parisian *Academie Gallante* and setting forth the story of a disappointed Casanova. This, in which two gay ladies deceived the *roué* and preserved their virtue, would hardly have been suitable for Presbyterian elders in the 1790's, and would have had to stay unused on a twentieth-century editor's desk; but it probably suffered little inattention from other of Mr. Wyeth's masculine readers. After it came—to indicate the internationalism of early Harrisburg, if not its Jacobinism—under "Foreign Intelligence," an item of contemporary French comment on recent legislation in the United States Senate and House of Representatives. Next appeared, under the caption "National Assembly," French comment on politics in France and English King George III's attitude toward the safety of King Louis XVI, a monarch for whom men had once tried to name Harrisburg, and for whose first son the county had been in 1785 enduringly named. There followed, as of late August, English comment on Continental affairs; and after it, "American Intelligence." Headed under the latter was what Boston had to say about Lafayette held in prison in Austria; what Providence, Rhode Island, thought of Americans held prisoners in Algiers; what Philadelphia was thinking about the uprisings of Highlanders in Scotland against their oppressive landlords, or about the dreadfulness of a plague which had reduced the population of Athens, Greece, to scarce a hundred inhabitants.

Commentary from an initial allusion to Frederick the Great turned into an eloquent editorial on the soundness of republican government and republican principles as related to "true and rational knowledge," and concluded with an anecdote of an unintimidated—and therefore unpunished—Austrian peasant who warned an Austrian officer that he was going to have to lead his regiment of Uhlans over a mountain of three million patriotic Frenchmen "who had sworn to prefer death to slavery."[2] Then, that venture into political science ended for what John Wyeth knew would not be an unappreciative audience of Susquehanna river-side folk, the man set up the last few columns of the third issue of the *Oracle* with an essay by Dr. Gregory on the importance of compassion as a virtue for children; with a "Melancholy Tale of a Drunkard" (not so likely to be esteemed among men as the earlier culling from the *Academie Gallante*); with a half-dozen lines on a German priest who leads religiously minded peasants over their fields and tells them brusquely that better than songs and prayer for a soil is manure; with a selection of poetry; with a picture of the punishment of the irreligious Tamerlane; and, finally, with one of Dr. Percival's *Moral and Literary Dissertations* illustrating the "Right Ideas of Truth and Faithfulness."[3]

Indeed, it would seem the first newspaper in the borough of Harrisburg started off with a healthy awareness of the capacities of human life and full sense of the passions and tastes through which man can be educated to a catholicity of judgment.

Not that John Wyeth intended to eschew frolic or sentiment, or that he would be indifferent to reprehensible prejudices. The fourth number of the *Oracle* carried the announcement of the marriage on Thursday, November 8, of Mr. William Kelso and Miss Betsy Chambers,[4] both of Cumberland County across the river. The nephew of Michael Simpson, keeper of the log of a voyage down the Mississippi in 1782, had taken a wife. The editor made no mention of either William's prowess or Betsy's charms, but he did not omit below the wedding notice a proper deference to the nuptial tie. Appropriately there he quoted:

> Though fools spurn Hymen's gentle pow'rs,
> Those who improve his golden hours,
>   By sweet experience know
> That Marriage, rightly understood,
> Gives to the tender and the good,
>   A Paradise below.[5]

Moreover, in the same issue he enjoyed entering an anecdote of a countryman whose pastor demanded of him one day why he did not attend church.

"Well there's two things there I don't much approve of," the rustic replied.

"How so? What are they?"

"Why, in the first place you keep all the talk there is to yourself; and, in the next place, I hate singing without drinking."[6]

When the *Oracle* was launched, its founder, of course, knew no more than another man just what pattern life in western Pennsylvania would take in the next biennium or what would be the course of the French Revolution in the decade then beginning. Disinterestedly enough he published at the end of November a report issued two months earlier from the National Convention in France. That body had decreed, "Royalty is abolished in France"; and "all public acts shall be dated the first year of the French Revolution."[7] In December he accorded liberal space to a description of the operation of the Jacobin Club in France. Its four thousand societies, dispersed over every part of that nation, debated in the most free and open manner all public and constitutional questions. From these emanated the majority of the opinions which the new government presently turned into the decrees of state; representatives of the people gave every decree final and solemn discussion.[8] Republicanism might seem to John Wyeth's readers in veritable flower.

No doubt, most of Dauphin County read news out of Paris with the same first credulity as their editor's. They neither believed that the National Assembly of France was governed by a mob nor that Lafayette had become a traitor to his country. They hoped he had not; for they entertained grateful remembrance of the services which the Marquis had rendered in America and they knew he had been a first proponent of revolution in his own country. But, republicans as they were in their convictions, it was easier for them to believe an individual, even a Lafayette, had been led into error than "that nine hundred representatives of a wise and enlightened people can do wrong."[9]

Those were the days when, wherever conversation was indulged in any company on public affairs, voices were heard saying: "The doors of the Senate room should be open"; and when Jock Blunder ironically insisted they should be kept closed: "It would be very imprudent," Jock scoffed, "to open them before the pictures representing the pitiful Louis XVI and the plotting Antoinette, with the dust on them, were removed."[10] He did not wish to "give patriots a dreadful cough" by their entering and breathing the *aristocratical* dust;[11] he thought it a risk to create any more foul currents to cease the decay of the opposition. Furthermore those were the days when republican Scotch-Irish Harrisburg read with avid eyes the story of the "new Christening" of Louis Philippe Joseph, former Duke of Orleans. That event had occurred on September 15, "in the 4th year of liberty for France, and the 1st of equality."[12] It was something to republicans to learn from the *Oracle* on December 3, 1792, that a great French prince had adopted by law the new name *Egalité*—perhaps more than that, on the same day when 'Equality' became his appellation "in public registers and notarial acts," the garden of the Palais Royal in Paris became by the same authorization "The Garden of the Revolution."[13]

If they were days of short-sightedness and error in the little borough, they were not wholly given to extravagant thinking. Men there could admire George Mason of Gunston-Hall, lately opponent in the Virginia Convention of the Ratification of the Federal Constitution, more recently author of most of the adopted first amendment and Bill of Rights. With sober eyes and sense of truth they read in the *Oracle*— just one week after their hearts had gone out to Louis Egalité—clauses from Mason's will. He recommended his sons avoid public office. If they could not do that, he charged them at the least "never to let the motive of private interest or ambition induce them to betray, nor the terrors of poverty and disgrace, nor the fear of danger or death, deter them from asserting the liberty of their country, and endeavoring to transmit to their posterity those sacred rights to which themselves were born."[14]

So Harrisburgers readied themselves, with the aid of their one borough press, for the two years ahead. Like other Pennsylvanians they now had a bicameral legislature. To them that was as *de facto* as the Constitution of the United States; and it had come about considerably more by the consent of frontier Pennsylvania political leaders. Among them moved occasional officials of the new government under the State Constitution of 1790. A new courthouse was rising; judges appointed by their elected Governor Thomas Mifflin were functioning in periodic sessions. Few citizens in Harrisburg repined that the chief executive for the commonwealth was not subject to review of his actions by a Board of Censors as had been the Presidents of the Executive Council under the Constitution of 1776.

Yet not unwelcome to their Jacobin sympathies was a paragraph of ironic eloquence with which John Wyeth indulged himself and them on December 24, 1792:

> The school for political morality is now opened upon the French frontier, and every father anxious for the virtuous education of his son sends him to the great master, the Duke of Brunswick. There he is to be taught that the soul of man is the property of the state, and that the proper use of reason is to teach him to be a slave; that for plain men to be free is inconsistent with the rights of kings and lords; and that to exercise our natural faculties is in violation to our allegiance; that to think is unbecoming to our station in society; and that the most honorable condition for man is to stand to the right, to wheel, to march, to load, to present, and to fire in the face of his fellow creatures, at the word of command.[15]

And, as 1793 came in, they were ready to read every comment which appeared in the *Oracle of Dauphin* on the subject of excise. For, if two things filled the minds of Scotch-Irish descendants in Harrisburg during that year, they were the latest episodes in the French Revolution and the reactions within their own commonwealth to Secretary Alexander Hamilton's concepts of taxation.

Debate was launched on January 7 by the correspondent "M.S." That writer was not ignorant of the fact that in June, 1791, the State Legislature had passed resolutions warning their representatives in the United States Senate to oppose every part of the excise bill then before Congress which should "militate against the rights and liberties of the people."[16] He knew that there had been a meeting of protest against Hamilton's law at Redstone in the summer of 1791 and at Pittsburgh in the August of 1792.[17] He had little doubt of the temper of constituencies in western Pennsylvania and of what was expected by them of their legislators in opposition to an unpopular Federal statute. He deplored not only the determination of officialdom to act in open contempt and disregard of the people's inclination, but he resented reports that they intended to bring about "an obedience to the diabolical hydra by force of arms."[18]

Indeed, as "M.S." looked upon veterans of the American Revolution —and Dauphin County, like Bedford, Westmoreland, Washington, and Allegheny, was full of them—they were "the living monuments of their own liberty," a liberty which they did "not mean to relinquish without their own proper consent."[19] Not for them was it to be said that they could not have laws to please themselves. Not for them was it to search into "musty records" to find precedents for an excise. Fervently he denounced aristocratic attachment to that sort of law as a borrowing "from the most enslaved part of Europe, Ireland."[20] In that country he pictured exactions of thousands "by the excise and the bayonet, its natural concomitant, from the unhappy people."[21] "Money," he warned, "would hire soldiers, and soldiers would dragoon people into compliance with any law."[22] Philosophically he remarked, "A law which gives universal satisfaction needs not the daring front of a soldier to give it weight or efficacy."[23]

On January 14 the *Oracle* carried a second contribution, this one going more immediately to the point of objection. The law was but a measure for exempting one class of citizens and taxing another. It benefitted "men of fortune"[24] who had engrossed immense tracts of land which were ever increasing in value; it shouldered the taxes off them on the small farmers—"on others, as if they were beasts of burden and insensible of the imposition."[25] Why, "M.S." demanded, should "gentlemen of opulence, real property, and fortune be precluded from paying" on their land, the only material possession of men which could be called "permanent and valuable?"[26]

His two offerings, as was right for a community in which the press stood for free circulation of ideas, brought rejoinder promptly. On January 21 *Veritas* of Fayette County, *E.Z.* of York County, and *Silanus*—who made no point of his residence—sprang to the challenge. The anonymous York Countian brought in mathematics to show how little collection of excise taxes would cost a government in comparison with the cost of collecting taxes on land. Twenty-two officers could collect by the one simple means what 2,257 would have to be employed to collect by the more difficult procedure. Furthermore, said *E. Z.*, distillers were then making more on a 3 shillings, 9 pence cost with a 6 pence tax than they had made with no tax on a 2 shillings, 9 pence earlier price. Less statistical in his rebuff, *Silanus* replied mirthfully. If his friend *M. S.* had to throw out "hints on the excise law,"[27] he must not withhold his mite of comment. Though *M.S.* might properly enough rate himself above him in learning, he would admit no inferiority to that rhetorician in drinking:

> I would never confess
> His head was stronger, or my belly less.[28]

But the man who had discharged the first two salvos in the *Oracle's* newspaper war was to be silenced by neither figures nor travesty. Energetically he came back on January 28. If, as *E. Z.* reasoned, distillers were getting more profit, they were getting it because the duty on foreign imported spirits had been making those less purchasable by the ordinary man. Besides, if they were getting it, their profits were coming from the common farmer on whom the rich wished to have the tax kept. As to *E.Z.'s* 2257 necessary collectors of land-taxes, 14 times 2257, or 31,598, officers would make "a sizable dot of people— especially with a firm military at their backs to be supported out of a treasury established by borrowed money and a funding system."[29] For *M.S.* dreaded two things for the citizen of the United States in 1793: he wished no standing army in the country, and he feared for a republic that might have to maintain itself by a partial taxation.

In fact, he was so serious that he ventured no glee in response to *Silanus*, his more amiable challenger. It was enough to reply that, if he desired to know who it was that reprobated the excise law, the answer was "all the people who live west of 110 miles from the seaports."[30] M. S. made no boast, in retort, of his own prowess in drinking.

Late winter receded before an early spring. The excise remained a topic for animated conversation in Harrisburg, but other interests appealed to readers. At his printery Mr. Wyeth had on display an offering in books. There stood not only the new *Reflections on Courtship and Marriage, in Two Letters to a Friend, to Which Are Added A Letter to a Young Lady on Her Marriage,* by Dean Swift, and *An Essay on Jealousy, in Two Discourses* by Joseph Addison, Esq.; persons less interested in secular literature could buy Dodd's *Reflections on Death;* Doddridge's *Rise and Progress of Religion in the Soul;* or *The Life of God in the Soul of Man.* Besides there were available for children Testaments, primers, and a *History of the Holy Bible;* and for older folk, beyond Watts' *Psalms and Hymns,* volumes which would counsel them against unwise love or guide them into cheerful entertainment: *Precipitate Choice, or the History of Lord Ossory and Miss Rivers; Fanny, or the Happy Repentance;* and *Julia, or the Adventures of a Curate's Daughter.* Happily too, on the shelves were copies of the *New Robinson Crusoe* and Sterne's *Sentimental Journey.*[31] Burghers did not have to remain boors.

Moreover, men could talk of what happened in France. So it turned out that the March 25, 1793, number of the *Oracle* was full of up-to-the-minute interest. It bore not merely an emphatic polemic on the excise, by *A Freeman* writing from Mifflin County, but the report of the execution of the King of France. The latter item of news had arrived in Philadelphia nine days before, coming by way of Lisbon, Portugal, and the ship, *Dominic Terry.*[32]

Abundant space was accorded it. Louis XVI, old friend of America, father of an infant prince from whom the county took its name, had been beheaded in the court of the Temple, on January 21, at Paris, between 10 and 11 A.M. No detail was omitted. Every first available comment was printed. French *émigrés* in Lisbon put on mourning as soon as they learned of the decapitation. The courage of the king as he mounted the scaffold was noted. He tried to speak to assert once more his innocence. French troops, however, on orders beat their drums and sounded their trumpets to prevent his being heard. Accordingly he could make but quiet reverence to all around him and lay his head on the block. Immediately it was severed. Then, the execution completed, the spectators gave three huzzas and threw their hats into the air. The executioners—"it was said"—and many near the scaffold dipped their buttons in the monarch's blood for sign of victory and triumph. Rumor from Lisbon added that the Queen and the

King's sister were in jail, committed to civil justice for examination and sentence, already put to death.

Impartially the editor continued with accounts. The incident, it was expected, would lead Spain to join Great Britain and Holland against France. "The Duke of Orleans, M. Egalité, was mentioned as having been the third signer to the sentence."[33] Mr. Wyeth promised to publish in the next issue of the *Oracle* what he could not include in the present number.

Much room, indeed, was needed for *A Freeman*, who was now taking up the cry which *M. S.* began in January. The contributor from Mifflin County vented his scorn on the recent asseveration that "the people appear very well satisfied" with the excise law, and were "willing to comply with the restrictions and requisitions contained in it."[34] From vitriolic anger with officers of government who expected country folk to be "supple as spaniels,"[35] he moved on to his belief that these were already undermining the Constitution recently framed to guard against arbitrary encroachments on liberty. What they were aiming at, he foresaw, was the creation of a standing army and the usurpation of monarchical powers. And why achieve a standing army, when men remembered what had happened in November, 1791, under the fatal generalship of St. Clair?[36]

His fervor extended itself also to means for raising taxes, although it somewhat divided his logic. He was for levying duties on the use of European luxuries which were "degrading to the virtuous spirit of American Republicans";[37] but he failed to explain how the government should thrive after it should have driven that corruptive source for revenue out of the country. The WELL BRED, who were now escaping the effects of the excise act, should be required to pay on their importations of "cards, dice, and billiards";[38] for the time when they stopped importing, he had no alternative suggestion for ways of meeting the financial needs of the state.

But *A Freeman*, however short-sighted his tactics in the art of persuasion, had his heart in the right place. He resented tyranny; he did not despise a gallant autocrat.

On April 1 the *Oracle*, keeping John Wyeth's promise, printed under "Foreign Intelligence" further accounts from France. From Paris, as of January 22, it published a more official report than had emanated from Portugal. Louis had been conducted to the guillotine in the mayor's carriage. His confessor and two gendarmes had accompanied him. He ascended the scaffold with firmness and made sign that he had something to say. But a great noise of drums and trumpets kept spectators from hearing anything except "I die innocent" and "I forgive you all."[39] As the sentence was executed, "Vive la Nation!" resounded on all sides. The whole Place and the Avenues were filled with troops of the line. At a coffee-house, however, a member of the Convention who had voted for Louis' death was attacked and killed. Paris feared that that rash act might be the beginning of lasting bloodshed.

Besides the advice containing such items the newspaper printed full report of the long January meeting of the French National Convention. Observation that Egalité was the fourth voter to pronounce Louis XVI guilty, it did not omit; and it recounted the horror of every member present when the former Duke of Orleans gave his vote "for the death of his king and relation." That "execrable branch of the House of Bourbon," it repeated from Paris, had had 20,000 livres from England to defray the charge of the assassins "whom he and Robespierre had now in pay."[40]

A week later the citizen from Mifflin appeared again in the *Oracle*, this time in a passage worthy of Thomas Carlyle:

Louis, then, has at length ascended the scaffold!—is at length—BEHEADED!—Cruel fate!—Humanity supposes the *crown* might have sufficed —supposes that, stripped of the trappings of royalty—deprived of regal power—Louis might, nay, ought to have been permitted to live—a citizen of France. However perfect the republican system of France may be; however conducive to the establishment of universal liberty; it will be viewed with horror by posterity, when found sealed with the blood of Louis XVI. Insult does not, cannot constitute republicanism.[41]

The writer was horrified at executioners who withheld from the unfortunate monarch the privilege commonly granted to the vilest criminals to address spectators before he died. An insult like that to a man whose "soul hovered upon the verge of eternity,"[42] with drums and trumpets drowning out his last words, was an instance of contempt never exhibited before. It was derogatory to the character of French republicans, and fixed an indelible blot on the historic page of France. Might such conduct never be imitated!

There need be little doubt that good folk among his readers along the Susquehanna were willing "to drop the tributary tear"[43] which *A Freeman* asked to the memory of the fallen king. Many in Harrisburg must have concurred in his belief that the "real service" which Louis rendered them in their recent "struggles for freedom" was "alone sufficient to counter balance all the political errors of his life," and that it demanded their "warmest gratitude."[44] In the diminutive county seat of Dauphin Jacobinism had suffered a blow. A republican who stood against the excise, as *M. S.* did, also stood for the law of humanity in nations.

But the issue between government and the Scotch-Irish attitude in Pennsylvania toward excise laws was about to be joined. No temporary allaying of sentiment in Harrisburg was to stop it.

General John Neville had accepted the position of chief inspector for the federal government in the western counties of Pennsylvania, and was making his residence—newly unpopular—in Pittsburgh. Violent resistance to the operation of the excise began. Robert Johnston, collector for Washington and Allegheny Counties was seized suddenly, shorn of his hair, tarred and feathered, left without his horse, and obliged to find his way home afoot.[45] In April an armed party attacked the house of Collector Wells in Fayette County, compelled the owner to give up his books and commission and publish his resignation in two weeks or have his house on the third attack burnt.[46] James Kiddoo and William Cochran, docile citizens, to their neighbors' disgust entered their stills in a revenue officer's books, only to bring local wrath on themselves.[47] Cochran had his still promptly destroyed, his mills all but ruined, and perforce published in the Pittsburgh *Gazette* an account of his misfortunes as a warning to other submissive folk.[48] John Lynn, who let a collector establish an office in his house, just escaped a hanging and was suffered to pass with no more than a tarring and feathering and the promise to get rid of his tenant.[49]

Fortunately no such scene occurred along the Susquehanna, and debate in Harrisburg during the spring of 1793 was chiefly journalistic. One contributor to the *Oracle* told an anecdote of a party of gentlemen in a neighboring county drinking grog, "big with the exalted idea of defraying their part of the duty on whiskey,"[50] but sober enough to banter a collector of revenue in their company of the name Sturgeon with the question whether he was a fish or an exciseman. Another offered "Intelligence Extraordinary" to the effect that "The excise act is taken dangerously ill and, despite her attendance by several eminent political physicians, is not expected to survive—which he prayed "God might of his infinite mercy grant."[51] A third responded in a retort that by latest report of her physicians the constitution of Mistress Excise is "still sound and unimpaired,"[52] her malady only "a slight eruption at the extremities."[53]

The spring and summer of 1793 passed with some lull in the excitement to the west, and a lessening of the work of the quills in central Pennsylvania. But that the fire was doing more than smoulder was indicated by a broadside published in the *Oracle* in September. This came in pure irony as "A Proposal for the Increase of the Revenue," penned by a Mifflin County writer masquerading as "An Exciseman." Facilely it pictured an aerial inspector.

"An hydrometer with him to prove all the Nectar." Mockingly it prayed for his early translation to "renowned Philadelphia," freighted with his collections in such sums, for the treasury there,

> As would pay the Assembly the dollar a day
> Which, in wisdom, they voted themselves the last session.[54]

Then both came for citizens in western Pennsylvania and along the Susquehanna and the Juniata Rivers in the year 1794. In fact, it might be said they brought it.

In June, Collector Wells, who had given up his office in Fayette County and opened one in Westmoreland, suffered another attack, and with the inmates of Philip Regan's house repelled it.[55] In mid-July a two-day fracas occurred in Pittsburgh. On July 16th an armed party of thirty-seven men surrounded Inspector John Neville's mansion in Pittsburgh; drew fire from within it and from the General's Negro quarters; and dispersed, carrying away six wounded companions.[56] On the 17th a much enlarged cohort, numbering both burghers and countrymen, attacked and destroyed the residence except for one outhouse, spared by them in charity because in it was stored the Negroes' bacon.[57] Such leniency, however, they did not extend to the Inspector's liquors. Rather they rolled these out of his burning cellar to drink with delight.[58] General Neville got away safe, and with him Marshal Lenox. But the episode was riot, and the consequences of it not to be dismissed lightly by the five-year-old federal government.

Washington and Secretary Hamilton were aware of nothing less than rebellion, and one of the two scented treason. Firmness was necessary. From Philadelphia the President issued a proclamation on August 7, declaring the state of riot and rebellion in the western parts; instanced the attack upon the house of John Neville, Inspector of Revenue for the Fourth Survey of the District there; enumerated other examples of disorder; and called for the services of the militia from the States.[59] In the same city on the same day Governor Thomas Mifflin, always considerate of the opinions of commoners and no great friend of the excise law, reluctantly ordered the Pennsylvania militia to prepare to join with the forces being raised by the President, and summoned the Legislature of the commonwealth to support him in the emergency.[60]

Beyond that, compliance was not by any means immediate. The

frontier had not bowed either to Philadelphia or George III. The spirit of the veteran of the Revolution was still bent scrutinizingly on any invasion of what it deemed its prerogatives. News of the measures of government came into central Pennsylvania in the second week of the month. At Carlisle, on the 14th, citizens met and drew up vigorous resolutions of protest. They objected in firm clauses to the sale of "back lands" in great quantities to land companies; called for repeal of the Funding Act, lest "speculators profit from it"; denounced the excise law as "unjust in principle, oppressive in operation, impractical in execution" and unworthy of a republican government. They frankly advised Congress to "lay a tax upon all warranted and patent lands";[61] to raise funds to defray the public debt and support the national government; and they called for a second meeting of themselves.

Harrisburgers were slower to foregather. A body of them met on September 5 at the courtroom of the borough. Dissatisfaction aired itself with respect to the excise; and objection was registered to "the wages of the officers of the federal Government."[62] But moderation prevailed in a town now more tamed than Carlisle. Good folk thought it unwise to countenance in any way the outrages committed in the "several more westwardly counties."[63] The danger of the hour was considered; and, discretion being the better part of valor, the assembly broke up without drawing any resolves. Then in malicious glee, "Daniel Discord, Chairman," and "Francis Fomenter, Clerk" presented to the next number of the *Oracle*[64] certain resolutions as of Dog Days 35th, 1794. Indeed, these two, parodying the intransigents of Carlisle, resolved on several recommendations. Let the pay of privates be made equal to that of the highest officers. Let all forms of property be taxed to support government except those which legislatures from time to time made objects of taxation. Let the people elect only such officers as will make "such laws as are agreeable to every individual citizen."[65]

Yet that travesty was not an exact equivalent to the swan song of resistance in the seat of Dauphin County. *Farmer* voiced a last appeal for a direct land tax in the *Oracle* in September 8; stabbed away at great landholders; anticipated (volubly) taxes on "our cyder, and our bread and butter." Republican veterans still read with content of the successes of the French in their war against England; still thought the happiness of their own country was implicated in the war of liberty against despotism; rejoiced in the defeat of the Duke of York.[66] More than that, even as local militia officers were mustering their three companies of men to serve with George Washington on his progress to the west, they kept the flag of France flying over the courthouse.[67]

Only on the advent of the President himself on October 3, did Alexander Graydon—to his Federalist satisfaction—see that emblem being lowered by the troops of the countryside.[68]

Burgesses Conrad Bombaugh and Alexander Berryhill delivered an address of welcome to the famous guest of the town and his aide, Colonel Hamilton, on that day; and with dignity proffered the best endeavors of themselves and the citizens "to support the happy constitution and wise administration of government."[69]

Far beyond the Susquehanna, the Western Insurrection, or the so-called Whiskey Rebellion, was stemmed. The crisis involved in the problems and vexations of that episode was dispelled by initial firmness and subsequent lenity. The solution of the Gordian knot of excise revealed the right use and right wisdom of government, and had its proper effect in the establishment of sound and workable law for a union of states. For that eventual consummation—in scenes quite apart from Harrisburg, and by the agency of persons quite other than Scotch-Irish—Washington justly drew honor to himself rather than to Alexander Hamilton. Amnesty succeeded where bungling and dragoon behavior, particularly on the part of New Jersey militiamen, had failed. Injury too often misconceived and protest too blindly misinterpreted came to an end. Pennsylvania and the United States got over a first and trying hurdle in the history of commonwealth and nation.

President Washington himself needed to go no farther towards the scenes of commotion than Bedford. On his way back from Bedford in the fourth week of October, 1794, he availed himself of the hospitality of Militia General Michael Simpson at that gentleman's home "Cherry Orchard," at the foot of the Cumberland Valley overlooking the Susquehanna. For the night of the 25th of the month[70] he was the guest of a man whose dying brother William, a private of Matthew Smith's company, he had visited in the hospital back of Plowed Hill in Massachusetts in 1775.[71]

Of the episode there must have been mention between the great Virginian and his Pennsylvania host. What we may doubt is that the owner of Simpson's Ferry explained to his one-time general and new-found friend that his initials were *M.S.*—and that *M.S.* had his own views as to the wisdom and justice of the excise law. Moreover, Washington probably never read *The Oracle of Dauphin*.

CHAPTER 24

NEIGHBORS AND EL DORADO

When the excitements of the Western Insurrection were in the air of Paxton Township, in July and August, 1794, John Wyeth advertised a greatly enlarged list of books as available for sale at his office on Mulberry Street. Contributions from the presses of the Old World might be drawn upon, as it were, to allay the passions and disappointments of politics. Many items had "just arrived from England" —although *Precipitate Choice, or The History of Lord Ossory and Miss Rivers* still remained from the stock of the previous season on the bookseller's shelves—and the array of volumes was a goodly one. Here now for the religiously minded were additional titles, beyond Bibles and Testaments, like *Milton's Works*, Milton's *Paradise Lost* and *Paradise Regained*, Bunyan's *Heavenly Footman* and *Pilgrim's Progress*, Neckar's *"On Religion,"* Pope's *Essay on Man*, besides numerous less eminent writers' works in commentary. Harvey's *Works*, his *Dialogues* and his *Letters* were at command. Near them were the *New Manual of Devotion*, the *Episcopal Prayer Book, The Christian Parent, The Parental Monitor*, and *Reflections on Death*. Not unaware that his Scotch-Irish patrons were commonly students of the principles of law, the printer offered no fewer than thirteen legal titles. Harrisburgers could buy of him Burns's *Justice* in 4 volumes, Burns's *Law Dictionary*, Blackstone's *Reports*, Croke's *Reports*, Cowper's *Reports;* could have from his shop *Powel on Powers* and *Powel on Mortgages*, Talbot's *Cases*, Wood's *Institutes*, the *Crown Circuit Complete*, Hale's *Pleas: Crown*, or even the *Conductor Generalis*. Mr. Wyeth had, apparently, little doubt of the intelligence of his customers.

Although he advertised such "religious mirrors" as *Devotional Addresses, Sermons to Young Women*, and *A Catechism of Nature*, he exhibited no indifference to secular tastes. Fashionable Philadelphians could hardly have craved a larger stock of mundane literature to select from. Here at Wyeth's printery for the less sophisticated folk of a borough were *Gil Blas;* Gay's *Fables;* Gay's *Poems;* the *History of Tom Jones, a Foundling* in four volumes; *The Vicar of Wakefield; Jockey Club, Or a Sketch of the Manners of the Age* in 3 volumes; *Essay on Old Maids, By a Friend to the Sisterhood; Fatal Follies, Or the History of the Countess of Stanmore* in two volumes; *Lucy Wellers,* 2 volumes by a Lady; *Tour in Holland;* Montague's *Travels;* Thomson's *Seasons; Robinson Crusoe; The Spectator* in 8 volumes; the *Sorrows of Werther; Surprises of Love, Exemplified in the Romance of a Day, Or An Adventure in Greenwich Park Last Easter;* and *School of Virtue, to Which Is Added the Fair Solitary.* Every topic of possible interest: sentiment, sex, etiquette, wit was represented. Harrisburg and Dauphin County readers had the culture of Europe, as it were, spread before their eyes and purses. Add *Aesop's Fables; Arabian Night's Entertainment;* the *Beauties of Creation; Of History; Of Fielding; Of Swift; Of Johnson;* the novel *Clarissa Harlowe;* Denham's *Poems,* Dryden's *Poems,* Donne's *Poems; Sanford and Merton;* Varro's *Husbandry;* a selection of texts in music; another in mathematics; Baron Steuben's *Military Exercise, with Cuts;* dictionaries of English, Latin, and Greek; spelling books; "a variety of favorite copperplate prints"; and playing cards—and Mr. Wyeth's client had opportunity to become macaroni, dilettante, gentleman, humanist, or scholar as he chose. The heir to the back inhabitant or the Paxton Boy could be off to new worlds of intellectuality, refinement, pleasure, aestheticism, and knowledge. By him might even be risked the taint of the drama if he thought to buy for himself, for his wife, or his daughter, *Charlotte, A Tale of Truth,* "wrote by Mrs. Rowson, of the New Theatre in Philadelphia, author of *Victoria, The Inquisitor,* and *Fille de Chambre,*" which was "a new and much admired novel" to be had at 5 shillings.[1]

To be sure, had he survived until mid-summer of 1794, the Rev. Mr. John Roan, Pastor of "New Side" Derry Church, would probably have objected to John Wyeth's stock-in-trade. By his will, drawn on July 28, 1775, that eloquent clergyman bequeathed to his son Flavel, in case the then fifteen-year-old lad should later appear to the Rev. George Duffield and his father's executor "to be religiously disposed,"[2] all his Latin, Greek, and Hebrew books, together with Henry, Flavel, Burket, Howe, Ridgely, Keach, Cruden, and Charnock. At the disposal of his heir, should he choose the sacred calling his father had embraced, were to be not only the main portion of Mr. Roan's estate but also the precious works on divinity. Even if all the other books should be sold in the settlement of the several bequests, for Flavel were to be preserved the volumes written by a theologian whom John Roan had so much loved that he named his only surviving son for him—an heir who came after a long and disappointing sequence of daughters and an older son who died in infancy.

Yet the fact was that Flavel Roan's tastes would wander far from John Flavel's *Fountain of Life, in Forty-Two Sermons,* from that celebrity's *Method of Grace* and his *Token for Mourners.* The youth's older cousin, Archibald Roan, who by his clerical uncle's will had been promised twenty pounds towards his education if he was "religiously disposed," turned to the law and began a career destined to take him far in politics, into a governorship in Tennessee and the early sponsorship of Andrew Jackson. Flavel was still more unregenerate. He took to teaching, to the ways of the world, and to occasional verse.

He should have been an absorbed reader of the literary columns of the *Oracle,* and one of Mr. Wyeth's most frequent customers. But, unhappily for wits in Harrisburg and Dauphin County, the Rev. Mr. Roan's son responded to old impulses, and frontiers farther on appealed to him as to his cousin. In 1794 Flavel, matured but unmarried and advancing towards middle life,[3] was a resident of Lewisburg sixty miles up the Susquehanna. There he had settled in Buffalo Valley near not only to his sister Jenny and her husband William Clingan but near to half the former population of old Derry Township. And not far away from him was A. Kennedy, printer of *The Sunbury and Northumberland Gazette,* and an editor not notably averse to scribal bawdry.

Through Wyeth, Kennedy, and Flavel Roan comes down to us the flavor of old-time broad Scottish comedy.

The Harrisburg editor quoted under "Poetry":

> Dr. Aldridge's Five Reasons for Drinking
>
> Good wine; a friend; or being dry;
> Or lest we should be, bye and bye;
> Or—any other reason why.[4]

For more indelicate innuendo he ventured, unsigned:

> Paraphrase
>
> An amorous youth, inclining to wed,
> Ask'd Socrates' notion of the marriage bed,
> When answered the sage, and wittily said:
>
> "Dear youth, if to marry or not you design,
> Ere life's at an end, you will surely repine—
> Both states have their curses. I know them by mine.

"If single, your passions unconquered will sway;
And lonesome you'll pass your hipp'd moments away,
Till a stranger inherits what yours is today.

"If married, your skull may be crack'd by a Pot,
"How dare you be absent, you drunken old sot?
While you father the brat you never begot."[5]

But with neither pseudonym nor anonymity the Sunbury publisher
A. Kennedy accepted from thirty-four-year-old bachelor Roan his un-
inhibited "Advertisement":

I am an old man, my case is quite common,
I want me a wife, a likely young woman.
I late had an old one, but three years ago,
She sickened and died, and left me in woe;
  I whin'd; J. B. preached a sermon when she was buried;
Wore my old wig a fort'night, then long'd to be married.
  If any one knows where a wife's to be had,
Such as seventy wishes when reason is dead:
A girl that will warm my old bones in the winter,
Let them leave the intelligence with Mr. Printer.[6]

For essentially Flavel was the Scotch-Irish man-about-town of the
Buffalo Valley, always receptive to entertainment, everywhere welcome. Neighborliness and hospitality shone for him.

The journal which he set down in his meticulous and delicate hand
was voluble as it was capricious and fun-loving. Like himself, it
missed nothing: barn-raising, burial, sermon, dance, butchering, election, cradling of wheat, dinner party, exchange of bottles or of cups
of cheer, bedrooms at hostelries, dalliance of lovers or libertines. For
many years it told all. Flavel lived to be the teacher of Governor
Simon Snyder's son, "Prince John of the Isle of Que,"[7] he attended
public exhibitions[8] of the speaking abilities of Mr. Hood's scholars;
but his interests were certainly as social as they were intellectual.

If Colonel Chamberlin[9] at above seventy-three had a young son,
his twenty-third child born to him by a young wife, the diarist recorded it. If he himself clerked at an auction sale, which held over till
tomorrow and necessitated his sleeping with the cryer, he did not fail
to note that four ladies and a child slept in a bed in the same room.
If he went to Methodist meeting at Derrstown, it was not to be un-
observant when he saw "Hamer squeezing Nancy McDonald behind
the stove."[10] Nor was his pleasure spoiled when, quartered in a good
"bed at the fire" at taverner Smelcher's, he beheld "sparking going

on"[11] elsewhere in the room. His sentences are commonly punctuated or interrupted with the drinks of whiskey which he took, and his fondness for "cider royal" he did not deny. But into Flavel Roan's journal went mention of Baptist Preacher Smilie's sermon at Jaysburg "on the fruitful vine";[12] and he approved the fact that "not two bottles" were drunk when at the cutting of William Clingan's wheat the squire got a harvest of 700 dozen, while the Rev. Mr. Thomas Hood cradled with the others as capable as any.[13]

Thoroughly catholic was the diarist's love of pastimes. He liked dining and dancing and was always present when the quality of the Valley foregathered for such pleasures. But his zest was equal for shows of rope-dancing,[14] boat launchings, selling pawns, singing matches, tea with ladies, weddings, tramping frolics, elections for militia field-officers, bridge-building across the West Branch at Northumberland, fights, and religious camp-meetings. Where young folk were, Schoolmaster Roan was always willing to be—whether at his cousin Roan McClure's, at Clingan's, at Samuel Maclay's, or George Clark's. He admired the ear rings or baubles which their fathers or uncles brought back with them as gifts on return from journeys to Philadelphia or Lancaster. He never neglected to say whose daughters were belles. With animation he noted "Beaux Kremer, Haslet, Barber. 'Where the carcase is, thither will the eagles gather together.'"[15]

Nothing illustrates better, perhaps, the neighborliness in the Scotch-Irish than Flavel Roan's *Journal*. In it one sees the spirit of Derry and Paxton Townships of old Lancaster County translated up river. Many a veteran of the Revolution had migrated from abodes along Swatara or Conewago Creek into Buffalo Valley in the 1790's: Colonel Robert Clark, Captain Jonathan McClure, Sankey Dixon, families of Hayes, Wilsons, Barnetts, and Hutchinsons. New township after township, in what still remained Northumberland County, filled up with their kinsmen and friends. Localities, villages, taverns took their names. Matthew Smith came to live on the east bank of the West Branch, where still lived Captain William Gray and Colonel William Cooke who had known Valley Forge. The cameraderie of Pennsylvania's militia and the lore of the War for Independence remained in the air.

The deaths of heroes at home became events. General James Potter just failed of living into the decade. That hardy old aide of Washington throughout 1776 and 1777 prospered on broad acres for a decade after the Revolution and took to farming with as lively a will as he had taken to command. In September 1789 he joined in a new barn-raising on one of his own properties and was caught and maimed by an accidental crash of timbers, suffering internal injuries. He was borne to a daughter's home in Franklin County for care and rest. Death came to him at the end of November and burial at Brown's Mills,[16] faraway from the Northumberland County compatriots with whom his old doughtiness and his mischance persisted in vivid remembrance.

Fifty-four-year-old Matthew Smith, Freemason and earlier Paxton Boy, friend of James Gibson and Lazarus Stewart in 1763-1764, captain unloved of John Joseph Henry while Benedict Arnold's men were marching in 1775 through the wilderness to Quebec, slowed his once fleeting steps, quieted his voice, and bowed to illness and death in 1794 at Milton. State was made of his passing. A company of light infantry under Major Piatt and Captain James Boyd marched with his body the six miles to Warrior Run Burying Ground and laid the old talker in the earth. Tears were shed by the military escort. Three volleys were fired over his grave.[17] Memory of him dimmed—but his honor grew into history.

More striking yet were the circumstances at the close of days for Captain John Lowden. That heroic soldier and wader at the battle of Lechmere's Point in Massachusetts in 1775 had known many honors before his death in February, 1798. In 1776 he sat as the member for Northumberland County in the Supreme Executive Council of Pennsylvania. After the Revolution he became a great landholder at Buffalo Cross-Roads, owning almost a township. He was handsome of stature and countenance; wore like a patrician his cocked hat, blue coat, buff vest and breeches, silver knee and shoe buckles. He owned many slaves. But the wind which passes over man passed over him also; and his family decided on burial at Columbia near relatives buried far down the Susquehanna. Services were conducted at Buffalo Cross-Roads; the casket was set in motion for the long journey and voyage. The cortege could not cross flooded Buffalo Creek and Colonel Robert Clark's slave Mel stepped forward. There was consultation, then consent; and the funeral party watched the negro shoulder the coffin, walk firmly over the footlog, and bear the precious burden forward across the first barrier to its long pilgrimage. The funeral could not have been more dignified with clansmen and bagpipes in Scotland.[18]

Through the 1790's, indeed, the social climate of the County remained as it had been in 1785, when eighty Scotch-Irishmen's signatures were set down among eighty-eight on a Memorial to the Assembly of Pennsylvania appealing for consideration for Widow Katherine Smith of White Deer.[19] She had known much of adversity, but her neighbors had witnessed through the long years her thrift and industry. Left "in low circumstances"²⁰ with ten children to provide for, the pioneer woman had taken a location of 300 acres at the mouth of White Deer Creek on the West Branch. Frontiersmen told her it was just the place for a mill seat, and a grist mill and a saw mill were much wanting in the new country. Katherine Smith borrowed money and built two mills, completing them in 1775. Then came the War for Independence. Gun barrels were needed in 1776 for Northumberland County and the Continent as much as grist and boards. Katherine added a boring mill to her property, began turning out a great supply of the needed rifle bores, throve, and won honor.

The terrors of the Wyoming Massacre came in 1778, and the next year savages invaded the region of the West Branch. In July, 1779, Indians congregated around Katherine's property and burned the whole works. Her eldest son, greatest help to her in her labors, went off as a soldier defender of the frontier, and died—his mother believed—in some unreported contest with the red foe. After four years she ventured back with the rest of her brood and began rebuilding grist and saw mill.

Then came a new adversary. Messrs. Claypool and Morris of Philadelphia sent agents ordering Widow Smith off the great tract of land which they claimed. Veterans of a score of battlefronts heard in contempt the intruders. Men helped the unfortunate lady frame her petition to Government; men rode about the vast county on both sides of the river, far up in Penn's Creek Valley, along White Deer and Buffalo Creeks, along Warrior Run to the east, south of that to Muddy Run, and down to the Point, gathering names of subscribers to the brave widow's patriotism and industry. Into the document went the signatures of all the most notable frontier citizens: among many other names were William Blythe, Thomas McCormick, General James Potter, Captain William Gray, Colonel Robert Clark, Colonel Matthew Smith, Robert Martin, Colonel John Kelly, James Gibson, Henry Starrett, James Crawford, Thomas Robinson—and, to lend both variety and dignity, that of the kindly Jew, Aaron Levy.²¹

All was a fine array of old Scotia, and of Americanism. The voices of Philadelphia land buyers and speculators, however, were still powerful in 1785. Widow Katherine did not gain her appeal; and with her sad plight she has dwindled into only a musty record among the Post-Revolutionary Papers of the Pennsylvania Archives Office in Harrisburg. Yet a gallant circle of neighbors and heroes sought to be her champions,²² and their neighborliness went into the making of a countryside in the last decade of the eighteenth century.

Meantime, lower down along the old Susquehanna, citizens of Harrisburg turned so far into gentle folk as to form a "Dancing Academy" and promote a land company of their own. Three sons of old Parson Elder went in for the measures of the light fantastic, and with them a whole bevy of youths out of established Derry and Paxton families: Lairds, Robinsons, Berryhills, Burds, Gilchrists, Kelsos, and Forsters. Perhaps to see that these adhered with full etiquette to their rules for the entertainment and escort of ladies, Alexander Graydon, William Maclay, and John Wyeth added their names to the fellowship.[23]

Less given to diversion, but as enthusiastically entered into was The Harrisburg and Presque Isle Company. That material organization had for design "settling, improving and populating"[24] country considerably farther away from the Susquehanna than Lewisburg, Northumberland, and Buffalo Valley. William Kelso, the far voyager with Michael Simpson in 1782; Thomas Forster, grandson of a forbear who once looked for the body of Jack Armstrong up Juniata in 1744; Robert Harris, grandson of the first settler at the Ferry, were interested in a more distant El Dorado. The triangle on Lake Erie at the northwestern corner of the State had been purchased by Pennsylvania in 1792. Let the Scotch-Irish move into it now by due process of law. Ten men came into the company, each taking five shares at $200 of the $10,000 stock. Four of their number were quite as serious about the enterprise as they were about the Harrisburg "Dancing Academy." Late in 1796 the company bought through public sale at Carlisle 37 Erie inlots and 8 outlots, as well as 430 acres at the mouth of Walnut Creek on the Lake and other acres inland at Waterford. Thomas Forster and Richard Swan during the next spring took up tracts for themselves in those vicinities and to further the interest of their fellow stockholders in the Harrisburg and Presque Isle Company. Presently sons of farmers in Derry, Hanover, and Paxton were emigrating to break lands for themselves. Other Kelsos, Wilsons, Moreheads, Robinsons were seeking homes and livelihood, the spirit of quest not yet died out from their blood.

Elsewhere in the same decade other men revealed signs that their breed was not yet wholly tamed. Samuel Maclay was not the brother of William Maclay to be without a self-dependence of his own. He was to go far, to be Speaker of the Pennsylvania Senate in 1801 and 1802, and later to prove himself a more enduring United States Senator than William; and forthrightness was in him also.

Before the Revolution came on, in 1767 to 1769, Samuel was deputy surveyor to his elder brother. In those years, on a hunting trip with his friend William Brown, he visited once with the celebrated Chief Logan at his Indian camp. Wagers on marksmanship were presently ventured.

"Me beat you for a dollar a shot,"[25] said Logan to Maclay.

The young surveyor parried the challenge, then rose to accept it.

A target was set. Indian and white man took turns. Five times Samuel's bullet came closer to the centre. "You win," admitted Logan.

After supper the two guests made ready to depart. Samuel made no mention of his winning; but the hospitable Logan brought out from his peltry five deer skins. Young Maclay protested: "You have been our host, that is enough."

"Me bet to make you shoot your best," insisted the Chief; "me gentleman, and me take your dollar if me beat—you take my skins."[26] There was, under the circumstances, nothing else for the victor to do.

Unfortunately, honors were not so even in Samuel Maclay's contest thirty years later with the Rev. Mr. Hugh Morrison who was called to the united congregations of Buffalo, Sunbury, and Northumberland in May, 1787. The members of three flocks, in their formal summons promised to be subject to their pastor's "administrations and reproofs, should outfalls and miscarriages expose us thereto."[27] They would treat his person "with friendship and respect, and behave in all things towards you as becomes a Christian society."[28] But that was no reason why a dozen years later they should permit him at Buffalo Cross-Roads Presbyterian Church to upbraid them in his sermons for their Republican leanings. Yet openly Mr. Morrison commenced preaching at the offenses of Samuel Maclay (who was a wealthy support to the church) when the political election was hot. The Republican Samuel stood it for a time, then stopped attending worship—and so did his constituency, who made up the majority of the members!

It was not a rebuke which the Federalist minister accepted with dignity. Rather, Mr. Morrison went one Sabbath-Day to his meeting house with the sparse remnants of his flock, locked himself and those few followers out of the sanctuary, led them with him to the nearby schoolhouse, and preached there. Afterwards the report circulated that Samuel Maclay and his majority party had shut their pastor out of his own fold.

Thereupon the favorite of the hour—and of the neighborhood—said what he thought of Hugh Morrison's behavior. The end of the seventeen-hundreds came, and the mercurial clergyman brought civil suit against the hero of the contest. The case dragged on in the courts for more than a decade; but the dismissal of the pastor of Buffalo Cross-

Roads was more prompt. He was officially out of his pulpit when the new century came in; and within another two years the sinner who would not be chastised by him, was bringing laurels to himself in the Senate at Washington.[29]

But the forthrightness which marked Maclay's conduct occurred in other folk, too. If the Scot is capable of intensity, that flame of the spirit burns alike in a John Knox or a Robert Burns. The divine pours out his intellectual wrath in *The First Blast of the Trumpet against the Monstrous Regiment of Women;* Burns sheds the tears of his sensitive pity for the mouse whose field nest he has just shattered with his plough blade. "M. S.," who, in the *Oracle of Dauphin* belabors the excise with a Knoxian anger, contributes to that news sheet in the same season an essay on "Fish," blasting in it the wantonness of anglers along Susquehanna. "Fish," writes that gentle soul, "are a species of animals which ought to be exempt from our tyranny. They inhabit an element of their own; they encroach not on our rights; nor do they destroy our food."[30] How sad, then, that men who otherwise would neither practice nor justify deception should conspire against the harmless creatures of the water, torture and drag them from the bottom of their homes. How pathetic to see the "trout driven from one end of his habitation to the other in the most agonizing distress, till spent and breathless he yields to his destiny—and the savage arts of man."[31] At the least, one sentimental gentleman out of the strain of Scotland —and more akin to Saint Francis of Assisi than to Izaak Walton— could repine at details of the conquest being made by his fellows of the river which flowed by his father's old-time loghouse doors. The Rev. Mr. Elder must have known what he meant when in December, 1763, he said that the Paxton men who had acted so furiously at Conestoga and Lancaster were in their private lives "not cruel, but mild and merciful."[32]

So was it, indeed, with James Gibson, once the penman who set down that remonstrance of the back inhabitants to Deputy Governor John Penn and the General Assembly which was presented to the Chief Executive's emissaries in Philadelphia in February, 1764. That clerkly frontiersman served as a captain from Cumberland County during the Revolution,[33] married a wife, and begot sons who served their country in the War of 1812. Records of him and his movements are lost for a decade and a half. He may have been the James Gibson of Northumberland County who set his name close to Matthew Smith's in the Memorial for Katherine Smith in 1785. But certain it is that in November, 1799, he arrived at Youngstown, Ohio, far beyond the Alleghenies of Pennsylvania, his family and all their household goods carried over the mountains in wagons. In the group was a second son, born to the Ohio pioneer by his wife Anna Belle Dixon, and named for his mother's brother, Robert Dixon,[34] signer of the Hanover Resolves, and soldier-hero who died at Quebec in 1775.

And so was it, too, with Moses Barnett, youngest of the children of Joseph Barnett of Hanover, born after his oldest brother William was brought back home from among the Indians. That stripling turned into a wagoner, traveling now to Philadelphia, now to Pittsburgh, now down into Virginia, carrying one burden or another in his Conestoga wagon. The eighteenth turned into the nineteenth century, and Moses decided to settle down as a farmer. But the forks of Beaver Creek, confluent of the Swatara, no longer spelled romance for him. He also must have new scenes; and he knew how the Harrisburg and Presque Isle Company had cast its spell on Dauphin County friends and kinsmen. Walnut Creek, which emptied into Lake Erie, called to him. "Barnett's Conquest," his farm at the head of the diminutive Beaver, lost its appeal. He sold and moved to Fairview Township on the Great Lake. The eminence which came to the Kelsos, whose timber lot in the lake shore was a dozen years later furnishing the keels for Admiral Perry's fleet, did not become his. But there were bright memories in the man. His El Dorado was only a farmstead, and he did not forget his wagoning days.

Presently he was a grandsire, telling children stories out of the past, tales illuminated with the names of Valley of Virginia towns or filled with the wonders of the Natural Bridge where there were a fine lot of open and hearty people, many out of Pennsylvania itself.

Only once did he incline to worry about himself, he narrated to his grandson, Isaac Morehead:

It was when I took those nails down the Valley, and got the whole way on beyond Winchester and halfway to Staunton without selling enough to pay keep for myself and my horses. There I was in the tavern thinking how I'd make ends meet. In came a black man, and the landlord inquired: "Is the granary locked?"

"Yes suh.'

"Is the smoke-house locked?"

"Yes suh.'

"Is the spring-house locked?"

I turned to the tavern-keeper: "Do you think I have come to rob you?"

"Oh no, not that; the niggers are such thieves we have to lock everything up."

Then I told my host I was in straits for money; I would pledge him my lead-horse if he would make me an advance until I could get rid of more nails. Before he could answer, a voice interrupted: "How much do you need, young man?"

I looked up, saw a stranger I hadn't remarked before, and answered, "Twenty dollars."

"Come along to my house, young man, and I'll find it for you."

I went, he handed me the amount. I offered to leave some kegs of nails as security. He refused them and I offered my note. "No, sir," said the Virginian; "you are not a Yankee, and I'll trust you. If you mean to cheat me, you'll do it in any event."

So I took his money, got on Staunton-wards, found buyers for my load, and on my way back stopped at the man's house again. "You see I'm not going to cheat you," I said. He looked at me, said he knew I wouldn't. I paid him his loan back, thanked him, told him I was sorry I'd not be coming back to Virginia, and didn't know how I could ever have the opportunity to do him a favor.

"Well, sir," said the man, "don't let that trouble you; do it to somebody else."[35]

Little Isaac Morehead observed that Grandfather Barnett always wiped his eyes when he got to the end of that anecdote. When Isaac, who also was Scotch-Irish, was older, he knew why.

CHAPTER 25

SEAT OF GOVERNMENT

IN MARCH 1787, came the first indication that Pennsylvania would ever put into public use the "certain lot or piece of ground in the town of Harrisburg"[1] set aside for the purposes of the Legislature by John Harris nearly two years before. For a brief time it seemed that their five-shilling trust might be enlarged into reality for Jacob Awl, Joshua Elder, Andrew Stewart, James Cowden, and William Brown. William Findley, still active leader in the old unicameral Assembly of the Commonwealth, bided his time. Other fervid supporters of the Constitution of 1776 were as ready as he to get the seat of government out of Philadelphia—the nearer to the frontier counties the better. On March 3 they took their conservative Eastern and anti-Constitutionalist fellow-members by surprise.[2] Findley called for a vote in a resolution to remove to Harrisburg, and by a sectional division and a majority of four votes carried the day. The Western counties went solidly for a proposal against which Philadelphia City, Philadelphia County, Bucks, Chester, Lancaster, Montgomery, and Northampton Counties pitted their combined strength.[3]

But the victory was only tentative. More influential than western members was the Philadelphia press, and regretful and resentful were five conservative members who had been absent on the day of the vote. They were not for having the political centre of Pennsylvania moved off its commercial hub: two-thirds of the population lived east of the Susquehanna River; the City on the Delaware was the only logical location for the State's capitol. Their arguments inspired the Republicans and anti-Constitutionalists in the Assembly to remarshal their forces.[4] Although the four men appointed to draft the resolution, David McConaughy, Michael Schmyser, Thomas Kennedy, and Joseph Powell[5] were all from Western counties, they never brought their work out of committees; and the seat of government continued at Philadelphia. The five-shilling trust of the Paxtonians on the Susquehanna remained but a monetary figment.

[349

The Constitution of 1790 came into effect; and until 1795 the Quaker City could regard itself as the unchallengeable capital of Pennsylvania. Then in February the House of Representatives passed a resolution designating Carlisle as the seat of government.[6] But, almost before the late John Harris' friends could grieve for the loss of their hopes, the Senate defeated the brash bill by nonconcurrence.[7] The Cumberland County town was again suggested in 1796, as were Reading and Lancaster; but the Senate continued faithful to Philadelphia.[8]

Two more years sped on. In 1798 Westerners proposed Wright's Ferry, Lancaster County, on the east bank of the Susquehanna, or Wright's Town, just opposite on the west bank in York County—and failed of encouragement.[9] In the Senate the name of Harrisburg was inserted as a substitute in the measure, and the two houses fell into disagreement.[10]

Greater reason for losing heart came to the four surviving friends of John Harris in April 1799. On the third of that month Governor Thomas Mifflin signed a bill for the removal of the Seat of Government to Lancaster, in Lancaster County, prior to the first Tuesday of the next November.[11] Only hope that Harrisburgers could have of some day drawing the capitol into their midst was that the act of the two Houses of Legislature was phrased cautiously "until the permanent seat of the government shall be hereafter established."[12] Lancaster had not got a sure thing, even though $3,000 had been appropriated for the removing of the records of the several State offices to the new prospective site, and though all three gentlemen appointed to accomplish that duty, Matthias Barton, Jacob Strickler, and Thomas Boude, were Lancaster County men.[13] The trust-shillings might yet become lucky pennies.

Without State House either built or planned for, the Government of Pennsylvania was transferred to Lancaster and makeshift office quarters in the following summer and autumn months. The books of the Secretary of the Commonwealth, of the Register and Comptroller-General, of the Master of the Rolls, of the Land Office, of the State Treasurer, and of the Clerks of the two Houses were ushered into *ad temporem* housings; and on December 3 the General Assembly met in a capitol which remained its place of meeting for thirteen more years.

The western counties were restive during that interval. If Harrisburg was quiescent for a decade after 1799, Northumberland Town, at the point up Susquehanna, centre of old-time Scotch-Irish Revolutionary spirit, was not. What better location could be found for a civic metropolis than a triangle of fertile land in the forks of a great river? On January 4, 1809, then, sundry inhabitants presented through their fellow-townsmen Senator James Laird a petition pointing out to the Legislature the happiness of their central situation. They had room for public buildings, excellent accommodations for officers of the State and members of the Assembly.[14] The appeal went into committee; but, not to be caught napping, sponsors of it prepared a preamble and resolutions and presented them on the same day. Their argument was first that the departments of Government, particularly the Land Office, were in want of suitable buildings for the protection of their records; accidents and fire constantly threatened; the thing to do was to fix the "permanent seat" at Northumberland and erect suitable buildings there for offices and Legislature.[15] The position was doughtily taken, but the Senate was neither to be rushed into action nor to cast a prompt vote for Northumberland. At most the petition served but to make lively debate during the remainder of the session of 1808-1809. Thereafter out from one form or another of resolutions went the name of Northumberland; and into one form or another went the name of Philadelphia. Senator Jacob Sommer said he was as far as any man from being influenced by any local interest, but he wished the Government to be permanently fixed where it might conduce to the greatest advantage to the people. He believed Philadelphia to be that place; the seat of government should be at the metropolis of trade.[16] Senator John Dorsey observed that Philadelphia already had sufficient buildings to accommodate both the offices and the Legislature of the commonwealth. If the Government went there, no heavy expense would have to be incurred in construction of buildings. Yet he was not wholly for Philadelphia; in fact, he would be willing to vote for Pittsburgh if only he could get the Government out of Lancaster.[17] But in February, 1809, whatever might be Mr. Dorsey's individual opinions, there was no great mood for returning to the banks of the Delaware, when on the seventeenth the Senate met in Committee of the Whole. Only eight years could be had for putting Philadelphia into the blank space in the bill.[18]

James Laird sought to have the name of Northumberland restored, but his fellows in the Senate could not see that his home town was central enough. John Burrows pointed out that even Harrisburg, "twenty miles from the southern boundary of the State,"[19] was more central. Yet he had little wish to make it easy for the men of eastern Pennsylvania to roll in their coaches into Harrisburg to legislate while folk from beyond the mountains (Mr. Burrows represented constituents in present Lycoming, Centre, Tioga, Clearfield, McKean, and Potter Counties)[20] had to come with mere knapsacks on their backs.[21] Mr. Nathaniel Irish, western Pennsylvanian who represented a constituency in Allegheny, Beaver, and Butler Counties, and who had examined all the situations along the Susquehanna "from the mountains above Harrisburg down to Columbia," thought the best one was "near to Middletown."[22] A canal, he remarked, was contemplated which would connect water carriage for produce between there and Philadelphia. A site more effectual than Harrisburg to intercept trade and keep it from going down the river to Baltimore would, in his view, be more relevant. He urged that a committee be appointed to examine the Susquehanna again for locations, and to bring its report to the next Legislature.[23]

After he had spoken, the original question was put and lost. Only seven Senators gave yeas now for Northumberland.[24] The Committee of the Whole let Speaker Presly C. Lane of Westmoreland supply the phrase "borough of Harrisburg, in the County of Dauphin"[25] for the moot blank space; and by a vote of 14 to 10 the resolution was adopted for report to the Senate[26] when duly reconvened.

But that step failed to bring the matter to formal action. For Isaac Weaver, member for electors in Greene and Washington Counties, now proposed postponement and a substitute measure; and his proposal, which called for a purchase of 150 acres above Harrisburg by the State, was allowed precedence. Views had to be heard as to whether or not buying the recommended land of Abraham Huey would be giving the commonwealth's sanction to an unfortunate speculation. Mr. Sommer drew 13 yeas against 9 nays for striking out the possibility of consummating such a bargain. In rapid suit the section of the resolution appropriating funds for the erection of public buildings was voted against.[27] After that—and the removal of the words "first of November"[28]—the Senate decided to postpone all further discussion in the body to the next session, while the Pennsylvania House of Representatives refused to consider any such bill in their current assembly.[29]

Not until the following winter was any removal of the capital to be determined on. By that time, however, sentiment was definitely crystallizing. On January 13, 1810, *The Times,* Lancaster paper published by Hugh Hamilton, ruefully announced that on the eleventh a bill for removal to Harrisburg had been read for the first time in the Senate. This, reported the weekly, authorized the Governor to purchase 10 acres of land from William Maclay (son and heir of a more famous father) and appropriated $1,000 for that purpose, besides $2,000 to defray the expenses of removing the public offices. Fourteen days later *The Times* reported the passing of this bill in the Senate on a vote of 20 to 9, and observed that it would be the order of the day on February 5 for the House to hear it. On February 10 the same newspaper was able to write of amendments offered in the lower body requiring the erection of six fire proof offices and appropriating $30,000 to pay for them.[30] Moreover, as clear sign of the contemporary trend, it revealed that a motion to strike out Harrisburg and insert Lancaster had lost by a vote of 55 to 36, while the section including the name of the borough on the Susquehanna was by 60 yeas to 29 nays.[31] Full attendance in the House indicated more than interest.

On February 17, Mr. John Wyeth of Harrisburg had the pleasure of publishing in the *Oracle of Dauphin* an editorial of happy augury:

The Seat of Government

We cordially congratulate our fellow citizens of Harrisburg on the pleasing prospect of its shortly becoming the permanent seat of government for the great and respectable State of Pennsylvania. In gaining this long contested decision of our Legislature, this place has received a great deal of illiberal and unfounded obloquy both in and out of doors, but with what success a respectable majority of our friends have at last declared;—and while the ebullitions of jealousy and sordid disappointments are now working their own cure, the citizens of this borough and its neighborhood will, with their accustomed liberality, unite in rendering Harrisburgh not only a spot pleasant, healthy and enriched with every other accommodation befitting the seat of government, but also a seat of *hospitality* and *kindness*.

His confident Saturday issue preceded by three days the next issue from the press of his rival *The Dauphin Guardian*. On Tuesday the twentieth the editor of that journal, Jacob Elder, from "next door to the sign of the Seven Stars" on Second Street, expressed himself less effervescently. He could announce that the bill for removal had finally passed both houses. Beyond that he was annoyed that "a Lancaster paper" was ascribing the removal "to executive influence and patronage." He did not regard it in any case derogatory to Governor Snyder to look upon the measure with favor. Indeed, the nephew of Joshua Elder realized that the seat of government had long been in agitation. (Harrisburg had been waiting for it twenty-five years.) "It was full time to bring it to a decision." The only disappointment the publisher of the *Guardian* could have felt deeply was that when Simon Snyder signed his approval on February 21, the removal was set for October, 1812, a season yet two years and eight months away.

But one week later Mr. Elder declared himself more spiritedly. On February 27 he scored "the *malice* displayed in the *Lancaster Journal*" in consequence of the transfer of the capitol. The "torrent of abuse" to which "poor Harrisburg" had been exposed was "all perfectly natural." But "Let them laugh that win," he exulted; and of William Hamilton, editor of the *Journal* he demanded tersely: "Is it not so, Billy?" Moreover, newly serene in his own journalistic triumph he could insist that all statements made by Lancasterians derogatory to Harrisburg were going to operate tenfold in the latter town's favor. Aspersion "would work its own cure" for injury to the borough.[32]

If other citizens of the old Paxton community like Squire Joshua Elder or Judge James Cowden felt as cheered in the late winter of 1809-1810 as the thirty-year old editor, there was really good reason for their satisfaction. For markedly the bringing of the capitol to Harrisburg was both frontier and Scotch-Irish legislative victory.

The vote of the Senate on January 26 and that of the House on February 12, 1810, both told a transparent story.

The twenty affirmative votes cast in the upper body came from 3 men of German names, 14 of unmistakably Scotch-Irish names, and 3 of English or indeterminate origin. Thirteen Senators giving yeas to removal to Harrisburg were John Burrows, James Brady, John Connelly, Ezra Doty, William Erwin, Abner Lacock, James Lowrey, Francis McClure, Archibald Rankin, Jonathan Roberts, James Stevenson, James Wilson, and Presly Carr Lane, the Speaker. In the same fellowship of one-time Ulster names was Wilson Smith, son of that Colonel Matthew Smith who as a young man of thirty had marched with the Paxton Boys to Philadelphia in 1764 and with his companion James Gibson presented John Penn and the Provincial Assembly their own bill of rights for the Pennsylvania frontier. All, indeed, that broke the solid front of "Scotch-Irishry" on January 26, 1810, was the fact that their two fellows, James Laird and Nathan Palmer, representing Northumberland and Luzerne Counties, who desired to have the capitol up Susquehanna, could not see eye-to-eye with them. Those two disappointed champions of Northumberland cast their ballots with seven other bitter-enders from Philadelphia, Delaware, Chester, Berks, and Lancaster Counties. Every man from west of the Susquehanna River stood for transfer of the Seat of Government to Harrisburg.

Similar were the later tallies in the Lower House in February. There the decision was won by 57 to 28; and there again the Northumberland following, including Frederick Evans, Thomas Graham, John Murray, and Abraham McKinney, dissented from their Scotch-Irish fellows to take position with a solid opposition from the eastern counties. But carrying the day against them, and against York Countians who would have liked the capitol at Wright's Town, were not fewer than thirty-six men of old Scots lineage. Moreover, apart from the four men of York, not more than six men from west of the Susquehanna shared in that defeat of east by west which made Harrisburg the seat of legislation and law for the Commonwealth.[33]

But the Act signed on February 21, 1810, by Governor Simon Snyder, by no means established the new capital immediately. The first section of it designated October 1812, as the time for the removal of offices from Lancaster to Harrisburg. Another section appointed 3 commissioners, Robert Harris (son of John Harris, founder of the borough), George Hoyer, and George Geigler[34] (the latter 2 not men of exactly Scottish surnames) to superintend that duty of transfer. A third authorized the Governor to accept an offer from the younger William Maclay of 10 acres of land, at $100 an acre, adjoining the tract set aside by John Harris in 1785 for the Legislature's use. Other sections provided appropriations, arranged for details of purchase, called for three commissioners to invite plans from architects for the prospective public buildings, and designated the State officials who should have authority with these 3 in adopting an acceptable plan.

Initial action was punctual. Stephen Hills, Esq., won a premium of $400 for his plan and the assignment of architect for the Capitol.[35] As early as March advertisements calling for contractors and announcing that all bids must be in by May 15, 1810, were published in newspapers of cities and boroughs from Philadelphia to Pittsburgh. Jacob Elder of *The Dauphin Guardian* rather than John Wyeth of the *Oracle*, despite that Federalist's editorial congratulations to Harrisburg in February, drew into his columns the substantial notice of Commissioners John Dorsey, Edward Crouch, and Jacob Bucher[36] about intended letting.

But early punctuality did not eventuate into early construction. Nor had that begun when in the spring of 1812 the records of the several State departments were removed to Harrisburg, or when in December of that same year the two Houses began sessions in the Dauphin County Court House.

By those dates, indeed, Pennsylvanians were thinking more of the preservation of American liberties and of "the Second War of Independence" than they were of sites of buildings for documents, offices, and assemblies of law-makers. On June 18 Congress had declared war on Great Britain. "Free Trade and Sailors' Rights" was the slogan of the hour. Especially in the western counties did the ardor for freedom burn. In Dauphin County 13 companies of militiamen mustered. Youth was on fire, gunsmiths throve, gentlemanly raiment were left in the wardrobe, honor reigned in stripling's breasts. The sons and grandsons of the heroes of the Revolution took arms. The progeny of Timothy Green, Joseph Barnett, and Josiah Espy, authors of the Hanover Resolves in 1774; of James Cowden, who acted with Colonel James Burd in the Middletown Resolves of the same year; of the heroes of the Londonderry Liberty Company of 1775; of Matthew Smith's riflemen not many months later in the bitter woods of Maine or the snows of Quebec—these and the heirs of thousands of other once Scotch-Irish folk were ready for the front.

Yet few of them—such were the vicissitudes of inept history—won actual chance to emulate their sires and grandsires. Between the time in 1812, when the offices of Pennsylvania Government were first moving into Harrisburg, and January, 1822, when first the Pennsylvania Legislature could convene in the new Capitol built for it,[37] no unique glory was won for the commonwealth by any act of battle, and no new lustre for military achievement was added to the glories of Pennsylvania Scotch-Irishmen.

Testimony there is, however, that the old alacrity of spirit in that breed had not faded out in 1812-1813. Their luckless cousins and their neighbors' sons may have got no farther than from Pennsylvania to Baltimore, and may have come back from no action there led by their disappointed officers; but two younger generation Hanover riflemen had looked more particularly to their laurels. The tale of them could stand for time and attest their own and their fellow's quality.

The pair enlisted in the Union Company of Volunteers of Captain John McClintock down the Cumberland Valley at Chambersburg, and from that Franklin County Town marched over the Blue Ridge and the Allegheny Mountains: to Fort Loudon, to McConnellsburg, to Bedford, to Stoystown, to Greensburgh, to Pittsburgh, then up state to Erie.

At this point they feasted, drank, sang songs, and slept well. They pitched their tents in meadows which subsequently proved more "elegant" for wetness than for either posture or encampment. In one town they were entertained in private homes and by leading citizens, and basked in the smiles of daughters and sisters. At another they were treated with as "much stimulating drink as they could punish," and were less cordially received by well-bred maidens.

But at Erie, where companies converged from many points, they found Forsters, Wallaces, and Wilsons migrated from their own home county down Susquehanna, and they were welcomed by relatives and friends. Older ladies told them of beaux they had once had in Hanover or Derry Township. Younger ladies were more gracious to them for having come into a town where they could be introduced into families who had known their families. Autumn was happy and gay.

Yet progress in December 1812, northward for Buffalo was a severe experience, despite the warm mittens which Erie girls had knit for their hands and had showered upon them as they marched away from their Presque Isle camp. One of the two young Hanover men became very ill. Dr. Culbertson of Chambersburg, their Acting Brigade Surgeon, selected a small detail of men, including his friend from home and himself, to find shelter for the invalid. At seven miles from Buffalo on the Williamsville road they found the first hostelry.

Nightfall was at hand, the sick man was limp and exhausted; but suddenly the party were facing a surly, unsympathetic landlord. He stood beneath a tavern sign which flaunted his name and proprietorship; and emphatically he repeated his story of quarters already filled up. The second and physically fit soldier from Hanover found himself looking quizzically from a face which seemed familiar to the painted letters over the inn door. Then inspiration came.

He brushed forward of Surgeon Culbertson and confronted the tavern keeper.

"Oh, yes, Mr. Landis," he began crisply; "you are going to take every one of us in." And peremptorily he added: "I know you, and you'll have a bed for my friend without any more palaver."

"Who are you, youngster?" bellowed the astonished host in quick anger.

"I'll tell you, when I have told these men who you are," responded the determined militiaman. "Men, this is Landis; during the Revolution he was a Tory living north of Hummelstown back home. Township patriots there didn't love him. One day several of his Whig neighbors, tired of his nonsense, had a rope around his neck and were looking for a handy tree.

"Lucky for him, Colonel Timothy Green and Major Joseph Barnett happened along. They were a bit softer-hearted than other Hanover folk. They took the rope from his throat and quieted his escort. Then they advised Landis to find somewhere else to live. He followed their counsel and got out of that neck of the woods.

"Tonight I have discovered where he took up his new residence." The soldier drew a breath, and then closed neatly: "And I believe he has room for all of us in it."

"Who are you?" demanded Landis, changing mien and tone.

"I?" said the stripling. "I am Joseph Barnett, son of your old rescuer, the Major; and our patient here is Timothy Green Allen, grandson of Colonel Green. Find a room for him."

There was no more of either hesitation or argument. The hospitality of Landis and his family was heaped upon Dr. Culbertson's squad. Both the Hanover boys had beds on that December night; and one of them lived long afterward to tell of how a grandson of an earlier Joseph Barnett had outfaced a hard-visaged ex-Tory and New York taverner.[38]

The spirit of quest and of truculent wit had not died out of Scotch-Irishry during the War of 1812. That equivocal struggle brought paradoxical elements of fame to the Keystone commonwealth. Across the Susquehanna and down its forest paths the pioneer forbears of the outstanding general of the era and victor at New Orleans, Andrew Jackson, had once pursued their way into Virginia. Off the shores of its northwest boundaries Captain Oliver Perry won the Battle of Lake Erie fighting from ships which had been built from timber cut at Erie, much of it from the woodlots of John Kelso, scion of ferryman stock on the Susquehanna for a half-century earlier. Jackson's exploit and the flagship of Perry at Erie were to become part and parcel of Pennsylvania lore.

But chilling delay and frequent postponement, rather than romance and derring-do, accompanied the plans for the State's Capitol. Years passed: Legislatures met in the chambers of the Court House at Harrisburg; books and records of office had protection there or in divers accommodations about the borough. Simon Snyder passed out of office in 1817 with the seat of government still unerected.

Not until May 31, 1819,[39] did citizenry witness the corner-stone laying for Architect Stephen Hills's proud design. On that date Governor William Findlay, a chief executive appropriately Scotch-Irish, Mr. Hills, William Smith stone-cutter, assisted by Freemasons Valentine Kergan and Samuel White, led in a simple ceremony. A large concourse of Pennsylvanians looked on. Three discharges from a public cannon heralded the event. A Harrisburg band played festive music.[40] Generous Pennsylvania German Melchior Rahm, who had voted in 1810 to bring the seat of government to the borough,[41] provided a collation on the public grounds for commissioners, architect, stone-cutters, masons, carpenters, and civic guests.[42] The affair was gala. And the informed knew that into the interior of the stone had gone copies of Charles II's *Charter* to William Penn; *The Declaration of Independence; The Constitution of Pennsylvania* of 1776; *The Articles of the*

Confederation between the Several States; much of the *Act* of the General Assembly for indemnifying the heirs of William Penn when they lost their proprietary rights; *The Constitution of the United States* of 1787; *The Constitution of Pennsylvania* of 1790. As if to top the climax, Harrisburgers knew there was added to those documents a copy of the Act of Assembly which removed the government centre from Lancaster to their own town on the Susquehanna. And, last of all, folk were pleased that into the box within the stones went the names of the commissions, of the builders and workman, and of all Pennsylvania officialdom, besides those of President James Monroe and Vice-President of the United States Elbridge Gerry.[43]

At length, indeed, the enterprise of structure was afoot. Thirty-four years had elapsed since John Harris had put his trust-shilling in the hands of his five Scotch-Irish friends, twenty-eight since the founder's death, thirty-two since good William Brown's, twenty-six since Jacob Awl's, nine since James Cowden's. Only Joshua Elder survived among citizens of the borough to represent at the corner-stone laying the first commissioners for furthering Harris' wish. Andrew Stewart had left Paxton and Harrisburg twenty-seven years before. The dream of Susquehanna Riverside back inhabitants had been slow in fulfillment. Moreover, two-and-a-half additional years would pass before Architect Hills's achievement was ready for occupancy by the Pennsylvania Legislature.

Finally, on January 2, 1822, occurred the great ceremony of entrance and dedication. A great procession moved forward with dignity. First marched the architect and his workmen, two and two. Then came the Clergy; the Governor and the Heads of Departments; Officers and the Senate and their Speaker; Officers, Speaker, and Members of the House of Representatives, likewise two and two; the Judges of the State; the Civil Authorities of Harrisburg; and, ending the parade, a long queue of citizens. In front of the Capitol, Architect Hills and his masons and carpenters opened into two lines; and between them the dignitaries and townsfolk passed up the steps into the stately edifice,[44] nobler example of early American Republican architecture than any perhaps realized.

The seat of Government had an austere and beautiful home. Within it the Rev. Dr. Lochman offered invocation, his prayer solemnly reminding the members of the two Houses "that the welfare of thousands" would "depend on their deliberations," and that they were "accountable beings" who would "once have to give an account of their stewardship to the just and impartial sovereign of the universe."[45]

Discourse followed from the Reverend Mason, Principal of Dickinson College, whose last words both recounted history and pronounced injunction. Change had come. "Not sixty years," he reminded his audience, had elapsed "since the sound of the first axe was heard in the woods of Harrisburg."[46] Not long ago wild beasts and wilder men had occupied the banks of the Susquehanna. But the mildness of the descendants of William Penn and the industry of Pennsylvanians had wrought a difference. The wild men hunted deer and entrapped fish in regions far remote from the newly civilized community. Here in their stead was a seat for the legislation of a powerful State.[47]

To the General Assembly the Reverend Dr. Mason delivered exhortation: "Go on and prosper, carry the spirit of your improvements through till the sound of the hammer, the ship of the wagoner, the busy hum of man, the voices of innumerable children issuing from places of instruction, the lofty spires of worship, till richly endowed colleges of education, till all those arts which embellish man shall gladden the banks of the Susquehanna and the Delaware, and exact from admiring strangers that cheerful and grateful tribute, 'this is the work of a Pennsylvania Legislature.' "[48]

It was, indeed, a day of promise for the commonwealth. But January 2, 1822, when Pennsylvania embraced the joy of having a majestic Seat of Government, was no longer the day of the Scotch-Irish. With the heirs of that hardy brood of pioneers working shoulder to shoulder, hearts in no sense "clay cold" but warm and eager as any to be liberty-loving Americans, were the Pennsylvania Germans. A Governor of their stock, Joseph Heister, was the chief figure in the procession. Three more men of the race from which he sprang would be his successors in the gubernatorial office in the next seventeen years.

What has long been recognized in national history as "the Era of Good Feeling" was at hand. The Scotch-Irish and the Pennsylvania Dutch had become Americans beyond peradventure of a doubt. The kindred of St. Columba and of Sir William Wallace who had first conquered the great Susquehanna watershed for the uses of the white man could rest in peace and victorious trust.

EPILOGUE TO SCIONS

WERE THE English poet Thomas Gray to come back to earth and seek in America a burial place more quiet than the Stoke Pogis of his "Elegy," he could hardly find a spot more appropriate to reward his romantic quest than Hanover Presbyterian Churchyard in Dauphin County, Pennsylvania—fifteen miles from Harrisburg, a mile and a half off United States Route 22 which follows an eastward course for Allentown, Easton, and New York. A county road branches to the north from the four-lane highway; winds in and out, up and down, over projections of yellow shale, rain-washed accumulations of rough shards and ruts. Five minutes of jolting, then it dips deep into a bowl in the foothills of Blue Mountain and surprises you there with evidences of former dense habitation. How ever did that resting place of the dead get into so isolated a corner, you wonder?

You have risked tires and brakes to find it; you catch your breath on sight of it. And, as you alight from your car, you become aware that the location is beautiful.

A stone farmhouse and a springhouse, just beyond and at quite the bottom of the bowl, hint of a watering place for animals and men. During a hundred and forty years worshipers at Old Hanover refreshed themselves and their horses at the head of Bow Run. The stone church, for nine decades at the side of the graveyard, has been gone now for three quarters of a century. But you see the same brightness of sky, smooth rondure of cultivated slopes, grace of forest-tipped fields in the dale which greeted the eyes of the faithful as they came to and from the sanctuary.

Whatever the passion and storm of reproaches for sin in the sermon indoors, outside all was calmly idyllic. Help came from the hills, however unregenerate the thoughts of Presbyterian saints may have been on contemplation of fine grazing lands for brown cattle or Merino sheep as the devout issued from service. Worldling or pious com-

[361

municant yourself, you realize you are seeing all that remains of an ancient centre of Protestant Scotch-Irish Christianity.

To your right, where once the meetinghouse stood, is a plantation of shaggy pines. Before you is a stretch of stone wall capped with concrete. In that barrier is a steel gate, painted with a metallic composition which has been peeling—you would guess—for a decade at the least.

The two wings of the gate are closed. A long corroded copper padlock fastens them against your entrance to the hundreds of weed-surrounded tombs inside. You must climb the barrier if you wish to learn more or you have opportunity—if you regard it dignified—to enter by a great breach in the west wall, a hundred feet to your left.

Enter that way and you stumble, almost in an instant, upon the bricked-high ledger stone of the Rev. James Snodgrass. Over it you bend; and first scrutiny apprises you of dates of birth and death. Then, at the bottom of the epitaph, you read:

"Your fathers, where are they? and the prophets do they live forever?"

You turn to look farther; and you recognize other graves. The stone of John and Isabel Craig tells of their being killed by Indians in 1756. That of Squire Adam Reed reminds of the frontier marriage of his daughter to the founder of Harrisburg long before the second ferryman above the mouth of Paxton Creek dreamed of his post-Revolutionary borough. That of Brice Innis, Jun'r, sets you to reflecting on a youthful army surgeon who survived Washington's campaigns of 1776 and 1777 only to die of a consumption a year later at his home in Hanover Township.

The stone of James Dixon brings into mind his son Robert, signer of the Hanover Resolves in 1774, who in 1775 died at Quebec with his faithful friend Michael Simpson ministering to him in the last hours of agony. The marker of John Todd recalls a hero who marched with Matthew Smith and Benedict Arnold through the wildernesses of Maine and Canada on that same fruitless enterprise which took young Dixon to his death. Stewart stones set you to reflecting on a scapegrace kinsman who defied a Province, founded a second Hanover, and fell a victim of the Indians in the Battle of Wyoming up Susquehanna.

Other stones remind you of the long flight down the river from the Big Island on the West Branch after the Massacre which followed the battle. McCormick stones remind you of two modern plutocratic families in Harrisburg and Chicago, whose sires two centuries ago dwelt nearby on new-broken farms among the wooden hills of early Lancaster County. Barnett stones induce memories of a pioneer's seven-year quest of a son carried off by the Indians. Closing the epitaph of the father of a famous Dauphin County judge are the words:

"Precious in the sight of the Lord is the death of his saints."

The table of things bravely done, nobly hoped for, serenely trusted in, accompanies you as you move through weeds and high grasses, between cracked and crumbling memorials. But Mr. Snodgrass' text from Zechariah persists in your mind: *"Your fathers, where are they?"*

Where indeed?

If it be in the memories of their progeny on court bench, in lawyer's, legislator's, engineer's, professor's, minister's, banker's, or business-man's office, then why the neglect here? Why the thick growth of weeds? the breached wall? the locked gate in an empty countryside, too far away on back roads to attract vandals or tempt motor trucks to illegitimate dumping of refuse? Has something which was more important to their forbears than success in political, industrial, and commercial life died out of the hearts of descendants of the men and women of Hanover?

Back in the Capital City to the southwest countless tombs in marble and granite in the Harrisburg Cemetery commemorate later folk of Scotch-Irish descent, not a few bearing names which are in Hanover Churchyard. Proud and stately aisles there declare by means of sepulture the greatness of families. Eminent aristocratic names out of Scotland abound in inscriptions on pillar, shaft, and architraved block. Ivies, evergreens, pink dogwoods, an occasional oak or tulip poplar, lend a verdant, half-vauntful, half-pensive beauty. Affluence combines with the monumental; tombs on the western bluff gaze in the winter over the slums, the railroads, and the smoke of the Capital City. The pomp of heraldry, if not its grace and *noblesse oblige*, is in the great cemetery. Wealth vies with wealth. Origin and the past are forgotten.

"Your fathers, where are they?" Do they live in their sons?

But where, apart from graveyards, in the middle of the Twentieth Century are the sons of the Scotch-Irish? A latter-day name is little index to breed. Camerons whose sires married Pfoutzes, McCormicks whose forbears married Buehlers and Nagels, Flemings whose fathers married Saussers, are no more authentically of Scots breed than Lutzes who descend from Barnetts, Zimmermans who trace proudly the blood of Galbraiths in their veins, Kunkels who trace that of Espys and

Crains, Grosses who claim that of Elders, Fortenbaughs who claim that of Cowdens.

In Pennsylvania the "clay cold" heart of the eighteenth-century German immigrant has turned into fire through marital alliance with a daughter or son of the Scotch-Irish. The burning impatience of the Scotch-Irish back inhabitant of 1776 has been tempered by the plodding and enduring quiet of the Palatine German whose progenitors settled in Berks and Lebanon Counties and, in the course of time, through their children took for their possession most of Central Pennsylvania.

As in the Christ there is no difference between bond and free, so in the contemporary Keystone State there is no difference between names Celtic and names Teutonic. All are American. Weiser, Muhlenberg, Snyder, Pennypacker, and Brumbaugh are equated now and remembered with Armstrong, Whitehill, Potter, Maclay, and Forster.

Hanover Churchyard, overlooked in the new era, neglected by descendants of mixed blood whose ancestors lie in their ashes there, is made newly beautiful by every change of season. Men have forgotten it. Only nature is faithful to keep it fair, despite ruts in a dirt road, broken walls, weeds, and epitaphs disintegrating. *"The prophets do not live forever,"* is the only safe answer to the questions posed on the tombstone of Mr. James Snodgrass.

Unless one add a few words from *The Book of Zechariah*:

> *"Be silent, O all flesh, before the Lord; for He is raised up out of His holy habitation."* (Zech. 2, 13)

For, if the virtues of the Scotch-Irish have vanished from their twentieth-century offspring, there can be little hope of recovering them except through the power of God's righteousness and the native simplicity of honest human hearts.

Scions who do not emulate the truth and courage of Saint Columba, of Sir William Wallace, of the frontier defenders of Provincial Pennsylvania, of the back county Presbyterian patriots of the War for American Independence, do well to keep silent. Let him who would speak for the Scotch-Irish on the Susquehanna today attend well, lest he prove only a false prophet wearing *"a rough garment to deceive."* (Zech. 13, 4)

Precious in the sight of the Lord is the death of his saints.

NOTES

See abbreviations of Sources under Bibliography, pp. 385-387

1. PROVINCE LAW, 1728 (pp. 9-18)

1. PA, 4th, I, 423
2. Ibid., 420-421
3. Ibid., 425
4. PA, 1st, I, 213
5. Ibid.
6. Ibid., 210-211 (Instructions to J. LeTort and John Scull)
7. Ibid., 211
8. Ibid., 214-215
9. Ibid., 215
10. Ibid.
11. Ibid., 209-210
12. Ibid.
13. Ibid., 213-214 (Colebrook Township is today in southeastern Berks County. Falkner's Swamp was apparently West Swamp Creek, flowing from that county into Montgomery and emptying into the Perkiomen. The writer has not been able to identify Coshahopin.)
14. Ibid., 217-218
15. Ibid.
16. Ibid., 215-216
17. PP, III, 41
18. Ibid.
19. Ibid.
20. Ibid.
21. Ibid.
22. Ibid.
23. Ibid.
24. Ibid.
25. Ibid.
26. PA, 1st, I, 219
27. Ibid., 221
28. Ibid.
29. PA, 4th, I, 437-440
30. Ibid., 440-442
31. PA, 1st, I, 222
32. Ibid.
33. Ibid.
34. PA, 4th, I, 442-447
35. Ibid., 445
36. Ibid., 446
37. Ibid., 446-447
38. Ibid., 447
39. Ibid.
40. PA, 1st, I, 224
41. Ibid.
42. PA, 4th, I, 447-450
43. Ibid., 449
44. Hist. Ches., 407
45. Ibid.
46. Ibid.
47. Ibid.
48. Ibid.
49. Ibid.

2. IMMIGRANTS (pp. 19-34)

1. Con. Weis., 40
2. Ibid.
3. D.Sc.-I, 144
4. Ibid., 34 and fn. 16
5. D.Sc-I, 34 and fn. 17
6. H.Sc.-I, I, 62-63
7. D.Sc.-I, 36
8. Ibid.
9. Ibid., 36-37
10. Ibid., 37
11. Pa. Gaz., Nov. 20, 1729
12. D.Sc.-I, 35
13. Ibid.
14. Ibid.
15. PA, 8th, III, 1807
16. PA, 4th, I, 453-454

17. Ibid., 454
18. Ibid.
19. Ibid.
20. Ibid.
21. Ibid.
22. Ibid.
23. Ibid., 455
24. PA, 8th, III, 1939-1940
25. Ibid.
26. Ibid.
27. Ibid.
28. PP, III, 67
29. Ibid.
30. Ibid.
31. Cuth. Diary

3. SUSQUEHANNA
(pp. 35-51)

1. Resumé of John Smith's Narrative, WT, I, 26
2. Ibid.
3. Ibid.
4. Ibid.
5. Ibid.
6. Ibid., illustration opposite p. 26
7. Version of story of Susquehannocks and Col. John Washington based upon WT, I, 49-51
8. WT, I, 40
9. Locations based upon Appendix Map, WT, I
10. WT, I, 200
11. Version of Walking Purchase based on Con. Weis., 96-99
12. Penna. Land Office Records
13. Ibid.
14. PP, VIII, 59
15. To identify John Elder's hand one has only to examine Elder. Pap.
16. This, with quotations preceding and following, follows the MS. in PP, VIII, 59
17. PP, VII, 61
18. Ibid.
19. Con. Weis., 179-183
20. Ibid., 180
21. Ibid., 180-183
22. PP, VIII, 62
23. Ibid., 63
24. Ibid.
25. Ibid.
26. Ibid.
27. Mem. Dav. Br., 235

28. Ibid.
29. Ibid.
30. Ibid., 235-236
31. Ibid., 236
32. Ibid.
33. Ibid., 239

4. TRADERS, RIVERMEN, SETTLERS
(pp. 53-66)

1. Penna. Magazine of History and Biography, XVI, 366; "Baptismal Records of Christ Church: "1728. Sept. 22 Harris s John and Esther 11 months"
2. PA, 2d, VIII, 783
3. John Harris' Receipt-Books
4. WT, I, 174
5. PA, 1st, II, 131-132; and PP, XII, 62
6. WT, II, 216
7. PA, 1st, II, 131
8. Ibid.
9. Ibid.
10. PP, XII, 62
11. Ibid.
12. Ibid.
13. Ibid.
14. PA, 1st, II, 131-132
15. PP, XII, 62
16. Ibid.
17. WT, I, 165-188
18. Ibid., 175
19. Ibid.
20. Ibid., 174
21. Ibid.
22. Ibid., 177
23. Ibid., 178
24. Ibid., 177
25. Ibid.
26. Ibid.
27. Ibid., 178
28. Ibid.
29. WT, II, 255, n. 1
30. WT, I, 178
31. Ibid., 250
32. Ibid., 252; and II, 373
33. Ibid., II, 373
34. Ibid.
35. Ibid.
36. Ibid., 374
37. Ibid.
38. Ibid., I, 210-211

39. CR, IV, 630-633
40. Ibid., 631
41. Ibid., 633
42. Ibid.
43. Ibid.
44. Ibid.
45. WT, I, 248
46. Penna. Land Office Records
47. CR, V, 440-441
48. Rich. P., 105 ff
49. Ibid., 107
50. CR, V, 441
51. Ibid.
52. Ibid., 441-442
53. Ibid., 442
54. Ibid.
55. Ibid.
56. Ibid., 443
57. Biog. Dau., 55
58. CR, V, 444

5. BACK INHABITANTS (pp. 67-80)

1. Pa. Gaz., July 25, 1754
2. Ibid.
3. Ibid.
4. WT, I, 223
5. Ibid., 231-232
6. Ibid., 224-226
7. Ibid., 226
8. CR, V, 440-441
9. WT, I, 226
10. An. Har., 36 (Andrew Montour to Richard Peters, Dec. 30, 1754)
11. Ibid., 31 (John Harris to Gov. James Hamilton, Oct. 2, 1754)
12. Ibid., 32
13. Ibid.
14. Ibid.
15. Ibid., 31
16. Ibid., 33
17. WT, I, 227-228
18. Ibid., 228
19. An. Har., 35
20. Ibid., 36
21. Ibid.
22. Ibid., 35
23. WT, II, 214 and n. 3
24. An. Har., 37-38
25. Ibid., 39-41
26. Ibid., 42

27. Ibid., 41-42
28. Ibid., 42
29. Ibid.
30. Ibid., 40
31. WT, I, 234
32. An. Har., 40
33. Ibid.
34. Ibid.
35. Con. Weis., 397
36. An. Har., 42
37. Ibid., 40
38. Ibid., 42
39. Ibid.
40. WT, I, 236, n. 1
41. Ibid., 236
42. Ibid.
43. Ibid.
44. An. Har., 45
45. CR, VI, 681 and 685-687
46. Rich. P., 210-211
47. Ibid.
48. FF, I
49. Ibid., 354-363
50. Ibid., 10-11
51. Biog. Dau., 55-56
52. FF, I, 28-29, 37
53. Ibid., 29-30 and 37-40
54. Ibid., 30
55. An. Har., 49-50
56. FF, I, 41-47
57. Ibid., 605-611
58. Ibid., 608

6. BY FAVOR OF PROVIDENCE (pp. 81-95)

1. Biog. Frank., 1
2. PP, VIII, 59
3. FF, I, 9
4. Biog. Frank., 1
5. CR, VI, 118-123
6. Ibid., 120
7. Ibid., 119
8. Ibid.
9. Ibid., 257
10. Ibid., 256-257
11. Ibid., 259-261
12. Ibid., 259
13. Ibid.
14. Ibid.
15. Ibid.
16. Ibid.

17. Ibid., 259-260
18. Ibid., 260
19. Ibid.
20. Ibid.
21. Ibid.
22. Ibid.
23. Ibid., 260-261
24. Ibid., 323-324
25. Ibid., 368-369
26. Ibid.
27. PA, 1st, II, 773-775
28. Ibid.
29. Ibid., 767
30. Ibid.
31. Ibid.
32. Ibid.
33. Ibid.
34. Ibid.
35. Ibid.
36. Ibid.
37. Ibid., 768
38. Ibid.
39. Ibid.
40. Ibid.
41. Ibid.
42. Ibid.
43. Ibid.
44. Ibid., 769
45. Ibid.
46. Ibid.
47. Ibid., 770
48. Ibid.
49. Ibid., 769
50. Ibid., 770
51. Ibid.
52. Ibid.
53. Ibid.
54. Ibid.
55. Ibid., 771
56. Ibid.
57. Ibid.
58. Ibid.
59. Ibid., 772
60. Ibid.
61. PA, 4th, II, 590-593
62. PA, 1st, II, 772
63. Ibid.
64. FF, I, 527-533
65. Ibid., 530
66. Ibid.
67. Ibid., 530-531
68. Ibid., 531

7. YOUTHFUL EBULLITION (pp. 97-109)

1. PP, XXIV, 62
2. Ibid.
3. PA, 1st, IV, 114-117
4. Ibid.
5. Ibid., 115-116
6. Ibid.
7. Ibid., 112-113
8. Ibid., 113
9. John Elder to the Gov'r, Aug. 24, 1763; Eld. Pap.
10. Elder to the Gov'r, July 6 and 29, 1763, Eld. Pap.
11. Elder to the Gov'r, Aug. 24, 1763, Eld. Pap.
12. Elder to the Gov'r, July 29, 1763, Eld. Pap.
13. Elder to the Gov'r, Sept. 30, 1763, Eld. Pap.
14. Ibid.
15. Ibid.
16. Timothy Green to Elder, Oct. 5, 1763, Eld. Pap.
17. Ibid.
18. Ibid.
19. PA, 8th, VI, 5477
20. Ibid.
21. Ibid., 5481-5482
22. Ibid.
23. Ibid., 5478
24. Ibid., 5486
25. Ibid., 5484
26. Elder to the Gov'r, Oct. 25, 1763, Eld. Pap.
27. Ibid.
28. Ibid.
29. Ibid.
30. Ibid.
31. PA, 1st, IV, 132
32. Ibid.
33. Ibid.
34. Rich. P., 209 and 258
35. CR, IX, 89
36. Ibid., 88-89
37. Hist. Dau., 61
38. Ibid.
39. "Smith's Narrative of the Massacre"; An. Har., 56
40. Ibid.
41. Ibid.
42. Elder to Gov'r John Penn, Dec. 16, 1763, Eld. Pap.; and PA, 1st, IV, 148

43. An. Har., 58
44. Ibid.
45. Ibid.
46. PP, XXXIII, 58
47. PA, 1st, IV, 147-148
48. Ibid., 100
49. Elder to the Gov'r, Eld. Pap.
50. CR, IX, 95-96
51. Ibid., 97
52. Ibid.
53. Ibid., 100
54. Hist. Dau., 63
55. PA, 4th, II, 594-597
56. John Harris' Receipt-Books

8. AFTERMATH OF MASSACRE (pp. 111-122)

1. CR, IX, 102-104
2. PP, XXXIII, 59
3. Consp. Pon., II, 378-379
4. CR, IX, 102
5. Ibid., 103-104
6. Ibid., 102
7. Ibid.
8. Ibid., 103
9. Ibid., 106-108
10. Ibid., 107
11. Ibid., 104-105
12. Ibid., 105-106
13. Ibid., 113
14. Ibid.
15. Ibid., 110-113
16. Ibid., 118-119
17. Ibid.
18. Ibid., 119-120
19. Ibid., 120
20. Ibid., 124
21. Ibid., 125-127
22. Ibid., 126
23. Ibid.
24. Ibid.
25. Ibid.
26. Ibid.
27. Ibid., 125
28. Ibid., 127
29. Ibid., 127-128
30. Ibid., 128-129
31. Ibid., 131-132
32. Ibid., 131
33. Ben. Fr., 310-311
34. Consp. Pon., II, 389; and Pa. Gaz., Feb. 11, 1764

35. Ben. Fr., 310
36. Ibid.
37. Ibid.
38. Ibid.
39. Ibid.
40. Ibid.
41. CR, IX, 134
42. Ibid.
43. Consp. Pon., II, 386
44. Ibid.
45. Ibid.
46. Ibid., 157-158
47. Ibid., 157
48. Ibid.
49. Ibid., 159
50. Hist. Dau., 68; and Consp. Pon., II, 387
51. Consp. Pon., II, 387
52. Ben. Fr., 310; and Consp. Pon., II, 160
53. Consp. Pon., II, 160
54. Ibid., Appendix, p. 388
55. Ibid.
56. Ibid.
57. Ibid.
58. Pa. Gaz., Feb. 11, 1764
59. Ibid.
60. Hist. Dau., 64
61. Ibid.
62. Ibid., 63
63. Ibid., 64
64. Ibid.
65. CR, IX, 107
66. John Elder to Joseph Shippen, Feb. 1, 1764; Eld. Pap.
67. Ibid.
68. Ibid.
69. Ibid.
70. Ibid.
71. Ibid.
72. Ibid.
73. Consp. Pon., II, 380
74. Ibid.
75. PP, XXXIV, 15-16

9. PERVERSITY OF FAME (pp. 123-140)

1. CR, IX, 138-142
2. PP, XXXIV, 15-16. Also the text of this manuscript is printed in Consp. Pon. II, 392-399
3. PP, XXXIV, 15-16
4. Ibid.

5. Ibid.
6. Ibid.
7. Ibid.
8. Ibid.
9. Ibid.
10. Ibid.
11. Ibid.
12. Ibid.
13. Ibid.
14. Ibid.
15. Ibid.
16. Ibid.
17. Ibid.
18. Ibid.
19. Ibid.
20. Ibid.
21. Ibid.
22. Ibid.
23. Ibid.
24. Ibid.
25. Ibid.
26. Ibid.
27. PA, 8th, VII, 5548-5553
28. Ibid., and Consp. Pon., II, 399-404
29. Consp. Pon., II, 400
30. Ibid.
31. Ibid.
32. Ibid.
33. Ibid.
34. Ibid.
35. Ibid., 401
36. Ibid., 403
37. Ibid.
38. Ibid.
39. Ibid.
40. Ibid., 404
41. Ibid.
42. Ibid.
43. Ibid.
44. Ibid.
45. Ibid.
46. PA, 8th, VII, 5549
47. Depositions in Consp. Pon., II, 375-379; and in Hist. Dau., 75-77
48. Hist. Dau., 76
49. Ibid., 75-76
50. Ibid., 75
51. Ibid.
52. Ibid.
53. Ibid.
54. Ibid., 76
55. Ibid.
56. Consp. Pon., II, 377
57. Ibid., 375

58. Ibid.
59. Ibid.
60. Ibid., 375-376
61. Ibid., 378-379
62. Ibid., 378
63. Ibid.
64. Ibid.
65. Ibid., 379
66. Ibid.
67. Ben Fr. Writ., IV, 289-314
68. Ibid., 290
69. Ibid., 310
70. Ibid., 314
71. W. B. Sprague, Annals of the American Pulpit, III, 218
72. Egle in Hist. Dau., 77-78, enumerates the Pamphlets written. See p. 77 for a description of the "The Paxton Men Impartially Represented."
73. Consp. Pon., II, 390-392
74. Ibid., 390
75. Ibid., 392
76. Hist. Dau., 77
77. Ibid., 78
78. Ibid.
79. Ibid.
80. Ibid.
81. Ibid., 68
82. Ibid.
83. Ibid.
84. By "Agricola"
85. Ibid.
86. Consp. Pon., II, 381-383
87. Ibid.

10. BACK INHABITANT LAW (pp. 141-156)

1. CR, IX, 450-451
2. Ibid., 453
3. Ibid., 453-454
4. Ibid.
5. Ibid.
6. Ibid.
7. PA, 4th, III, 350 ff.
8. Ibid.
9. CR, IX, 450
10. Ibid.
11. Ibid.
12. Ibid.
13. Ibid., 451
14. Ibid.
15. Ibid.
16. Ibid.

17. Ibid.
18. Ibid.
19. Ibid.
20. PA, 4th, III, 371-372
21. Ibid., 372-373
22. Ibid., 380-382, 394-400; and Pa, 1st, IV, 296
23. PA, 4th, III, 388-389
24. Consp. Pon., II, 378-379
25. PA, 8th, VII, 6087
26. Ibid., 6088
27. PA, 4th, III, 365-366
28. Ibid., 402-405
29. Hist. W-B., I, 453-456
30. Ibid., 460-461
31. Ibid.
32. Ibid., 462-463
33. Ibid., 465-466
34. Ibid., 508-510
35. Ibid., 507-508
36. Ibid., II, 626-627
37. Ibid., 627-628
38. Ibid.
39. Ibid., 629-630
40. Ibid., I, 511-512; and Sus. Co. Pap., III, 176-177
41. Sus. Co. Pap., III, 177
42. Ibid., 176
43. Ibid., 177
44. Hist. W-B., II, 639
45. Ibid.
46. Ibid.
47. Ibid., 640-644
48. Sus. Co. Pap., IV, 6, ftn. 4
49. Hist. Dau., 71
50. Ibid.
51. Ibid.
52. Hist. W-B., II, 644
53. Ibid.
54. Ibid., 645
55. Ibid.
56. Ibid.
57. Ibid., 647
58. Ibid., 648
59. Ibid.
60. Ibid.
61. Ibid., 633
62. Ibid., I, 480-487
63. CR, IX, 678-680
64. Ibid., 682
65. Ibid.
66. Ibid.
67. Ibid., 682-683
68. Ibid.

69. Ibid., 683
70. Ibid.
71. Ibid.
72. Ibid.
73. Ibid.
74. Ibid.
75. Ibid.
76. Ibid.
77. Ibid.
78. Ibid., 682-684
79. Ibid., 684
80. PA, 4th, III, 430-431
81. Ibid., 431
82. PA, 1st, IV, 378-379
83. Ibid., 378
84. Ibid.
85. Ibid.
86. Ibid.
87. Ibid.
88. Ibid., 378-379
89. Ibid., 379
90. Ibid.
91. Ibid.
92. Ibid.
93. Ibid.
94. Hist. Dau., 69-70
95. Ibid., 69
96. Ibid.
97. Ibid.
98. Ibid.
99. Ibid.
100. Ibid.
101. Ibid.
102. Ibid.
103. Ibid., 70
104. Ibid.
105. Ibid.
106. Ibid.
107. Ibid.
108. Ibid.
109. Ibid.
110. Ibid.
111. Ibid.
112. Ibid.
113. PA, 1st, IV, 383-391

11. BOUNDEN DUTY AND DISTANT RIVERS (pp. 157-173)

1. Morison and Commager, The Growth of the American Republic, I, 159
2. Ibid.

3. PA, 2d, XIII, 271
4. Ibid.
5. Ibid., 271-272
6. Ibid.
7. Ibid., 272
8. Ibid., 271
9. Ibid.
10. Hist. Dau., 79
11. Ibid., 79-80
12. Ibid., 80
13. Ibid.
14. Ibid.
15. Ibid.
16. PA, 2d, XIII, Frontispiece
17. Ibid.
18. PA, 5th, II, 43-46
19. Growth Am. Rep., I, 159
20. Arn. Camp., 1
21. Route of march based on "Journal of Capt. Wm. Hendricks," PA, 2nd, XV, 25-30
22. Arn. Camp.
23. PA, 5th, II, 43-46
24. Arn. Camp., 12-13
25. PA, 2d, XV, 26
26. Ibid., 27
27. Ibid., 27-29
28. Ibid., 28
29. Ibid., 30
30. Ibid.
31. Wilkinson: Memoirs, I, 17-18
32. PA, 2d, XV, 30-31
33. Arn. Camp., 12
34. Ibid., 14
35. Ibid., 15
36. Ibid., ftn. 1
37. Ibid., 15
38. Ibid., 16
39. Ibid., 18
40. Ibid.
41. Ibid., 19
42. Ibid.
43. Ibid., 22
44. Ibid.
45. Ibid., 23
46. Ibid., 24
47. Ibid., 40
48. Ibid., 48
49. Ibid.
50. Ibid.
51. Ibid., 52-56

12. FEAT WITHOUT LAURELS
(pp. 175-185)

1. Arn. Camp., 56
2. Ibid., 56-57
3. Ibid., 62
4. Ibid., 67
5. Ibid., 75-76
6. Ibid., 71
7. Ibid., 71-72
8. Ibid., 73
9. Ibid.
10. Ibid.
11. Ibid., 77
12. Ibid.
13. Ibid., 77-78
14. Ibid., 79
15. Ibid., 79-80
16. Ibid., 80
17. Ibid.
18. Ibid.
19. Ibid., 81
20. Ibid., 81-82
21. Ibid.
22. Ibid., 82
23. Ibid.
24. Ibid., 83
25. Ibid.
26. Ibid.
27. Ibid., 85
28. Ibid.
29. Ibid., 86
30. Ibid., 87
31. Ibid., 88
32. Ibid.
33. Ibid.
34. Ibid.
35. Ibid., 90-91
36. Ibid., 94
37. Ibid.
38. Ibid., 95
39. Ibid., 107
40. Ibid., 130-131
41. Ibid., 131
42. Ibid., 134-135
43. Kenneth Roberts: March to Quebec, 33
44. Ibid.

13. FIRST MONTHS OF LIBERTY
(pp. 187-201)

1. PA, 2d, XIII, 260-268
2. Ibid., 253-257
3. Ibid., 259-260
4. Ibid., 260-267
5. Ibid., 262-263
6. Ibid., 263
7. Ibid.
8. Ibid., 264
9. Ibid., 264-265
10. Ibid., 266-267
11. Ibid., 266
12. Ibid., 267
13. Ibid.
14. Ibid., 263
15. Ibid., 259
16. Ibid., 307-317
17. Ibid.
18. Ibid., 267
19. Ibid., 307-308, 310-311, 313
20. Ibid., 309-310
21. Ibid., 313-314
22. Ibid., 311-312
23. Ibid., 315-316
24. Ibid., 318-321
25. Ibid., 322-323
26. Ibid., 323-324
27. Ibid., 343-344
28. PA, 5th, II, 332-335
29. PA, 2d, XV, 195-218
30. Ibid., 195
31. Ibid.
32. Ibid.
33. Ibid.
34. Ibid.
35. Ibid.
36. Ibid.
37. Ibid.
38. Ibid., 196
39. Ibid., 197
40. Ibid.
41. Ibid.
42. Ibid., 198
43. Matthew Arnold, quoting from Ossian in "On the Study of Celtic Literature"
44. PA, 2d, I, 519-522 and 511-516
45. Ibid., 522
46. PA, 2d, I, 515
47. Lewis Burd Walker: The Burd Papers, 90

48. Ibid., 91
49. Ibid.
50. Ibid.
51. PA, 2d, I, 520-521
52. PA, 2d, XV, 198-199
53. PA, 2d, I, 630-631
54. Ibid., 631
55. Ibid., 630
56. Ibid., 631
57. Ibid.
58. PA, 5th, VII, 352-356
59. Ibid.
60. Ibid., 352
61. Ibid., 355
62. Ibid., 352
63. Ibid., 353-354
64. PA, 2d, XV, 200-202
65. Ibid., 200
66. Ibid., 200-201
67. Ibid., 201-202
68. Ibid., 202
69. Ibid.
70. Ibid.
71. Ibid.
72. Ibid.
73. Ibid.
74. Ibid.

14. OUT FROM A SETBACK
(pp. 203-210)

1. PA, 5th, VII, 356
2. PA, 1st, V, 212
3. RP, VII, 96
4. Ibid.
5. Ibid.
6. Ibid.
7. Ibid.
8. PA, 1st, V, 151
9. Ibid.
10. PA, 1st, V, 133
11. Ibid.
12. Ibid., 164
13. Ibid.
14. Camp. Pr., 59; and PA, 2d, XV, 203
15. Camp. Pr., 45-47
16. Ibid., 49
17. PA, 2d, X, 314-315
18. Ibid., 315
19. Ibid.
20. PA, 2d, XV, 202-203
21. Ibid., 203
22. Ibid.; and PA, 1st, V, 157; and Camp. Pr., 60

23. PA, 2d, XV, 203
24. Ibid., 202-204
25. Ibid., 203
26. Ibid., 204
27. Ibid.
28. Ibid.
29. Ibid.
30. PA, 1st, V, 158-159
31. Ibid.

15. NORTHUMBERLAND
(pp. 211-222)

1. PA, 8th, VII, 6748
2. Ibid., 6749
3. Ibid., 6848
4. "Genealogical Map of the Counties"; and Hist. North., 149
5. Hist. North., 445
6. Ibid., 202
7. Ibid., 179 and 202
8. Ibid., 203-204
9. Ibid., 210
10. An. Buf. Val., 44
11. Ibid., 44-45
12. Ibid., 50
13. Ibid., 64
14. PA, 5th, II, 29
15. PA, 2d, XIII, 266-267
16. Ibid.
17. PA, 5th, II, 30
18. Ibid.
19. Heber G. Gearhart: "Northumberland County Troops in the Continental Line," North. Co. Pr., V, 32
20. Ibid., 32-35
21. An. Buf. Val., 82
22. Ibid.
23. Ibid.
24. Ibid.
25. Ibid.
26. Bat. Am. Rev., 157, 166-167
27. North. Co. Pr., V, 33
28. Ibid.
29. Ibid.
30. Ibid., 33-34
31. Ibid., 34
32. Ibid., 33-35
33. Ibid., 35-36
34. Ibid., 35
35. Ibid., 36
36. Ibid., 47-49
37. Ibid., 37
38. Ibid., 38

39. PA, 1st, V, 133
40. North. Co. Pr., V, 38
41. Ibid., 41-42
42. H. Cowpens, 71-79
43. North. Co. Pr., V, 41
44. Ibid., 44
45. Ibid., 45-46
46. PA, 5th, II, 33
47. North. Co. Pr., V, 42
48. Bat. Am. Rev., 305 and 320
49. Ibid., 324
50. Ibid.
51. Ibid., 324-325
52. Ibid., 332-333
53. Ibid., 341; and H. Cowpens, 110-111
54. Bat. Am. Rev., 341
55. Ibid.
56. H. Cowpens, 113-116
57. Ibid., 80
58. North. Co. Pr., V, 43
59. Ibid.
60. H. Cowpens, 106-107
61. Eleanor Taylor: "Schoharie County in Legend and History," including "Timothy Murphy," by Henry H. Eddy, 33
62. Ibid.; and H. Cowpens, 122
63. Bat. Am. Rev., 350
64. Hist. Dau., 438-439

16. NO SHINING GLORY
(pp. 223-233)

1. PA, 2d, XIII, 472
2. Ibid., 474
3. Ibid.
4. Ibid.
5. Ibid., 476
6. Ibid.
7. Ibid.
8. Ibid., 476-477
9. Ibid., 477
10. Ibid.
11. Ibid.
12. Ibid., 478
13. Ibid.
14. Ibid.
15. Ibid., 479
16. Ibid.
17. Ibid., 480
18. Ibid.
19. Ibid., 481
20. Ibid.
21. PA, 1st, V, 558-561

22. Ibid., 559
23. Ibid., 560
24. Ibid., 559
25. Ibid.
26. Ibid.
27. Ibid., 559-560
28. Ibid., 624-625
29. Ibid., 624
30. Ibid.
31. Ibid., 625
32. Ibid.
33. Ibid.
34. Ibid.
35. Ibid.
36. Ibid., 628-629
37. Ibid.
38. Ibid., 634
39. Ibid.
40. Ibid., 572-573
41. Ibid., 572
42. Ibid.
43. Ibid., 598
44. PA, 2d, XIII, 482
45. Ibid., 483
46. Ibid.
47. PA, 1st, V, 768-769
48. Ibid.
49. Ibid., 769

17. "AND DEVIL TAKE THE HINDMOST!"
(pp. 235-245)

1. PA, 1st, VI, 122
2. Ibid.
3. Ibid., 123
4. Ibid.
5. Ibid.
6. Ibid.
7. Ibid., 151
8. Ibid.
9. Ibid., 168
10. RP, XIX, 66
11. PA, 1st, VI, 159-160
12. RP, XIX, 82
13. Ibid.
14. Ibid., 63
15. Ibid., 68
16. Ibid.
17. Ibid.
18. Washington, II, 58
19. Ibid., 519
20. RP, XVIII, 40
21. Ibid.

22. Ibid.
23. PA, 1st, VI, 175-176
24. Ibid., 176
25. Ibid.
26. RP, XIX, 25 (President Wharton to Col. Samuel Hunter, Jan. 19, 1778)
27. PA, 1st, VI, 194-195
28. Ibid.
29. Ibid.
30. RP, XIX, 40
31. Ibid.
32. Ibid.
33. RP, XIX, 55
34. Ibid.
35. Ibid.
36. Ibid., 34
37. Ibid.
38. Ibid.
39. Washington, II, 59-61
40. Ibid., 60
41. Ibid.
42. Ibid.
43. Ibid., 61
44. Ibid.

18. WYOMING
(pp. 247-259)

1. Washington, II, 82
2. Plumb: History of Hanover Township and Wyoming Valley, 148-154
3. Ibid., 154
4. Hist. W-B, II, 956-960
5. Ibid., 960-963 and 972-973
6. Ibid., 956
7. Ibid., 960-962
8. Ibid., 975
9. Ibid.
10. Ibid., 976-977
11. Ibid., 978
12. Ibid.
13. Ibid., 978-979
14. Ibid., 979
15. Ibid., 981
16. Ibid., 982
17. Ibid., 986-987
18. Ibid., 988
19. Ibid., 988-989
20. Ibid., 989
21. Ibid., 990-991
22. Ibid., 991
23. Ibid.
24. Ibid., 991-992
25. Ibid., 992-993

26. Ibid., 996-1002
27. Ibid., 999-1002
28. Ibid., 1003-1004
29. Ibid., 1009-1010; and Miner: History of Wyoming, 219 and Appendix, pp. 20-21; and Pearce: Annals of Luzerne County, 117
30. Hist. W-B, II, 1006
31. Ibid., 1007-1009
32. Ibid., 1007
33. Ibid., 1010-1011
34. Ibid., 1006
35. Ibid., 1012
36. Ibid., 1014
37. Ibid.
38. Ibid., 1016
39. Ibid.

19. "WITH WHAT MEASURE YOU METE" (pp. 261-279)

1. Hist. W-B, II, 1016
2. Ibid., 1018-1019; and Miner: History of Wyoming, 226
3. Pa. Gen., 194
4. PA, 5th, VIII, 646-647
5. Pa. Gen., 194
6. N. & Q., series 3, III, 262
7. Ibid.
8. PA, 1st, VI, 632-633
9. Ibid.
10. Ibid.
11. Ibid., 633
12. Ibid.
13. Ibid.
14. Ibid.
15. Ibid.
16. Ibid.
17. Ibid., 634
18. Ibid.
19. Ibid.
20. Ibid.
21. Ibid.
22. Ibid.
23. Ibid.
24. Ibid., 351
25. Ibid.
26. Ibid., 635-636
27. Ibid.
28. Ibid., 636-637
29. Ibid., 650
30. Ibid., 649
31. Ibid., 660-661
32. Ibid., 665
33. Ibid., 674
34. Ibid.
35. Ibid.
36. Ibid.
37. Ibid., 687-688
38. Ibid., 688-689
39. Ibid.
40. Ibid., 689
41. Ibid.
42. Ibid.
43. Ibid., 729-730
44. Ibid., 770
45. Ibid., 773-774
46. PA, 1st, VII, 3-4 and 5-9
47. Ibid., 5-6
48. Ibid., 1
49. Ibid.
50. Ibid., 3
51. PA, 1st, VI, 680
52. Ibid.
53. Genealogical and Biographical Annals of Northumberland County, 693-694
54. Inferred from PA, 5th, IV, 500 (Daniel McMath)
55. PA, 1st, VI, 730
56. PA, 2d, XV, 219-253
57. Ibid., 257
58. Ibid., 255-288
59. Ibid., 263
60. Ibid.
61. Ibid.
62. Ibid., 267
63. Ibid., 268-269
64. Ibid., 275
65. Ibid., 264
66. Ibid., 265
67. Ibid., 259
68. Ibid.
69. Ibid., 257-258
70. Ibid., 258
71. Ibid.
72. Ibid., 271
73. Ibid., 272
74. Ibid.
75. Ibid., 273
76. Ibid., 274
77. Ibid.
78. Ibid., 275
79. Ibid., 275-276
80. Ibid., 277
81. Ibid., 279
82. Ibid., 280

83. Ibid.
84. Ibid., 283
85. Ibid., 285
86. Ibid., 285-286
87. Ibid.
88. Ibid., 139 and 244
89. Ibid., 244-245
90. Ibid.
91. Ibid.
92. Ibid.
93. Ibid., 245
94. Ibid., 139-140
95. Ibid., 245
96. Ibid., 138
97. Simms Fr., II, 246
98. Ibid.
99. Ibid.
100. PA, 2d, XV, 245
101. Ibid., 248-249
102. Ibid.
103. Ibid., 248
104. Ibid.
105. Ibid., 249
106. Ibid.

20. TRUE TO HERITAGE (pp. 281-294)

1. Pa. Gen., 542
2. Ibid.
3. Ibid.
4. PA, 2d, XV, 295-334
5. Ibid., 297
6. Ibid.
7. Ibid., 298
8. Ibid.
9. Ibid., 299
10. Ibid.
11. Ibid.
12. Ibid.
13. Ibid.
14. Ibid.
15. Ibid., 299-300
16. Ibid., 300
17. Ibid.
18. Ibid.
19. Ibid., 300-301
20. Ibid., 301
21. Ibid., 302
22. Ibid.
23. Ibid.
24. Ibid.
25. Ibid.

26. Ibid., 303
27. Ibid.
28. Ibid.
29. Ibid., 304-305
30. Ibid.
31. Ibid., 331
32. Ibid., 332
33. Ibid., 332-333
34. Ibid., 320
35. Ibid., 321
36. Ibid., 322
37. Ibid., 326, 327, and 331
38. Ibid., 322
39. Ibid., 326
40. Ibid., 323
41. Ibid.
42. Ibid., 326
43. Ibid., 323
44. Ibid., 329
45. Ibid., 307
46. Ibid., 310
47. Ibid., 314
48. Ibid.
49. Ibid., 321
50. Ibid.
51. Ibid.
52. William Kelso: "Diary of a Trip to New Orleans via the Mississippi"
53. Ibid.
54. Ibid.
55. Ibid.
56. Ibid.
57. Ibid.
58. Ibid.
59. Ibid.
60. Ibid.
61. Ibid.
62. Ibid.
63. Ibid.
64. Ibid.
65. Ibid.
66. Ibid.

21. LAWMAKERS AND FOUNDERS (pp. 295-307)

1. PA, 4th, III, 629
2. Ibid., 647-649
3. Selsam: The Penna Constitution of 1776, 148-149
4. Ibid., 149
5. Ibid., 206

6. Ibid. and Penna Evening Post, Oct. 10 and 19, 1776
7. PA, 4th, III, 627-648
8. Biog. Dau., 168
9. Encyclopedia Britannica, 11th Ed., XVIII, 101-102
10. PA, 4th, III, 629
11. Ibid., 634
12. Ibid.
13. James G. Marshall, The Marshall Family of Bellefonte, Pa., 74-76
14. PA, 4th, III, 632
15. Hist. Dau., 104-105
16. Hist. Leb., 50-52
17. Ibid., 50
18. Ibid.
19. Ibid.
20. Ibid.
21. Ibid.
22. Ibid.
23. Ibid.
24. Ibid.
25. Ibid.
26. An. Har., 72
27. Biog. Dau., 174
28. Hist. Dau., 96-97
29. Biog. Dau., 184
30. Cuth. Diary, 105 and 110
31. Rich. P., 312
32. Biog. Dau., 178
33. Ibid. and PA, 2d, XIII, 271-272
34. Penna Manual, 1947-1948 (No. 88), 504
35. Ibid., 503; and Biog. Dau., 168
36. An. Har., 72
37. Ibid., 71-72
38. Ibid., 72
39. LP, III (1785-1790), 14-18
40. Ibid., 15
41. Ibid., 16
42. Ibid., 16-17
43. Ibid., 18
44. An. Har., 82-83
45. Ibid., 75
46. Ibid., 76
47. Ibid., 13-14

22. ILK OF DOUBTING THOMAS
(pp. 309-321)

1. Great R.
2. Ibid., 186
3. Counter-R., 207
4. Ibid.
5. Ibid.
6. Ibid.
7. PA, 4th, III, 647
8. Ibid., 647-648; and Counter R., 207-208
9. Pa. Gen., 353
10. Ibid.
11. Great R., 185
12. Counter-R., 216
13. Ibid.
14. Minutes of Assembly, 1785-1786
15. Ibid.
16. Ibid.
17. J. Wm. M., 1-401
18. Ibid., 343
19. Ibid., 3
20. Ibid., 1
21. Ibid.
22. Ibid., 2-3
23. Ibid., 5
24. Ibid.
25. Ibid., 24-25
26. Ibid., 9-10
27. Ibid., 10
28. Ibid., 10-11
29. Ibid., 29
30. Ibid.
31. Ibid., 95
32. Ibid., 96
33. Ibid., 114
34. Ibid., 99
35. Ibid., 219
36. Ibid., 221
37. Ibid., 227
38. Ibid., 240
39. Ibid., 321
40. Ibid.
41. Ibid.
42. Ibid.
43. Ibid., 332
44. Ibid., 335
45. Ibid., 336
46. Ibid.
47. Ibid.
48. Ibid., 349-350
49. Ibid., 350
50. Ibid., 353
51. Ibid., 265-266
52. Ibid., 376
53. Ibid.
54. Ibid., 401
55. Ibid., 231

23. EXCISE AND FRENCH REVOLUTION (pp. 323-336)

1. Oracle, Nov. 3, 1792
2. Ibid.
3. Ibid.
4. Ibid., Nov. 10, 1792
5. Ibid.
6. Ibid.
7. Ibid., Nov. 26, 1792
8. Ibid., Dec. 10, 1792
9. Ibid., Nov. 10, 1792, quoting from the Federal Gazette
10. Ibid., Dec. 3, 1792
11. Ibid.
12. Ibid.
13. Ibid.
14. Ibid., Dec. 10, 1792
15. Ibid., Dec. 24, 1792
16. West. Ins., 20
17. Ibid., 22
18. Oracle, Jan. 7, 1793
19. Ibid.
20. Ibid.
21. Ibid.
22. Ibid.
23. Ibid.
24. Ibid., Jan. 14, 1793
25. Ibid.
26. Ibid.
27. Ibid., Jan. 21, 1793
28. Ibid.
29. Ibid., Jan. 28, 1793
30. Ibid.
31. Ibid., Mar. 11, 1793
32. Ibid., Mar. 25, 1793
33. Ibid.
34. Ibid.
35. Ibid.
36. Ibid.
37. Ibid.
38. Ibid.
39. Ibid., Apr. 1, 1793
40. Ibid.
41. Ibid., Apr. 8, 1793
42. Ibid.
43. Ibid.
44. Ibid.
45. West. Ins., 28
46. Ibid.
47. Ibid.
48. Ibid.
49. Ibid., 28-29
50. Oracle, Mar. 25, 1793
51. Ibid.
52. Ibid., Apr. 1, 1793
53. Ibid.
54. Ibid., Sept. 16, 1793
55. West. Ins., 29
56. Ibid., 41-42
57. Ibid., 48-49
58. Ibid.
59. Oracle, Aug. 18, 1794
60. Ibid.
61. Ibid., Sept. 1, 1794
62. Ibid., Sept. 8, 1794
63. Ibid.
64. Ibid.
65. Ibid.
66. Ibid., Aug. 18, 1794
67. An. Har., 106 and 108
68. Ibid.
69. Ibid., 106-107
70. Hist. York, 624
71. *Supra.* See note 31 of Chapter XI ("Bounden Duty and Distant Rivers")

24. NEIGHBORS AND EL DORADO (pp. 337-348)

1. The inventory of volumes was advertised first on July 14; but the text here is based on the *Oracle* of Aug. 25, 1794.
2. For Pastor Roan's will see N. & Q., series 1 and 2, II, 342-343
3. John Roan in his Account Book (Dauphin County Historical Society) records Flavel's birth as on July 31, 1760, "at 1½ af."
4. Oracle, Aug. 25, 1794
5. Ibid., Jan. 14, 1793
6. Reprinted in An. Buf. Val., 242
7. An. Buf. Val., 383
8. Ibid., 379
9. Ibid., 383
10. Ibid., 382
11. Ibid., 360-361
12. Ibid., 361
13. Ibid.
14. Ibid., 360
15. Ibid., 363
16. Today Brown's Mill Graveyard, where also lie his wife, his daughter Elizabeth, and her husband, Capt.

James Poe, a soldier of the Revolution.
17. An. Buf. Val., 293
18. Ibid., 314-315
19. Post. Rev., XXIII, 16
20. Ibid.
21. Ibid.
22. The whole story of Widow Smith and her champions is perceptible in the Memorial.
23. Dancing Academy By-Laws (Dauphin County Historical Society)
24. Hist. Erie, 216
25. An. Buf. Val., 401 402
26. Ibid.
27. Ibid., 249
28. Ibid.
29. Account of Maclay and Morrison based on An. Buf. Val., 249-251, 296, 318, and 329
30. Oracle, May 6, 1792
31. Ibid.
32. John Elder to John Penn, Dec. 27, 1763, Hist. Dau., 62
33. PA, 5th, VI, 242
34. W. T. Gibson: "Captain James Gibson and Anna Belle, His Wife, etc."
35. The story of Moses Barnett and his grandson is based upon Egle's "Barnett Family" in Pa. Gen. and Isaac Moorhead's Occasional Writings.

25. SEAT OF GOVERNMENT (pp. 349-360)

1. An. Har., 76
2. Minutes of Assembly, Mar. 3, 1787, p. 132
3. Counter-R., 197
4. Ibid.
5. Minutes of Assembly, Mar. 3, 1787, p. 133
6. Barr Ferree: Pennsylvania, A Primer, 44
7. Ibid.
8. Ibid.
9. Ibid.
10. Ibid.
11. Ibid.
12. Statutes at Large of Penna., XVI (1798-1801), 239-241
13. Ibid.
14. An Har., 136
15. Ibid., 136-137
16. Ibid., 137
17. Ibid.
18. Ibid.
19. Ibid., 137-138
20. Penna. Manual, vol. 88 (1947-1948), 514
21. An. Har., 138
22. Ibid.
23. Ibid.
24. Ibid.
25. Ibid.
26. Ibid.
27. Ibid., 138-139
28. Ibid., 139
29. Ibid.
30. Hugh Hamilton's paper says that the amendments were offered by "Mr. Spayd," but official records in the Penna. Manual reveal no membership for a man of that name in 1809-1810. Hamilton's error might have been a misprint for George Spangler, then a member from York.
31. The Times, Lancaster, Feb. 10, 1810
32. Dauphin Guardian, Feb. 27, 1810
33. The analysis of the votes in the Senate and the House given above has been carefully drawn from the tallies and the rolls of names entered in the Senate Journal for Friday, Jan. 26, 1810, and in the House Journal for Monday, Feb. 12, 1810. The Christian names of members and the enrollment by counties have been compiled by comparison with the rolls of legislators presented in the Penna. Manual, vol. 88, 503-621
34. An. Har., 140
35. Ibid., 143
36. Dauphin Guardian, April 3 through May 1, 1810
37. An. Har., 151-152
38. The story of Timothy Green Allen and Joseph Barnett has been adopted from two versions: one in an old undated Harrisburg news clipping owned by a descendant of the Barnett family in West Virginia, Mrs. Thomas R. (Mabel Barnett Cowden) Moore, of Charles-Town; the other in Isaac Moorhead's Occasional Writings, pp. 236-240. Young Allen, according to Moorhead's ac-

count, died at the Landis hostelry; and his body was prepared for the grave by Mrs. Landis.

A tombstone, cut in Pennsylvania and sent on to mark Timothy's resting-place, was set up and cared for by George Rogers, a gentleman of an earlier Hanover Township family.

39. An. Har., 145

40. Ibid., 145-146
41. Senate Journal, Jan. 26, 1810
42. An. Har., 145-146
43. Ibid., 146
44. Ibid., 151-152
45. Ibid., 152-153
46. Ibid.
47. Ibid.
48. Ibid.

BIBLIOGRAPHY AND SOURCES

BIBLIOGRAPHY AND SOURCES
with abbreviations

An. Buf. Val. . . . . John Blair Linn: *Annals of Buffalo Valley*, Pennsylvania, 1755-1855, Harrisburg, 1877

An. Har. . . . . George H. Morgan: *Annals . . . of Harrisburg*, Harrisburg, 1858

Arn. Camp . . . . John Joseph Henry: *Arnold's Campaign against Quebec*, Albany, 1877

Bat. Amer. Rev. . . . . . Henry B. Carrington: *Battles of the American Revolution*, 1775-1781, New York, 1876

Ben. Fr. . . . . Carl Van Doren: *Benjamin Franklin*, The Viking Press, 1945

Ben. Fr. Writ . . . . Albert Henry Smith, Ed.: *The Writings of Benjamin Franklin*, The Macmillan Company, New York, 1906, 10 vols.

Biog. Dau . . . . *Biographical Encyclopedia of Dauphin County, Pennsylvania*, Runk and Company, Chambersburg, 1896

Biog. Frank . . . . *Biographical Annals of Franklin County, Pennsylvania*, Chicago, 1905

Camp. Pr. . . . . Alfred Hoyt Bill: *The Campaign of Princeton*, 1776-1777, Princeton University Press, 1948

Consp. Pon. . . . . Francis Parkman: *The Conspiracy Of Pontiac*, Little, Brown and Company, Boston, 1908, 2 vols.

Con. Weis . . . . Paul A. W. Wallace: *Conrad Weiser, Friend of Colonist and Mohawk*, University of Pennsylvania Press, 1945

Counter-R . . . . Robert L. Brunhouse: *The Counter-Revolution in Pennsylvania*, 1776-1790, Pennsylvania Historical Commission, Harrisburg, 1942

CR . . . . *Colonial Records of Pennsylvania*

Cuth. Diary . . . . S. Helen Fields, Ed.: *Register of Marriages and Baptisms Performed by Rev. John Cuthbertson, Covenanter Minister, 1751-1791, with Index to Locations Visited*, Washington, D. C., 1934

D. Sc.–I ....Wayland F. Dunaway: *The Scotch-Irish of Colonial Pennsylvania*, University of North Carolina Press, 1944

Elder Pap ....*John Elder Papers*, Public Records Office, Education Building, Harrisburg

FF ....*Frontier Forts of Pennsylvania*, 2d Edition, Harrisburg, 1916, 2 vols.

Great R ....Carl Van Doren: *The Great Rehearsal*, Viking Press, New York, 1948

H. Sc.–I ....Charles A. Hanna: *The Scotch-Irish, or The Scot in North Britain, North Ireland, and North America*, Putnam's, New York, 1902, 2 vols.

H. Cowpens ....*The Hero of Cowpens, A Centennial Sketch*, A. S. Barnes and Company, New York, 1881

Hist. Ches. ....J. Smith Futhey and Gilbert Cope: *History of Chester County, Pennsylvania*, Philadelphia, 1881

Hist. Dau. ....William Henry Egle: *History of Dauphin County*, 1883

Hist. Erie ....*The History of Erie County*, Warner, Beers and Company, Chicago, 1884

Hist. Leb. ....William Henry Egle: *History of Lebanon County*, 1883

Hist. North. ....Herbert C. Bell: *History of Northumberland County*, Chicago, 1891

Hist. W-B ....Oscar Jewell Harvey: *A History of Wilkes-Barre*, Wilkes-Barre, 1909, 4 vols.

Hist. York ....John Gibson: *History of York County, Pennsylvania*

J. Wm. M. ....*The Journal of William Maclay* (Charles A. Beard, Ed.), Albert and Charles Boni, New York, 1927

LP ....*Laws of Pennsylvania*

Mem. Dav. Br. ......*Memoirs of the Rev. David Brainerd, Missionary to the Indians on the Borders of New York, New Jersey, and Pennsylvania*, Jonathan Edwards and Sereno Edwards Dwight, Editors; S. Converse, New Haven, 1822

North Co. Pr. ......*Northumberland County Historical Society Proceedings and Addresses*

N. & Q. ....*Notes and Queries*

Oracle ....*The Oracle of Dauphin*, 1792-1794, Harrisburg

PA, 1st ....*Pennsylvania Archives*, first series

PA, 2d ....*Pennsylvania Archives*, second series

PA, 4th ....*Pennsylvania Archives*, fourth series (Papers of the Governors)

PA, 5th ....*Pennsylvania Archives*, fifth series

PA, 8th .... *Pennsylvania Archives,* eighth series (Votes of Assembly)

Pa. Gaz. .... *The Pennsylvania Gazette*

Pa. Gen. .... William Henry Egle: *Pennsylvania Genealogies,* Harrisburg, 1886

Pa. Prim. .... Barr Ferree: *Pennsylvania, A Primer,* New York, 1904

PP .... *Provincial Papers,* Pennsylvania Public Records Office

Post-Rev. .... *Post-Revolutionary Papers,* Public Records Office

RP .... *Revolutionary Papers,* Public Records Office

Rich. P. .... Hubertis Cummings: *Richard Peters, Provincial Secretary and Cleric,* University of Pennsylvania Press, 1944

Simms Fr. .... Jeptha R. Simms: *The Frontiersmen of New York,* G. C. Riggs, Albany, 1883, 2 vols.

Sus. Co. Pap. .... *The Susquehanna Company Papers,* (Julian P. Boyd, Ed.), Wilkes-Barre, 5 vols.

Washington .... *Nathaniel Wright Stephenson and Waldo Hilary Dunn: George Washington,* Oxford University Press, 1940, 2 vols.

West. Ins. .... H. M. Breckenridge: *History of the Western Insurrection in Western Pennsylvania, Commonly Called the Whiskey Rebellion, 1794,* Pittsburgh, 1859

WT .... Charles A. Hanna: *The Wilderness Trail,* Putnam's, New York, 1911, 2 vols.

OTHER SOURCES

"Agricola," *The Squabble; A Pastoral Eclogue.* (Philadelphia, 1764). In the Paxtang Collection of the Presbyterian Historical Society

By-Laws and Membership of the Dancing Academy. Dauphin County Historical Society, Harrisburg

"Genealogical Map of the Counties." Pennsylvania Department of Internal Affairs, 1933.

Harris, John; *Receipt-Books.* Pennsylvania Public Records Office.

Kelso, William; "Diary of a Trip to New Orleans via the Mississippi." In the *Kelso Papers, 1782-1816.* Pennsylvania Public Records Office, Harrisburg. (Original in the possession of Robert F. Kelso, Esq., Zanesville, Ohio.)

Roan, Rev. John; *Account Book.* Dauphin County Historical Society, Harrisburg

Wilkinson, James; *Memoirs of My Own Times,* 3 Vols. (Philadelphia, 1816)

INDEX

INDEX

[391